THE CHILD
FROM FIVE TO TEN

THE CHILD
FROM FIVE TO TEN

Arnold Gesell, M.D.

Frances L. Ilg, M.D., and Louise Bates Ames, Ph.D.

In collaboration with
Glenna E. Bullis

REVISED EDITION

HARPER & ROW, PUBLISHERS, New York
Grand Rapids, Philadelphia, St. Louis, San Francisco
London, Singapore, Sydney, Tokyo, Toronto

Library of Congress Cataloging in Publication Data

Gesell, Arnold Lucius, 1880-1961.
  The child from five to ten.
  Includes bibliographical references and index.
  1. Child development. I. Ames, Louise Bates, joint author. II. Ilg, Frances Lillian, 1902-   , joint author. III. Title.
HQ767.9.G47 1976   155.4′24   76-5123
ISBN: 0-06-011501-7

90 91 92 17 16 15

CONTENTS

LIST OF ILLUSTRATIONS AND TABLES

PREFACE TO THE REVISED EDITION

There always comes a time for revision, especially after thirty years, and even more so now when so much is happening so fast. But at the same time we are amazed that so much of this volume holds up as it was written in 1946. The child of five to ten still grows in the same way and acts in relatively the same way as he did thirty years ago, and did for many years before that.

In fact, it appears to be not so much the child as the culture that has changed. Five-year-olds seem still to be for the most part well adjusted, calm, and thoroughly delightful. Sevens are often withdrawn and thoughtful, somewhat unhappy. The eight-year-old is still expansive, speedy, and evaluative. Ten is calm, collected, and appreciative. And so for the ages between. They remain very much as we saw them back in 1946.

But the culture itself has changed in many ways. World War II, mentioned frequently in our earlier volume, has long been over, even though the world is far from at peace. Space travel has become almost commonplace. Civil rights efforts have made us increasingly aware of the interests of all minority groups. Inflation has added to the burdens of many families. Television, in its bare beginnings when the original book was under research, now plays a prominent part in most households in this country.

Schools, too, have changed. Our special concern for the many children who experience learning difficulties has led to much experimentation in our schools and to elaborate efforts at compensatory education.

This whole area of school and school behavior is one that we did not explore fully in our original edition. It was covered adequately only after we established the Gesell Institute of Child Development after leaving Yale and before Dr. Gesell's death, and took on a clinical service in addition to carrying out our research studies.

Necessity was indeed the mother of invention. Through this clinical service we began to see the child more in his own right, to appreciate his individual growth, especially in response to the demands of his school environment. Previously we had separated the child from his school, relating him to what he did in school but not to his total school program.

We had viewed the *preschool* child vis-à-vis the nursery school group, perhaps because we had a nursery school of our own, which most of our research subjects attended. But we had slipped up on seeing the school-age child fully in relation to his school group.

When we finally started our study of school behavior in 1956, we found that a large proportion of the children were developing and behaving at a slower rate than was expected of them by the school, and that they needed to be well into their age to be able to function fully at the anticipated grade level.

Our investigations led to our book *School Readiness*, by Ilg and Ames, published by Harper & Row in 1965. But this was still only a beginning. The work goes on, however, and we shall report to you what we consider our very important findings on the whole question of "developmental school placement." Our position is that each child should be allowed to develop at his own rate and not be put under undue stress to satisfy the demands of a school system. The schools' present greatest need, as Jonathan Kozol stated so aptly, is to treat each child as a human being and not as a subject who must be made to fit into preconceived patterns which are all too often not relevant to the individual.

The growth of a child is slow but steady. We need to be willing to await its manifestations. The growth of an idea or a book is not on as sure ground as the growth of a child. But if we stick close to the laws of nature and of growth, we are bound eventually to find our way.

It was a pleasure to us to reread the preface to the first edition of this book, written in 1946. Those involved in the writing of the book had all viewed the child from his or her earliest beginnings, from birth itself. We had experienced the basic and dramatic phases of development as they expressed themselves in remarkably patterned and lawful progression. We came to respect growth and to enjoy each new manifestation. But as the child grew older and received the many new stimuli from a school environment, we anticipated that these clear-cut growth patterns might not be as easy to define.

The opposite was actually the case. It was during the study of the ages from five to ten that we finally saw clearly the flow of stages (six, on present count) within each of the larger cycles. (We have defined the major cycles of growth that take place from two to five, five to ten, and ten to sixteen, and in each we see the same sequence of alternating stages of equilibrium and disequilibrium, inwardizing and outwardizing of behavior.)

All seemed to fall so easily into place. There is the smoothness of five and finally once again of ten years of age, the outer limits of this cycle, when all appears to be in good equilibrium. Then there is the breakup stage at five and a half to six. Six and a half is a moment of equilibrium between the breakup of five and a half and the inwardizing of seven. Seven in some ways represents the trough of the wave, when so many subtle and even dark forces are at work. But this, too, passes and the glory of the crest of the wave comes at eight, when all is released and the child is, as we describe it, expansive, speedy, and evaluative. Then comes a further period of inwardizing and anxiety at nine, followed by the beautiful equilibrium of ten.

This new awareness of the orderliness and meaning of the stages made us want to look back into the earlier years of life to see if the same stages occurred. Sure enough, they were all there, but expressed at greater speed. The same six stages had been traversed in three years only, from two to five. Behavior during these earlier years is described in this volume on pages 29–48.

We can report that when we carried out our study on the older ages, from ten to sixteen, we resisted the concept that the stages within a cycle would continue; it seemed almost too pat. But the more we doubted, the more clearly the stages manifested themselves. We now have no doubt that a similar patterning takes place throughout the entire life span.

Our special thanks must go to the Ford Foundation's Fund for the Advancement of Education, which so patiently supported our efforts over the critical ten-year period in our institute's history from 1957 to 1967. Fortunately also at that time, Title III programs supported by the federal government were going strong and allowed us to continue our work in many school systems all over the country. It was this work that clarified our feelings about the growing child in school.

We shall discuss our ideas about the child in school in its own proper chapter. But first we need to establish the groundwork of the growth process and maturity traits in all other aspects of living.

Frances L. Ilg, M.D.

Louise Bates Ames, Ph.D.

INTRODUCTION

How this book is built and how it may be used*

Books have origins. And origins often help answer the inevitable questions as to aims, scope, and method. This particular book was not written with design deliberately aforethought, nor yet as a mere afterthought. In retrospect we have become aware that it grew from some inner necessity as a developmental sequel to the earlier volume, *Infant and Child in the Culture of Today*, first published in 1943 and revised in 1974. The two volumes supplement each other and are further supplemented by a third—*Youth: the Years from Ten to Sixteen*. All three may be considered companion volumes, but each is constructed to stand independently.

Our continuing interest in children whom we had studied during their infancy and preschool years led to annual follow-up observations of the same children during the years from five to ten. The present volume, therefore, is in large measure a biographic-developmental study of the patterning of behavior throughout the first ten years of life. The approach is definitely longitudinal, and our findings are presented in the form of *growth gradients* embracing some eighteen age levels and ten major fields of behavior. For convenience of reference, as well as to aid interpretation, the findings are also presented in cross-sectional age summaries.

---

* Some readers may prefer to skip this introductory material and move directly to Chapter 5, *Five Years Old*, p. 49.

In the Preface we alluded to the favorable circumstances that surrounded this survey of the psychological growth of the school child. The cohesion and cooperativeness of the staff over a long period of years enabled us to do some group thinking in the interpretation of our voluminous data. One-way-vision-screen facilities made auxiliary observations possible, while the basic contacts with the children and their parents were highly individualized. These contacts, moreover, were cumulative, so that children, observers, examiners, and parents all came to understand one another. The organic growth of mutual understanding and rapport over a period of ten years or more must be mentioned as an important element in the validity of our investigation.

Fifty or more children were examined at five, five and a half, six, seven, eight, nine, and ten years of age. Most of these children were of high-average or superior intelligence, and came from homes of good or high socioeconomic status. Three-fourths of the children had attended the guidance nursery of our clinic; some had also been developmentally examined during infancy. Nearly all the children attended a public elementary school, and were in this sense representative of a prosperous American community. A special group of fourteen children, who attended an excellent private school in a small Connecticut town, were examined at semiannual intervals from ages six through nine. These children were not only examined individually, but were observed as members of their schoolroom groups. There were numerous observations and discussions with the teachers relative both to individual and to group behavior. Children from the public schools in Woodbridge, Connecticut, collaborated in responding to our questions about television and grandparents, in preparation for the revision of this volume.

The case record for each child grew to considerable size before the end of the study. It included for each periodic contact the following materials: (a) a psychological examination based on the Gesell developmental schedules and Stanford Binet scale; (b) performance tests, including the Arthur series; (c) reading-readiness tests, including Monroe; (d) visual-skills tests, including pursuit fixation, fusion, acuity, etc.; (e) naturalistic observations of the child's play behavior and incidental postural and tensional behavior; and (f) a wide-ranging interview with the mother, concerning behavior at home and at school. The incidental, naturalistic observations often proved revealing when brought into relation with the more formalized observations. All the records were carefully analyzed, age by age, situation by situation, and child by child. Percentage frequencies were noted, but were not made the sole basis for the final conclusions, and are not reported in this volume. The ultimate criterion of credibility and validity was developmental: Does the given behavior have an assignable status in a gradient of growth as indicated by the converging evidence of the total data for all the children of all the ages?

This criterion is frankly clinical, but due care was exercised to secure ample objective data. The gradients, the individual items of the gradients, and the growth trends were discussed in detailed conferences. All this involved subjective estimates, but with self-correcting safeguards. The very complexity and diversity of the data required that we use the method of progressive approximation. An unqualified statistical report of frequencies would not have served our purpose. Our task was to make the data intelligible and to extract meanings, so that the reader might gain a better insight into the nature of child development. Although we have made a survey which has taken years of application, our primary purpose is not to report the findings as mere facts, but to give the reader the benefit of what we have learned through the unique opportunities of the investigation.

The construction of the book, therefore, explains itself. For this is a book that was at every step built with the interests of the readers in mind, particularly parents and teachers; also physicians, nurses, and others who are professionally responsible for safeguarding the developmental welfare of children from five to ten.

Part One is intended to give the reader preliminary orientation to the central theme of development. Since this section of the book is somewhat theoretical, some readers may prefer to start right in with Part Two, which discusses each specific age in concrete and practical detail.

Part Two describes the progressive stages in the growth of the child's mind, by means of a series of cross-sectional characterizations. The mental growth of the first four years is summarized in twelve thumbnail sketches. The purpose of this summary is to give foundation and perspective to the portrayal of the years from five to ten. Each of these yearly age levels is treated more elaborately and always with systematic reference to ten major fields of behavior: 1. Motor characteristics. 2. Personal hygiene. 3. Emotional expression. 4. Fears and dreams. 5. Self and sex. 6. Interpersonal relations. 7. Play and pastimes. 8. School life. 9. Ethical sense. 10. Philosophic outlook.

These ten categories are fairly comprehensive. They were not decided upon in advance. They were the natural outgrowth of the data when the basic records were analyzed. They determine the *Maturity Traits* which are concretely formulated in the double columns of chapters 5–9. For convenience of reference they are always identified by the same sectional numbers.

The maturity traits are *not* to be regarded as rigid norms, nor as models. They simply illustrate the kinds of behavior (desirable or otherwise) that tend to occur at this age. Every child has an individual, unique pattern of growth. The behavior traits here outlined may be used to interpret the child's individuality and to consider the maturity level at which he or she is functioning.

Each of the age levels covered in Part Two is treated as a unit, but not as an independent unit. Throughout we have emphasized the dynamic sequences that preserve the continuity of the total stream of development. The reader who wishes to get acquainted with any given age period will probably be interested to read the two adjacent periods to perceive the past and the future trends.

The chief aim of this volume is to impart a sense of growth trends. Although the subject matter is arranged by ages, our purpose has *not* been to set up rigid age norms or a static yardstick. Growth is motion. We should be mainly concerned with the position of the child in a forward-moving cycle.

Part Three deals with the total growth complex. We take the reader onto ten closely connected platforms, in order to impart a panoramic view of the flowing slopes of development, with trends that date back to infancy. These trends are also formulated in tabulated *gradients of growth*. The platforms represent the ten major fields of behavior (chapters 11–20). Each field constitutes a terrain of growth territory distinguishable enough to be considered as a separate topic. To comprehend a landscape one must look at it from varied angles. So these chapters often reveal a single subject in different aspects. It will be found, for example, that motor characteristics affect emotional expression and tensional outlets. They may even enter into the sense of self, and thereby influence interpersonal relations, which in turn concern ethics and school life. It is very important to grasp the unitariness of the growth complex. We hope that the very multiplicity of the growth gradients (over forty in number) and the parallelisms among them will throw light upon the growth process as a living integrated reality.

Here again we would emphasize that the gradients are always relative and not absolute. They are *not* offered as norms of absolute ability, but as approximate norms of developmental sequence. The gradients will become an aid to child guidance only if they are used to locate the position of a child with respect to certain aspects of behavior in the total growth complex. Your problem, as a lay person, is not to measure the mind, but simply to get a sense of direction.

Do not be surprised if you find that your child does some things that are not even mentioned in the book! We know that every child is an individual and that he travels by his own tailor-made time schedule. Nevertheless, we have given you in the characterizational profiles the descriptive maturity traits and in the seriated growth gradients a frame of reference to consult. If you do not use this reference frame too rigidly, it should help to make your child more intelligible; and if he is at all normal, as he probably is, then you will have the reassurance that he is steadily (though not evenly) moving forward to higher levels of maturity. This reassurance will also place you in a better position to give the backward-mindful and forward-constructive guidance best suited to him at a particular phase of his development. And you will always be confronted by a phase at a time! The total ground plan is beyond your control. It is too complex and mysterious to be altogether entrusted to human hands. So nature takes over most of the task, and simply invites your assistance.

PART ONE

GROWTH

... Could you tell me
how to grow,
or is it unconveyed,
like melody or witchcraft?

EMILY DICKINSON

CHAPTER 1

THE CYCLE OF DEVELOPMENT

The years from five to ten occupy an important position in the scheme of human development. To appreciate their significance we may look down two vistas; one vista reaches into the past, the other into the future. A diagram will help us see these middle years of childhood in true perspective.

It takes, on the average, somewhat over twenty years before a newborn infant becomes an adult. Birth was itself preceded by ten lunar months of growth, in which the zygote became an embryo and the embryo a fetus. Soon after the beginning of the fetal period—that is, eight weeks after conception—the nervous system and the muscular system show signs of organization. The fetus stirs with body, head, arm, and leg muscles. Presently eyes and hands become active with mild but patterned movements. By the twentieth prenatal week the future infant is already in possession of the billions of nerve cells that are to govern his behavior throughout life.

As early as the eighth week of intrauterine life the beginnings of the differences between a boy and a girl become recognizable. Long before birth the future infant is already stamped with individuality. Every child is born with potentialities peculiar to him or to her. Each child has a unique pattern of growth, determined by these potentialities and by environmental fate.

There are, however, certain basic traits and growth sequences that are typical of the human species in a modern culture. These general characteristics are indicated in the accompanying diagram, which

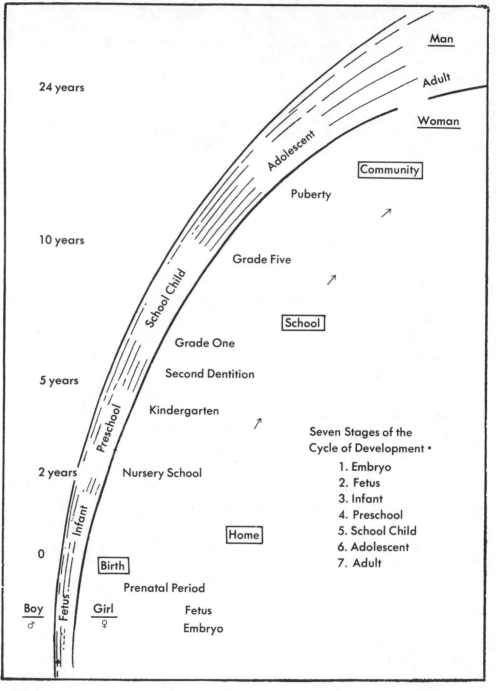

Figure 1
Seven Stages of the Cycle of Development

is so drawn that one may look into the long vista that stretches toward the future and also into the deep vista that reaches downward into the formative past.

The general course of development is similar for both sexes, but girls mature somewhat more rapidly and earlier. Our diagram, therefore, shows two separate curves.

Seven stages are pictured. They correspond only partly to Shakespeare's seven ages of man. The distant stages of senescence and senectitude are not included. Emphasis is placed on the progressive developmental advance, which proceeds as follows:

1. Stage of the embryo (0–8 weeks)
2. Stage of the fetus (8–40 weeks)
3. Infancy (from birth to 2 years)
4. The preschool age (2–5 years)
5. Childhood (5–12 years)
6. Adolescence (12 to 20–24 years)
7. Adult maturity

Man, of all creatures, has the longest period of relative immaturity. He is so complex that it takes him over twenty years to grow up, physically and mentally. Not without reason was the right of franchise in our democratic culture postponed for many years.

The years from five to ten occupy a middle position in this long span of immaturity. These middle years are intermediate both in a biological and in a cultural sense. During them the child sheds his milk teeth, a biological event. At six years he cuts his first permanent tooth, a molar at that. We may call it a school-entrance molar, for it punctuates his induction into the elementary-school system, which is a sociological event.

Puberty is the next great landmark on the pathway to development. It marks the beginning of adolescence, which continues for some ten years, until the attainment of maturity. They are years of completion; the first five years of life are years of preparation. The middle years of childhood lie between. They can be understood only in terms of the past in which they are rooted, and in terms of the future toward which they trend.

Being intermediate years, they lack the dramatic vividness of infancy on the one hand and of adolescence on the other hand. In consequence, the psychology of the five-to-ten period has been somewhat slighted. The literature reflects a tendency to generalize for the period as a whole without recognizing the age difference within the period. The elementary school, to be sure, promotes its children on an annual basis; but curriculum and methods are too largely determined by a narrow psychology of learning instead of a liberal psychology of development. The institutional pressures of the school tend to obscure or to overlook both the individual and the age differences in growth processes. The child is not only advancing in strength and skills, but changing in the interior patterns of private psychology.

Knowing too little about these subtle and hidden changes, parents are prone to blame the school for maladjustments; and teachers in turn are prone to blame child and parent. Often no one is to blame. Ignorance of the ways of growth lies at the basis of many of our difficulties. If only the child could tell us more about how he or she feels, thinks, acts. We judge too much by the superficial evidences of "success" or "failure," and then further distort our judgments by an overweening attitude of competitiveness projected upon the child. Here, again, more insight into the laws and the concrete ways of growth will humanize our adult-child relationships.

Perhaps people have exaggerated the perturbation of adolescence and also the steadiness and stability of childhood. Although some refer to the years between five and the teens as the "latent period," actually more goes on than meets the eye: there are alternations of relative equilibrium and of transitional disequilibrium; there are rhythms of accent in introverted versus extroverted activity, in home versus school, in self versus group interests, in fine motor versus gross motor movements, in the to-and-fro shifts, in the delicate controls of eye movements. Only by identifying the developmental shifts in such counterbalanced traits can we arrive at a more accurate picture of what these somewhat inscrutable boys and girls are really like. Development does not advance on a straight line.

Man was not made in a day. It took vast ages to bring to their present form his capacities to walk and talk, to manipulate with his hands, to contrive with his brain, to see with such rich perception, and to foresee with far-reaching imagination. In some condensed way the child must retraverse these immense ages. This, too, takes time. The organism must gather up and reweave the essential ancestral threads. In the vast complexities of his or her nervous system the child matches the vastness of his ancestral past.

At the age of five the child has already come a long way, has surmounted a hilltop. No longer a mere baby, he or she is almost self-dependent in the elementary routines of life at home, and is often ready for the simple community life of a schoolroom. In emotional traits, and in general intelligence and adaptability, he or she evinces a well-organized, well-rounded action system. It is as though Nature had momentarily completed what she undertook to create. The five-year-old at least presents a preliminary version of the ultimate adult, perhaps registering in a dim way what was once a plateau of full maturity in the remote racial past.

Five, therefore, is a nodal age. For a brief period the child remains in a phase of balanced adjustment to self and to the environment. It is as though the problem of development had been solved. But the push of growth and the pressure of cultural demands build up new tensions. Sometimes these demands are excessive. It is as though the culture were bent on appropriating the child—who is also bent on assimilating the culture; because, of course, the child is destined to graduate from five-year-oldishness.

It is not, however, easy to strike a smooth and steady balance between the child and his or her multifarious environment. At five and a half to six years, the child seems less integrated than at three years, being more like the two-and-a-half-year-old, who has not fully found either self or environment and is therefore in a fluctuating two-way equilibrium. The five-and-a-half-to-six-year-old likewise is in a bipolar phase, trying simultaneously to find himself and to find out his new environment. Choice and reconciliation between the two poles create tensions and hesitations; new problems of development are being solved. This is the key to understanding some of the difficulties and instabilities of the child at the threshold of formal education.

The seven-year-old is under better self-control. The child at this age shows less lability and a greater capacity to absorb and organize new cultural experiences. He or she establishes more firm relationships with companions and with teachers, is decidedly more unipolar, is better able to take what comes: there is less disequilibrium. This is, comparatively speaking, an absorptive and assimilative phase. Day by day the child grows in mental stature.

By the age of eight, the budget of income and outgo shows new balances. The child has built up a firmer body of experience and is able to give as well as to take. Showing more initiative and spontaneity in going out to meet the environment, he or she can fraternize with coequals. At nine the child is becoming still more detached from apron strings and domestic tethers. With a mounting indifference to elders when away from them, he or she dwells in a self-selected culture.

By the age of nine and ten this indifference reaches new heights. Boys and girls alike are amazingly self-dependent. Their self-reliance has grown, and at the same time they have acquired intensified group feelings. Identification with the juvenile group promotes the complex process of detachment from the domestic family group. This is part of the method of maturing.

At the same time the divergence between the sexes is widening. By the age of ten, the tendency toward segregation is well defined. Girls somewhat earlier than boys enter upon the prepubertal period, marked by changes in body proportions, metabolism, and endocrine secretions. These changes become yet more marked during adolescence, which is a prolonged period of diminishing immaturity. The child thus becomes a youth, the youth an adult.

For boys the stage of adolescence lasts about ten years, for girls a year or two less. Adolescence, therefore, is almost as long as infancy and childhood combined. From a cultural standpoint it is an extremely critical period; because it is that time of life when youth is progressively initiated into the responsibilities of citizenship and into the meaning of marriage. With marriage the first great sector of the cycle of development comes full circle. For then a new home is founded. A new infant is born. A new generation starts on its life career, which again pursues the age-old sequence of infancy, childhood, adolescence, and parenthood.

We can scarcely expect the carefree child to contemplate the full sweep of this cycle of development. He or she is deeply immersed in the present. Parents and teachers must make up for this lack of foresight. Being adults, they can better understand the scope and the trends of the cycle. They can have confidence in these trends; they can use knowledge and skill to direct the trends. In countless ways they can give infant, child, and youth intimations of the future that is in store.

For all these reasons it is extremely important that teachers and parents see the whole cycle of development in its imposing perspective. A developmental outlook upon the everyday problems of child behavior imparts meaning and dignity to these problems. It lessens their irritation. We cannot comprehend child life with a sense of proportion or of humor unless we see that life through the stereoscopic lenses of development.

When we put on those lenses we see things in their third dimension: the shortcomings, strivings, and immaturities of children take on new meaning. Each child's behavior is then appraised in terms of his or her development history, his or her unique patterns of growth. External pressures will be modulated to the individual's changing growth needs. He or she will be reared through guidance based on sympathetic understanding. The purpose of this volume is to increase understanding.

A pageant of changes comes with the years. We shall characterize these changes in some detail. None of the changes is ushered in with dramatic abruptness, and there are numerous personal variations in tempo and in timing. But it will be profitable to delineate the changes, so that we may have a frame of reference which will bring the growth processes into focus.

This makes it necessary to adjust our own interpretive lenses from year to year; because the six-year-old child *is* significantly distinguishable from the seven-year-old, and the seven-year-old in turn from the eight-year-old. When we can define the trend of these year-by-year differences, we can adapt our practices and our expectations to the nature and the needs of the individual child.

How else can we avoid the ever-present dangers of authoritarianism in home and school? How else can we realize the spirit of democracy, which above all pays tribute to the dignity of the individual?

CHAPTER 2

THE GROWING MIND

"I wish to understand my child." This is the desire of every right-minded parent. "I wish to understand so far as possible the individuality of each of my pupils." That is the goal of the modern teacher. Such understanding requires some appreciation of *how the mind grows*. This book deals with the minds of growing children.

The mysterious relationships between mind and body need not concern us. It is enough to know that the psychology of the child, which includes the total behavior, is inseparably bound up with the nervous system, and indeed with the entire organism. We cannot separate the "mind" from the total child; and it would lead us far astray if we considered the psyche an occult force, which operates behind the scenes. The child is a unit, as the product of the nervous system.

The growing mind is part and parcel of a vast network of living tissue. The mind grows because the tissue grows. Neurons have phenomenal powers of growth. They multiply rapidly in the embryonic and fetal periods, when the foundations of behavior are laid. The five-month-old fetus is already in possession of the full quota of twelve or more billions of nerve cells which make up the nervous system. These cells continue to grow and organize throughout the cycle of development.

One may think of the child's mind as a marvelous fabric of some kind—a growing fabric. Physically its structure is represented by a great maze of nerves and nerve tracts, and a microscopic feltwork of branching fibers and exquisite fibrils. Functionally the mind consists of propensities and patterns of behavior. We cannot see the under- lying feltwork, but we *can* see the outward behavior patterns. These patterns have so much design and are so lawfully related to one another that the mind is indeed comparable to a fabric that is richly woven and interwoven—an organic fabric which continues to grow, creating new patterns while it grows.

Parents and teachers who think that a child is so plastic that he or she can be made over by strenuous outside pressure have failed to grasp the true nature of the mind. The mind may be likened to a plant, but not to clay. For clay does not grow. Clay is molded entirely from without. A plant is primarily molded from within, through the forces of growth. The present volume will stress these forces.

Intelligent guidance begins with the concept of growth. To under- stand a child, whether in infancy or in the school years, one must become acquainted with the gradients of growth which determine the trends and patterning of his behavior.

What is a growth gradient? It is a series of stages or degrees of maturity by which a child progresses toward higher levels of be- havior. A few concrete illustrations will show how growth gradients operate in the first year of life, in the preschool years, and also in the years from five to ten.

For example, consider a simple six-step gradient in the field of *reading behavior*. The fifteen-month-old child who has just attained the sensorimotor skill of building a tower is also at the lower threshold of reading. He can already help to turn the pages of a picture book. He can definitely identify the circular hole in a circle- triangle-square form board. Surely this is the growth rudiment of the capacity to recognize the round letter *O*, which is the begin- ning of all reading. Moreover, he can read some of the pictures in a book to this extent: he pats a picture he recognizes. Our illustrative growth gradient begins with that pattern of behavior—an ele- mentary perception of a picture on a printed page.

READING BEHAVIOR

1. 15 months   Pats identified picture in book.
2. 18 months   Points to an identified picture in book.
3. 2 years   Names three pictures in book.
4. 3 years   Identifies four printed geometric forms.
5. 4 years   Recognizes salient capital letters.
6. 5–6 years   Recognizes salient printed words.

As a child grows older, his patterns of behavior become more complex, and they seem to embody to an increasing degree the impress of cultural influences. The mechanisms of development, however, do not change, and the child remains true to his or her unique patterns of growth and adaptation. We may illustrate this with still another six-step gradient, which outlines certain progressions in the field of *acquisitive behavior*. Under this term we include patterns and propensities that concern the appropriation and ownership of material things and the collection of possessions.

This acquisitiveness gradient no doubt ought to begin with prehensory behavior, because the infant is a very grasping creature! He seizes and holds objects with intense avidity. Often he resists removal of an object that he has acquired; but his possessive relation to the object is so fleeting that we scarcely think of him as the owner of his toys! They simply "belong" to him. He does not have a strong sense of personal ownership. In the five-year-old, however, we see a personal pride in *his* belongings, which bespeaks an altogether higher form of acquisitive behavior. The growth gradient for the next five or ten years runs somewhat as follows:

ACQUISITIVE BEHAVIOR

1. 5 years   Takes pride in certain personal possessions
             (e.g., a hat or a drawing of his own).
2. 6 years   Collects odds and ends rather sporadically
             (e.g., Christmas cards).
3. 7 years   Collects with purpose and specific, sustained interest
             (e.g., post cards).

4. 8 years   Collects with zeal and has strong interest in size of collection (e.g., comics, paper dolls).

5. 10 years   Collects more formally, with specialized, intellectual interests (e.g., stamps).

6. 15 years   Saves money with discriminating thrift and interest in money values.

Analysis of the foregoing gradient will show that the cultural determinations are not as powerful as they appear to be on the surface. To be sure, hats, post cards, comics, stamps, and moneys are cultural goods. But the value the child instinctively places on these goods, how he collects and cherishes them, how he disposes of them—all this depends upon his developmental (and temperamental) characteristics. A similar relationship between maturation (biological) and acculturation (environmental) will prove to hold in all fields of behavior. The primary growth gradients hold the key to the wisest methods of guidance and education.

In Part Three of this volume we shall assemble numerous gradients, covering a wide diversity of behavior areas.

Growth gradients are frames of reference which can be used to locate the stage of maturity a child has reached in a given field of behavior. These gradients are not applied to ascertain a mental age or to measure the child in an arbitrary way. Rather, the purpose is to find his or her approximate position in various sequences of development. That enables us to estimate the developmental ground he has already gained and the ground that lies just ahead. Educational and guidance measures can then be adapted to the maturity of the child. Failure to interpret an individual's maturity status leads to wasted effort, harmful interference, and unjust discipline.

Sometimes, of course, the child's behavior is so unexpected and so contradictory that it is very difficult to understand. It must be remembered that the mind does not grow on a straight and even front. The course of development is uneven (in some children more so than in others). It zigzags, and sometimes it spirals backward in a way that suggests retreat and regression. But if the child is normal, the ultimate and all-over trend is toward a higher level of maturity. Development is like a stream: it carves the best possible channel; it flows onward; it reaches a goal.

A child may be making good progress even when his or her development seems to be taking a devious course. This is transparently shown by the manner in which a baby learns to creep. Careful observation has disclosed that a baby goes through some twenty stages or substages in achieving this locomotor ability. Ten of these stages are pictured in the accompanying pictographic gradient. The developmental goal is forward locomotion, prone progression on all fours. But note how often the behavior at a given stage seems to fall short of the goal and even appears contrary to it. Yet in due season the child scoots across the floor on hands and knees, then on hands and feet, and yet later on feet alone.

The following stages are depicted in the diagram (over a dozen intervening stages are omitted):

Stage	Behavior Pattern	Progression	Code
A	Lifts head—legs passive	None	x
B	Swims (head rears, legs extend)	None	x
C	Pivots (arms alternately flex and extend)	Circles	x
D	Crawls backward (arms push)	Backward	→
E	Kneels creepwise (lifts trunk)	None	x
F	Creeps backward (lowers trunk)	Backward	→
G	Rocks (in high creep position)	Oscillates	⇆
H	Creep-crawls (pitches forward)	Forward	←
I	Creeps (on hands and knees)	Forward	←
J	Creeps plantigrade (on hands and feet)	Forward	←

From the foregoing sequence, which is virtually universal for the human species, it is clear that Nature does not always go directly to her goal. She takes a roundabout path, and sometimes she seems to be poised midway as though she did not know where to go! At stage G the child is all set to go places, but instead rocks back and forth, oscillating between two alternatives. At stage C he spun around in a circle; at stages D and F he actually went backward;

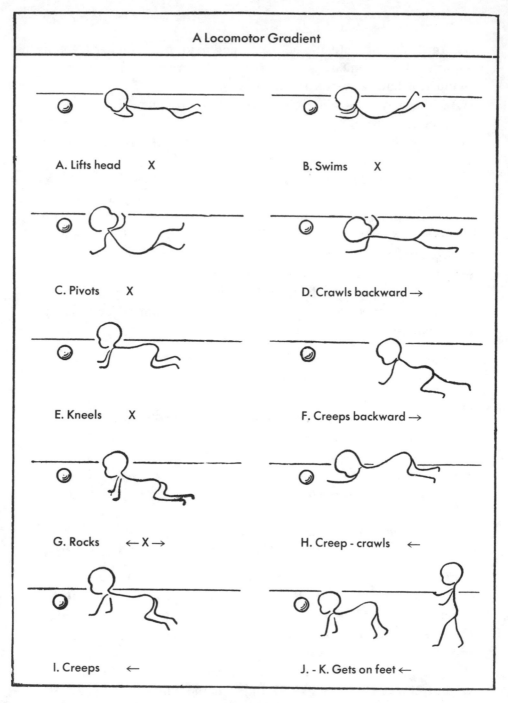

Figure 2
Locomotor Gradient

at other stages he remained completely on location. And yet when we view the entire gradient in perspective we know that he was making *developmental headway* all the time, even when he was pushing himself backward. Nature has a devious cunning which is beyond our logic.

The child is so closely in league with Nature that we must respect his innate gradations of growth. Who would think of punishing an infant because he propelled himself backward instead of forward, or because he vacillated between forward and backward; or because he combined crawling and creeping patterns instead of adopting the "proper" method of locomotion? In the naïve immaturities of the infant's prone behavior we see that Nature herself needs time to refashion in the individual a complex type of behavior which required eons of evolution in the race.

The patterning of prone behavior supplies an instructive example of the mechanisms that govern child development at all ages. The baby betrays immaturities while solving the problems of locomotion. A school beginner will be confronted by other problems, but will exhibit comparable immaturities. In his writing he will go in wrong directions, will produce astonishing reversals, and at times will seem to make no progress at all. But ultimately he achieves the necessary coordinations of posture, eyes, and hands that will enable him to write straightforwardly. Rate of progress will always depend primarily upon the maturity of the child's nervous system. It is doubtful whether anyone should be "disciplined" for motor shortcomings. And in interpreting "failures" in writing, reading, and arithmetic, it is well to recall the tortuous gradations by which the baby "learns" to creep.

From this preliminary discussion it is clear that the significance of a child's behavior depends upon the position of that behavior in a developmental sequence. In any given situation we ask: What growth preceded? What growth is likely to follow? In the management of children, we do not so much need rules of thumb; we need orientation. Growth gradients will give us bearings in the latitude of maturity levels and in the longitude of age.

As a child advances in age, he or she not only gains in height and weight, but body proportions, and even body chemistries, undergo change. Most important of all, the behavior equipment changes. The changes are gradual; so gradual, indeed, that they often escape notice. They come as softly as a thief in the night.

For each year from five to ten we have drawn up in Part Two a type portrait which delineates the distinctive behavior characteristics of that age. It is not assumed that this portrait will snugly fit any one child; but it will suggest the traits by which he or she may be appraised. A series of such annual portraits will also define the concrete trends toward maturity. Just as the eye needs two overlapping images in order to see depth, so we need two adjacent maturity levels to secure a stereoscopic view of the child's development.

These year-by-year behavior profiles provide the basic points of departure for the growth gradients assembled and codified in Part Three. The profiles outline a total behavior picture. The gradients are designed to serve as *interpretational devices*. Properly applied, they will help the adult appraise the problems of growth with which every child is faced. The child can scarcely formulate his problems for us. We must watch his behavior and use it as a clue to understanding. If he reverses his digits he may well be in the equivalent of a backward-crawl stage in locomotion.

A growth gradient may tell us where he has arrived and where he is going. By applying several gradients to their several fields of behavior, we get a better view of the child's total maturity status. We may even get an indication of his strongest assets—and his characteristic liabilities if he has any. We do not necessarily expect a child to be equally advanced in all behavior fields. We know that there are many entirely normal variations in the chronological age at which school abilities are attained. We know that every child has a unique pattern of growth. And just because basic development proceeds in sequences that are nearly universal, the growth gradients help us to discover and describe that unique pattern.

The child is his own best norm. He is never so much like himself as when he is changing, because his growth characteristics are the truest index of his individuality.

Growth gradients also tell us something about the psychological differences between boys and girls. Girls are more advanced and more generalized in some types of behavior. Boys are more intense and more channelized—for example, in certain aspects of acquisitive behavior. Some of these differences are subtle, but they are significant and should influence our attitudes as parents and educators.

Growth gradients deal with relativities rather than with absolutes. Nothing can be more misleading than an absolute, particularly in the management of children. Absolutism leads to authoritarianism and this in turn leads to blindness—a blindness toward the developmental status and to the developmental needs of the child. From an absolute standpoint, "stealing" is always *stealing*, but even a crude use of a simple gradient of acquisitive behavior will indicate that there is a difference between the "pilfering" by a seven-year-old and a specific "theft" by a ten-year-old.

Growth gradients therefore make possible a developmental outlook upon the frailties of human efficiency and of childhood conduct. Far from encouraging a policy of indulgence, a developmental philosophy reinforced by concrete growth gradients will make us more alert to the developmental needs of children. Such a philosophy has far-reaching implications for the harmony of relationships between parent, teacher, and child.

CHAPTER 3

THE PARENT-CHILD-TEACHER RELATIONSHIP

When a baby is born he is still almost completely merged with the cosmos. Which is to say that he has no sense of self-identity, no sense that distinguishes between the *World of Things* and the *World of Persons*. As the child matures he gradually makes distinctions. He learns to discriminate between what is animate and inanimate. Slowly he discovers his physical self. He becomes dimly aware of his personal self. He discovers his parents. He differentiates friends from strangers, children from adults, aggressors from benefactors. He finds that he is a personal agency who acts and is acted upon.

He does not say all this in words, but he builds interpersonal attitudes into his growing personality, chiefly through his experiences with other persons. Indeed, personality is the end product of all the interpersonal relationships in which an individual becomes involved. When this intricate web of relationships is wholesome, the personality tends to be wholesome. Needless to say, the basic organization of personality takes place in the first five years of life.

The parent-child relationships, therefore, are of determining importance in the early patterning of personality. A well-ordered home which provides normal parental care is the best guarantee of mental health in the growing child. The school naturally can accomplish maximum results only when it works in harmony with such a home. But this should be a two-way harmony, with the child more than an innocent bystander. In fact, the child from five to ten is at the apex of a triangle of interpersonal forces. Life apparently would be easier for him if he had to adjust only to his parents or only to his teachers. But he has to adjust to both sets of adults. Sometimes the task is doubly difficult when the home and the school adults fail to see eye to eye.

Perhaps the best way to understand the meaning and mechanism of the teacher-pupil relationship is to compare it with its prototype, the relationship between parent and child. What are the similarities? What are the differences?

1. The parent-child relationship is based on heredity, or kinship. The teacher-child relationship is based upon authority conferred by the state. This authority is very august. From an educational standpoint it confers upon the teacher a certain advantage, because it puts him or her in a position to regard the problems of child development in a realistic manner.

2. The teacher's "family" is large. This, of course, confers a fundamental advantage upon the parent-child relationship. But when we recall that only a portion of the parents' time can be devoted directly to the task of rearing children, we see that the advantages are not all in favor of the home. The teacher, moreover, has the tremendous psychological reinforcement that comes from the impact of the school group upon the individual child. She can use the group to influence the child.

3. The intimacy and the restricted size of the home give parents maximum opportunity to become acquainted with the characteristics of their children. But here again the teacher is not at a complete disadvantage if she has been professionally trained to perceive individual differences. Moreover, the teacher observes the child as a member of a social group. This brings to light characteristics the home cannot reveal.

4. During the early school years the emotional bonds between parent and child are more intense than those between teacher and child. A wise teacher respects this difference and does not try to function as a substitute mother. She has an enlightened platonic affection, which she metes out to assist the developmental needs of

her pupils, apportioning more to some than to others. Hers is a wholesome, human friendliness. Unfortunate is the child who attends a schoolroom where the very atmosphere is so unhomelike and so domineering that his sense of security is weakened.

If, then, we analyze the psychology of enlightened parent-child and teacher-pupil relationships, we find three common components: (1) considerateness, (2) a sense of humor, and (3) a philosophy of growth.

1. *Considerateness.* Considerateness is the first essential. The very word considerateness conveys the idea of respect for the dignity of the individual. Considerateness, it has been well said, is in itself a social system. It certainly favors the development of democratic attitudes.

If parents (and teachers) begin with the assumption that they can make over and mold a child into a preconceived pattern, they are bound to become somewhat autocratic. If, on the contrary, parents begin with the assumption that every baby comes into the world with a unique individuality, they are bound to become more considerate. For their task will be to understand the child's individuality and to give it the best possible chance to grow and find itself. The same holds true for teachers.

Considerateness, as we use the term here, is not merely a social or domestic grace. It is something of an art, a kind of perceptiveness and imaginativeness, which enables one person to understand the attitudes of another person. It is an alert kind of liberalism, which acknowledges distinctive characteristics in other individuals. It is an active form of courtesy.

2. *A sense of humor.* The sense of humor is a pliant sense of proportion. Its function is to keep the individual from becoming mechanized and hardened. It is a play of the mind akin to the spirit of freedom. When a teacher has it, she protects her own mental health and that of her pupils. Humor is a safeguard against undue tensions and the severities of unwise discipline. An overserious schoolroom violates for children the Jeffersonian right of pursuit of happiness.

3. *A philosophy of growth.* The child's personality is a product of

slow and gradual growth. His nervous system matures by stages and natural sequences. He sits before he stands; he babbles before he talks; he says "no" before he says "yes"; he fabricates before he tells the truth; he draws a circle before he draws a square; he is selfish before he is altruistic; he is dependent on others before he achieves dependence on self. All his abilities, including his morals, are subject to laws of growth. The task of child care is not to mold the child behavioristically to some predetermined image, but to assist him step by step, guiding his growth.

This developmental philosophy does not mean indulgence. It is instead a constructive accommodation to the limitations of immaturity. Lacking such a philosophy, a teacher may use harsh methods of discipline, and false methods of instruction, designed to subdue her pupils and to bring them to a uniform level. Lacking such a philosophy, a mother may unjustly accuse the teacher of not keeping her child up to the normal standards of achievement and conduct.

These are the broad considerations that make the improvement of the parent-child-teacher relationship so vital to our culture. It is a three-way relationship. The child with his double bonds is an intermediate link, creating a third bond of responsibility between teachers and parents. The responsibility cannot become mutual without a common outlook upon the developmental welfare of the child. This requires more than academic-achievement tests, intelligence scores, and graded report cards. Home and school alike must lay less stress on competition and be more genuinely concerned with the nature and the needs of the child's personality.

A Special Word to Fathers*

A new era is opening for fathers. The status of children is changing, and the role of father in the home is coordinately changing. Not long ago he was truly a monarch. His word was law, and the

---

* Written in 1946, this still applies today.

law was stern. He held himself apart from the plain, everyday affairs of his children, reserving his powers for higher occasions of discipline and admonition. He did not unbend. Even during the long prenatal period he maintained a befitting detachment.

All this is now shifting under the irrepressible tide of cultural forces. Fathers are actively sharing in the numerous everyday tasks that go with the rearing of children. Participation rather than detachment is the trend. The careful mutual planning that now characterizes pregnancy and maternity hygiene marks a great advance in our ways of living. With the aid of the famous old Broadway success *Life with Father*, we wave a gay goodbye to the paterfamilias of the good old days.

The modern father is now in the process of finding his new role. He has already discovered that he is not satisfied merely to give emergency help with night feeding and laundry, or to have sketchy contacts with his children on evenings or Saturday afternoons. He is somewhat amazed to find that at times his child does not respond to his well-meaning and affectionate approaches. He discovers that at some ages the child seems to be better than at others. Perhaps he especially enjoyed the three-year-old or the five-year-old period, and was simply dumfounded by six-year-old behavior. Many fathers do not get on a comfortable, companionable basis until a son reaches nine or ten years of age, when they arrive at a man-to-man rapport.

Some ages are indeed smoother and pleasanter than others, but all are equally interesting and significant. The father-child relationship will not be on a fully enlightened level until both parents make a joint effort to understand the ever-changing characteristics of the child at each advancing stage of maturity. This demands a developmental outlook upon all the problems of child care and child management. It demands an increasingly penetrating acquaintance with the *mechanisms of growth*.

We live in a technological age and need not be frightened by the concept of mechanisms. Fathers readily think in terms of atomic structures, electronic orbits, short and long waves, and frequency modulation. They would like to know what makes the child tick.

It degrades neither child nor father to bring mechanical concepts to bear upon the manifold wonders of the child's behavior and individual development. These concepts do not solve the mystery of life, but they do strengthen our faith in the lawfulness of life and growth.

They help us to understand why the pathways of child development are so tortuous and yet so patterned and ballasted by an overall trend toward optimal realization. This kind of insight leads to a deeper understanding of individual differences. It makes for philosophic tolerance and a more vital appreciation of the meaning of infancy and childhood. May this new knowledge not only be of interest to fathers, but also be put to use by them. Many fathers have a hard time correlating their child's maturational age with his placement in school. When a child needs extra time, many fathers resist this possibility of slowing down the child. Somehow their pride is hurt. (More of this in our chapter on school.)

We respectfully invite fathers who read this volume to regard it as an introductory manual in psychotechnology, which deals with the mechanisms of child development and thereby with the improvement of parent-child relationships.

PART TWO

THE GROWING CHILD

Growth of Man like growth of Nature
Gravitates within,
Atmosphere and sun confirm it
But it stirs alone.

EMILY DICKINSON

CHAPTER 4

THE FIRST FOUR YEARS

The cycle of human development is continuous. All growth is based on previous growth. The growth process is therefore a paradoxical mixture of creation and perpetuation. The child is always becoming something new; yet he always summates the essence of his past. His psychology at the age of five is the "outgrowth" of all that happened to him during the four years after birth—and the forty weeks prior to birth. For all the past was prelude.

The Newborn Infant

Birth marks the arrival but not the beginning of an individual. The true beginnings trace back to the embryonic and fetal periods, when the tissues and organs of the body take form and when even the shape of the behavior to come is profoundly foreshadowed. Types of body build are prefigured: square and firm; round and soft; spindly and delicate. Modes of reaction characteristic of varieties of physique are likewise laid down.

The patterning of behavior gets under way remarkably early. By four weeks after conception, the heart beats; by eight weeks, head and trunk make minimal movements; by twelve weeks, the hands flex; by twenty-four weeks, the chest is capable of rhythmic movements; by twenty-eight to forty weeks, all physiological functions may be sufficiently mature to ensure survival in the event of birth.

Once the infant is born he must struggle for his very existence.

With the assistance of nature and caretakers, he must bring his various physiological functions, such as respiration, temperature regulation, digestion, excretion, sleeping, and waking, into adequate coordination. While making these early life adjustments the infant appears unsteady, unstable. His thresholds of reaction are low and inconstant. He startles, sneezes, quivers, cries on slight provocation. His breathing and body temperature are irregular. He may even swallow in the wrong direction! Normally, he weathers the storms of adaptation and settles down to relative stability in a few weeks. But so exacting are these early transitions that we may say a baby is really not full-born until four weeks of age.

No sharp line can be drawn between "physiological" and "psychological" functions. A baby's satisfactions, needs, interests, and drives are determined by the status of the entire organism, including metabolism, the chemistry of body fluids, and the tonus of the muscular system. Throughout infancy much of the behavior is directly related to the complex functions of feeding, sleeping, and elimination. The acquisition of speech even involves a recombination of feeding and breathing behavior patterns—a recombining which it took the race literally millions of years to perfect. The "lower" vegetative functions are thus incorporated into the growing action system. They color emotional patterns and temperamental trends. The autonomic nervous system, which presides over these functions, operates in close conjunction with the cerebrospinal nervous system, which governs sensation and motion. The newborn baby is already in possession of the basic equipment for feeling, sensing, and moving. Mental growth is well under way.

In the next four years the child will make prodigious progress. Never again will he advance with the same speed. He is laying the wide base of a pyramid which continues to ascend in the years from five to ten. During the first half of this first decade he is preeminently a home child. During the second half he is both a home and a school child. In rapid succession he progresses from bassinet to crib, to highchair, to playpen; to porch, sidewalk, nursery, and schoolroom; to first, second, third, fourth, and fifth grades. In a growth sense, it is a long as well as a swift journey.

The present chapter will briefly characterize the developmental ground covered during the first four years, with milestones at four, sixteen, twenty-eight, and forty weeks; twelve, fifteen, and eighteen months; and two, two and a half, three, three and a half, and four years.* The child does not linger at any of these milestones, so we shall emphasize the unremitting sweep which bears him on his forward course. But with the aid of ten stop-motion sketches we can get an impression of his transforming behavior make-up as he travels toward his consecutive destinations.

Four Weeks Old

The month-old baby is no longer a mere neophyte in the elementary art of living. He breathes with regularity, his heart has steadied its pace, his body temperature has ceased to be erratic. His muscle tone is less fluctuant than it was in the days of long ago when he was only a newborn. He has reserves of muscle tonus. He taps the reserves and responds with motor tightening when you pick him up. This makes him feel less molluscous and more compact. By virtue of his heightened muscle tonus he is already more competent to meet the buffetings of fate.

His or her reactions since birth have become more configured. The baby sleeps more definitely, wakes more decisively. He opens his eyes wide and does not lapse so much into shallow, ambiguous drowsing. When awake, he usually lies with head averted to a preferred side. Often he extends the arm on that side, crooking the other arm at shoulder level in a sort of fencing attitude. He holds and activates this tonic neck-reflex posture from time to time as though it is a developmental exercise, and indeed it is. Nature is laying a foundation for a coordination of eyes and hands.

In a few more weeks the baby will begin to look in the direction

---

* For a detailed account of these stages of development, the reader may refer to the companion volume *Infant and Child in the Culture of Today,* by Gesell, Ilg, and Ames, rev. ed. (Harper & Row, 1974).

of the extended arm and catch sight of his hand. Even now he will see and briefly follow a moving object dangled near his eyes. But his hands remain fisted. He is not yet ready for reaching.

He gives attention only insofar as his behavior capacities permit. This will always be true, even after he reaches school age. Just now he manifestly attends to the sensations of gastric well-being that suffuse him after a meal, and to the massive warmth of a bath. Sometimes he immobilizes with interest as he regards the face of his mother. His emotional patterns are very simple, if we may judge by the general impassiveness of his physiognomy. Nevertheless, he reacts positively to comforts and satisfactions, and negatively to pain and denials. He cries. He listens. Occasionally small throaty sounds emerge from his larynx.

In all these behavior tokens we see the germs of language, of sociality, perception, intelligence, body posture, and even locomotion. The neuromotor system is organizing apace. The mind is growing.

Sixteen Weeks Old

By sixteen weeks the neuromotor system has so elaborated that the child is no longer always content to lie on his back. He likes to be held for brief periods in a seated position, so that he may face the world eyes front. So held, he can erect his head. This is the first component of the upright posture, which in another year will enable him to walk alone. Command of head and eyes comes before command of feet.

The sixteen-week-old infant has gained considerable control over the six pairs of searchlight muscles that move his eyes in their sockets. The eyes focus upon his own hand; they shift their focus to an object nearby; they pursue a dangled toy moving through a 180-degree arc. Eyes are becoming nimble.

There is something prophetic in the way in which the sixteen-week-old infant relishes the sitting position. His eyes glisten; his pulse strengthens, his breathing quickens, and he smiles as he is translated from horizontal to perpendicular. This is more than an athletic triumph. It is a widening of the visual horizon; it is a social reorientation.

Social behavior both personal and interpersonal has greatly expanded. He or she coos with personal contentment, chuckles, laughs aloud. The child used to smile only on gastric occasions, but now imitates a social smile, and also smiles responsively and vocalizes on social approach.

The hands are no longer predominantly fisted. They are uncurling, and soon they will be able to reach out. But at present the baby reaches with his eyes. He inspects, he looks expectantly; he even singles out small details in his visible environment. He associates sight and sound. He "notices" when he hears and sees his food prepared. He reacts to cues and clues. This always remains the essence of wisdom.

The sixteen-week-old child is usually well adjusted both to the world of things and to the world of persons. This is partly because he derives such great satisfaction from the free use of his eyes. He frets when his visual hunger goes unappeased. He quiets when ocular and social stimuli combine to feed his appetite for visual experience. But new demands are in the making. Soon he must satisfy the eagerness of his hands as well as that of his eyes.

Twenty-eight Weeks Old

Touch hunger follows visual hunger. Or, rather, the two now combine; for the twenty-eight-week-old baby is bent on manipulating everything he can lay his eyes and hands on. Whether he lies on his back or sits in his highchair, he must have something to handle and to mouth. He likes to sit up, for he is gaining control of his trunk muscles—another step toward the attainment of upright posture.

Note with what concentrated attention the baby exercises his growing powers. He sees a clothespin on his play tray. He grasps it in an instant, brings it to his lips and tongue for tactile impressions, bangs it on the tray for sound and motion, transfers it from hand to hand and back again for manipulatory experience, inspects it with a twist for visual perception. Such avid attention is born out of growth needs. The baby's play is work and his work is play.

So engrossing is his self-activity that he can amuse himself for long periods. But he can smile at onlookers and is usually friendly both with familiars and strangers. Indeed, he presents an amiable union of self-containedness and sociality. He alternates with ease between self-directed and socially referred activity. He listens to words spoken by others; he listens also to his own private vocalizations.

At this age the child's abilities are in good balance. His behavior patterns and trends are in focus. He is so harmoniously constituted that he causes few perplexities on the part of his caretakers. It is a period of short-lived developmental "equilibrium." There will be similar periods in his later growth career, but they likewise will be transient. The growth complex never fully stabilizes. New thrusts and new tensions of development produce imbalances which are in turn resolved and replaced by another temporary stage of comparative equilibrium.

The twenty-eight-week-old baby has numerous new problems of posture, locomotion, manipulation, and personal-social behavior to meet before he or she reaches the age of forty weeks. The course of true development cannot always run smoothly.

Forty Weeks Old

Horizons widen with each advance in motor maturity. The forty-week-old infant can creep, and this greatly expands the scope of his initiative and of his experiences. But significantly enough, he tends to keep head erect and eyes front while he creeps. He shows a special interest in vertical surfaces, by which he pulls himself to his feet; for the upright posture is his developmental goal. He is nearing this goal in gross motor control; he can sit quite alone and he can stand with support.

Fine motor control also is advancing. Place a string on a table: the baby grasps it with prompt, exact pincer prehension. At twenty-eight weeks he slapped the string with his flat palm. If he is more discriminating now it is because uncountable millions of delicate connections have silently organized in his network of neural and muscular fibrils. Nature is perfecting particularly the acuteness of his sensitive fingertips. He is under an irrepressible propensity to poke and pry and palpate with his extended index finger.

This is another method for widening the psychological horizon. By his inquisitive poking he probes into the third dimension of depth. He discovers the physical secret of container and contained. Place a cube in a cup: he thrusts his hand in and fingers the cube. His perceptual world is not as flat as it used to be.

The forty-week-old child is also penetrating more deeply into the social environment. He discriminates more sharply between familiars and strangers. He imitates gestures, facial expressions, and sounds. He heeds "No! No!" He echoes "Da-Da." He probably has learned a nursery trick. But if he now pat-a-cakes to everyone's delight, it is due not so much to the teaching of his elders as to his own developmental readiness. At twenty-eight weeks it was quite impossible to teach him this nursery game.

Twelve Months Old

Since the baby was born, the earth has completed one full revolution around the sun—chronological age: one year. The baby can now place a cube in a cup and release it—developmental age value: one year. A baby is as old as his behavior. From the standpoint of guidance and education, he must be appraised in terms of the maturity level of his or her abilities. When one year old, he can usually cruise around his playpen by himself, but in walking he needs the guiding help of a supporting hand.

Gross motor skills show more individual variation than fine motor and adaptive behavior. Again place a string on a table. The baby plucks it with deft thumb and forefinger opposition and dangles an object tied at the end of the string, thus giving evidence of increasing perceptiveness of relations. He puts one and one together. He holds one cube and contacts another cube with it; or he puts a cube into a box; or into the receiving palm of his mother's hand.

Left to his own devices with a dozen cubes, the child exhibits a very instructive behavior pattern. He picks up one cube and drops it; he picks up another cube and drops it; he picks up still another and drops it. All this is done in a somewhat disorderly manner; but by all the canons of development this one-by-one cube manipulation must be set down as the first step in the gradient of mathematics! It is nothing less than rudimentary counting. This remarkable behavior pattern is not the result of imitation nor of cultural impress; although the culture in due season will supply the appropriate labels, 1, 2, 3, 4, 5. . . . In time the labels will be true symbols and the child will entertain corresponding concepts—but not yet!

In social situations, too, the yearling child puts one and one together. He likes an audience; he repeats performances laughed at; he enjoys all sorts of to-and-fro household play. This social reciprocity is based on his increasing emotional perceptiveness, which enables him to read more accurately the emotions of others.

Fifteen Months Old

At fifteen months the behavior picture seems to lose its harmony and equilibrium. This is the dart and dash and fling age. The give-and-take of to-and-fro rapport is superseded by one-way behavior. The fifteen-month-old child is no longer a mere creeping and cruising baby. He strains at the leash with his new-found powers of walking and toddling. He likes to overturn wastebaskets; he likes to pull off his shoes.

His gross motor drive is powerful: he is ceaselessly active, with brief bursts of locomotion, starting, stopping, starting again, climbing and clambering. It is as though he were an aggressive jeep putting himself through all its paces.

If confined to a pen, he or she is likely to pick up each toy and fling it outside. This is a gross type of prehensory release—a casting pattern which needs practice—at least in the child's own estimation. Developmentally, crude casting precedes more highly coordinated forms of throwing. But this casting is not altogether crude, because the baby is casting with eyes as well as with hands. He is using his eyes alertly to see where an object falls, as it falls. This is a significant exercise in distance perception, in ocular accommodation and convergence. It requires agile coordination of the various eye muscles.

The fifteen-month-old child is not all bluster and bumble. Surprisingly enough, he can poise one cube over another and release it with sufficient neatness to build a tower of two. In the ancient history of the race this was an important construction feat. It is a significant achievement in the history of the individual.

The release pattern is now so refined that the baby can pluck a pellet and drop it into the mouth of a small bottle. He does this without instruction or demonstration. We simply place the pellet beside the bottle; he responds with immediate spontaneity. Spontaneous behavior is often a key to developmental readiness.

Eighteen Months Old

The fifteen-month-old toddler strains at the leash. The eighteen-month-old runabout is on the loose, colliding with new physical and cultural problems at every turn. The one-year-old, by reason of his locomotor immaturity and relative docility, is protected from excessive impacts of the culture. But the eighteen-month-old child is no longer a "mere" baby, and life is not so easy for him. Larynx, legs, hands, feet, bladder and bowel sphincters are all, concurrently, coming under cortical control. With such an extraordinary diversity of behavior patterns to coordinate, it is no wonder that he functions in brief spans and pulsations of attention.

His attention is sketchy, mobile, works in swift brief strokes. He lugs, tugs, dumps, pushes, drags, pounds, runs into nooks and corners and byways; goes up and down stairs; by one device or another pulls a wheeled toy from place to place, abandons it—and then resumes with variations, including walking backward.

He attends to the *here* and *now*. He has little perception for far-off objects. He runs into them headlong, with scant sense of direction. He has little perception for far-off events. No need to talk to him about the future. He may, however, understand and even execute a simple commission within his motor experience, such as "Go and get your hat." He has a few favorite expressions of his own: "All gone," "Bye-bye"; "Oh, my!"

Although he has meager pre-perceptions, he has a significant sense of "conclusions." He likes to complete a situation. He puts a ball in a box with decision and caps the performance with a delighted exclamatory "Oh, my!" He closes a door; he hands you a dish when he has finished; he mops up a puddle—all with an air of conclusiveness, as if to say "now that's done."

Two Years Old

The two-year-old is graduating from infancy. Since the age of eighteen months he may have grown two inches, gained three pounds, cut four teeth. He can run without falling; he can turn the pages of a book singly; he can pull on a garment; he can keep a spoon right side up as he puts it into his mouth; he can frame a two-word phrase or a three-word sentence; he can even use words to express and to control his toilet needs.

But concessions must be made to his developmental immaturity. He is still an infant-child. There is a residual stagger in his walk. His running is amateurishly headlong. He can not slow down or turn sharp corners. (Motor abilities are rarely modulated while they are still new.) He delights in the grosser forms of muscular activity—romping and rough-and-tumble play. He tends to express his emotions massively in dancing, clapping, stamping, or captious laughter.

The facial muscles of expression, however, are more mobile. The muscles of the jaw are under better control. Chewing is no longer as great an effort as it was at eighteen months, and mastication is becoming rotary.

The fine motor coordination of the two-year-old is obviously de-limited by certain selective immaturities of his or her nervous system. He can build a tower of five or six cubes, but cannot rearrange them in a horizontal row to build a wall. He also has difficulty in making a horizontal stroke with crayon, even though he imitates a vertical stroke with the greatest of ease. This predilection for vertical over horizontal is based not on chance but on a foreordained geometry of growth. When somewhat older, the child will show a comparable predilection for the horizontal. Yet older, he will be in full command of both dimensions. At the age of three he can build a bridge that combines both vertical and horizontal components.

Similar developmental delimitations show themselves in the sphere of personal-social behavior. He has a robust sense of *mine*, but a very weak sense of *thine*. He can hoard, but he cannot share.

Two and a Half Years Old

The two-and-a-half-year-old also has difficulties with *thine* and *mine*—difficulties which, by the way, have not been entirely mastered even by the adults of the human race. The two-and-a-half-year-old, however, has developed a stronger awareness of persons other than himself. He will bring a favorite toy to nursery school to display it with pride; but he finds he cannot quite surrender it to his play-mates. He will also be seized with an intense impulse to acquire a coveted toy; but once in possession, he abandons it with indifference. The sense of ownership is evidently in a transitional, unmodulated phase of development.

The two-and-a-half-year-old does not have himself well in hand. He is reputed to be variously impetuous, imperious, contrary, hesitant, dawdling, defiant, ritualistic, unreasonable, and incomprehensible. He does lack the equanimities of the classic self-containment of twenty-eight-week-old maturity.

His difficulties are due to the fact that he is just discovering a new realm of opposites. Life is no longer a one-way street as it was at eighteen months. Life is charged with alternatives. Every pathway in the culture has become a two-way street. He has a great deal of intermediating to do between contrary impulses, and yet he has to become acquainted with *both* opposites. Being inexperienced as well as immature, he often makes two choices where he should make one; or he makes the wrong choice; or he makes none at all. Hence his reputation. Hence the impatience of his disciplinarians.

For the time being, his action system is in a stage of relatively unstable equilibrium. He has yet to acquire skill in balancing alternatives and in thinking of one alternative to the exclusion of another. He reminds us of the two-way rocking and the creep-crawl stages in the patterning of prone locomotion. Yet we know that he is forging ahead developmentally and we can predict that at the age of three years he will have himself in hand.

Three Years Old

The three-year-old has himself in hand because he has come out victorious in his struggle with diametric opposites. He is no longer as paradoxical and unpredictable as he was at two and a half. He has captured the power of judging and choosing between two rival alternatives. In fact, he likes to make a choice, within the realm of his experience. He is sure of himself. He is emotionally less turned in on himself. He takes his routines more sensibly and does not insist on rituals to protect himself. He has more flexible personal relations. Self-dependence and sociality are well balanced. Accordingly, he seems to fit into the culture more comfortably. His whole action system, for the time, is in good working equilibrium. Hence his good reputation. Hence the approval of his elders.

Three is a nodal age, a kind of coming of age. The conflict of opposites which a half year ago expressed itself in "negativism," "willfulness," and "contrariness" gives way to a new realization of social demands. Far from being contrary, he tries to meet and to understand these demands. He even asks, "Do it dis way?"

Much of this social amenability is based on sheer psychomotor maturity. He is more sure and nimble on his feet; he no longer walks with arms outstretched (he swings them like a grownup); he can dodge, throw, stop-go, and turn sharp corners. He has attained to the developmental rule of three: he can count to three; he can compare two objects, which requires a three-step logic; he can combine three cubes to build a bridge; he can combine a vertical and horizontal crayon stroke to make a cross; he can barter commodity a for commodity b, which also requires a three-step logic; in play and games he can wait his turn.

For all these reasons you can bargain with and on the three-year-old. He marks both a culmination and a prophecy in the cycle of child development.

Three and a Half Years Old

Three is conforming, but three and a half is just the opposite. Refusing to obey is perhaps the key aspect of this turbulent, troubled period in the life of the young child. It may sometimes seem to his mother that his main concern is to strengthen his will, and he strengthens it by going against whatever is demanded of him by that still most important person in his life, his mother.

Even the simplest occasion can elicit total rebellion. Dressing, eating, toileting, getting up, going to bed—whatever the routine, it can be the scene for an all-out, no-holds-barred fight. Techniques and tricks formerly foolproof can no longer be guaranteed to work.

One may fairly and in all friendliness describe the three-and-a-half-year-old boy or girl as being inwardized, insecure, anxious, and above all determined and self-willed. This self-will does not seem to be rooted in a strong personal security, as one might expect, but rather seems based on a pervasive insecurity. This insecurity is evidenced even in physical ways: the child stutters, stumbles, trembles. And tensional outlets of all varieties are conspicuous at this age. Even vision may pose a special problem, and many now show a marked fear of heights.

Emotional as well as physical insecurity is often expressed. He tells his parents, "Don't look," "Don't laugh," "Don't talk." But he may say "Don't look" at one moment and the next become very angry if not given full attention.

Rebellion against parental commands can be so strong at this time that many mothers find that their child does better with a baby-sitter than with them. Inconsistency makes trouble, too. The child may be extremely shy one minute and overbold the next. This is not an easy age.

Four Years Old

The three-year-old is conforming. The three-and-a-half-year-old is anxious. The four-year-old is assertive and expansive. He bursts with motor activity: racing, hopping, jumping, skipping, climbing. He bubbles with mental activity, manifested in an abandoned use of words and in flights of fable and fancy. The four-year-old tends to go out of bounds, notably in his or her speech and in imaginative antics. He is blithe and lively, but is more firmly based than may appear on the surface. Emotionally and intellectually he comes back to home base; he does not get too detached from his moorings. The uncertainties of three and a half are now brought together in a new surety of action. The mental consolidations achieved at the age of three serve to stabilize.

The key to the psychology of the four-year-old is high drive associated with a mental organization that is mobile at the margins. His mental imagery is almost mercurial. It moves from one configuration to another with great agility. In his dramatic play he doffs and dons his roles with the greatest of ease. In his drawing he is often a downright improviser. He designates his drawings during and after execution rather than in advance. His drawing of a man is scarcely recognizable as such, and readily metamorphoses into something else with free comments.

The four-year-old is voluble, because the architectured neuron network that underlies language is literally burgeoning with "outshoots" which take the form of new conjunctions, new adverbs and adjectives, expletives and novel syntax: *maybe; I guess; not even; enormous; suppose that; really; I bet you can't do this, I hope!* Order finally emerges out of this linguistic luxuriance; but at four years we must expect some developmental exaggeration. Even though he can scarcely count to four, the four-year-old blithely talks of seventy-seven.

This is a growthsome stage. He or she tells tall tales, brags, tattles, threatens, alibis, calls names. But this bravado is not to be taken too seriously; his attractive traits more than compensate. He is fundamentally striving through these impulsions to identify himself with his culture and to penetrate its unknown. Sometimes he seems to be almost conscious of the growing-up process. He is much interested in becoming five years old; he talks about it a lot.

We have now characterized in rapid sequence thirteen ascending levels of maturity in the first four years of life. In succeeding chapters we shall describe at length six more maturity levels, embracing the years from five to ten. At these later ages we shall encounter many new and interesting patterns of behavior, but we do not expect to find new mechanisms of development. The fundamental mechanisms have already revealed themselves in the transparent naïvetés of infancy and preschool childhood.

A panoramic view of the thirteen early stages of maturity gives us a deepened appreciation of the surety and the lawfulness of child development. Although there are innumerable complications in the environment, we see that the growth complex moves forward with certainty toward specific ends. Every child is unique; but every child is also a member of one human species. Obedient to these species characteristics are growth sequences which are rarely or never circumvented. The motor control of the eyes precedes that of the fingers; head balance precedes body balance; palmar prehension precedes digital prehension; voluntary grasp precedes voluntary release. Banging comes before poking; vertical and horizontal hand movements before circular and oblique; crawling before creeping; creeping before upright walking; gestures before words; jargon before speech; nouns before prepositions; solitary play before social; perceptions before abstractions; practical before conceptual judgments. These are but a few simple examples of the sequential order inherent in the structuralization of child behavior, from its lowest to its highest manifestations.

The structuralization of behavior is an important concept. It means that we must visualize the action system of the child as a living structure, which is ingeniously fabricated through the architecture of growth. The lines of this construction are suggested by the behavior profiles we have sketched.

From these sketches it is evident that the mind does not grow like an onion, nor like an artichoke, by the addition of successive layers. It grows by weaving unimaginably complex patterns which correspond to the multiplicities of a world of things and of persons. All these patterns are incorporated into a single individuality.

The process of this incorporation is intriguing to everyone who wishes to understand the dynamics of psychological growth. The action system (the corpus of behavior) develops as a unitary whole. In general, its organization proceeds in a head-to-foot direction; and from the central axis outward. The trunk is innervated before the shoulders; the shoulders before the arms; the arms before the hands. Opposed members and counterpoised functions must be brought into balance: flexor versus extensor muscles; right and left extremities; eyes and hands; forward and backward movements; vertical and horizontal movements; grasp and release; mine and thine; self-activity and sociality; good and bad, etc.

As it matures, the action system reconciles and counterbalances a host of opposites. But this process is so intricate that growth cannot take a straight-line course. It seesaws, emphasizing now one and now another opposed function, but finally coordinating and modulating both. Self-regulatory fluctuation and reciprocal interweaving are outstanding methods of child development.

As we have seen from the thirteen maturity profiles in this chapter, the growing action system is in a state of formative instability combined with a progressive movement toward stability. Growth gains are consolidated in periods of relative stability. There is a somewhat rhythmic trend toward recurrent equilibrium. Witness the relatively stable equilibrium at sixteen weeks, twenty-eight weeks, fifteen months, and three years. Contrast the relatively unstable equilibrium at two and a half years and three and a half years.

The trends of development tend to repeat themselves at ascending levels of organization, as though the cycles of development took a spiral course. It is an onward spiral, but the child at a given stage may show a strong resemblance to what he was at an earlier stage.

These parallels in the developmental spiral are very instructive. They indicate the logic of growth changes. Although the child always remains true to himself, we must expect him to pass through varying phases. It helps us to understand his behavior if we recognize that there are nodal periods when he is in focus, and other periods when he is in transition. Although we shall never apply age norms arbitrarily, it gives us a sense of perspective to know that there are fundamental correspondences in the dynamic make-up of the child

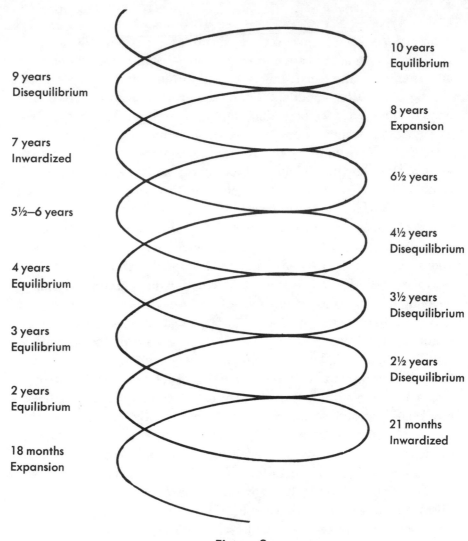

Figure 3
The Spiral of Development

Figure 4

Sequence of Stages

Cycles	Stage 1 Equilibrium	Stage 2 Disequilib.	Stage 3 Equilibrium	Stage 4 Disequilib.	Stage 5 Equilibrium	Stage 6 Disequilib.	Stage 1 Equilibrium	Duration
	Smooth, Consolidated	Breaking Up	Rounded, Well-balanced	Inwardized	Vigorous, Expansive	Neurotic, Inwardized, Troubled	Smooth, Consolidated	
1st	4 weeks	6–12 weeks	16 weeks	20 weeks	24–28 weeks	Birth	4 weeks	0.7 years
2nd	40 weeks	44–48 weeks	52–56 weeks	15 months	18 months	32 weeks	40 weeks	1.2 years
3rd	2 years	2½ years	3 years	3½ years	4 years	21 months	24 months	3 years
4th	5 years	5½–6 years	6½ years	7 years	8 years	4½ years	5 years	5 years
5th	10 years	11 years	12 years	13 years	14 years	9 years	10 years	6 years
						15 years	16 years	

at sixteen and twenty-eight weeks; at three years and five to five and a half years; at two and a half years and five and a half to six years. The maturity characteristics of the infant and preschool child may well serve as touchstones for a more sympathetic insight into the inner psychology of children of school age.

In fact, we have determined a rather complex sequence of stages of alternating equilibrium and disequilibrium, starting actually in infancy and continuing on through adolescence. Figures 3 and 4 illustrate, graphically and in words, the patterned way in which not only equilibrium and disequilibrium but whole sequences of phases of behavior repeat themselves as the child matures.

CHAPTER 5

FIVE YEARS OLD

How can we best portray the rich and varied developmental transformations that take place in the growthsome years from five to ten? Most of these transformations come so stealthily that we are scarcely aware of them at the time at which they occur. Yet they come with such unremitting surety that each birthday marks a significant advance. Each year brings changes in the maturity picture.

Ages and Stages

In the chapters that follow we shall attempt to outline the patterns of these progressive changes. What behavior is like in the first four years has just been summarized. Our next task is to characterize the succeeding years in terms of their *developmental essence*. This means a series of descriptions which will define the directions and destinations of development. Incidental comparisons between adjoining stages of maturity will give a further insight into development as a process.

The concept of maturity, when applied to children, is, of course, relative. A three-year-old is normally more mature than a two-year-old. A one-year-old is extremely mature when compared with a sixteen-week-old baby. Indeed, the maturity difference between them is very much greater than that between a six- and a seven-year-old child; *for the rate of development has already slowed down by the age of five.*

The developmental changes that occur in the years from five to ten, therefore, are not as striking as those that occur in infancy. Being less dramatic, the changes are easily overlooked, both at home and at school. To become more aware of the developmental forces that bring about these changes, we need a frame of reference. Above all, we need to know that the forces are working day in and day out, year in and year out. Growth is a process.

Our task is to point out the influence of age on the growth of behavior. The psychology of a child is determined by his or her maturity and experience. The experiences in turn are determined by maturity as well as by the culture in which the child lives. The variations both in child and culture are, of course, enormous. A child may be reared in Patagonia or on Park Avenue. That must make some difference. His color may be white, black, or brown. In terms of endowment, he may be idiot or genius. In physique he may be endo-, meso-, or ectomorphic. In temperament, viscero-, somato-, or cerebrotonic. In life career he may have enjoyed the affection and security of a happy home; or he may be one of those culturally disinherited "five-year-old people" from war-torn countries "who look like seventy because they have seen things no child should see."

With such a multiplicity of variables, it would be fatuous to look for mathematical averages. It is possible, however, by comparing one age group with another, to single out distinguishing behavior characteristics and developmental trends. On the basis of such systematic comparisons, we shall draw up a series of *behavior profiles*, devoting a separate chapter to each age level.

The profiles will present behavior characteristics that are typical of intelligent children of favorable socioeconomic status in our American culture. A profile does not attempt to portray either an individual child or a statistical child. Each profile is a composite character sketch which incorporates intimate cross-sectional and longitudinal studies of a wide range of children. As such, the behavior profiles may be used to identify and interpret the changing developmental status of actual children as they mature in the years from five to ten. Our first profile outlines the developmental essence of the five-year-old. Five is a nodal age which marks both the end and the beginning of a growth epoch. FIVE, himself, seems to be conscious of a culmination, for he announces somewhat assertively, "I am five!"

Behavior Profile

The five-year-old has come a long distance on the upward-winding pathway of development. He will have to travel fifteen years or more before he becomes an adult, but he has scaled the steepest ascent and has reached a sloping plateau. Although he is by no means a finished product, he already gives token of the man (or the woman) he (or she) is to be. His capacities, talents, temperamental qualities, and his distinctive modes of meeting the demands of development have all declared themselves to a significant degree. He is already stamped with individuality.

But he also embodies in his young person general traits and trends of behavior that are characteristic of a stage of development and of the culture to which he belongs. *These underlying pervasive traits constitute his five-year-oldness.* They are the maturity traits that make him somewhat different from the four-year-old and from the six-year-old.

Five is a nodal age; and also a kind of golden age both for parent and for child. For a brief period the tides of development flow smoothly. The child is content to organize the experiences that he gathered somewhat piecemeal in the less deliberate fourth year. As an expansive four-year-old he was constantly going out to meet the environment, making his thrusts in an almost harum-scarum manner. In contrast, the five-year-old is self-contained, on friendly and familiar terms with his environment. He has learned much; he has matured. He takes time to consolidate his gains before he makes deeper incursions into the unknown. At the age of about five and a half a new form of developmental restlessness makes itself apparent.

Meanwhile there is an interlude when he feels quite at home in his world. And what is his world? *It is a here-and-now world*: his father and mother, especially his mother; his seat at the dining room table; his clothes, particularly that cap of which he is very proud; his tricycle; the backyard, the kitchen, his bed; the drugstore and the grocery store around the corner (or the barn and the granary if he is fortunate enough to live in the country); the street, and perhaps the big kindergarten room, with other children and with another "nice lady." But if his universe has a center, it is his mother who is that center.

He does not tolerate even a kindergarten well, if it makes too many pioneering demands upon him, as it is likely to do if he is not fully ready. (We shall discuss this matter of readiness at length later in this volume.) Just now he is not in a pioneering phase of development. He has a healthy intolerance for too much magic and too much fairy tale. He has just barely discovered his actual world, and this has enough novelty and reality on its own merits. He is even something of a homebody. This is not because of abnormal dependence, but because the home is a complex institution, which invites and rewards his consideration. He is happy to play house, with all its domesticities, by the hour, which is not to his developmental discredit. And if while he is in kindergarten he particularly enjoys the dramatization of domestic situations, we cannot be amazed. He must make the familiar more familiar to himself; the familiar world is still new.

Even his infancy is relatively recent. He likes to have the experiences of his earlier childhood revived for him by his mother. He talks baby talk to his infant sister or brother. All this helps him detach himself from his babyhood and become more completely identified with his present, immediate environment.

His rapport with the environment is very personal. He is not yet ripe for the conceptual detachments and the abstract notions that adult ethics aspire to. He has a fairly robust sense of possession; for things that he likes he even has a pride of possession; but it is with reference to his *own*. He does not have a general notion of ownership. He tends to be realistic, concrete, and first-personal; without, however, being aggressive and combative. "Do dogs run?" a five-year-old was asked. "I don't have a dog!" was his polite answer.

Yet within the limits of the familiar and a narrow fringe of the unknown, he will ask questions of his own. Some of the favorites are: What is it for? What is it made of? How does this work? Why does the bus come around this way?

The five-year-old makes a favorable impression of competence and stability, because he does not go off on wild tangents. Nor is he overdemanding. He likes to function well within the realm of his abilities. Although his spontaneous play is not stereotyped, it tends to restrict itself to small, conservative variations. But these variations are numerous and in time they yield substantial developmental gains.

Self-limitation is almost stronger than self-assertion. Accordingly, he demands adult help where needed. He likes little responsibilities and privileges to which he can do full justice. He is best managed on that basis rather than through challenges to efforts still beyond him. He may respond with little flashes of resistance or sensitivity if overtaxed, but quickly resumes his habitual poise. There is often a vein of seriousness. He is much more deliberate than a four-year-old. He thinks before he speaks.

Nevertheless, the five-year-old may have a vein of humor. He likes to plan a "surprise joke," even in the realm of moral conduct. His father asks him, "Have you eaten your dinner?" He says "No!" already betraying advance amusement in his deception. He adds, "And I won't eat it!" Presently on investigation, to everyone's great joy, it proves that he has already eaten his dinner, every bit of it!

Five-year-olds like to fit into the culture in which they live. Their spontaneous activity tends to be under good self-control. They seek adult support and guidance. They accept adult help in making unfamiliar transitions. They are eager to know how to do things that lie within their capacity. They like to be instructed, not so much to please their elders as to feel the satisfactions of achievement and social acceptance. They like to practice the social convention of asking, and waiting for, formal permission. And they like to be "good." A five-year-old may tell his mother, "Today I'm going to do all the good things and none of the bad things." Another may start the day with the cheerful prediction, "This is my lucky day."

This docility, however, does not mean that the five-year-old, with all his or her attractive traits, is a highly socialized individual. He is too deeply immersed in his world to have a discriminating perception of his self among his peers and superiors. His cooperative play is usually limited to a group of three, and is conducted with chief concern for his individual ends rather than the collective ends. Boys and girls accept one another freely regardless of sex; though not without hierarchical competition as to who in housekeeping play should fill the role of mother and who that of the baby. Not being unduly aggressive and acquisitive, the five-year-old tends to get along peacefully with playmates in simple group play.

The emotional linkage to his mother is strong. He obeys her readily. He likes to help about the house. He enjoys being read to by his mother. Should things go wrong, he may use her as a scapegoat, blaming her as a "mean mommy." On the other hand, he will also accept punishment from her with a temporary change of course.

These emotional patterns are, of course, subject to great individual variations; but they suggest a strong matriarchal orientation. The mother, after all, is a rather important figure in the small world of the five-year-old. She is obviously the great executive agent of the household, from whom proceed all blessings and authorizations. He is discovering the outlines of the social order—outlines which emerge in the home. And he signals his new social insight by asking his mother to marry him!

This proposal reflects the intellectual limitations as well as the emotional patterns of a typical five-year-old. He represents an interesting combination of practical realism and primitive naïveté. He has some appreciation of yesterday and tomorrow, but he understands *me, now, here* better than *you, then, there.* He is so completely immersed in the cosmos that he is unaware of his own thinking as a subjective process separate from the objective world. He is factual and literal rather than imaginative. He can distinguish his own left hand from his right but lacks that extra bit of projectiveness which would enable him to distinguish left from right in another person. Although he is beginning to use words with great facility, he is so self-in-cosmos engrossed that he cannot well suppress his own point of view to realize by reciprocity the point of view of others. Yet he has an elementary sense of shame and disgrace. He seeks affection and applause. He likes to be told how nicely he is doing. He likes to bring home something he has made at school.

The five-year-old is practical rather than romantic. He defines in terms of use: "A horse is to ride. A fork is to eat." Fairy tales with excessive unrealities vex and confuse him. He is serious, empirical, direct. Give him a crayon and he will draw a man with head, trunk, extremities, eyes and nose. He may even supply five fingers, for he can count to four or five. He can also copy a square. If he copies a few capital letters, he is likely to identify them very closely with persons and objects. He almost makes personalities for certain words. His mechanics and his astronomy are likewise tinged with animisms. He is very innocent in the realm of causal and logical relationships. Clouds move because God pushes them, and when God blows it is windy.

FIVE is a great talker. The volubility of the fourth year yielded an increased vocabulary of perhaps two thousand words. He has overcome most of his infantile articulation. He uses connectives more freely when he narrates an experience. He can tell a tale. He may exaggerate, but is not given to overfanciful invention. His dramatic play is full of practical dialogue and a kind of collective monologue. He is using words to clarify the multitudinous world in which he lives. In language perhaps more than in any other field of behavior he shows a slight tendency to ramble out of bounds.

In general, the emotional life of the five-year-old suggests good

adjustment within himself and confidence in others. He is not without anxieties and fears, but usually they are temporary and concrete. Thunder and sirens awaken dread. Darkness and solitude
cause timidity. Many a five-year-old has fits of fearfulness lest his
mother leave him, or be gone when he awakens. His dreams may be
pleasant, but he is often more subject to nightmares, in which terrifying animals figure more prominently than persons.

All things considered, however, the five-year-old in his waking
hours is in excellent equilibrium. His health is usually good. Psychologically he is comfortably at home in his world, because he is at
home with himself. He may be pushed off balance, but he tends to
return to counterpoise. Ordinarily he does not go off on tantrum
tangents. A brief stamping of feet and a "No, I won't!" suffice. Although fond of climbing and gross motor activity, he shows composure in his standing and sitting postures. He does not shift or
fidget while in a chair. Often we see unconscious grace and skill in
both gross and fine motor coordinations. There is a finished perfection and economy of movement—which again suggests that five is a
nodal stage toward which the strands of development converge to
be organized for a new advance.

Indeed, the psychological nature of five-year-oldness becomes
most apparent when we halt at this milepost and look back at the
developmental path by which the child reached his or her present
estate. It is a winding, spiraling pathway. There were similar mile-
posts in the past: there will be others in the future. Five-year-oldness
compares with three-year-oldness and with twenty-eight-week-old-
ness in its general configuration and quality. Ten-year-oldness will
resemble five as will sixteen. These are brief periods in which the
assimilative, organizing forces of growth are in ascendancy. During
intervening periods, at four, six, and eight years, the expansive,
fermentive, forward thrusts of development are more prominent.

Needless to say, these alternations in the accents of development
are not sharply defined. The growth continuum is like the chromatic
spectrum: each phase, each color, shades by imperceptible gradations into the next. Yet the seven colors of the rainbow are dis-

tinguishable. In a similar way the maturity traits of the five-year-old are distinguishable from those of the six-year-old.

And be forewarned—you will not understand your six-year-old unless you make the distinction!

Maturity Traits

A behavior profile aims to give us a composite picture of the child as a whole. We cannot do justice to his psychology unless we think of him as a total unit, as an individual. If we try to take him apart, he vanishes; he ceases to be a person.

Nevertheless, he is so many-sided that we cannot attend to every aspect of his complex behavior equipment at one glance. We must look at him from different angles, and seek out those characteristics which are of special significance. Since the child is a unified personality, we shall find that all his or her traits are more or less interdependent.

For practical purposes, we can group these traits into ten classifications, which are shown on the accompanying table. We call them *maturity* traits because the emphasis, throughout, is not on the abilities of the child, but upon the stages and mechanisms of his or her development.

The list of traits is fairly comprehensive and covers the most important areas of behavior with which home and school are concerned. Under the various headings we shall cite concrete examples of behaviors that we have encountered at the yearly age levels. The examples are not always typical, but they do illustrate the kinds of behavior and the degrees of maturity that parents and teachers have to reckon with in relatively normal children.

The maturity traits are set forth in brief, informal statements which reflect the everyday happenings of home and school life. We do not set up these traits as norms, but rather as indicators of the child's behavior equipment at a given level of maturity.

Figure 5

Classification of
Maturity traits and Gradients of Growth

1. **Motor Characteristics**
   Bodily Activity
   Eyes and Hands

2. **Personal Hygiene**
   Eating
   Sleep
   Elimination
   Bath and Dressing
   Health and Somatic
      Complaints
   Tensional Outlets

3. **Emotional Expression**
   Affective Attitudes
   Crying and Related
      Behaviors
   Assertion and Anger

4. **Fears and Dreams**
   Fears
   Dreams

5. **Self and Sex**
   Self
   Sex

6. **Interpersonal Relations**
   Mother–Child
   Father–Child
   Siblings
   Family and Grandparents
   Manners
   Teacher–Child
   Child–Child
   Groupings in Play

7. **Play and Pastimes**
   General Interests
   Reading
   Music, Radio, Television,
      and Movies

8. **School Life**
   Adjustment to School
   Classroom Demeanor
   Reading
   Writing
   Arithmetic

9. **Ethical Sense**
   Blaming and Alibiing
   Response to Direction, Pun-
      ishment, and Praise
   Responsiveness to Reason
   Sense of Good and Bad
   Truth and Property

10. **Philosophic Outlook**
    Time
    Space
    Language and Thought
    Death
    Deity

The foregoing areas of behavior
in ten major sectors of child
development are treated by ages in
chapters 5–10 and by gradients in
chapters 11–20.

Sometimes behavior that occurs is undesirable and preventable. Every stage or age has its negative as well as its positive aspects. If the reader understands the developmental import of the behavior, he or she can usually work out a method of management suitable to the child's maturity. Child guidance must always be adjusted to the demands of development. Occasionally specific guidance measures are suggested. Generally the guidance will be implied in the statement of the traits and will not call for detailed formulation. For convenience, a standard set of ten rubrics will be used in presenting the illustrative maturity traits at each age.

We begin with *motor characteristics*. Basically the child is a system of muscles with which he executes motions in time and space. We are interested in the course, the form, the symmetry, and the direction of these motions. How do his motor coordinations change with age, as revealed in body posture, in handedness, in drawing, and in the use of eyes and hands?

The child is also a physiological organism which must replenish and sustain itself, which is subject to illness and outward stresses and inward tensions. Under *Personal Hygiene* we include the behaviors and adjustments relative to eating, sleeping, elimination, and physical well-being.

Affective attitudes and threats to the organism are manifested in various forms of *Emotional Expression* and in *Fears and Dreams*.

The forces of self-conservation, however, are strong. The child builds up a sense of self, he differentiates himself from the opposite sex, he comes into increasing command of sex factors which concern his own life and his relations with others. Significant growth changes occur in the area of *Self and Sex*.

He actually works out the detailed architecture of his sense of self through social rather than private activities—through a vast web of associations with his elders, his parents, his teachers, and his peers— the web of *Interpersonal Relations*.

Much of his activity, both personal and social, is playful, experimental, gamesome, recreational. His *Play and Pastimes* reveal his spontaneous energies and interests.

But modern culture has willed that the child from five to ten must also go to school. He has much to learn about the sciences, the arts, and the amenities of civilization. The patterns of his *School Life* reveal how he reacts to the demands of the culture.

In school hours and out-of-school hours he is constantly thrust into the necessity of adjusting to other persons, friends and strangers, young and old, threatening and kind. Thereby he weaves a web of personal-social relationships which express themselves in various labels and values: "thine and mine," "good and bad," "do and don't," "right and wrong," "you are to blame," "I am to blame," "be a good boy," "be a nice girl." Here is the source of the *Ethical Sense*.

Philosophy has been defined as the knowledge of things divine and human and the causes in which they are contained. Even a child makes his own formulations in this vast field of knowledge. His formulations undergo interesting transformations with age. We shall describe these transformations in terms of the child's *Philosophic Outlook*.

The following maturity traits are **not** to be regarded as rigid norms, nor as models. They simply illustrate the kinds of behavior—desirable or otherwise—that tend to occur at this age. Every child has an individual pattern of growth, unique to him. The behavior traits here outlined may be used to interpret his individuality and to consider the maturity level at which he is functioning.

1. MOTOR CHARACTERISTICS

BODILY ACTIVITY

FIVE is poised and controlled. He is well oriented to himself. Posturally he is less extreme and less extensor than he was at four. He is closely knit. His arms are held near his body. His stance is narrow. In kicking a ball he may throw and kick simultaneously. Eyes and head move almost simultaneously as he directs his attention to something. He is direct in his approach, facing things squarely. He goes directly to a chair and seats himself. He appears to be well oriented to the four points of the compass as he turns a quarter to left or to right or even to the back as he is seated in a chair.

Gross motor activity is well developed at five. Although the child of this age may walk with feet pronate, he can walk a straight line, descend stairs alternating his feet, and skip alternately.

His alternating mechanism is put to

practice in much of his behavior. He loves his tricycle and is adept at riding it. He climbs with sureness and from one object to another. He shows a marked interest in stilts and roller skates, although he cannot sustain a performance for long.

FIVE's economy of movement is in contrast to FOUR's expansiveness. He appears more restrained and less active because he maintains one position for longer periods, but he changes from sitting to standing to squatting in a serial manner. He is nonetheless active. Although he plays longer in one restricted place, he is a great helper who likes to go upstairs to get something for mother, or go back and forth from kitchen to dining room to put things on the table.

EYES AND HANDS

FIVE sits with trunk quite upright, his work directly before him. He may move to right or left slightly to orient his body, and he may stand and continue. His eye-hand performance appears as capable as an adult's, although actually the finer patterns have yet to develop. His approach, grasp, and release are direct, precise, and accurate in simple motor performances. He utilizes his preschool toys more skillfully and purposefully. A familiar puzzle is done in a mercurial manner.

He is becoming more adept with his hands and likes to lace his shoes, fasten buttons that he can see, "sew" wool through holes on a card by turning it over. He likes to place his fingers on the piano keys and strike a chord. He now shows a preference for blocks of various sizes and colors, with which he builds simple structures. He also likes to copy from a model.

FIVE likes to observe. He watches mother make something, then he tries it. He needs many models and likes to copy designs, letters, and numbers. He also likes to have outline pictures to color, trying to keep within the lines.

In spontaneous drawing he makes a single outline drawing with few details. He may attach the back and front door to the sides of a "house" or he may draw a square for a house, making an indentation at the top and bottom for the doors. He recognizes that his result is "funny."

Handedness is usually well established by five, and the five-year-old can identify the hand he uses for writing. His initial approach is with the dominant hand and he does not transfer a pencil to the free hand as he did at three and a half to four years. In block building he alternates the use of the hands, but the dominant hand is used more frequently. This is also true when he points to pictures.

When maintained in a sedentary position he becomes restless, lifts his buttocks from the chair, turns to the side or stands, but remains within the radius of the table and chair. Tensional outlets are brief. With his free hand he may scratch, brush, poke, or touch any part of his body (on the same side as that hand)—parts of his face as well as arm, leg, and clothes. He may also sneeze or have to blow his nose. Sneezing may be so common that one wonders if he has a cold. Toilet tissue is needed at a moment's notice.

2. PERSONAL HYGIENE

EATING

Appetite. The shift to a better appetite begun at four and a half is fairly well established by five. This does not, however, mean that all meals are uniformly better. Two meals a day are good and the third one, usually breakfast, may be relatively poor. An illness or an operation does not upset this established appetite, as would have been the case at an earlier age.

FIVE is interested in completions, even to the extent of cleaning his plate. He is slow in accomplishing this, but he is persistent. His appetite is better than his ability or interest in feeding himself; so he not only accepts help, but often asks for it.

Refusals and Preferences. FIVE likes plain, simple cooking. For his main meal he may prefer meat, potatoes, a raw vegetable, milk, and fruit. Gravies, casseroles, and even puddings may seem too complicated and artificial to him. Cooked vegetables, especially the root vegetables, are in special disfavor. Cereal is continued mainly through the will of the parent and may be accepted only if fed by the parent. The child is influenced, however, both in his preferences and in his refusals, by the example of others.

He is also influenced by television programs. He may accept new foods at a restaurant, at a picnic, or when a guest joins the family group.

Self-Help. FIVE is expected to feed himself and on the whole does a fairly skillful though slow job of it. Many FIVEs, however, still need help, especially toward the end of the meal or with foods, like cereal, to which they are not partial. FIVE is beginning to use a knife for spreading, but he is not yet ready to cut his meat, nor will he be ready for some years to come.

Table Behavior. Manners take on little significance until the child has a good appetite and is able to feed himself completely. Therefore, FIVE still has a little respite before the torrents of criticism begin.

If he eats with the family, including dinner at night when father is at home, he usually wiggles in his chair. He does not get up and run around or ask to go to the bathroom, as he did at age four. But he usually brings his conversational ability to the table and tends to monopolize the conversation. This interferes with his eating and slows him down considerably. If it can be arranged for him to eat the main course in advance of the family meal, he eats better, and can handle dessert with the family. However, FIVE likes to conform and will if reprimanded make an effort to improve his behavior, though he may need very frequent reminders. He may still wear a bib, though many now wear a napkin tucked in at the neck.

SLEEP

Nap. A fair proportion of five-year-olds still nap occasionally. The nap seems to be an antifatigue adjustment. A five-year-old may nap if he goes to morning kindergarten, or if he goes to afternoon kindergarten may nap on Saturday and Sunday only. Or he may nap on rainy days. In any case, he does not usually have more than one or two naps a week. Boys are more likely to nap than girls, and a few may nap as often as five out of seven days, and for one to two hours.

The majority of five-year-olds who do not nap usually do not take a rest period spontaneously. They may, however, ask to go to bed early at night. They do not resist a planned "play nap" of half an hour to one hour if provided with something interesting to do (coloring, modeling with plasticine, building structures with Tinker toys and Lincoln Logs). The child especially enjoys an alarm clock set to ring when his play nap is ended.

Bedtime. The 7 P.M. bedtime persists with many; some delay until 7:30 or 8 o'clock. Usually the child has been read to before he starts for bed. He often prefers to have his mother precede him to turn on the lights. Getting ready for bed usually goes smoothly. Some continue to take a toy animal or doll to bed with them, but many have given this up. However, this does not

mean that the child will not return to his pets at a later age when he needs them more.

Some who do not fall asleep quickly ask to "read" or to color for a while. Others fall asleep at once without any desire for presleep activity. Still others like to lie quietly in the dark, singing to themselves or carrying on a conversation with an imaginary child. These conversations often deal with feats of prowess such as beating up another child or shooting wild animals.

A few still get up frequently, demanding a drink, something to eat, or the bathroom, but most can take care of their own needs without bothering their parents, though they report what they are doing. Usually FIVE falls asleep about half an hour after he starts to bed. A few remain awake until 9 P.M. Sleep may be delayed because of a too exciting day, the presence of company, or anticipation of the parents going out for the evening. If the child has trouble getting to sleep, it sometimes helps to put him in his parents' bed, removing him later to his own bed.

Night. Some children sleep through the night, but many have their sleep interrupted by need for toileting or by dreaming. This is the age when parents often waver as to whether the child should be picked up routinely to be toileted, or whether he is ready to sleep through the night. A trial of not waking him up reveals either that he no longer needs to be toileted or that he awakens by himself, usually after midnight, and calls for his mother. Some actually toilet themselves, but feel that they must report to their mother before going back to bed. Usually there is little difficulty in getting back to bed and to sleep.

Dreams and nightmares definitely invade the sleep of many five-year-olds. Frightening animal dreams predominate. Many children awaken screaming, have difficulty in coming out of their dream even with their mother by their side; finally, with the help of shifting to another room or being toileted, they wake up, realize where they are, and go back to sleep again. Usually it is difficult for the child to tell you much about this type of nightmare. It is amazing to see how quickly the child quiets at his parent's touch or voice. The five-year-old is beginning to talk out loud in his sleep, possibly naming his mother or a sibling.

Morning. Most five-year-olds awaken at 7 to 8 A.M. after an eleven-hour sleep. They often obligingly sleep later on Sundays. The earlier-than-7 A.M. risers are often those who continue to take naps or those who are put to bed very early. At this age children may be expected to take care of themselves on waking, to close their window, put on their bathrobe and slippers, toilet themselves, and occupy themselves in bed with coloring or books until it is time to get up. A five-year-old can often be very helpful with a younger sibling, even to the extent of changing wet pajamas. He no longer demands to go to his parents' bed in the morning, for he is now quite occupied by his own activities.

ELIMINATION

Bowel. It is customary for the five-year-old to have one movement a day, usually after a meal. This is most commonly after lunch, and if not then, more often after supper than after breakfast. The four-year-old's tendency of interrupting a meal to have a movement is not characteristic of FIVE. But the child may, at the end of a meal, complain of a "terrible" pain, which is usually related to a need to have a bowel movement. Those children who are reported to function at "any old time" often show increased constipation and a tendency to skip a day or two. This is more true of girls, who need to be checked more carefully. They are helped by the suggestion that they must sit at the toilet long enough to function. Prune juice or some mild laxative may be needed. There is less interest in reporting on their movements than there was at age four. A number are still in need of help in being wiped.

Bladder. Although FIVE takes fairly good responsibility for toileting, he urinates infrequently and is likely to put off going to the toilet when he actually needs to go. Wriggling and hopping on one foot are obvious clues to the adult. Some children perhaps will need to be interrupted during a morning or afternoon play period with a bathroom reminder before it is too late. They may resist this interruption, but come more willingly at the prospect of a snack or in answer to a bell.

Certain girls need to be watched for sore, reddened genitals. This is easily controlled with a bland salve. This condition may possibly be related to masturbation, but may also be a developmental or individual characteristic.

Many children are now dry at night, with or without a pickup. Many others, even when picked up for midnight toileting, are still wet by morning.

BATH AND DRESSING

Bath. The bath is now accomplished with a fair amount of speed and real child participation. The child cannot yet draw his own bath water, but this is in part related to his fear of the hot-water tap. He definitely wants to help wash himself, especially his hands and knees. He is apt to get stranded on one knee, washing it over and over, and needs to be shifted to his other knee or to some other part of his body. Many mothers prefer to bathe the child themselves and have it over with; others use this as a reading period, at the same time supervising the child part by part throughout his bath. A few five-year-olds still cling to boat play during their baths.

Dressing and Care of Clothes. Parents commonly report that "he can but he doesn't" dress himself. Undressing is still easier than dressing. FIVE does

better at dressing if his clothes are laid out singly on the floor. Otherwise he is still apt to get them on backward. He can now handle all but back buttons. Shoelace tying is usually beyond him, and those who are able, tie too loose a bow.

A fair number of five-year-olds handle the task of dressing without too much prodding. Others are self-motivated only when they are eager to be ready for the next happening, or to surprise their parents. Some are able to choose two or three days a week when they will be responsible for dressing themselves. The other days are the mother's days, when she will be completely responsible. His own days may be marked on a calendar; he is becoming interested in the calendar as a guide and record.

Children take little responsibility about their clothes at this age, either in selecting them, laying them out, picking them up after they have been removed, or keeping them in good condition. Even those girls who are clothes-conscious and proud of their appearance do not take good care of their clothes.

HEALTH AND SOMATIC COMPLAINTS

On the whole, the five-year-old's health is relatively good with the exception of the communicable diseases, which increase in number from the fourth year on. Whooping cough and chicken pox take the lead. Measles, once in the lead, is now better controlled. Some will have only one or two colds during the winter months, which is in startling contrast to the repeated colds of the four-year-old.

Stomachaches are fairly common and are related both to the intake of food and the need to have a bowel movement. Stomachache may follow the ingestion of foods the child does not like, or the too rapid taking of food. If the child is pressed to finish his meal in a hurry, he may vomit.

TENSIONAL OUTLETS

The majority of tensional outlets are related to presleep activity. Thumb-sucking may still occur in a few children, but only prior to sleep. With some it occurs only once a week or once a month. Others use comfort objects such as sheets, blankets, pillows, or toy animals to help them go to sleep more quickly. Many are reported to have given up these habits or are in the process of giving them up.

FIVE may be a good age to plan to terminate thumb-sucking. Parents need to differentiate between the child who is going to be able to handle it by himself and the one who needs help. Maybe the voluntary giving up of the object related to the thumb-sucking will break up the pattern. Then the child may need help in going to sleep, such as having his mother sit beside him or having her return the sleep-inducing object if he cannot get along without it. Covering the thumb with a Band-aid, or planning for some much-desired object (such as a kitten),

may provide the necessary motivation. In any event, the plan should not be imposed, but should be so fully discussed with the child that it becomes his own plan.

The hand-to-face response manifested in nose-picking, nail-biting, or any hand-to-mouth gesture is fairly common at five. Sniffling may be so repetitive as to resemble a tic. Those who do not show their tensional outlets in these restricted ways do so in their interpersonal relations, especially with their mothers. They are either stubborn and resistant, or whiny and cranky. Others are still expressing four-year-old out-of-bounds tendencies. They continue to be overactive and noisy, and may take a slight flaw in a toy as a reason to destroy it completely. Personality factors influence the ways in which tension is released.

3. EMOTIONAL EXPRESSION

FIVE has largely overcome his four-year-old out-of-bounds, runaway, neighborhood visiting tendencies. Home is to him preferably indoors and also preferably within earshot of his mother. He is said to be very helpful. Though he is often a great talker, he deliberates before he speaks and does not plunge in headlong as he did at four. FIVE is often seeking an answer. He is not only helpful, but often truly cooperative. He does not act before he asks permission. Though he may have been jealous of a younger sibling, he now may adore this same sibling and be protective and helpful in taking care of him.

FIVE is poised. He has new inhibitory controls and anticipates immediate happenings well. Nevertheless, he may be too excited by an anticipated event if he is not prepared long enough in advance. His eating and sleeping may be disturbed and he may become very shy or overactive when the actual event occurs. He has given up most of his four-year-old brashness, and no longer shows off before company.

The ringing of the telephone may induce him to answer it. When he was younger, his mother answered, while he seized the occasion to run for the cookie jar.

This inhibitory poise makes FIVE capable of a new kind of determination —a positiveness which he uses to get his own way and to follow through his ideas. It also makes him a little dogmatic, so he sees only one way to do a thing, only one answer to a question. It is important to recognize this as a temporary and perhaps useful growth trait. If you contradict him or try to make him more broad-minded, he will contradict in turn and will argue as long as you allow him to. You usually lose the argument, or at least you should lose. If he is pushed too far he will become angry and then cry or call names, for instance calling his mother a "bad girl," "dirty rat," etc. If he is spoken to sharply or scolded he will usually cry. But for the most part he tries to hold his own ground and is less likely than formerly to rush off to seek comfort in one of his special comfort toys. His mother can help him control a wayward action by interjecting a magic word such as "tent" (the word may work like magic if the child is very eager at that time to have a tent given to him).

Some FIVEs do not function well unless they get off to a right start. You can often get the child to adjust to your demand if you help him to carry out your idea in his own way. That is the manner in which your way and his way mix. He cannot change in midstream; he must start all over again. One five-year-old who had started a day on the wrong foot and had kept in this groove finally wept when the day was half spent, and said, "I wish I could start Sunday all over again."

4. FEARS AND DREAMS

FEARS

FIVE is not a fearful age, nor is it an age of overawareness. Even though the child has been previously frightened by tales of witches, ghosts or bogymen, he may no longer fear them because they have so little reality for him. Dogs are somewhat less feared than formerly. He may still say he is afraid of things, though his fears are actually receding in intensity. FIVE is, however, beginning to have some fears that may be more extreme at five and a half and six years of age, such as the fear of certain elements: thunder, hard rain, and the dark.

His outstanding fear is that he will be deprived of his mother—that she may go away and not come back, or that she may not be at home when he returns from school or may be gone when he awakens in the night. This may be a difficult period for the mother because it confines her to her home even when the child is asleep. It is essential, however, to work out a satisfactory adjustment with the child so that his fear will remain under his control. He may be induced to accept the protection of some other person in his mother's absence. Or it may be that all he needs to make him feel secure is the telephone number that will reach his absent mother.

Nighttime heightens his fears. Thunder and sirens at night are far more frightening than in the daytime. He is less afraid of the dark, but he still likes to have his mother precede him upstairs at bedtime. He often likes a light on in the hall or bathroom and likes to have his door a little ajar. If his mother tries to talk him out of it he may say, "But the darkness gets into my face."

DREAMS

FIVE's sleep is often broken with dreams. These are usually unpleasant, and are frequently about wolves and bears that get into bed with him. They may bite and chase him, but this active aggressiveness is more common at five and a half and six years. Often FIVE wakes screaming because of the frightening quality of his dream. He is usually quieted fairly easily, though it may take some time to awaken him

from a nightmare and to get him back to sleep after being awakened.

The dream may be reported at once or in the morning. Other dreams are only reported if some daytime experience helps the child to recall them. For example, one child was reading with her mother a story about a green frog, when she suddenly stopped and said, "Green, green like the woman. You know, I don't think she should pop out from the floor and frighten me." Some who have nightmares are unable to report anything about their dreams. Others, judging from the elaborateness of their reporting, are probably making up the dreams they report.

Wild animals and strange or bad people that frighten the child are most conspicuous in five-year-old's dreams. There are also dreams of activity in connection with the elements, flying through the air, jumping into water, being near a fire. These occur usually in a rather unpleasant, frightening connection. Everyday events and familiar persons (mother and playmates) are beginning to appear in dreams, but they are not yet taking a prominent role.

5. SELF AND SEX

SELF

FIVE is more self-contained than he was at four; he is more of a person. He is serious about himself and is much impressed with his own ability to take responsibilities and to imitate grown-up behavior. He is rightly spoken of as more mature. He may not seem as independent as he was, but he is more aware of the relationship of his acts to people and to the world around him. He is shy in his approach to people, but he builds up a slow, steady relationship which makes five one of the favorite ages of childhood for the adult. With things as with people, FIVE likes to prepare and plan for happenings in the near future rather than to have them sprung on him.

He is secure in his relationship with his mother. She is as much himself as he is. It is essential for him to hold an even give-and-take with his mother. He is naturally obedient, wants to please, wants to help, and asks for permission even when it is not necessary.

FIVE shows a remarkable memory for past events. He can hoard thoughts as he hoards things. Through his questioning he builds up an impressive fund of information. And as with everything else about FIVE, there is a certain orderliness to what he thinks as well as to what he does.

FIVE lives in a here-and-now world, and his chief interest in the world is limited to his own immediate experiences. He likes to stay close to home base.

SEX

FIVE as a rule does not dwell upon sex questions as he did at four. His interest in sex is chiefly in the baby, in the having of a baby. This interest is manifested even in FIVE's mothering tenderness toward a younger sibling. Although he may have asked in an earlier year, "'Where do babies come from?" he re-asks this question at five. All he wants to know is that the baby grows in its "mommy's tummy." He is rarely interested in how the baby started. The use of the words "seed" or "egg" reminds him of vegetables and chickens and may confuse rather than help him. He readily accepts a statement as it is given and then repeats it with little meaning. One five-year-old introduced his baby brother to some visitors thus: "This is my baby brother. He came from a seed."

Some FIVEs still cling to the idea that you buy a baby from a hospital. They may even solve the problem of the sex of the baby by declaring that the hospital gives out boys on certain days and girls on other days. Very few FIVEs are aware of the enlarging abdomen of pregnancy, nor do they grasp the idea of the growth of the baby within the mother. A few girls are concerned about how the baby gets out and may spontaneously think that it comes out through an appendix scar if they have seen one.

The real interest of the five-year-old is in the baby rather than in its antecedents. Boys as well as girls desire to have a baby of their own. Some FIVEs relate themselves back to the time when they were in their mother's stomach. They like to talk about this and to ask their mother if she remembers all about it. Or they like to relate themselves to the future when they are going to have a baby of their own.

Or on noting a slight distension of the stomach in themselves, will conclude that they are going to have a baby, or maybe a doll. A child may dramatize the birth process by suddenly bringing forth a doll tucked between the legs. Another child of similar age may have a more critical sense of the realities. One five-year-old was heard to ask another, "Are you old enough to have a baby?" "Goodness, no," was the reply. "I can't even tell time yet."

FIVE rarely plays the game of "show," exposing genitals or buttocks. In fact, FIVE has become rather modest, especially about exposing his or her body to strangers. He may even display modesty before a babysitter or a younger sibling. He is aware of the sex organs in others when exposed and also of accessory sex characteristics such as pubic hair or breasts. Although he knows that difference in sex is indicated by the sex organs, that is not the usual method of differentiating girls from boys. There is still some perplexity in the minds of some FIVEs as to why a sister does not have a penis or why a father does not have breasts. Some FIVEs may express a desire to become the opposite sex. Others emphasize their own sex by discarding any plaything they possess that may be related to the opposite sex. Boys, for instance, may emphatically refuse to play with such feminine toys as dolls or ironing boards.

6. INTERPERSONAL RELATIONS

FIVE is that delightful stage when the child takes life as it comes. On the whole, he does not ask too much of life, nor does he give too much. His life problems are restricted in scope and easy for him to handle. His mother finds him a joy to have around the house. He is helpful, is always within earshot, and keeps her posted about his activities by always asking permission. He has endearing ways of showing how much he adores her. One five-year-old girl who had some difficulty about her mother's departures expressed it this way: "My stomach hurts. I begin to cry; and when you come back, oh, I'm so happy!" Another FIVE, who was trying to be more obedient, whispered in her mother's ear, "I've got a surprise for you. I'm going to say okay every time you speak to me."

Fathers also come in for their share of a five-year-old's affection. The father, however, is rarely the preferred parent. FIVE is fond of his father, proud of him, may obey him better than the mother, but he may not take punishment as well from his father as from his mother. In the insecurity of the middle of the night he wants his mother most of all. If, however, the mother is ill or absent, some FIVEs who have been slow to build up a relationship with their fathers will now accept them. Fathers may not receive as much affection from the child as do mothers, but on the other hand they do not receive as much disparagement. It is the mother who receives the brunt of the child's outbursts. It is the mother who is threatened with "I'm not going to play with you any more. You're a bad mommy."

Grandparents are much appreciated by five-year-olds, though admittedly the things children like best about them is that they give them toys and other gifts and provide favorite foods.

FIVE is showing greater ability to play with others. He may play very well with a younger or an older sibling. He is less bossy and is now helpful and even devoted to a younger sibling. He is protective and mothering. Often a five-year-old boy is said to adore his younger sister; nothing makes him more fighting mad than the threat to take her away.

But life is not always smooth between siblings. Indoor play is poorer than outdoor play and needs supervision and planning. FIVE has moments of jealousy when a younger sibling is receiving all the attention, and he is capable of blaming some of his acts on the younger sibling. Because FIVE adjusts so well to a younger sib, parents sometimes overlook the fact that the younger child can be too much of a strain on a docile five-year-old.

FIVE likes best to play with children of his own age. Some FIVEs prefer their own sex, some the opposite sex, and others readily accept either. FIVE, since he or she is such a homebody, is fairly dependent upon the children who are available in the neighborhood. Most FIVEs play best outdoors.

Some play best on their own home grounds, others away from home or in some neutral spot such as a park. A group of two is optimal. Whenever there are three in an unsupervised group, two often gang up on the third. It is wise for the parent to hold to the simple rule that the child may invite only one child at a time until he is able to handle more, which is at seven or more usually at eight years of age.

Sometimes FIVE responds best to an older child and may even take a minor part in the neighborhood group play, accepting the role of baby in house play and leaving when he does not wish to compete. The bossy FIVE usually does best with a younger child who will accept being bossed. But even the bossy FIVE will take turns in playing other children's ways if part of the time they will concede to play his way.

Certain pairs of children from five to eight years of age prove to be incompatible in play. They seem to find no common ground except arguing and fighting. These very same pairs may become bosom friends at the age of eight or nine. Thrusting them together too often before they are socially ready does them no more good than to give them complicated reading material before they are ready for it. Some amenable FIVEs need to be protected from being held too long in a social situation, because they may explode in a savage manner which might easily have been prevented if the parent had recognized the emotional fatigability of the five-year-old.

Twenty minutes can be a long time for a five-year-old.

7. PLAY AND PASTIMES

GENERAL INTERESTS

When FIVE is asked, "What do you like to do best?" he or she is likely to answer with simply one word: "Play." And he is indeed a good player. He has his body under more smooth, skillful control and is therefore capable of play without too much adult assistance. With increasing age, differences in personality and sex become more evident in what the child chooses to play.

FIVE shows a craving for the standard kindergarten materials. He paints, draws, colors, cuts, and pastes. He especially enjoys cutting things out and is happy when provided with an old wallpaper book. Sometimes he cuts paper into shreds simply for the sake of cutting. On occasion he slips over from paper to cloth and takes gouges out of his clothes. He still needs to be watched when using scissors.

Blocks continue to be highly favored play material for both boys and girls. Girls build houses for their dolls and project personal situations, whereas boys build roads, tracks, bridges, tunnels, and use their houses for tanks, airplanes, army trucks, and fire engines. Houses play an important role in five-year-olds' play behavior. FIVE likes to make big houses with big blocks, or tent houses of chairs draped with blankets. He wants to get into them, but he does not really play in them after he has entered.

Babies are another outstanding interest of the five-year-old. Dolls are used as babies. And this interest is by no means restricted to girls. Boys, too, want to play with dolls, dressing them, putting them to bed, and most of all taking them for rides in their carriages. Unhappy is the five-year-old boy who craves a doll for Christmas and finds a stuffed animal in its place. The culture is unknowing in the ways of development or it would not act so arbitrarily. (More boy dolls are now on the market than were formerly.) The interest in dolls is so strong that it is briefly shown at this age even by those girls who later scorn dolls.

FIVE's interest in houses is also expressed in his imaginative reenactments of domestic happenings. Boys join in this play as well as girls, but many boys prefer war games to the milder forms of house play. Hospital play is not as strong as it was at age four, and school play is not as strong as it will be at six.

Gross motor activity is a favorite with FIVE. He rides his tricycle with speed and adroitness. His tricycle moves freely, less hampered by the trailing equipment he so delighted to hitch on when he was four. FIVE swings, climbs, skips, roller skates, and jumps from heights. He may take to climbing trees or jumping rope. He may attempt acrobatics, trapeze tricks, and even stilts.

Girls are likely to prefer sewing; boys, carpentry. Boys already may show a well-defined interest in tools.

Their earlier tendency to destructiveness, their interest in taking things apart, may now be expressed in play with tools.

READING AND NUMBERS

There is nothing a five-year-old likes better than being read to, although he may spend considerable time looking at books himself and may even pretend to read. He prefers stories about animals that act like human beings. He shows marked fondness for first-grade readers that tell about occurrences in the lives of children. A few FIVEs may like to listen to a reading of comic strips, regardless of whether they understand them.

FIVE is becoming more aware of the rudiments of reading and arithmetic. He is interested in copying letters and numbers. He enjoys playing simple letter and number games with his parents. Often this type of spontaneous interest is not satisfied in the home for fear that the school methods of teaching will be interfered with. The school might well recognize that home and school methods are not necessarily in conflict and that they can be used together advantageously. Any child who shows this spontaneous type of interest at home should have it satisfied.

MUSIC, RADIO, AND TELEVISION

FIVE prefers his own records to the radio. He likes to play them over and over again. He likes a combination of music and words that tell a story. He may listen to the radio a little, show-ing a preference for the advertisements —he likes the catchy songs and the repetition. But most prefer television to either. Most admit that they watch television a lot. Children claim they are allowed to watch as much as they want to, but admit that parents help decide what programs to watch.

Some FIVEs can pick out tunes on the piano. They like to be taught how to play a few familiar melodies and they are apt to play the same song over and over again. They may sing with their records, or they may translate the music into dancing. FIVE enjoys dancing, especially at the bedtime hour.

8. SCHOOL LIFE

Being such a homebody, FIVE is well adjusted at home and is ready for the experience of being with children his own age, especially in a supervised group. He usually adjusts with relative ease even when he has not had previous school experience. He may want his mother to accompany him to the threshold on the first day, but may not want her to enter the schoolroom. The adjustment to one adult at a time is easier for him. Girls are more apt to want continued support of this kind for several days or even a few weeks. An older child may substitute for the mother until the child is ready to go on his own. Going on a school bus sometimes solves this problem.

Girls are more apt to like school than boys. Boys complain when they are not provided with enough outdoor activity or when they do not have "large blocks." Spirited children may complain that "the teacher makes me do things," "the teacher makes me stay in line," or "I want to draw what I want to."

On the whole, the health of the kindergartener is remarkably good. Some show fatigue every ten or fourteen days and a day at home with mother may be welcomed. With some children it may be advisable to plan for a four-day week, either with Wednesday at home, allowing a two-day span, or with Monday or Friday at home.

Sometimes a miraculous change occurs at school and the very child who may be "bad" at home becomes "good" at school. The opposite is also possible and usually indicates that the child is not yet ready to adjust to a group situation unless he is permitted and helped to participate only on the outskirts of the group.

There is less carry-over from home to school and school to home than there was at four or will be at six. So FIVE takes fewer things to school, although he may still like the security of a favorite toy, which he clutches en route and then stores in his cubby. A few bring books for the teacher to read to the class. FIVE takes his handiwork home from time to time, but he is more interested in securing his teacher's immediate recognition than in taking things home for his mother's approval.

FIVE usually is not communicative about his school life. He may report that another child hit or pinched him,

that the teacher made him do something. Parent and teacher can profit on occasion through communicating by telephone in regard to an episode that may have occurred at home or at school.

On arrival at school, FIVE goes directly to his room and teacher. He needs some assistance with the removal of clothes and asks the teacher when he needs help. However, dressing for outdoor play or for going home is quite a different matter. Many children are not ready to take this responsibility and need to be dressed entirely. An older child who calls for him may take over.

FIVE enjoys a routine, and adjusts well to an activity program that allows freedom of movement and yet maintains control of the sequence of separate activities. The morning may start with a free play period when he chooses blocks, carpentry, puzzles, painting, coloring, clay, or house play. He changes from one activity to another. He usually completes a task, although his attention may shift to watch another child at work, or he may go to the teacher to tell her of a personal experience or to show her his product. Boys as well as girls play house. Daily routines such as washing, telephoning, shopping, with occasional episodes of doctoring, are enacted. Boys prefer blocks; girls, house play.

Transitions are fairly easy for FIVE. With a word of warning from the teacher he completes his task, and with some help from her he puts materials away. He is then ready for the next activity, perhaps a discussion and a music period followed by a snack. A simple song or story may accompany a short relaxation period.

The group enjoys a directed activity period of about twenty minutes in which a simple task can be completed. This directed time may also be utilized for copying or recognizing letters, learning to print one's own name in capitals, or counting objects in the room.

Much of FIVE's reading and number work is closely associated with his play, both at home and at school. He can pick out capital letters, first at the left or right of a page and then at the beginning of a sentence in the text. Later he reads letters in combination, such as "C-A-T," and asks what they spell. Signs are of particular interest to him and he may like to add a sign to his block structures. He may also add wooden letters for people, such as A for Ann or S for Susan. He likes to identify repetitious words in a familiar book such as sounds the animals make or exclamatory words. At five and a half some children pretend to read from a book that they have memorized; others like to underline the words they know.

FIVE enjoys counting objects; he tells how many toys he has. He can copy numbers and may write some from dictation. During the year he learns to identify a penny, nickel, and dime. Attempts to add or subtract within five are made with or without using fingers or objects. Being five has tremendous significance to him. He is more likely to tell you that he is five years old than to tell you his name.

The directed activity period may be followed by story time, which is a highlight for FIVE, particularly when the story is dramatized after the reading. Stories with repetitive action and phrases are favorites, especially stories about animals, trains, or fire engines.

Outdoor play usually comes at the end of the morning, but is variable according to season and weather. Since FIVE is very much aware of both, it is helpful to have an outdoor space where most of his activities can be carried on during clement weather. Sandbox, swing, large blocks, and Junglegym are favorites. Sometimes an excursion is planned to a nearby place of interest.

The five-year-old's morning at school is on the whole quite smooth. The here-and-nowness of FIVE requires immediate attention and thus the teacher circulates about the room, ready to help, listen, or handle an emergency such as paint spilling. She provides the setting and materials for his experiences and is sought for approval and for affection.

FIVE works in short bursts of energy. He shows the same tendency when he suddenly shoves, strikes out, or throws blocks or stones. He may learn to inhibit impulsive attacks by being told that "it hurts." His play is predominantly on his own even though he likes to be in a group. He goes from one activity to another, usually completing each. Similarly, he changes his postural orientation: he sits in a chair for one activity, stands for another, sits on the floor or on a table for another. He resents interference with his materials, but he may be very obliging and provide an article on request. Some children may need to be separated from the group in play, but at this age they usually can be removed to the outskirts without actual isolation.

The teacher's voice can ordinarily be heard above the chatter in which the children tell one another what they are doing, or repeat what a neighboring child has just said. Typical remarks are:

"Guess I'm through with that side."
"I'm going to do my work."
"Going to do your work, Susie?"
"I can't."
"Tommy, did you say I can't?"
"Look at my house."
"Look at her house."
"Now make the grass."
"Da-da-da-da; dum-dum-dum."
"I want to save mine."

A desire for toileting is announced and a response may be expected from the teacher. FIVE may wait until the last minute but can care for himself. Boys may grab at their genitals and girls may wriggle or place hands on thighs. If FIVE holds off too long, particularly when outdoors, he or she may have an "accident." A boy may on occasion urinate outdoors. FIVE, however, accepts a suggestion to go to the toilet before it is time for outdoor play.

Kindergarten activity is not always highly social. In free play, two, three, or four children may sit at the same table to crayon or to mold clay but may work independently and readily leave for play in another part of the room. The same grouping is evident at the sandbox. Housekeeping may hold a larger number together for a while. With added experience, two children may be found building cooperatively on the same block structure.

9. ETHICAL SENSE

FIVE's poise is sustained because his own needs and the environmental demands are rather equally balanced. FIVE is a part of his environment and his environment is a part of him. Thinking of him in these terms, it becomes easier to discern the quality of his ethical sense, which is so new and so tentative that it can hardly be classified as such.

FIVE enjoys helping his mother and running errands. He likes to please, to do things in the right, accepted way. He does not usually resist a request with "I won't," as he did at four, but he may hesitate between a refusal and an acceptance. He may refuse to do things because he cannot do them, or because he is too busy to do them. Sometimes he is motivated by a simple reward. Although he likes praise, his need of it is not as great as it will be at six. His asking for permission or his telling what he is going to do indicates how much he has identified himself with his environment. An answer to his request seems often to be needed as a starter.

Making up his mind is not too difficult, for he has not many alternatives to choose between, and he is apt to make a conforming choice. He can, however, change his choice, for he is susceptible to reason or to an explanation. And since he wishes to oblige, he may shift to his parents' side. A few FIVEs are more rigid and by a simple device can be jostled into line.

FIVE is often spoken of as being markedly good, "like an angel." His sense of good and bad, if he has any, does not differentiate right from wrong. He either takes his behavior for granted, or thinks only in terms of his practical relationships to other persons. FIVE is "good" because he loves his mother and wants to please her. He does not want to do "bad" things, because such conduct annoys people and makes them uncomfortable. A few FIVEs are unusually concerned about being called bad. This is worse than a spanking to them, and they may appear to be ashamed of it. But at the same time they may compulsively handle their fear of being called bad by playing "bad school." In "bad school" they jump on tables and run around the room screaming—behavior which they believe not to be acceptable in school.

If FIVE does something he should not do or did not want or mean to do, he is likely to blame the nearest person. If his mother is close by, the child may accuse her with a "Look what you made me do." A sibling, a dog, or another child may be blamed when they are a part of the scene of action.

There may be more validity to this accusation than one at first realizes. When a child is running down a hill and meets another child, there is no doubt that he may show an unsteadiness in his running and finally fall. The other child did not push him, but the other child's presence did remove his attention from his running. He could not do the two things at once—both look at the child and run. It is very significant that during the preschool years serious accidents do occur when the mother is right beside the child and yet not giving her full attention to him. He becomes dependent upon her if she is there, whereas if he had been on his own he might have exercised his usual caution and not come to grief.

FIVE enjoys the possessions he has. He is not as eager for presents as he was at four, nor does he brag about his possessions as he did earlier. This does not mean that he is careful about his possessions.

A few children take things home from school, such as toys or books, but readily and willingly return them. At home the five-year-old may take things from the kitchen, or a girl may desire and take some of her mother's powder or perfume.

On the whole, FIVE is relatively truthful. He believed his fanciful tales at four, but by five he knows that he is fooling, and has his tongue in his cheek. Sometimes his tales are self-protective, though oddly so. One five-year-old who was late for dinner told his parents that "a big boy said he was going to kill me so I couldn't come home." Other fanciful tales may indicate a wish not yet fulfilled. The five-year-old girl who reported that her teacher said she read well enough to read with the first grade was obviously expressing an unsatisfied longing.

10. PHILOSOPHIC OUTLOOK

DEATH AND DEITY

The vast intangible creative force called God is often grasped rather well by the mind of the four-year-old. But FIVE does not soar as high and has a tendency to bring God within the scope of his everyday world. He asks very specific questions about what He looks like, is He a man, what does He do and where does He live? He also conceives of God's world as having modern equipment and therefore asks if you can call Him up on the telephone and if He makes cars.

Some FIVEs are more aware of God's presence and may even fear that He sees whatever they do. One five-year-old thought that God pushed him whenever he fell. Others may be rather critical of God and His reported handiwork, for they feel that "God made a mistake when He made a mosquito."

Death likewise is taken in a fairly matter-of-fact way. FIVE seems to recognize dimly the finality of death and may speak of it as "the end." The dead person is to him one without living attributes: "He can't walk, he can't see, and he can't feel." He is interested in the posture of someone who falls dead—"Did he fall on his back or his face?" If he is told that dead people go to heaven after they die, he wonders why they don't fall out of heaven.

He has linked up the facts that when you are old you die. He is not usually concerned about his own personal relationship to death, or the possible deaths of those around him. He does, however, recognize the eventual possibility that others will die and states the fact that "When I grow up all you people will be dead." Though he has not as yet conceived of his own death, he readily enters into the game of playing dead when he is shot.

TIME AND SPACE

FIVE in his sense of time is concerned chiefly with the NOW. It is difficult for him to conceive of himself as not having existed or as dying. Time for him is largely his own personal time.

The more common "time" words used by adults are now a part of the child's vocabulary and he handles them freely. He knows when events of the day take place in relation to one another. He can answer correctly such questions about time as the following:

"How old will you be on your next birthday?"

"What day is today?"

"What day does Daddy stay at home all day?"

"What day comes after Sunday?"

"What day do you like best?"

Many FIVEs are very much interested in the calendar and the clock. A few copy the numbers on the clock's face and may read them. They are especially proud of possessing an alarm clock of their own, and accept the ringing of the alarm as the time to get up or to terminate a play nap.

FIVE's chief spatial interest is in what is HERE. He is extremely focal, is interested in the space he immediately occupies. He has little insight into geographic relationships, but does recognize some specific landmarks. He likes to draw roads on very simple maps of his immediate neighborhood. He can now cross neighborhood streets by himself and likes to do errands at the nearby store. His interest in more-distant places depends upon his personal associations with them.

CHAPTER 6

SIX YEARS OLD

Behavior Profile

"He is a changed child!" Many a mother has said this ruefully when her former five-year-old begins to lose his angelic five-year-oldness. "I don't know what has gotten into him!"

There is some mystification about this change. At five he was such a well-organized child, at home with himself and at home with the world. But as early as the age of five and a half he began to be brash and combative in some of his behavior, as though he were at war with himself and with the world. At other times he was hesitant, dawdling, indecisive; and then again overdemanding and explosive, with strangely contradictory spurts of affection and of antagonism. At other times, of course, he was quite delightful and companionable. What *has* gotten into him?

Perhaps nothing more or less than six-year-oldness!

The sixth year (or thereabout) brings fundamental changes, somatic and psychological. It is an age of transition. The milk teeth are shedding; the first permanent molars are emerging. Even the child's body chemistry undergoes subtle changes reflected in increased susceptibility to infectious disease. Otitis media comes to a peak; nose and throat difficulties occur more frequently. The six-year-old is not as robust or as staunch as he was at five. There are other important developmental changes which affect the mechanisms of vision, and indeed the whole neuromotor system.

These changes manifest themselves in new and sometimes startling psychological traits—traits that begin to make their appearance at five and a half. The six-year-old proves to be not a bigger and better five-year-old. He is a different child because he is a changing child. He is passing through a stage of transition similar to the paradoxical stage of the two-and-a-half-year-old. He also has much of the fluidity and forthrightness of the four-year-old. Combine the paradoxical and labile qualities of the two-and-a-half-year-old and four-year-old and you have an indication of the maturity traits of the six-year-old.

In describing these traits we shall emphasize those that make the six-year-old distinguishable from the five-year-old. These traits do not descend upon the child with a sudden onrush. The colors of a developmental spectrum shade into one another by imperceptible gradations. But to paint a vivid and usable maturity portrait we must dip our brush where the pigment is strong. With this much apology to the six-year-old, we shall now attempt to do him developmental justice—remembering that such justice tends to bridge the chasm between angels and demons.

The action system of the child is now undergoing growth changes, comparable in their way to the eruption of the sixth-year molars. New propensities are erupting; new impulses, new feelings, new actions are literally coming to the surface, because of profound developments in the underlying nervous system. These changes probably hark back to psychological increments which were slowly evolved through eons in the remote prehistory of mankind. In the individual, the essence of the racial increments is crowded into the brief space of months and years. The five-year-old has already come into a fundamental portion of the racial inheritance. The six-year-old is coming into a later portion. *This* is what has gotten into him!

Psychological inheritance, however, does not come in neat packages. It comes in the form of behavior trends and dynamic forces which must be reconciled and organized within a total action system. It takes time to pattern and balance conflicting trends of behavior as they well up in the sixth year of life. Some conflict is a normal accompaniment of developmental progress, so we may take a constructive and optimistic view of the developmental difficulties the six-year-old encounters.

He tends to go to extremes—under slight stress, whenever he attempts to use his most recently acquired powers. As an actively growing organism, he is entering new fields of action. The new possibilities of behavior seem to come in pairs. He is often under a compulsion to manifest first one extreme of two alternative behaviors and then its very opposite. Diametric opposites have almost equal sway over him, because both propensities have only recently arrived upon the scene. He is inexperienced in their management and meaning. It is hard for him to choose between evenly competing opposites. When he is away from home, he may even be overtaxed by the simple proposition: "Will you have chocolate or vanilla ice cream?" A difficult choice—and one that will not be decisive even after it is made; for an immature child will not completely forego the vanilla after he has chosen the chocolate. Decisions that were easy or judicial at five have become complicated with new emotional factors, for he or she *is* growing. The complication signifies increased maturity. The indecisiveness signifies immaturity if we allow ourselves a paradoxical distinction between maturity and immaturity.

Let a poem by Edna St. Vincent Millay bear witness to the duplexity of life situations at the age of six:

> Come along in then, little girl!
> Or else stay out!
> But in the open door she stands
> And bites her lips and twists her hands
> And stares upon me trouble-eyed:
> "Mother," she says, "I can't decide!
> I can't decide."

A two-and-a-half-year-old displays a similar difficulty in handling opposites—in deciding between *yes* and *no*, *come* and *go*, *fast* and *slow*, and many another *do* and *don't*. The child oscillates between two alternatives, chooses the wrong; or in quick succession chooses the wrong, the right, the wrong, the right; dawdles, or reaches an impasse, stymied by the two-way possibilities. It is almost as if he were seeing two images and plagued with the inability to suppress one image for the sake of clear single vision. Our six-year-old is suffering from a similar (and likewise temporary) developmental duplexity. He is afflicted with bipolarity—a seesaw awareness of both ends of a dilemma.

The six-year-old manifests his bipolarities in many different ways. He flies quickly from one extreme to another. He cries, but his crying is easily diverted into laughter, and his laughter into crying. He sidles up to his mother and says, "I love you," but in another breath he may say, "I hate you, I'll hit you." He will mutter as much to a total stranger. Indeed, if we note the psychological shallowness of his brash verbalizations, his epithets ("Stinker!"), his profanity ("Aw nuts!" "Dope!"), we can allow with a smile of sympathetic humor that there is a certain naïveté in his madness. We must discourage his irresponsibilities, and yet recognize that these warring intensities and impulses are new experiences for him. Sometimes he seems bent upon defining what *not* to do by doing it.

Certainly he is as inexpert in handling complex human relationships as he once was inept in putting a spoon into his mouth. He frequently misses the mark. Watch him in his social approaches to his baby sister. He may be very good to her, and also very bad, all in the same afternoon or the same half hour. To attribute his badness to sheer perversity or even to jealousy may be a mistake. The inconsistencies of the six-year-old's conduct, his tendency to bolt in and out and to slam, his verbal aggressions, his intense concentrations, his abrupt terminations, his explosive atttacks upon situations —are all cut from the same cloth. An outstanding characteristic of the six-year-old is his meager capacity to modulate. But we need not despair. With the help of the culture and the help of time he will improve that capacity.

His difficulty in making a ready distinction between two-way possibilities is not limited to situations that are emotional or ethical in nature. In his early efforts to print letters of the alphabet he is prone to reverse them. His *B* looks backward. This tendency to reverse letters and numbers is one of the many reasons why we prefer to delay the beginning of any formal teaching of reading, in school or at home.

Life is charged with double alternatives for all of us, even after we are grown up. The six-year-old in our complex culture happens to be in a phase of development where these alternatives crowd upon him rather thickly. He is at a crossroads where he has to intermediate between contraries. When he does the wrong thing, he is called bad, but there is no use in asking him why he was bad; he has not yet made a clear distinction. He is not fully oriented. He is in new territory. He does not have command of his motor impulses nor of his interpersonal relationships. At the age of five awareness and capabilities were in better balance. The six-year-old is aware of more than he can well manage. He often overdifferentiates (going to extremes), or he underdifferentiates. He is overemphatic, or he hesitates and dawdles, or attempts things that are too hard. He wants to be first. He always wants to win. This makes him quarrelsome and accusing on the playground. Yet he wants to be loved best. At Christmas he wants a good many presents, but doesn't always know exactly what they should be. He is so active and acquisitive for new experience that his manners are likely to be hasty and sketchy— a quick "Come in," or "Thank you"; but no prolonged deference or formality, as in shaking hands.

It follows that a birthday party limited to six-year-olds is not a model of decorum. Even under adult supervision with a master plan, such a foregathering tends to become a kaleidoscopic medley of high-pressure activities—short-shrift amenities as the guests arrive, a pouncing seizure of presents, an excited exchange of favors, everyone expecting the first prize, bubbling bravadoes, scrambles, and hullabaloo with interludes of silence induced by ice cream. At no other age are children more insistently interested in parties; at no other age, perhaps, are they less competent to produce a party agreeable to adult ideals of decorum. Characteristically enough, the eagerness of the six-year-old is not matched by his capabilities, particularly under social stress. A philosophic observer will detect evidences of constructive, adaptive behavior even in the confusions and diffusions of a high-spirited party. A prudent parent will limit in advance the complexity of the party.

A primary-school teacher will see in such a party a display of the same rich energies with which she deals every day as she guides her group of first-graders. A schoolroom represents the tool and the technique by which our culture attempts to pattern these abounding energies. Fortunate are those children who are entrusted to a teacher capable of interpreting their enthusiasms as symptoms of a growth process which needs skillful direction. Such a teacher creates in her schoolroom a cheerful atmosphere of tolerance and security which is hospitable to a certain dramatic quality in the six-year-old.

What do we mean by this dramatic quality? Not an artificial, stage-like make-believe, but a natural tendency to express and to organize new experience through frank muscular reactions. A healthy six-year-old is supple, sensitive, alert. He reacts with his whole action system. He not only smiles—he fairly dances with joy. He cries copiously when unhappy, kicks and shakes with his grief. Even during sleep he pitches his whole organism into his dreams; hence the gross arousals of his nightmares, which come to a peak at the age of six. During the waking day he tries on and throws off moods with facility. He uses body postures, gestures, and speech to give expression to emotions and ideas that are taking shape within him.

We must remember that the six-year-old is not simply trying to perfect abilities that he had at the age of five. Nature is adding a cubit to his psychological stature. He is moving into altogether strange domains of experience, using his muscles, large and small, to pioneer new pathways.

Dramatic self-activation is at once a method of growth and of learning. It is a natural mechanism whereby the child organizes his feeling and thinking. But the task is too great for him alone. The school is the cultural instrument that must help him enlarge and refine his dramatic self-projections. Instinctively he identifies him-self with all that happens about him, even with the pictures and the letters in his book and the numbers on the blackboard. Just as he must pick up a block and handle it to learn its properties, so he must project his motor and mental attitudes into life situations. Emotions are not formless forces; they are patterned experiences. The function of the school is to provide personal and cultural experiences that will organize simultaneously the growing emotions and the associated intellectual images.

Naturally, this can be done effectively only through activity programs and projects that will set into operation the child's own self-activity. He learns not by rote but by participation and a creative kind of self-activation. His teacher takes him and his schoolmates on a trip to a dairy. The children talk it all over sometime later, after an interval of assimilation. As an individual and as a tenuous member of a group, the six-year-old translates his experience by building a ground plan of the barn with building blocks. He plans with the group to reenact part of his experience by dramatic representation. Through all these means of expression he clarifies meanings and relationships. There are endless opportunities for similar dramatic assimilation—*pantomime* of simple actions ("I am chopping wood"); *portrayal of moods* (a lost child, a tired boy); *tableaux and self-initiated dramatic skits* (school and home life); *dramatized stories with simple plot* (Mother Goose and very simple puppet plays). The ordinary six-year-old mind is not ready for purely formal instruction in reading, writing and arithmetic. These subjects can be visualized only through association with creative activity and motorized life experiences. Such dramatic expression must not be confused with rehearsed theatricals or formalized kindergarten play-acting. It is a developmental form of self-expression, which must be evoked impromptu and by ingenious indirection. Once a primary teacher has grasped this fundamental principle, she can establish a mutually delightful rapport with her pupils.

For a disadvantaged child a well-conducted school is a haven. For the average school beginner, the understanding teacher becomes a kind of auxiliary mother on whom he or she fixes affection. The teacher does not displace the mother, nor does she aspire to become a substitute mother. But she strengthens the child's sense of security in the strange world beyond his home. He derives a new confidence in this world from her daily welcomes and assurances, and from the sheer satisfaction of his broadening experiences and the protectiveness of a partially standardized environment.

He does not wish this environment to deviate much from a familiar, set pattern. He likes some social routines. He has to assimilate so many new experiences that he prefers psychological landmarks that remain fixed. He is fond of the rituals and conventions that are reliably repeated each day. He rather likes to see his teacher in a customary location when the program of the day begins. (Sometimes he may even have a passing regret if she changes her hair style!) Perhaps because he is constantly making new discoveries, he craves a few fixed points in his mental universe.

It is easy to forget that this young discoverer has to adjust to two worlds: the world of home and the world of school. The school provides certain simplifications and group controls which the home lacks. His emotional anchorage remains in the home, but he has to acquire a modified set of emotional moorings in school. The two orientations are neither interchangeable nor mixable. Being inexpert in emotional modulations, the school beginner cannot always shift readily within the two worlds. An ill-timed visit at school from his mother, a mysterious conversation between his mother and his awesome new teacher, may produce some jangle of images and attitudes. Often it is hard enough to make the transition when the two worlds are physically separated. In the morning the child may have difficulty in leaving his true mother; he may be teased on the trip to school, because a six-year-old is an easily frightened and teasible victim for the eight-nine-ten-year-old upperclassmen (hat snatching and verbal detractions). And the new customs at school may be so rudely strange that they baffle and disorient.

Parents, teachers, and school administrators may be unaware of the complex of factors both inherent and environmental which can undermine the morale of a school beginner. Sometimes the transition to school is so blundering that it produces gastrointestinal symptoms and severe emotional reactions. Here individual differences count. The sensitive and immature children suffer most. Difficulties of adjustment are exaggerated if the teacher has a cheerless, disciplinary personality, if the methods of instruction are overrigid, with excess stress on academic proficiency, competitiveness, and school marks. In some of these instances the tensions of school entrance are so abnormally weighted against the child that his mental health is overtaxed. School entrance is no simple transition and it should be tempered by flexible arrangements of attendance and program.

We have already alluded to certain primitive features in the maturity traits of the six-year-old. These traits are vaguely characterized by such adjectives as impulsive, undifferentiated, volatile, dogmatic, compulsive, excitable. His spontaneous drawings are crude but realistic, and sometimes suggestive of the graphic renderings of early man, in their portrayal of action, of sky and earth, and of ornamental design. He likes to draw a house with a tree beside it. Wild animals, darkness, fire, thunder and lightning figure in the fears and dreams of the six-year-old. Boy and girls alike are naïvely proud to lose their teeth and have a ready faith in dental fairies, elves, and other supernatural agencies.

Although his intellectual processes are concrete and even animistic, the six-year-old is highly dependent upon the direction and guidance of adult authority. Witness the modern version of primitive magic in which the incantatory parent counts "one, two, three, four, five, six, seven," with the advance understanding that when the magic "seven" is intoned, the required deed will be done by the obedient child. The magic works. It is not based on pure gullibility. The deliberate counting, which can be shortened or lengthened to suit the needs, gives the child an opportunity to mobilize the adjustment that he cannot accomplish by himself. Like any other guidance device, it should be used judiciously, but it turns a neat trick in overcoming the hobbling effect of the child's bipolarity.

In the long run, neither home nor school will rely upon magic, but upon the utilization of the dramatic potentialities of the six-year-old, to lead him into new ways of self-control. His dramatic self-projectiveness is one of his most significant maturity traits; and it is constantly available. By means of it he maintains his own spontaneous contacts with the culture; by means of it, also, the culture lays hold upon him and directs him into new participations and anticipations. Much environmental influence comes through automatic imitation and incidental suggestion, both of which are related to his dramatic qualities. The total process of assimilation, whereby the child acquires his ways of life, is called acculturation.

Since he is given a share in the process, he does not become a mere figment of the culture. Through his projections, he does not merely reduplicate portions of the culture; he reappraises and reorganizes himself in relation to the culture. He begins to see himself and his bipolar opposites in their social contexts. He thus lays the basis for self-appraisals and evaluations which come to fuller flower in the seventh and eighth years.

These inward processes of assimilation and reconstruction rise to higher levels as the child matures. We shall see some interesting growth transformations in the seventh year. But the transitional sixth year must come first.

Maturity Traits

The following maturity traits are **not** to be regarded as rigid norms, nor as models. They simply illustrate the kinds of behavior—desirable or otherwise—that tend to occur at this age. Every child has his own pattern of growth, and his own timetable. The behavior traits here outlined may be used to interpret his individuality and to consider the maturity level at which he is functioning.

1. MOTOR CHARACTERISTICS

BODILY ACTIVITY

The composure of FIVE is no longer characteristic of FIVE AND A HALF, who is said to be restless at home. He plays indoors or outdoors and does not seem to know which place he wants to be. He occupies himself with digging, dancing, and climbing. He rides his tricycle downhill. He carts things about in a wagon. Sand, water, and mud play keep him occupied. Household tasks provide many motor activities. He likes to set the table and help his mother by getting things for her. When asked what he plays, he may say, "Just one thing after another."

SIX is an active age. The child is in almost constant activity, whether standing or sitting. He seems to be consciously balancing his own body in space. He is everywhere—climbing trees, crawling over, under, and about his large block structures or other children. He seems to be all legs and arms as he dances about the room.

He approaches activities with both more abandon and more deliberation, and he may stumble and fall in his efforts at mastery. He may like the "cleaning-up" job at school, brushing the floor, pushing furniture about, albeit he is somewhat clumsy and not too thorough. He enjoys activity and does not like interference.

There is a good deal of boisterous, ramble-scramble play. He likes to wrestle with his father or a sibling, but this may end in disaster, for he does not know when to stop. Indoors his ball play may become a menace as he bounces, tosses, and tries to catch. He is also interested in stunts on a trapeze bar; he likes to pull himself up on a rope and swing. Swings are favorites; he sits with more freedom and balance and he loves to swing as high as he can.

SIX overextends in much of his motor behavior. He likes to build blocks higher than his shoulder; he tries to do a running broad jump without minding if he falls. His own yard may not be as attractive to him as a neighbor's.

EYES AND HANDS

There are also noticeable changes in the eye-hand behavior of the five-and-a-half-to-six-year-old. He seems more aware of his hand as a tool and he experiments with it as such. He is reported to be awkward in performing fine motor tasks, yet he has a new demand for such activities. Tinker Toys and tools are especially intriguing to him. He may be interested less in what he accomplishes with the tools than in manipulating them. He likes to take things apart as well as put them together. Girls especially like to dress and undress dolls at this age.

The child now holds his pencil more awkwardly and he changes his grasp on it. He likes to draw, print, and color as he did at five, but he adheres less closely to a model. Filling in with color may occupy him for a considerable period. In coloring, he is awkward, shifts his body position as well as his grasp of the crayon, and tilts his head. He may stand and lean way over the table and continue to draw or he may rest his head down on his arm. He may say that his hand "gets tired" and bring the free hand to it briefly. With his attempts at finer manipulation he is often found standing or even walking as he is working.

SIX is as active in sitting as he is in the standing position. He wriggles on a chair, sits on the edge, may even fall off. There is a good deal of oral activity: tongue extension and mouthing, blowing through and biting lips. He bites, chews, or taps his pencil. Pencil grasp is less awkward than at five and a half years, but his performance is laborious.

Eye and hand now function with less of the speed and close relationship that they showed at five. In building a tower of small blocks, SIX makes a more deliberate, regardful approach and tries to place the blocks accurately. But they may not be as accurately aligned as they were at five. At another time, SIX may build with such careless abandon that the blocks fall repeatedly.

He touches, handles, and explores all materials. "What do you do with this?" He wants to do everything. There is often more activity than actual accomplishment. But he cuts and pastes, making books and boxes, and molds clay into objects.

SIX can move his eyes more facilely and he shifts his regard frequently from the task at hand. He is easily distracted by the environment and his hands may continue to work as he watches another's activity.

In carpentry he needs a good deal of assistance. The saw bends and gets jammed. He pounds and pounds in driving nails, but often fails to hit them on the head and may even break the board. He may hold the hammer near the head. He can, however, make crude structures.

2. PERSONAL HYGIENE

EATING

Appetite. The good appetite of FIVE continues into six and may become tremendous. Some children are said to eat all day long, and are reputed to eat better between meals than at them. Breakfast continues to be the poorest meal and may be accompanied by stomachache, nausea, and infrequently by vomiting (especially if school demands are excessive). A liquid diet of milk and fruit juice is definitely preferred.

In contrast to his poor morning meal, the six-year-old often feels hungry just before he goes to bed and may eat a sizeable snack with real enjoyment. He may even awaken in the middle of the night and request food.

SIX's eyes are often bigger than his stomach, and he is apt to ask for bigger helpings than he can handle. He should not be held too closely to his initial request. If he does not agree to have two helpings, with the chance of refusing his planned second helping, he may be allowed to divide the food on his plate into two portions. Face-saving devices for both parent and child should be made quickly available as they are needed. Such devices gather legitimacy and meaning when one realizes that the six-year-old is characteristically good at starting things and definitely poor at finishing.

A boost in appetite is often accomplished by some new experience, some change in routine. Thus a visit to grandmother's, or a meal at a restaurant with the family, often brings about an improvement, even though it may be only temporary.

Refusals and Preferences. SIX continues to prefer plain cooking. Though he may have a fairly wide range of food likes and is willing to try new foods, his likes and dislikes are usually very definite. He may refuse meat because he once was served a piece with a little rim of fat on it, or because he doesn't like to chew. He may refuse foods by spells. What's "in" is strongly in and what's "out" is completely out. This is the age when peanut butter begins its rise toward its seven—eight-year-old pinnacle of preference. Many of the cooked desserts, especially rice pudding and custard, are perhaps refused for themselves alone, but often the six-year-old goes "off desserts." If they came at the beginning of the meal he might perhaps eat them with relish. He usually prefers raw vegetables to cooked ones. Textures are extremely important: lumpy, stringy foods are commonly refused.

Self-Help. Many children return to finger feeding at six. Eating implements seem to be an unnecessary intrusion between them and the food, and are manipulated awkwardly. Even such foods as mashed potatoes are finger fed. These children should be given more whole foods so that they may finger feed themselves. The fork is often preferred to a spoon and will be used if the food can be speared. At the opposite extreme are the fastidious children who would not think of touching their food with their fingers or of spilling a drop. These children eat with care and precision and use implements deftly.

Table Behavior. It is not an edifying experience to have a six-year-old at the table, especially at the evening meal. He really does not belong there, and would much prefer to have a tray beside the television set while he is watching his special program.

His motor control is very erratic in sitting as well as in standing. The minute he sits down his legs are likely to start swinging. If your leg or the table leg is within range, the force of his thrust will be duly imprinted. If he must come to the table, he might be allowed to come in his stocking feet. After his initial attack upon his food he begins to dawdle and to wriggle. He reaches for a carrot and knocks over his milk. His arms jerk and he spills his food. Pretty soon he is teetering on the back legs of his chair or even on only one leg. Father is slowly losing patience and has perhaps already said too much in his attempt to hold the child in line.

When the six-year-old does eat he stuffs his mouth too full and is apt to talk with his mouth full. If his total body is not active, he is at least likely to talk too much. If he is criticized for his behavior he is apt to find the same flaws for which he is criticized in his siblings or parents.

Leaving him alone at the table produces almost the opposite effect to the desired one. He dawdles even more. Taking the food away from him either makes him angry or produces tears. The return of the food may tip the scale in the right direction, but the best stimulus, if he is at the family table, may be to race with him, making sure that he will win.

Needless to say, not all six-year-olds are composites of this picture, but most of them show at least some of its features. A few children actually eat better with the family group than alone, but a surprisingly large number request supper in bed, or a tray by the TV. They seem to sense what is best for them; for when allowed to come to the table on occasion, they handle the situation much better, showing pride in accomplishment. It is unfortunate to send a child from the table as a punishment for failure. If he insists on being with the family group regularly, he is usually quite satisfied to sit at his own little table, preferably with another sibling.

A napkin is still a cultural tool beyond his competence. The child now refuses a bib and may also refuse to have the napkin tucked in under his chin. If the napkin is beside his plate he forgets to use it and if it is on his lap it quickly falls to the floor. He may be aware of food around his mouth and may deftly remove it by a sweep of the back of his hand. Some use a napkin on being reminded, but on the whole clean hands and clean faces are still the responsibility of the adult and not of the child.

SLEEP

Nap. A very few five-and-a-half-year-old children cling to a half-hour nap on occasion. By six, if there still is any desire to nap it is cut into by afternoon school attendance.

Bedtime. The five-and-a-half-year-old in his presleep patterns shows a very real developmental shift in behavior. He is definitely tired and rarely resists going to bed at his usual bedtime (7–8 P.M.) or even earlier. Some children like to get ready for bed before supper and to have a tray in bed, though they do not actually go to bed to sleep before their usual bedtime. They are more fearful at this age, want the companionship of their mother even after the lights are turned off; may ask to have an adult remain on the same floor with them, to sleep in the same room with a sibling, or to have the hall light on. There is a return of interest in taking stuffed animals and dolls to bed with them, even to the number of two or three. They treat these toys as though they were real people keeping them company. Prayers have an unusually quieting effect upon some children and should be seriously considered especially with the fearful child.

The six-year-old's bedtime behavior is not as fearful as that of the five-and-a-half-year-old. He goes to bed quite easily and enjoys some quiet activity or music after he is in bed. He especially likes to be read to or to look at books for half an hour. This is an excellent time to stimulate a child's interest in reading. He enjoys picking out single letters, especially capital letters, or even words in the story his parent is reading to him. After the lights are turned out he is fond of telling about the day's happenings and about things that are on his mind. He is very spontaneous at this age: all the mother needs to do is to listen.

Some children enjoy having father

put them to bed, and respond more smoothly to him. Others, however, are overstimulated by the father. As a rule, the mother is still preferred, especially for the good-night chats.

Night. There is an increasing number of six-year-olds who are said to be "wonderful sleepers." But there are still quite a few, though fewer than at five, whose sleep is disturbed by toilet needs or by "bad dreams." Strange men and women are beginning to appear in their dreams, and the dream animals that are still frequently present are becoming active, especially in biting.

When a terrifying nightmare occurs, the child may be unable to quiet until his mother gets into bed with him. Those who are able to awaken by themselves, crawl into bed with their parents, especially with their mother. Some return to their own bed after telling the dream; others after a short reassuring snuggle.

Very few children are toileted routinely at this age. Some of those who still need to get up must report to their parent after they have functioned, but an increasing number care for themselves and get back into bed by themselves.

Morning. Morning waking at five and a half years of age shows two extremes: the early wakers (5:30–6:00 A.M.), and the late wakers (8 A.M.). The latter may even have to be awakened. By six the extremes are not quite so wide. The usual waking time is be-

tween seven and seven-thirty, and the child no longer needs to be wakened. The five-and-a-half-year-old sleeps about eleven and a half hours; the six-year-old eleven hours.

On rising, the six-year-old toilets himself, and usually becomes more interested in his morning play activities than in his dressing. If, however, his clothes are laid out singly on the bed for him, he may carry through after a reminder to begin.

ELIMINATION

Bowel. The general pattern of the five-year-old persists—one movement per day, perhaps after lunch. There is a tendency to shift this function to the earlier half of the day rather than the latter half. A few shift to before breakfast or after bedtime. Two movements per day may occur, but these are often two installments of one movement, since the child may not sit long enough to complete the evacuation. The parent needs to help with a little supervision to see that the child remains long enough to finish.

As a rule, functioning is rather rapid; in fact, if the child has waited until the latter part of the afternoon, it may be so rapid that he makes a mad dash for the bathroom and may arrive there too late. With some children the movement seems to occur almost involuntarily before they can do anything about it. These episodes of incontinence affect the parents almost more than the child. The child may be ashamed and may crawl off into some recess, though frequently he tries to set things right by changing his pants and cleaning himself up.

Ability to function easily on the school toilet may not come until about the age of eight years. The six-year-old therefore often comes to grief while loitering on his way home from the afternoon session unless a parent meets him to expedite his return home, or forestalls the episode at the noon hour. Spanking and undue "shaming" are poor measures of control.

Most children take care of their own needs without reporting before or after they have functioned. Some are more aware of the function and report, as they did earlier, on the size, shape, and number of the movements; or they do the opposite and withdraw themselves completely by locking the bathroom door.

Swearing and name-calling are definitely related to the bowel function at this age. "Stinker" is a term in common use and may well stem from a realistic experience.

Bladder. Day or night wetting is now rare. As at five, a child may delay too long and have to make a mad dash. Frequently such episodes can be averted by reminding the child to go to the bathroom at a favorable time— e.g., before he goes out to play or before he goes on a trip. A few children suddenly wet or dampen their pants just as others suddenly have an impulsive bowel movement. They feel bad and often say, "I don't know when I do it." These lapses might be controlled by a little more planned reminding.

A fair number still need to get up for toileting, usually taking care of their own needs and going back to bed without reporting to their parents. However, night wetting is not uncommon even at six. Some parents like to try one of the commercial conditioning devices in hopes of achieving night dryness, though we prefer to wait for this until the child is seven.

The urinary function, especially the sound of this function, may stimulate giggling and teasing between two children at this age. One child in the bathroom at a time is a simple rule, easily adhered to. Peripheral and preventive control thus takes the place of directed control. In the male six-year-old, the urinary function may be used verbally in a humorous or an angry attack: "I'll pee in your eye!"

BATH AND DRESSING

Bath. The nightly bath is now being resisted by some children, especially boys. The child may say he is too tired to bathe, which is true in part, for he might have bathed without resistance at five o'clock with the plan to have supper in bed. A bath every other night may be accepted fairly readily. Some children still show no interest in washing themselves. Some try to bathe themselves completely. Others limit their efforts to legs and feet. Nearly all need help in drawing the water and with regard to finishing touches in the head and neck region.

Often a bath goes more smoothly with father than with mother. Dawdling in the tub is the rule and it is hard to get the child out of the tub. He can be hastened by simple techniques such as pacing, counting, or planning an interesting bedtime activity.

Most children of this age wash hands and face reasonably well but not spontaneously, and with some, the face is just the nose. Although beginning to be aware of dirt on another person, many SIXES are not too much concerned about dirt on themselves and they may resist washing themselves, though they will accept help. More casualness about washing up would help a good deal to make home life smooth. A mother's self-rebuke (after a meal!), "Oh, I forgot to remind you to wash your hands!" gives the child a wonderful lift—the legitimate kind of lift one gets from knowing that others also err.

Dressing and Care of Clothes. Wanting to dress is half the battle, but many six-year-olds have not as yet acquired this desire. That is why SIX still needs to be handled in part like a five-year-old. Though he often will not allow his mother actually to assist him, her mere presence seems to help. It is a good time for spelling or arithmetic games or "I see something" games. He also loves to race with a parent. If he ties his shoelaces he does it too loosely. A child may need less help on the more leisurely mornings when he does not attend school. Undressing is accomplished with considerable speed.

SIX is a clothes-conscious age. Specific styles and colors, often red, are demanded. Six-year-olds often need help with their boots and also with the second sleeve of their coat.

Although SIX is interested in his clothes, he does not take very good care of them. As one mother expressed it, "She likes to have things right, but she doesn't do anything about it." At five and a half, when the child peeled off his clothes he often threw them to (or at) his mother. At six he flings them all about the room, often in a humorous way or to test how many places and directions he can throw. This can easily be turned into a useful game of collecting the clothes, or dirty clothes may be thrown into a corner— more fun than to throw them into a hamper.

"Shoe trouble" is a very real trouble at six. The six-year-old boy especially wants to take off his shoes when he is in the house, but he is apt to leave one in one room and the other in another, and all too frequently the entire household is set on a hunt the next morning so that he can go to school with his shoes on. His parents actually prefer to have him take his shoes off at the table because he kicks. Here are multiple grounds for preventive strategy. Why not do as the Dutch do, have the six- and seven-year-old take off his shoes as he enters the house, and let him go around in his stocking feet?

Some boys are becoming interested in combing their hair. Girls may rue the day that they insisted on long hair, but they do not want to give it up in spite of all the discomfort that combing causes. The scalp is very sensitive at about this age, but the child may occupy herself with a book, or coloring, or piano, during the process.

HEALTH AND SOMATIC COMPLAINTS

It is not only the general behavior of the six-year-old that goes awry, but the working of his physical bodily structure as well. The five-and-a-half to six-year-old is full of complaints— legitimate ones that should be listened to seriously. At five and a half his feet "hurt" him. He may walk as though lame. By six his legs hurt him, occasionally his arms, and frequently the back of his neck. He says he has a "crick" in his neck. Rubbing and massage bring both comfort and alleviation of pain.

He complains of being hot, so hot that he would like to go outside in winter without any outer clothes on. He perspires readily. His mucous membranes seem to inflame easily. The mucous membranes of his eyes may become reddened and he may develop styes. His throat not only hurts, but it becomes red and infected, and the infection frequently spreads to his ears and his lungs. Otitis media again reaches a peak, as it did at two and a half. In addition to the more common communicable diseases as at five —chicken pox and whooping cough—

German measles and mumps show an increase. Diphtheria and scarlet fever reach a peak as it will in preadolescence. Pediatric care with immunizations is fortunately controlling more and more of these diseases.

Allergy responses are high. These may be in the form of a return of past allergic responses or a new development of hay fever. The mucous membrane of the nose is sensitive and congests readily. A number of girls complain that their urine burns, and they have reddened genitalia which need intermittent care with bland salve. The skin may be very sensitive in the head and neck regions. Hair-combing is a painful process for some girls at this age. Boys may react with half-painful convulsive laughter when washed by an adult, because of hypersensitive face and neck. If the child washes himself he is far less sensitive. Boils may develop on face, neck, or arms.

The child of this age tires easily; in fact, he wilts. Yet he may hate to give in by resting. Rather free use of the bed will prevent undue fatigue and even illnesses. The bed should be psychologized in the child's mind as a pleasant haven of rest and of relaxing activity.

SIX does not make transitions easily. The immediate future often looms up as something almost too much to cope with. He may not want to get up on school days. He may say, "I don't feel well," but makes a dramatic recovery as soon as the school bus, if he travels by bus, has passed his house. Or when he is at breakfast he may complain of a stomachache, and even vomit. Significantly enough, these symptoms do not occur over the weekend. A little help, by not requiring him to eat too much at breakfast, and the added interest of having an older and admired child call especially for him or her, may well control these symptoms. A stomachache may still, as at five years, be related to an imminent bowel movement.

The clumsy headlongedness of SIX makes him susceptible to falls. He is fairly safe in trees, but is not too well balanced on fences, which he insists upon climbing. He is apt to break a fall with his arm, and thereby is liable to break his arm as he falls.

This is the age when the word "sissy" looms up as a possible reality in the minds of many fathers, in regard to their sons. The sight of blood may be upsetting to the six-year-old and the removal of a splinter by his mother may bring a hysterical reaction. Fathers should not too readily construe this as "sissy" behavior, and should realize that it is part of the child's emotional bond with his mother. If the parent feels that the splinter must be removed at once, the child may gather control by being allowed to pinch his mother as much as it hurts. But why does the splinter need to be removed at once? Sticking on a sanitary adhesive ensures an oozing and healing around the splinter, which often comes out with the adhesive tape as it loosens in the bath. A child is more likely to report his scratches, slivers, and blisters if he can tolerate the treatment. Serious infections usually are the result of delayed reporting and absence of care.

TENSIONAL OUTLETS

Tensional manifestations rise to a peak at five and a half to six years of age. They include outbursts of screaming, violent temper tantrums, and striking at the parent. The child may so completely lose control that the mother needs to intervene and take him bodily to his room, leaving him there for a brief period and then returning to help him get over his difficulty. Left alone, he might go on indefinitely to a point of exhaustion. Skillful distraction helps.

After the storm has passed, the mother analyzes what brought on the outburst, and how she might have avoided it. She may be able to discuss this with the child when he is in a receptive mood. By six years of age he may be snapped out of his outbursts with a humorous twist not related to himself and may shift his crying and screaming into laughter, though before this age the use of humor may well make matters worse.

The mother needs to realize that at this temporary maturity stage the child wants his way just for the sake of having his way, and that he will be more open to suggestion by six or six and a half years. She must also realize that the child again needs to be protected from himself, just as he did at two and a half. Free access to candy may have to be stopped for a time, and drawers and closets may again need to be locked; or a rigid schedule may have to be set up, stating how many pieces of candy are allowed, and the conditions under which they are allowed.

Besides violent outlets, there is a diffusion of tensional energy into diverse channels—swinging legs and wriggling, biting or tearing off fingernails and toenails, scratching, grimacing, grinding teeth, chewing on hair or pencils; picking the nose, and even eating nasal incrustations. These various behaviors are likely to occur when something is demanded of the child—or by the child of himself—which is not yet within his competence, or when he is waiting for something to happen, or even when he is trying to go to sleep. If pronounced, the tensional behavior may indicate that the child's task should be lightened. The disgusting aspect of nose-picking can at least be alleviated by seeing that the child thoroughly cleans his nose before he starts out for school.

At night he might not fight sleep so much if he were read to or allowed to listen to music, or had a chat with his mother after lights are out. He may want to talk about things that are on his mind—things that he cannot think through without his mother's help. He likes to hear about God. Finally he lets his mother go after prayers are said and he has had a goodnight kiss.

In some children the tensional outlets are less marked—a sigh, bringing fingers to mouth, hair to mouth, or hands to hair. With some the tensional escape is verbal or expletive—"Hell"; "Damn"; "Ugh"; "Hum"; "Stink." Yet others manifest repetitive muscular releases, ticlike in nature: blinking, throat-clearing, twitching of one side of the face, or head-shaking. If such reactions occur mainly at dinner when father is at home, the child should probably have his meal on a tray in his room. This does not imply that the father is the specific cause of these reactions. It may simply mean that the child is so immature that for the time being he is not up to the family group at mealtime.

In a few children, epecially boys, who stutter, there is a marked exacerbation at six, with a genuine difficulty in getting started to talk. By six to six and a half these same children are aware that they stutter. As one boy expressed it, "No use fooling me, I know I stutter." The best handling is preparedness. Knowing how to act and what to say in new social situations reduces sensitiveness and a tendency to withdrawal.

3. EMOTIONAL EXPRESSION

During the period from about five and a half to six years, the child is in a more or less constant state of emotional tension and even ferment. His emotional reactions reflect both the state of his organism and its sensitiveness to his environment. His emotional expressions may be likened to the magnetic needle of a compass, which reports an exact position. The parent needs to realize that a child of this age is very accurate in expressing the exact position and direction of the course that he is taking. It is very difficult to alter this course by external pressure. For that reason, preventive handling, or a constructive giving in, are often the only two ways of dealing effectively with the child. Fortunately, by six and even more by six and a half, behavior begins to lose its rigidity. It becomes more susceptible to shifts in direction, both inwardly motivated and outwardly stimulated.

Although the emotional trends of the five-and-a-half-to-six-year-old may be considered as rigid and as going in one direction, he can veer to the opposite direction and become rigid in that direction. That is why he is so often described as "sunshine and shadow," or "either-or," "utterly sweet or utterly horrid." He "adores his dog but is cruel to him"; he "adores his baby sister but threatens to kill her." He may meet a new experience with shyness and then with sheer abandon. He may refuse to answer a question for lack of knowledge and yet declare, "I know about everything." Reportedly he is "wonderful" at school and "terrible" at home, or vice versa.

Many of the difficulties of the five-and-a-half-year-old arise out of an inability to shift and to modulate behavior. He is not so much persistent as unable to stop; so he cries continuously once he has begun. He stays with things so long that he becomes fatigued and often cannot leave them of his own accord without an emotional explosion. Children who are poor fine-motor performers and who are more interested in people and in gross motor activities readily become moody, bored, and restless with indoor confinement. They wander around and do not know what to do. Dawdling—which reaches a peak at this age—may be regarded as a persistence of aimlessness. When the child tries to make a difficult choice he "gets all mixed up," but if he does make up his mind he becomes adamant. He is completely unable to consider a compromise and neither bribes nor punishments produce their usual results. Nevertheless, he does have good days as well as bad. It is important to build up behavior on these good days when he is responsive.

The child of five and a half to six years responds to impersonal handling, such as the counting technique, to which he can be trained to react automatically. Also such smooth-the-way phrases as "A good thing to do," or "First do it your own way, then do it mine" may forestall the child's usual resistance. He takes criticism badly, but thrives on praise and approval. He likes to do things on a game basis. One child expressed this mode of cooperation nicely when she said, "My mother isn't angry; we're doing things together!"

On the bad days the parent may wisely let things go, and figuratively "head for the woods." You do not demand much from the child on these days and you utilize as much as possible the automatic releases that have taken hold on the good days.

If emotional explosions do come,

they come very rapidly, and in different ways. Some children merely cry; some attack both verbally and with their hands and feet; some have an all-over temper tantrum as though their bodies were firing from all points. The children who "burst into tears" are perhaps the most sensitive. They cry because things are not going right, because their feelings are hurt, because their mother spoke sharply to them or to one of their siblings. The children who strike out physically or verbally are more excitable and impetuous in disposition: they feel that their course of action is suddenly impeded. Their verbal missiles of attack are short and terse: "I won't"; "I'll scream"; "I'll hit you"; "Get out of here"; "Keep quiet"; "I'll shoot you." Such verbal defiance at least inhibits a physical attack.

In a temper-tantrum type of response the lower centers seem to take over completely. Parents say, "He gets so mad he's almost insane" or "He becomes positively furious!" In these rages the child may throw a vase or rip a hole in a chair. The swing back to equilibrium is achieved differently by different children. Some can respond to help from the parent, especially if the outburst has occurred because of a misapprehension or lack of information. The majority finally respond to distraction, but a few seem to have to continue until their energy has been spent.

When a child feels sorry after a violent episode and attempts to make amends, he may well be moving away from outbursts to a higher organization, but the surest means of promoting his organization is for the parent to handle the child preventively. In all these outbursts it is usually the little things of life that light the fuse. The child got a word wrong at school, the mother couldn't tie the child's shoelaces the minute he asked, or he stubbed his toe. The big things of life, real demands, may be handled with relative ease. There is a marked decrease of these explosions by six, and still more by six and a half years of age. The child is then more receptive to teaching and can at least ask for help.

The fresh, rude, "ready for a fight" attitude in the six-year-old's voice and bearing is unduly distasteful to many parents. This attitude actually denotes a step forward, in the sense that the organism is now trying to act on its own even though it may be by defiance. The child gets a new leverage by pulling away from the parent. With hands on hips and that saucy look on her face, a six-year-old girl defies her mother with an "I won't." Or maybe, while seated at the table, she crosses her arms and looks haughtily at her mother without speaking—but fortunately gives a clue by glancing down to the side of her plate, where the mother forgot to place a spoon.

When asked a question, SIX may reply, "Why do you want to know?" or when given a reason, he voices his repeated phrase "So what!" He domineers and he argues; especially does he argue when he undertakes to show his mother where she was wrong. He may become very noisy, boisterous, and easily excitable. On such occasions he may quiet if you read to him or have him listen to records.

Girls especially are full of buffoonery; they giggle and grimace, and act silly, often with the intent to make others laugh. They might go on endlessly unless diverted to some new interest. When company comes, both sexes are most irrepressible. They want to be the life of the party. They monopolize the conversation, do gymnastics, act foolish, kick up their heels, laugh, and interrupt without seeming to be aware that anyone else is talking. It might be better if they were given some attention and allowed to do their tricks with an audience response. Then they could be more readily transferred from the scene. Perhaps the mother has planned in advance on something for them to do or someplace for them to go, or maybe one of the guests will join the child in his room to see his things and play with him.

The excitement of a party is frequently too much for SIX and he either crawls off into a corner, withdraws from the scene, or becomes unrestrained in actions or talk. He may say wildly, "I'm going to eat the radiator" or "I'm going to eat the bathroom." An ideal party at six might consist of an exchange of presents—the guests to receive as well as to bestow gifts—and a feast of ice cream and cake.

The six-year-old's initial response to any personal demand made upon him is usually "No," but given time and a few detours, he will come around to the idea almost as though it were his own. He may freeze into immobility if asked to "hurry up." Sometimes he is willing—especially if asked in the proper tone of voice—but he does not carry through. Then he needs to be given three or possibly four chances. If this fails, one can often get him started by counting—a device that usually works like magic. He resents authority that is arbitrarily imposed. He also resents punishment or being reprimanded before company, and rightly so. If he rebels, as he may, about school, it would be wise to look into possible causes. Maybe he has had one unfortunate experience which he cannot get off his mind, but which could easily be made right; or maybe he isn't ready for first grade.

Praise is an elixir to SIX, but correction is poison. However, he can accept a correction if it is postponed long enough after the event. With some children the necessary postponement is only a few hours or less. In some households such discussions become related to a specific time of day, as after lunch, at rest time, or at bedtime. But with a few children, several days must elapse before discussion can take place. Too many events in the life of the child are left dangling and unresolved at this age. One parent reports that she kept a dated record of disturbing events, using the notebook to help the child recall and finally to resolve his difficulties. This method of handling is comparable to storing away for future reference the squeaky toys the infant once feared. Finally, when he is ready, the toys are brought out again. It is wonderful for him to discover that now he can handle and enjoy these very toys.

The shift in emotions from five and a half to six and a half is almost as though the child were passing through an emotional spectrum from dark to light. The new sense of self that is emerging at five and a half years is working pretty much in the dark. Gradually, with further organization, there is a real shift from the more negative emotions into a positive zone. By six the child is becoming happier. He laughs and squeals. He has a "twinkle in his eye" when about to tell a story; a "glow of satisfaction" after he has talked on the telephone. He seems to feel the beauty of a sunset, the grandeur of clouds, and the mysteriousness of insect sounds in the summer twilight. He is said to be angelic at times, to be more generous, to be companionable and sympathetic. Although he may have strong likes and dislikes, his preferences may show real taste.

But these new positive emotional forces are still under crude control. He trembles with excitement. He boasts that he is the best. He praises himself as he says, "I did an awfully good picture at school." He is inquisitive to the point of destructiveness. And most of all he shows pride in his acts, his accomplishments, his clothes, his family possessions, and his siblings. But he may also be most jealous of the very sibling of whom he is most proud.

By the age of six and a half years, joy begins to figure more strongly in his emotional life. Parents report a new kind of enthusiasm: he "loves" to do things. He "enjoys books," he "enjoys the effort of working on a thing," and most of all, "he enjoys surprising his parents." Despite these positive and pleasant trends, there are recurring and less happy episodes, reminiscent of the five-and-a-half-to-six-year-old stage of immaturity. However, the overall trend toward equilibrium is so strong that after an episode, the child can plan and resolve to be "good" the rest of the day! There are also precursor signs of SEVEN, when the child looks too far within himself and begins to worry.

4. FEARS AND DREAMS

FEARS

The terrific newness and incompleteness of behavior patterns at five and a half to six years of age show their reality in a marked increase of fear responses. Some of the preschool fears, such as fear of dogs, may show a temporary rise, but the child may now confine his fear to big dogs. He may be able to touch little dogs and may be thinking ahead to the time when he can have a dog of his own. Wild animals may still be a fearful reality. The upstairs becomes inhabited with lions and tigers, but oddly enough these creatures do not invade his mother's room. That is why the five-and-a-half-year-old may go to sleep so quickly in his mother's bed. But ridding his own room and closet of wild animals by the dramatic wielding of sticks, especially by his father, makes his room safe again. Wild animals, especially bears, also inhabit woods, and the forest is accordingly to be feared. Tiny insects also are to be feared, because of both their noises and their bite or sting. The reading at school of a story about Foxy-Loxy, who eats you up, or one about bees, which sting, may be the true source of a child's refusal to return to school.

The elements thunder, rain, wind, and especially fire are all fearful in their separate ways, but especially because of the sounds they make. Man-made sounds like sirens, static, telephones, the toilet flushing, angry voices on TV, all may induce fear until they are localized and identified. The child may provide his own protection by putting his hands over his ears. Helping some other person to control a fear is the surest means of resolving a fear. Even a kitten may be protected from a possible fear of thunder by a child's comforting words: "Don't be afraid—that's only thunder."

The imagined subhuman witches and ghosts that come through a wall are also feared by the six-year-old. He compulsively grapples with these creatures in dramatizing play in the dark, but by the fearful tones in his voice as he plays one knows that he has not yet conquered his dread. A few six-year-olds, especially if over-indoctrinated, are afraid of God, and think that God is watching everything they are doing.

Human beings also are feared. The man under the bed, the man in the woods, takes on characteristics human and subhuman. There is a comparable fear of deformities. A broken leg in a cast or a spastic child fearsomely offends the six-year-old's idea of the normal human. Some six-year-olds— and these are readily picked out and tantalized by the very children they fear—are afraid that other children will attack them. The fear that something might happen to mother, which began at five, persists into six, and now includes the fear that she may die.

A fear that is difficult to understand and often makes the child "go to pieces" is his fear of even a slight injury to his body. A sliver, a scratch, the prick of a hypodermic, the sight of blood, all may produce a response out of all proportion to the cause. The child's control comes later when he is able to take care of his minor injuries.

With the undoubted reorientation that the five-and-a-half-to-six-year-old child is experiencing in space, he becomes more aware of upper and nether regions. Boys particularly are frequently afraid of the cellar and occasionally of the attic. Dark is to be feared because it moves in space, and destroys all spatial relationships. The lighting of a candle in the dark is something to be cherished because it brings back spatial relationships, even though it may also produce shadows that possess a frightening form. The presence of another human being or animal is especially needed at the five-and-a-half-year-old stage, when cellars and attics or being alone on the second floor are fears to be conquered. The presence of light may be enough to allay the fear, but by no means always before age six. A flashlight under the pilllow, a night light in the room which produces a diffuse, nonshadowy light, a light in the hall, all help to dispel these fears which are so much a part of the child's incompleteness, and a relatively normal expression of his immaturity.

There are "time fears" as well as "space fears." The fear of being late for school may appear in a few children who have overresponded to an experience of being late. A fear arising from some single experience is rather common at six, but it would not occur were the child not susceptible to that specific stimulus. The primary occasion is often unknown, because there may be a delay even of two or three days before the child expresses his fear either in words or in a dream. That is why it is well for a parent to be informed about his child's experiences both at home and at school.

It is imperative for the parent of the six-year-old to understand the mechanism of fears. In general, fears may be thought of as "coming in" when a child becomes aware of something he cannot comprehend or handle. His first response is one of withdrawal. This withdrawal stage may last for a split second or may persist for months. This is the child's method of protection, of waiting until he is better organized to handle the situation from which he has withdrawn. Later, when

he is more ready to handle it he will go through a period when he approaches the situation compulsively.

All too frequently, experiences come to the child prematurely. An alert, knowing, understanding environment would protect him from experiences until he was relatively ready to handle them. This does not mean that he should live an isolated, sterile life. But it does mean that a six-year-old should not see movies with airplanes crashing or violent television programs, that he should not be read stories about children being eaten up by bears or princesses turning to stone, that a little girl should not be left loose to pick up with a strange man. And a little boy should not have paragraph-reading crammed into his brain when he has only a two-letter span.

Such protection does not preclude the fact that at a later age the child may seek the very experiences from which he now withdraws. At eight he cannot get enough of extreme action and gore. Thereby he will resolve his former withdrawal—by compulsive approach into the very areas from which he has earlier withdrawn. The length of a compulsion stage may well match the length of the preceding withdrawal stage. Therefore the environment should shorten the withdrawal stage if it can by a better timing of the initial experience. Sometimes the child becomes so fixed in a withdrawal stage, if the experience has been extremely premature, that the environment must actively assist in the resolution. The child cannot handle it by himself. According to the situation or the individual personality involved, the adult must either build up positive responses by minute stages or thrust the child into a compulsive approach stage which when satisfied may lead to resolution.

DREAMS

The dreams of SIX, like his waking behavior, tend toward opposite extremes: funny or ghastly, nice or bad, a jolly clown or an angry lion. Wild animals such as foxes, bears, tigers, or snakes are not only in his bed but they bite and chase him. Nevertheless, there are usually fewer wild-animal dreams than at five. Domestic animals such as the dog, cat, and horse are now beginning to inhabit the child's dreams. The dog may chase him—but these domestic animals are far less frightening and usually enter into his "nice" dreams.

The commonest element dreamed about is fire. SIX dreams that a house, or more specifically his own house, is on fire. He may also dream of thunder and lightning, or of war.

The near-human figures of ghosts and skeletons bring dream fright to the child, but dream angels also sing to soothe him. Girls especially dream about bad men who appear at their windows, or who threaten to get into their rooms, or who may actually be in their rooms hidden under a piece of furniture.

Human beings are now taking more of a place in the child's dreams. He dreams of his mother, his siblings, his playmates, of himself in relation to other people. Girls may dream that their mother has been injured or killed. SIX may dream that he has been abandoned by his parents, and is alone in the house with his dog. But when he dreams of his playmates, he dreams of happier things, of parties and play at the seashore.

SIX frequently laughs in his sleep or talks out loud. He calls his mother, siblings, and playmates by name and is apt to give orders in his sleep: "Don't do that" or "Put it down."

Nightmares are less common than they were at five, although some children, especially boys, continue to have nightmares without being able to tell what they are about. If SIX awakens, he is usually able to go to his parents' bed to seek comfort.

Within a series of dreams, some children hold on to a standard pattern, others show change from one dream to the next. Resolution is more quickly achieved when the dreams show a shift in pattern. SIX may dream that the house down the street is on fire, then that the house in the middle of the block is on fire, and finally that his own house is on fire. Another SIX may dream that her mother was killed, then that both she and her mother were killed, and finally that she alone was killed. Though it is difficult to find out what many nightmares are about, they probably have a stereotyped repetitiveness of pattern which needs to be jostled into variation to obtain a resolution.

5. SELF AND SEX

SELF

SIX is the center of his own universe. He wants, and needs, to be first, to be loved best, to be praised, to win. He believes that his way of doing things is right, and wants others to do things his way as well. He cannot lose gracefully or accept criticism. He does not care especially about pleasing others, but may please others to please himself.

SIX is his own one-sided, assertive self. He operates from a self-centered bias. He is bossy, wants his own way, dominates a situation, and is always ready with advice. A few SIXES may be somewhat aware of themselves as separate entities similar to others but unique in themselves. One articulate SIX was able to express this in writing the words "I am me." Another thought about the word "person": "Mommy is a person, daddy is a person, I am a person—three persons." SIX is also beginning to be interested in his own anatomical structure.

Though he may have glimmerings of a notion of himself as a person, SIX does not behave like a complete person. He is extremely possessive of his belongings, and shows a marked return to the use of the possessive pronouns "my" and "mine." This trait harks back to his two-and-a-half-year-old self. He is most secure when he is in control of a situation. Then he shows off, acts independently, boasts, changes any error into success by his qualifying remarks, and would like to play his father against his mother if he could. He often holds the sway of the dictator in the exercise of his new powers.

When the outside world impinges adversely upon his self, he is stubborn, obstinate, unreasonable, distractible. He dawdles, goes to pieces, pays poor attention, or becomes over-excited, especially as he relates himself to special events. Praise is the one impingement he can absorb with ease.

As a king needs his jester for a little relaxation, SIX seems to need to return, on occasion, to babyhood. Some SIXES carry on a conversation with themselves in a babyish fashion. Others talk only to a younger child or to a sibling with baby talk. Still others for a period talk baby talk at all times and to everyone, much to the exasperation of their parents. A few want to become a baby in more ways than just through speech, and may dramatically enact salient bits of a baby's life. Other children may wish to be babies, but may not dare to mention it to anyone until finally they are able to whisper it to their mothers, adding the reason, "So I won't have to do things."

The shift from present self to a former younger self, that is, to a baby self, is easily accomplished by the six-year-old, for he seems to have a power to pretend that he is almost anything. He may be an animal, an angel, a prince, a fireman, or a parent. He is most organized when he loses himself in some make-believe role. This practicing at being somebody or something else is probably an important step on the way to a full realization of his own sense of self.

The child's own sense of self is also probably in some way strengthened through his interest in the conduct of his friends. There is a tremendous interest at this age in the conduct of friends, whether or not they do things correctly, how they behave. SIX frequently projects his own feelings onto others and then criticizes them on this account. The adult feels that the six-year-old is "fresh," but SIX makes this complaint against his friends. "He's so fresh"; "She thinks she's everything." Or, in more detail, "She thinks she's a princess, but she isn't. You ought to see her drawing!"

SIX is also building up his sense of self by embroilment with his mother and his increasing separation from her. This is expressed in his frequent resistances and also in his somewhat contradictory responses to her—strong affection one minute and strong antagonism the next.

The six-year-old is beginning to experience an outside world when he attends school, and this extramural world may have standards and rules somewhat different from those he has met at home. Insofar as the authorities of school and of home conflict, he himself experiences conflict. Even when there is no marked conflict of authority, many SIXES have difficulty in orienting themselves to two distinct worlds: that of home-mother and that of school-teacher.

SIX likes and seeks new experiences, but he tends to be undifferentiated and undiscriminating. "Everything is everywhere" to him. He has limited appreciation of scale or hierarchy, and may be angry that his mother has more possessions than he.

SEX

The relative quiescence of the five-year-old vanishes at six. His sex interests spread and penetrate many new and varied fields. SIX is interested in marriage, the origin of babies, pregnancy, birth, the opposite sex, sex role, and a new baby in the family. The facts of intercourse are still beyond his grasp. A few children at this age who are told of this aspect by older children usually come to their mother to have her confirm or deny the facts. Then the matter is usually dropped and the child shows little interest until the age of eight or older. SIX may still be looking backward to the time when he was a baby and may try to recapture that state dramatically by reenacting some baby ways. These ways are easier to recapture if there is a baby in the household. SIX may go so far as to put on diapers and then wet them. He imitates a younger sibling and especially enjoys talking his version of baby talk.

SIX giggles, sometimes uncontrollably, over bathroom words such as "wee-wee" or "pee-pee"; he giggles over panties; over bathroom situations and exposure of a "bellybutton." There is hilarious humor for boys to pretend to "tee-tee" in their mother's lap or on each other; or for girls to pretend that they are boys in an attempt to urinate standing up. Boys especially are apt to expose their genitals before girls and girls are apt to take off younger children's pants. If an older child, especially an eight-year-old, is playing with a six-year-old, the play may elaborate into doctor play and the taking of rectal temperatures. A crayon, the eraser end of a pencil, the tip of an enema tube, or the wooden thermometer in children's doctor kits may be used. Since this play is often stimulated by the fact that rectal temperatures have been taken during the child's illnesses, it might well be better to have temperatures taken by mouth. By four years of age a mouth temperature is safe and can be secured, especially if the child is allowed to take his teddy bear's temperature at the same time. This type of sex play can also be fairly well controlled if the rule is made that only one child at a time is allowed to go to the bathroom.

Although the distinguishing roles and organs of the two sexes are fairly well defined in the mind of the six-year-old boy, he may still wonder why his mother has no penis. He knows that only females have babies, yet he, as a boy, may be upset because he can never have a child, or he may even be fearful that a baby is growing inside of him. A few SIXES still want to be the opposite sex. One six-year-old girl we knew dressed up in boy's clothing, tucked her hair under a cap, demanded to be called Johnny, and played with a truck.

SIX is definitely interested in marriage. One thing that was not clear in the preschool years he now is sure of—namely, that you marry a member of the opposite sex. But this member of the opposite sex may be his mother, his aunt, a sister, or a contemporary (or in the case of a girl, her father, an uncle, or a brother). Often multiple marriages are planned. There is some vague idea that babies follow marriage, but there may also be some question as to whether a woman could have a baby without being married.

SIX is more interested in how the baby comes out than in how the baby starts. He may spontaneously think that the baby is born through the navel, but he accepts readily the assurance that there is a special place between the mother's legs where the baby comes out when it is time. Some children are concerned about the mother's knowing when it is time for her to go to the hospital, and also if it hurts when the baby is born. The presence of the doctor "to help" seems to alleviate any overstress on pain. It is difficult for some to picture a possible opening for the baby to come through, and if the child sees the birth of puppies he may ask, "Who is going to sew up the hole?"

The pregnancy period is not of much interest to SIX. He still is scarcely aware of the enlarging abdomen, even though it may be his own mother's. It is unfortunate when SIX is told of a coming baby too long before the expected arrival. A month or two is quite long enough for him to wait.

SIX is at the beginning of interest

in knowing how a baby starts. If he has been told some story such as that God makes all babies, human and animal, he will find it difficult to reconcile this fact with his knowledge of dogs having puppies, cats having kittens, and the lady next door having a baby. He now seems to grasp the idea of the baby starting from a seed and is no longer confused by his relating the seed to the ground. One SIX, even without the usual stimulus of the seed, thought that he himself came from the ground. He counted backward from his present age, finally got to one year of age, and wondered where he was before that. He asked, "Did I come from the ground?" but readily accepted the fact that he came from his mother's "stomach." Inquisitiveness in regard to the father's role ordinarily does not appear before seven or eight.

SIX wants his mother to have another baby, even if there is already one baby in the family. He usually speaks of the baby as a brother or a sister. Some SIXES specify that they want a baby of their own or of the opposite sex, while others would be satisfied with either. A boy may be repudiated by a girl as a possible sibling because "they fight."

6. INTERPERSONAL RELATIONS

SIX is a trying age for many a parent. One of our parents reports that she dreaded to get up in the morning because it meant one continuous contest with her six-year-old—one long "fight, fight, fight." Another parent similarly reported that she could not

be off her guard for a single second, for "If he has a thousandth of a chance he will take it."

These comments may seem extreme, but they are true of the interpersonal tensions that are so peculiar to the period from five and a half to six years. No period makes a greater demand upon a sense of perspective and a sense of humor. If the parent recognizes the transitional character of this intense behavior, SIX becomes much more manageable and altogether less trying. Life is also made more complicated for him if his outbursts are taken sensitively. And the mother might wisely spare her feelings.

She had better count ten before she reacts too personally to his vehement "I don't like you. You are mean and wicked. I want to kick you!" All she did to earn this explosion was perhaps to change the angle of the pillow on his bed! But SIX has a delicate trigger psychology, which is more easily accepted than understood.

Spanking will do little good. The child will react with momentary regret or fury, but without any long-term improvement in his behavior. He would feel more at one with his mother if she told him a story about another little six-year-old who was very naughty. Maybe this other six-year-old said he would get an ax and chop his mother up, or maybe he wished that his mother and father would be killed in a fire. In any case, the story of the imaginary six-year-old should parallel the child's own acts and experiences. What the imaginary child's mother said and did to her child becomes very important to the intently listening six-year-old. Also, he may be able to grasp some idea not only of how children act at this age, but what kind of experiences pile up to make them act as they do.

The difficult, rigidly explosive behavior that the parent encounters in the five-and-a-half-year-old can best be handled by preventive means, by giving in or by suggesting the opposite of the desired behavior. Direct clashes of will between mother and child should be avoided whenever possible. Parents often use a strenuous direct approach which becomes exhausting for them. They report, "You need to clamp down, or be firm with him"; "You have to pound it into him"; or "He won't listen unless you're cross with him." An indirect approach or giving him several chances is more likely to set the child on the move. Doing with him what is requested may bring out his concealed but latent cooperation. He does not like to do things as a task, but he enjoys doing things with another person, especially with his mother.

SIX is sensitive to his parents' moods, emotions, and tensions, even though the parents may think they have hidden their feelings from the child. SIX also quickly detects any shift in facial expression and reacts badly to the raising of a voice. He cannot tolerate seeing his mother cry, becomes very sympathetic when she is sick, and may show anxiety about her well-being. Although SIX is often described as being "embroiled with" his mother, he is actually extremely ambivalent in regard to her. He may say "I love you" at one minute and "I hate you, I wish you were dead" at the next. He is most loving with his mother, yet most of his tantrums are directed against her. He craves her help, especially in domestic routines, yet he often refuses to accept it.

In sharp contrast to his sensitive awareness of the other person is the kind of behavior often described as fresh, nasty, insulting, impudent, bratty, rude, and argumentative. When this side of the child's nature is shown toward grandmother, for instance, unfortunate results may ensue. Grandmothers and relatives in general often take on rights that they might more wisely not assume if they realized in advance the possible results. SIX's mother, in spite of his frequent embroilment with her, is actually the one person who is his real support and need, and even she may have to "make" him do things. A mere relative therefore may expect such a reply as "I won't, and you're only my aunt and you can't make me."

SIX often assumes a "know-it-all" attitude which makes him seem domineering. A little deferential response from the parent will soften his imperiousness. Parents need to beware of SIX when he is corrected or criticized, for he is likely to turn on them in one way or another. A few children react with inward resentment, a few can change the subject, others may attack with words or fists.

Despite all this furiously assertive behavior, SIX still craves affection. He wants to be assured in words of his mother's fondness for him. He may soften to the extent of sitting on his father's lap when he is being read to. Sometimes he gathers a cloak of closeness around himself and one of his parents by having a secret, even in a "foreign" language. The other parent is not supposed to know anything about the secret. He likes to burst into a close feeling relationship with his parent by some pleasant surprise (such as drinking his milk without protest!).

Fathers can and should play an important role in the life of the six-year-old child. Girls are said to be "crazy about" their fathers and may demand a good-night kiss from them. Boys are building up a father-son relationship of affection and admiration. They may demand every minute of a father's time; they respond to pep talks from him; and if he accompanies them to the doctor's office they are less likely to cry. There is something delightful and exciting in doing things with your father: gardening, painting screens, going for a train ride, playing games, or just telling him all your troubles.

There may be a startling improvement in the smoothness and ease of bedtime when father puts the child to bed, especially in the absence of the mother. Baths even may be taken with little supervision, the father being instructed to read his paper while the child undertakes to bathe himself. Bedtime may be shifted back a half hour when father takes over. Even morning dressing takes on a new independence and comradeship when father is close by.

Since the response to father is so excellent, there is a danger that he will be expected to take over the lion's share. But this would be a serious mistake, for the child would then begin to respond to the father as though he were the mother, with all the attendant tugs and pulls, detours and explosions. Mother, however, would benefit if the father took over two or three bedtimes a week. With such relief, both mother and child would adjust better to each other; for although the child may not be able to get on with his mother, he also cannot get on without her. Growth itself brings its periods of relief, for suddenly, in the midst of trying behavior, a two-week interlude of angelic calm may descend as though from nowhere. Father tiptoes into the house at night and whispers his incredulous query: "Is he still the same?" Parents might well enjoy this lull, for it is sure to end!

Grandparents, if available, can still add a great deal to family living. Visits with them are enjoyed, though the child's expressed reason for liking grandparents sometimes remains somewhat commercial: "She makes good food"; "He gives us things."

SIX does not handle a younger sibling well without considerable planning and supervision on the part of the parent. A very few who have difficulty with their contemporaries play well with their younger siblings. They may be devoted to and proud of younger siblings, and eager to share a room with them at night, especially at five and a half, but as a rule they play well together only occasionally. Although they may talk baby talk to a younger sibling at five and a half, they become more interested in teaching him when they are six. They also like to evoke responses from him by making silly noises or by some other device. They may try to goad him into being bad in the hopes that he will be scolded.

SIX insists upon being first in everything, and his whole day may be spoiled if a younger sibling gets to the table in the morning before he does. He is jealous of any attention or present bestowed upon the younger child. If a guest unwittingly neglects him, he can be readily satisfied by a simple appeasement gift from his mother. One may need a reserve supply of such gifts on hand when there is a younger child in the household. A few SIXES go to the extreme of demanding a duplicate of many of the sibling's toys.

SIX may be bossy with a young sibling. He argues, teases, bullies, frightens, torments, makes him cry, hits him, gets angry with him, and may on occasion fight terrifically. Sometimes it is the younger sibling who irritates the six-year-old. SIX gets along fairly well with an older sibling, but is likely to be overstimulated.

Although some SIXES play well alone, SIX generally wants other children to play with. A fair proportion play well either with children their own age or with those somewhat older. A half hour of indoor play is usually maximum. Outdoor play is better sustained. Sex lines are not sharply drawn and preferences are often dependent on neighborhood availability.

Twosomes are the rule, but small groups are forming. The make-up of these groups shifts often and group activity may go on in a manner so unorganized that any individual child may leave the group without disturbing the play. There is a great deal of exclusion of a third child by two others, and concern about whom friends are playing with: "Are you playing with So-and-so? All right then, I'm not playing with you!" SIX does not get along too well with his friends in play, even though there is considerable interest in and talk about "school friends" and "playmates." Children worry a good deal about their friends' cheating or doing things the wrong way, and there is a good deal of "tattletaling."

As to younger children, SIX is apt to handle them in the same way that he handles a younger sibling. He bosses and teases, and if not watched, may lock a younger child into a small, enclosed space.

SIX is usually either in high favor and sought after by the other children, or he is disliked and excluded from play. Some SIXES buzz around a girl of comparable age as though she were the queen. She in turn may dismiss one after the other in a queenly fashion. Another dominant six-year-old may provoke crying in a whole series of children who have rebelled against playing "her way." Some SIXES are picked on, terrorized, or knocked down. Older boys may lie in wait to beat up a six-year-old. Older boys also tease SIXES to get rid of them, or they simply send them home. Some SIXES lose their appetites and others lose their tempers in response to such teasing.

SIX is often rough in his play. He threatens to go home, he quarrels, he calls names, he pushes, he (or she) pulls hair, kicks, and fights when things are not going the way he wants them to. Some SIXES do not know how to play roughly, are terrorized by physical combat and should be protected accordingly by teachers as well as parents until about the age of eight years, when a child is able to cope with rougher experience.

In view of SIX's multiple difficulties in interpersonal relationships, one may not expect him to be too much at ease with people or willing to meet them. The blank look, the inability to say "Hello," the unknowing impoliteness, are all a part of his callow nature. In another year he will be able to give a better account of himself—so why make excessive demands upon him a year too soon?

7. PLAY AND PASTIMES

GENERAL INTERESTS

In his play activities, SIX spreads himself as he does in everything else. At five years the play episodes were restricted and confined; they now have expansive scope and movement. SIX's mother says, "Whatever he is doing is all over the place."

SIX continues many of his five-year-old interests, but with more intensity of feeling. His mother reports that "he loves to paint and color." Cutting and pasting are done as needed. He draws more actively than formerly. Boys prefer to draw spaceships, airplanes, trains, train tracks, and boats with occasional persons; but girls prefer to draw people and houses.

There is a very real return to an earlier interest in earth and water. Six-year-olds revel in their "muck shops" and enjoy making mud roads and houses. Boys especially like to dig. Their holes become tunnels with boards for a roof over them. Digging may evolve into gardening and the planting of seeds. But having made the start, SIX usually finds it too difficult to continue the care of his garden.

One of the most positive new demands made by the five-and-a-half-to-six-year-old child is for a bicycle. Boys often demand an electric train. The urge for a bicycle at this age seems to be based on a need and a desire for locomotor leg exercise and body balance, rather than on mere possessiveness. Many children would be satisfied if they could borrow a small bicycle until they have learned and have had some successful experience. If this early urge were satisfied, ownership of a bicycle might be put off until the child is more ready for the responsibility.

Sex differences in choice of play are defining themselves more clearly. In gross motor and imaginative play both sexes, however, find a common meeting ground. Both sexes like to "tear around" in running games such as tag and hide-and-seek. Both like to roller skate, swing, swim, and do tricks on bars. Both indulge in ball play, though girls are apt to bounce a ball while boys attempt the rudiments of baseball. Girls delight in jumping rope.

The quick capacity of SIX to pretend greatly enriches his play life. A bed rapidly becomes a fort, a group of chairs a boat. Girls are more likely to play school, house, and library, but certain boys are often ready to join with them. Girls also like to dress up in costumes, including hats, slippers, lipstick, and housecoats, and may at times turn their play into a dramatic performance. At five and a half there is a good deal of doll play, which consists chiefly in the dressing and undressing of dolls. Nude dolls clutter the house and playroom. By six, doll play is at its height. There is much interest in the paraphernalia of doll play: doll clothes, suitcases, wash baskets, swings, stoves, and the like. Playing house that includes the use of dolls is a great favorite also. The mother role is definitely preferred, and there is a marked aversion to the impersonation of baby. Some younger child, if present, is usually forced to take this inferior role.

Boys may take part in school and house play, but they are more apt to play war games, cowboys, or cops and robbers. Shooting the enemy and getting under cover are two characteristic forms of play.

Boys show a marked interest in transportation and construction. Besides a very genuine interest in electric trains, they are interested in airplanes and more particularly in boats. Some girls may share with them an interest in blocks, tools, and workbench activity. At this age many children start the "collections" that will later use up so much time, energy, and space. At present these collections are extremely miscellaneous and undifferentiated, consisting of toys, fancy paper, Christmas cards, or mere odds and ends.

If asked what he likes to do best, five and a half will answer, "Play with my doll, bicycle, blocks, train, wagon, truck." Six answers, "'Play with soldiers" or "Play with dolls."

READING AND NUMBERS

SIX is taking a more active part in reading. Through his repeated hearing of favorite books, he may "read" stories from memory as though he were really reading the printed page aloud. He is also interested in recognizing single words in familiar books and in magazines. He enjoys printing his letters to spell real words and he also enjoys simple oral spelling as a game. Boys especially enjoy thinking about numbers, and like to read any number they see. Many of the table games that the six-year-old plays fit in well with his intellectual interests. The favorites are anagrams, dominoes, Chinese checkers, and simple card games that mainly demand matching.

SIX continues to like stories about animals, but he is also branching out into an interest in nature and birds. Many SIXES enjoy poetry. The book SIX would really prefer would be a diary about himself. Daily newspaper comics and comic books telling about animals are beginning to make a steady inroad into his life.

MUSIC, RADIO, TELEVISION, AND MOVIES

Although some children still prefer their own phonograph records, the majority of six-year-olds listen to the radio or watch TV for at least a few programs each week. When a choice needs to be made between television or outdoor play, the latter usually wins.

Few SIXES are ready for movies. They like short home movies about nature, and best of all film records of their own earlier years. If allowed to go to a movie they are likely to become restless, closing their eyes and stopping their ears to shut out any fighting or shooting. They may weep over sad scenes and finally have to leave the theater. Musicals and animal pictures are the best accepted.

Television is an important feature of the lives of most six-year-olds. Most watch "a lot," and most admit that their parents sometimes object to both the amount of viewing and to programs viewed. Nearly all have their preferred programs.

8. SCHOOL LIFE

SIX shows a positive anticipation of first grade. His mother usually accompanies him on the first day, but his adjustment is more assured if he has visited the teacher and has seen the room and materials previous to his induction into the group. The majority like school and want to do "real work" and to "learn." They like to do "everything"; they do "too much." Dislike of school often does not occur until the end of the year if the child for one reason or another has been unable to maintain his place in the group. Not infrequently, however, an unpleasant experience makes him refuse to go to school for one or several days. Perhaps he was frightened by a story, or was asked to put on his rubbers by himself, or was asked to count and pass the crackers! He may limit his refusal to a certain day when he knows there is to be an activity he does not like. He may wish to go to some other school, perhaps to one that he has formerly attended.

Even under the best of handling, SIX will probably be fatigued by his difficulties of adjustment and will have his share of colds. Absences may become a common occurrence throughout most of the year. But some controls can be instituted to alleviate these absences. The six-year-old is not ready for all-day attendance. He still profits by an activity rest period alone at home. He may adjust to an all-day session by Christmas time. In some groups Monday is the poor day after a weekend at home, in others it is Friday after a week at school. Adjustments are best planned according to the group.

The interrelationship of home and school is important to the six-year-old.

He brings many things to school: stuffed animals, dolls, flowers, bugs, shells, fruit, and especially books. These are for showing his classmates, or more especially his teacher. He may also bring a treat of cookies for the whole group. He takes things home as well, such as drawings and his carpentry. His parents' response means a lot to him. The thrill of the year comes when he takes home the first primer he has mastered. It is to be hoped that parents will not criticize any errors at this moment of triumph.

Parents often are disappointed that SIX reports so little about his school experiences. SIX is most apt to bear tales about bad things other children do or to boast beyond reality of his own accomplishments. The outstanding nonconforming child is sure to be reported upon by most of the children in the group. A bedtime chatting period is an excellent opportunity for the six-year-old to talk about himself and his school experiences.

Parent-teacher interviews by telephone or by appointment provide a means of reporting significant home or school behavior. Not only does the teacher gain from these interviews, but the mother comes to feel that she is more a part of the school family, ready to step in and help whenever she is needed.

In characterizing first-grade behavior, teachers comment as follows: "One day it is very exciting to teach first grade; the next day it is very dull." "Sometimes you have to work very hard; at other times you don't have to work at all." There are wide swings of behavior. "Things come in spells, like talking out loud all the time. You handle that specific behavior, try to counteract it as well as you can [whispering is the antidote], and suddenly the behavior has disappeared and all too soon something else takes its place."

Despite these ups and downs, these extremes, SIX wants to work. He would be continually happy if life were just one long series of beginnings. He gasps with excitement in his eagerness to tackle a new thing. It is the middle of a task that confuses him. He may want to give up, but with his teacher's help he may see the end and then he is thrilled to attack the end as a new beginning. Any help or praise from his teacher spurs him on; he is trying to conform and to please his teacher and himself. He likes an opportunity to show and talk about his finished product.

The activity program for six-year-olds includes crayons, paint, clay, carpentry, and large outdoor blocks— materials familiar from kindergarten days. These, however, are now approached more spontaneously and more experimentally. Products show a new creativeness, though the child may for a short period do the same picture or painting over and over again. He needs some simple direction and help to plan what he will do, and also needs guidance along the way. Direct interference, however, is not tolerated by SIXES.

Learning to utilize symbols in reading, writing, and arthimetic is his new challenge. SIX especially likes group oral work since he is such an incessant talker, but he is more flexible than he was at five, and likes a variety of approaches to learning. He likes to recognize words the teacher puts on the blackboard, and to write at his desk. (He cannot copy from the blackboard with facility as yet.) He begins to print small letters, although he tends to reverse them and to revert to capital letters. Capitals are simpler to form and have less reversibility. With certain children, capitals probably should be used throughout first grade, or at least until the child shows a spontaneous desire to shift to small letters. Writing as well as reading induces the typical tensional overflow of chewing pencils, hair, or fingers. SIX likes to write something for his mother or father. He may recognize his reversal of a letter, but he does not always stop to correct the reversal.

The six-year-old is learning to read combinations of words. He comes to recognize words out of their familiar setting and learns new words out of text before he approaches them in text. He makes a variety of errors: He adds words to give balance (the king and the queen). He reverses meaning (come for go). He substitutes words of the same general appearance (even for ever; mother for mouse, saw for was). He adds rather than omits words (little, very, y at the end of a word). There is also a tendency to carry down a word that he encountered on the line above. Pronouns may be interchanged (you for I).

Many children use a marker or point with their fingers at this age, and they may bring their heads closer as they continue to read. Mouthing of pencil, tongue, hair, or fingers is frequently seen, as well as wriggling or even standing up.

SIX still likes to be read to both at home and at school and will listen to almost anything you read to him. He takes his primer home to read, but may also try to read the books he had when he was younger.

SIX is learning number symbols (digits) as well as letters and they are similarly reversed. In writing numbers he may say: "I never do 2's so good." "Some people make 8's like this." "I wonder if I'm making these backward." "I'm tired. I'm hot, too." The one-by-one counting of objects is less evident; he begins to group objects into four of this and five of that. Balanced pairs such as $3+3$ or $5+5$ are favorites.

At this age girls are usually better in reading, writing, and drawing, while boys are better in number work and listening to stories.

SIX does not enter the classroom with the directness of FIVE. Some may even dawdle outside. The teacher is ready to greet the child, inspect what he has brought, or give him a reassuring word when necessary. He still needs some help with boots and difficult articles of clothing and the teacher should be ready to supply needed help. The better-coordinated children are often eager to help those who cannot manage by themselves. A few do best if they dress apart from the group.

SIX shifts from one activity to the next with comparative ease. He is willing to stop even though he is enjoying what he is doing, and can leave a task incomplete and finish it the next day. If there is too much slack between activities, the boys especially are apt to wrestle with each other.

Toileting is relatively easy, if the toilet adjoins the room. SIX can go by himself, although he may announce that he is going. He accepts the teacher's suggestion of a special time if he has not gone already. Girls and boys can use the same facilities. Single toilet units are preferable, two to a room. A sign set by the child can indicate when one is occupied. A good rule is to allow only one child at a time to use the facilities.

SIX is oriented to the whole room and to the whole group. He is constantly on the move or manipulating things. He is impatient when his flow of movement is interfered with unless by chance you are going in his direction. He talks of his own performance and that of others. Occasionally an argument between two children may attract one child after another until the whole class is attentive, but as a rule it dissolves as another child picks up a mere thread or word of the conversation.

Characteristic verbalization during free play is illustrated by the following:

"I won't be on your side if you do."

"Oh, I know that one."

"Look, Rosalie, this is the first page."

"Let's change places in the desks."

"Miss Hill, do you know what SF means?"

"I need an eraser and I can't find it and I need one."

"Miss Hill, I'm going to the bathroom."

"Oh, shoot the shoot pifs."

"I'll shoot the mess pot in the middle of the mess."

"You want red. I want blue."

"If he finishes it any more he'll ruin it."

"Hey, you started it" (snatches book).

"Give that right back" (snatches book).

"You know what I'm doing?"

"Fall. That's when you fall down. That's when the apples fall. That's why we call it fall."

"Hello, measles. Hello, chicken pox."

"Hello, whooping cough."

SIX enjoys the feel of the group. Groupings are often of twosomes and are frequently shifting. The activity partially determines a group, but emotional responses are now playing a stronger role. Certain children are apt to spoil group games. The proximity of the teacher may help, but often these children need to be kept apart and busy with something they enjoy doing, such as digging or building.

9. ETHICAL SENSE

The growth clock appears to be set backward at the very important age of five and a half to six years. In one sense this is true in reality, for the child is acting very much like his former two-and-a-half-year-old self. Both these ages, however, may be thought of as a backlash of reorganization preparatory to new organization. Parents need to feel what is happening within the child's organism and should adapt their demands to that organism, so that he can grow into more of an entity in himself, and thereby become more of an individual capable of further adjustment to his ever-expanding environment.

Girls, as a rule, with a greater fluidity of mental structure and a more flexible but continuing contact with their environment, do not experience the more extreme patterns of disorganization that boys exhibit. Girls are better at conforming. But the tendency of both sexes is to respond more slowly or to respond negatively to any direct demand put upon them. Given time, however, they may respond in their own way, even as though from their own initiative. Many children need to be reminded of a thing two or three times to build up a stimulus strong enough to secure response. The responses may vary with the child's wishes and moods.

If the parent tries to press a command with a firm tone of voice, she may anticipate an opposite response on the part of the five-and-a-half-year-old. The six-year-old under similar pressure will defy his mother with a "No, I won't" or "How are you going to make me?" If threat of physical punishment or actual physical punishment is resorted to after such defiances, the results are usually poor. The child becomes furious, mimics his mother during the punishment, and shows only a tendency to repeat the performance on future occasions. Preventive methods or the use of magic such as counting are far more effective. By six, the child responds better to some form of isolation—play in his room, for example, or sitting on a "thinking chair" (formerly known as a "naughty chair"). And how he loves to be praised! He preens himself like a peacock and his behavior is tremendously improved.

It is not easy for five and a half to make up his mind. It is almost as though he were held in a vise made of two opposing forces. This causes him to shift his decision back and forth. When SIX vacillates between two choices, he almost invariably ends with the "wrong" one. That is why the parent may need to make decisions and to state clearly what is to happen and how the child is to act. When SIX finally does make up his mind, rarely can anything make him change it, even on those occasions when he has made it up with relative ease. There are very few six-year-olds who can be reasonable about changing their minds; but there are a few others who are almost too conforming.

SIX is not only aware of "goodness" and "badness" in himself and in his acts, but he wants to be good—especially if it does not take too much effort. He asks whether he is good, and he wants his mother to prevent his naughtiness. "Badness" separates him emotionally from his mother. He shows his wish to be accepted by his mother when he asks, "Even though I've been bad, you like me, don't you?" or when he says, "Let's be friends, Mommy." He does not want to hurt people and he feels sorry and may even cry about it if he does. He is unusually aware of what in his estimate is "badness" in a younger sibling, and he may even go so far as to classify all people into "good people" and "bad people." In his way of thinking, it is parents who determine what is allowed and what is forbidden.

To the six-year-old, things that his parents allow are good things; things they forbid are bad things. An expressive five-and-a-half-year-old spontaneously dictated to her parent the following list of "Things to Do and Things Not to Do" which clearly defines her idea of good and bad.

Things to Do

1. Say "I think you are eating good things today."
2. Pleasant things are lovely to do:
   (a) Eat nicely.
   (b) Always say "please" and "thank you."
   (c) Always remember to say "Good morning, good afternoon, good evening."
3. Eat dinner by ourselves without having to be reminded.
4. Keep quiet and answer people when they are talking to you.
5. Keep clothes clean.
6. Keep watches going—wind them up.
7. Go to bed at 7:30.
8. Wake up at 7:30.
9. When people are breaking things tell them to stop.

Things Not to Do

1. Not to say, "I am not talking to you."
2. Not to say, "Give it to me."
3. Not to say, "Give me the biggest piece of anything."
4. Spill crumbs on floor.
   (a) Spill milk or water.
   (b) Get food on hands or faces.
5. Set fires anywhere.
6. Pulling away from someone when they are doing something nice for you.
7. Slamming doors.
8. Don't tear books.
9. Shouldn't keep windows open when it rains.
10. Don't tear clothes.
11. Don't break windows.
12. Don't call people when they are busy.
13. Don't break armchairs.
14. Don't pinch people.

Some SIXES are capable of accepting responsibility for their acts. Yet they may say, "It was an accident" or "I didn't mean to do it." But the six-year-old, and more particularly the five-and-a-half-year-old, is apt to blame siblings, other children, mother, an animal, or even some inanimate object. If the misbehavior was very serious, however—a football thrown through the living room window—the child is often able to take full responsibility. The big things of life are easy. It is the little things that cause the most trouble. Perhaps it wasn't so difficult for George Washington to confess that he had cut down the cherry tree!

FIVE AND A HALF and SIX are much better at winning than at losing, just as they love praise and cannot tolerate criticism. That is why they should not be put into positions where they are likely to lose; they may be forced into cheating in order to win. SIX loves to make up spontaneous games with rules that shift in the middle of the game. These are the kind of games he can handle. He has the controls and can shift the rules to his advantage.

Taking things belonging to others and telling tall tales are more common at SIX than the adult often wishes to believe. The distinction between mine and thine is almost as difficult for a six-year-old to make as it was when he was two and a half. "Mine" is uppermost in his mind and he easily grasps near objects that he desires, holds on to them, and adds them to his collection of just "things." Or he may have some real use for some of the objects he takes. Girls are likely to take their mother's jewelry, slippers, or a housecoat. If they ransack their mother's purse they rarely take money, but prefer keys or lipstick. Boys prefer pipe cleaners, matches, and little odds and ends from their father's desk drawer.

From school they take such innocent little items as a barrette, a piece of clay, a peg, a piece of black paper, or an eraser. Children who have taken things themselves are the first to criticize other children as "awful" when they take things. SIX is usually caught in the act, for he takes things with others looking on. But even with the evidence before his eyes, he will flatly deny any relationship to the object in question, or will alibi with some statement such as "Tommy gave them to me." SIX can least of all tolerate direct correction in matters of conduct. He cannot even accept it in the less personal fields of reading and arithmetic. But he will readily respond to an indirect approach if asked, "How did you break all those bottles?" or "Where did you find those matches?"

When he has told all—which is not difficult if he is not directly accused—he can plan with his parent how he can act better next time. Perhaps he needs things locked away to help him to remember; or he may need supervised experiences with fire. Or his teacher, in cooperation with his mother, might allow him to take certain things home from school. Then his mother can help him to return them when he is ready. If he takes things without permission, he is likely to destroy them. If he is made to return them, he can often best accomplish this with his mother by his side. Occasionally, at his request, it is advisable for his mother to return them for him.

A few children can handle their desire for new things by swapping. The bargain may be relatively fair—a rubber band for two pennies—but as a rule someone gets the poor end of the bargain unless an "even swap" of similar objects is made. SIX may also overdo his generosity, because of a greater interest in giving than in receiving. He needs to be protected from giving away his really valuable possessions.

SIX is eager for more and more possessions. He is a great saver. He wants toys for the toys' sake almost more than for his interest in playing with them. If a guest arrives at a six-year-old's home without a present he will probably receive criticism. Though SIX likes to have quantities of possessions, he is extremely careless about them, mislays and loses them. It is the six-year-old whom one sees downtown looking sad and bewildered while his mother demands, "Well, where did you leave it?" SIX is often destructive of his possessions, and if he is held responsible for the upkeep of his room he dawdles over or kicks his toys in the process of picking them up. He usually lives in a "mess," but he responds cooperatively if his mother helps him and occasionally he likes to surprise her with a tidy room.

Money is becoming of real interest to the six-year-old both in the form of an allowance and as a reward. Little chores such as emptying wastepaper baskets, putting out milk bottles, drying dishes, or even eating a good meal are done more willingly when a reward is in view. Some children want only to save their money, put it in the bank; others spend it for candy and cookies; others are extremely careless with it; but a few really want to put

it to use and buy something special. SIX may spend an hour in the ten-cent store trying to decide on a purchase, and finally come out with a roll of adhesive tape.

10. PHILOSOPHIC OUTLOOK

DEATH AND DEITY

The age of six is often the peak period in these middle years of the child's interest in a creative power to which he can relate himself. Although he at first found it difficult to comprehend a God who saw him, but whom he did not see, he now relates God in his mind to the larger sphere of creation. He grasps the concept of God as the creator of the world, of animals, and of beautiful things. He accepts these larger concepts at six, even though he will soon think them over, become skeptical, and need to have them explained further.

SIX asks to go to Sunday school. He likes to listen to Bible stories and could hear the same ones over and over again. He especially likes to participate in a short ritualistic service with balanced candles on an altar. By his acts in his very real attempt to conform to what is demanded of him, and by his facial expression, he shows that he feels the awe of this ancient group worship. He is now developing a feeling relationship with God. Prayers become important to him. He feels confident that his prayers will be answered.

God has his counterpart in the bipolar mind of the six-year-old. SIX may be unusually susceptible to any teaching about the devil, although such teaching is uncommon today. One six-year-old recognized two forces fighting within her and acknowledged that the one who had all the bad ideas usually won. She invented a name for this opposing force by pronouncing her own name backward. Having named it, she had more control over it. God similarly becomes his own counterpart when his name is used profanely. This is fairly common at six.

Death also becomes more related to SIX's feeling self. He is fearful that his mother will die. He is beginning to be aware of any deaths that may occur in his immediate surroundings or to relatives, and tries to penetrate the causes of these deaths. Besides dying from old age, one can be killed, he realizes. Also, he makes a slight connection between sickness, medicine, hospitals, and death. There may be a preoccupation with the appurtenances of death: graves, funerals, being buried in the ground. Children discuss these matters and may express dislike of the notion that their relatives or they themselves should be buried in the ground. SIX often needs to be protected from death experiences. Pictures of dead children may haunt his dreams. Seeing a dead animal is an experience he does not forget easily. He asks, "How long does it take to die?"

SIX may think that there is a reversible process to death, that you return to life after you are dead. He may say to a friend, "I wish you had never been alive! And then other times I don't feel like that at all." His best acceptance of death is that someone else takes the dead person's place: puppies take the place of dogs; and children the place of their parents. If SIX feels the immediate possibility that his mother might die, then he needs to think of someone, perhaps an aunt, as a possible substitute for his mother. One child became caught up in this process of dying and said, "First mother will die, then I will live with Nancy. Then Nancy will die and I will live with Helen. Then I don't know who I would live with if Helen should die. I think about it and it scares me."

TIME AND SPACE

SIX does not live as much in the Now of time as did FIVE. He wants to recapture time past, and shows marked interest in hearing about his own and his mother's babyhood. He penetrates the future by the sequence of significant holidays and family birthdays. Duration of an episode in time has little meaning for him. He shows little interest in learning how to tell time beyond the hours. He answers correctly such questions as:

"What time do you go to school?"

"What time do you come home from school?"

"What do you do in the fall? In the spring?"

"What grade are you in?"

The space of the six-year-old is definitely expanding beyond what it was when he was five. He is now interested not only in specific places, but in relationships between home, neighborhood, and an expanding community, including school. As at four, he likes neighborhood visiting. He knows the names of some nearby streets, and the location of some major points of interest. He may even be so aware of a special sequence of spatial relationships that he may fear he will get lost if he doesn't stay on a known specific route.

SIX is learning to distinguish his own left from his own right hand, but he cannot distinguish left and right in another person. His spatial concepts like so many others are relatively undifferentiated.

CHAPTER 7

SEVEN YEARS OLD

Behavior Profile

There is in many children a kind of quieting down at seven, but before we reach this quiet, sometimes even rather withdrawn, time of a young child's life, we can look forward to enjoying the pleasant experience of his being six and a half. Five and a half through six years of age is, indeed, in many a time of turmoil and confusion, a time of bipolar, opposite-extreme disequilibrium.

Fortunately, in the growing child any stage of disequilibrium tends to be relatively short-lived. As boy or girl reaches somewhere around six and a half years of age, on the way to seven, there often comes a marvelous period when the energy and enthusiasm of six is expressed in positive rather than in negative ways.

The six-and-a-half-year-old tends to relate strongly and warmly to those adults close to him. With his warmth, sensitivity, and enthusiasm, he can be a delightful and engaging companion. For a few short months, until the age of seven brings in its characteristically minor notes, the child seems briefly to be at his very top form, happy with himself, a joy to those around him.

Seven is something else again. The seven-year-old goes into lengthening periods of calmness and of self-absorption, during which he works his impressions over and over, oblivious to the outer world. Seven is an assimilating age, a time for salting down accumulated experience and for relating new experiences to the old.

By this token the seven-year-old is a good listener. He likes to be read to, he likes to hear a twice-told tale. Picture him huddled or sprawled before the television, endlessly observing. Picture his response to a sudden interruption; he resents intrusions on his ruminations; he feels ill at ease if he cannot bring them to a conclusion. All this means that he has already reached a higher level of maturity. Explosive bipolarity is giving way to inwardized consolidation. He therefore seems more introverted than the callow six-year-old. Parents often say, "He is a better child now!" Basically he is, of course, the same child in a new stage of growth.

Seven is a pleasant age, if one respects the feelings of the child. His feelings need a new and even subtle regard because he is prone to lapse into musing moods during which he orders his subjective impressions. This tendency to muse is a psychological mechanism by which he absorbs, revives, and reorganizes his experiences.

As adults we scarcely appreciate how much a seven-year-old still has to learn—not in factual knowledge, but in comprehension of the meanings of the manifold life situations that impinge upon him at home and at school. These meanings are essentially feelings. They do not emerge in definitive patterns; they must be "worked over," and practiced through mental activity. Just as a forty-week-old child exploits two cubes by tilting, tapping, and combining them, so a seven-year-old manipulates his new-found psychological materials through the exercise of reflective fantasy. This is a growth process. Thereby he learns to modulate the meanings of things and of persons. Thereby he overcomes the primitive impulsiveness of six-year-old maturity and advances further into the intricate culture that continuously invests him. Never forget how vast that culture is, and how innocent of its structure is the mind of the seven-year-old! He needs his moments of reflection as well as of action. Through his inner life as well as through his outward conduct he achieves his adjustments.

This inner life is the hidden subtle aspect which demands some deference from us. We cannot do justice to the psychology of the seven-year-old unless we recognize the importance of his private mental activities. They account for his occasional brooding, his heedlessness, the minor strains of sadness and complainingness, his sulks, his mutterings, his shynesses, a certain pensiveness which is not without charm. But at times his complaining does go rather far. *Everybody* hates him; he is *never* going to have a decent Memorial Day; these are not his true parents, he *knows* he is adopted. He really seems to enjoy his complaining.

He takes in rather more than he gives out. In another year he will be comparatively expansive, projecting himself into the environment. Now he mulls things over in terms of their repercussion upon his personal self. His thinking is more intensely active than appears upon the surface. He will be in a brown study and then suddenly light up with a flash of insight and dash off to proclaim or carry out the revealed idea. He is a good guesser, and he sticks to his guesses. Asked to explain his intuitional cogitation, he says, "You see, I just notion some way in my mind."

Although given to self-absorption, the seven-year-old is not an isolationist. He is becoming aware not only of himself but of others. He is increasingly sensitive to their attitudes. He is beginning to see his mother in new perspective. He achieves a measure of detachment from her by developing attachments to other persons. Very frequently he or she longs for a baby brother or sister. He shows a new interest in his father and in playmates of an older age. And usually he becomes very fond of his teacher. We can see his personal-social reactions deepening at home, on the playground, and in the schoolroom.

This socializing susceptibility is most transparently displayed at school. His joy is unalloyed when his teacher smiles upon him. He brings her a red apple. He likes to be near her, likes to touch her and to talk to her. He talks in order to establish a personal rapport, and to mobilize his abilities. At the beginning of a task he asks, "Shall I start now?" as though he could not begin without a verbal sanction. He seems very dependent upon reminders and verbal guidance. When he is older he will be more self-contained, more self-dependent, at least in the simpler school tasks.

In a genial second-grade room each child is likely to have a personal relationship to the teacher. In fact, he may even fall in love with her. The wise teacher recognizes this relation as a developmental mechanism. She quietly circulates about the room so that she may come into personal touch with and talk individually to her children. She knows that they need speech to make social contacts and to clarify their thoughts. She uses this individualized conversation as a technique to maintain rapport, to set up challenges, and to foster self-reliance. She does not rule from a throne. By setting up sympathetic two-way relationships, she exerts a powerful influence on the emotional organization of her pupils. Personality development is of great importance at this age. The second grade is peculiarly in need of sensitive and perceptive teachers.

At home as at school the child's personal-social behavior shows an increasing awareness both of self and of others. He is more companionable than he was at six and less likely to get into intense entanglements with his mother. He uses the mutual pronoun "we" in referring to himself and his mother. He likes to do things for her and for his father, if they do not hold him too long and too strictly at solitary tasks. He is better fitted for short tasks and needs the recurring support of friendly language. With such support he becomes a happy helper and errand-runner during an afternoon in the garden. He likes to please.

However, he also has a deepening vein of independence. Accordingly he will on occasion resist his mother with an argumentative "But, Mommy . . ." Sometimes he withdraws mutteringly into himself, hinting that he does not want to be a member of the family, and that the family does not like him! He can be "mad at mother" and assume a sulky mood. We may suppose that this "againstness," if not carried to extremes, is part of a normal process of developmental detachment—of self-weaning. It is a more mature form of behavior than the verbal aggressiveness and the direct physical attacks of a year ago.

In terms of development, it is entirely natural for the seven-year-old to be at times amenable and at other times assertive. Indeed, he is not so stably organized that he functions at one well-sustained level. There is considerable variability from day to day and within a single day. There are mood changes from sweet-and-good to cross-and-tearful.

His self-dependence, however, is not robust enough for highly cooperative play. His group play is loosely organized and individual ends are still the most prominent. Donkey-in-the-middle is a typical game that reflects his general level of cooperation. He is not a good loser. He tattletales. If a playground situation grows too complex and things go badly, the seven-year-old runs home with a more or less righteous declaration, "I'm quitting," followed by muttered aspersions of "gyp," "mean," and "unfair."

Let us be duly grateful for this budding righteousness. It is evident that the seven-year-old is developing an ethical sense. He is discriminating between good and bad in other children and even in himself. He is beginning to be conscious of the *attitudes* of his playmates as well as of their actions: "I don't want the kids to make fun of me!" He is ashamed to be seen crying. His crying is less infantile than it was at six; it comes more from the inside, often from wounded sensitiveness. Nevertheless, he is learning to pull himself together and to stop crying. He tends to be a more polite and better child when away from home, which also betokens a regard for the good opinion of others.

Tantrums are vanishing. Instead the child removes himself from the scene through fits of sullenness, or through a hasty retreat with a slam of the door. Alibiing and blaming others are common traits. The blaming is usually ill-founded; but the alibiing may have a touching trace of conscientiousness: "I was *just* going to do it."

With this degree of self-deception we may expect a certain amount of so-called lying. But there is an increasing concern over the wrongness of lying. The concern is, actually, in excess of the child's intellectual capacity to tell the truth and should not be imposed upon by severe appeals to his honor. His sense of property is likewise immature. He will appropriate pencils, erasers, and the music teacher's pitch pipe, with a nonchalance that would be amazing if we did not realize the complexity of ethical honesty. It is too early to label his shortcomings as thieving. If he fails to realize that the pitch pipe belongs to someone else, it is because he is too completely absorbed in the satisfaction of owning the pipe himself. In another year he will probably be able to project that feeling of satisfaction upon the true owner. And then he will make a culturally adequate distinction between thine and mine. He will consider the injunction "Thou shalt not steal."

It takes time for these ethical feelings of meaning to grow. Again we must recall the extreme complexity of modern culture and of the process of acculturation. By dramatic projection the six-year-old identifies himself with the culture chiefly in terms of action. The seven-year-old projects in terms of feeling as well as of action. He is coming to feel the import of actions both for himself and for others. He has some symptomatic worries. His developmental task is to adapt his emotional reactions to cultural sanctions and yet preserve his own identity. He must apprehend life emotionally as well as intellectually. His growing intelligence is manifested in insights; his growing wisdom in feelings of meaning.

At the age of seven there are new evidences of reasonableness and of critical capacity. The seven-year-old is more reflective; he takes time to think; he is interested in conclusions and logical ends. You can reason a little with him even in ethical situations that are charged with emotion. He himself uses language more freely and adaptively; not only to establish rapport, but to make running comments on the matter in hand. Often these comments are self-critical: "I can't do that." "I can't think of the next thing." "It may come out all right." "I haven't had that in school." "I think I know." "I can't figure it out." "Are you supposed to do that?" "Oh, wait a minute." "I'm stuck." "I got to think it over." "What's the matter with me! It's crooked—I can't make it straight."

And then out comes the eraser. Time and time again he expunges with rubber the valiant strokes of his pencil. We might almost call Seven the eraser age. Sometimes he mutters self-disparagement as he erases and blows upon his work; but he strives nonetheless for improved results. That the disparagement is touched with a trace of sadness is in keeping with seven-year-old character.

Part and parcel of this maturity is the child's *perseverance*; a tendency to continue and to repeat a behavior that affords satisfaction.

He watches television as long as he's permitted. He draws something that takes his fancy; he draws it over and over again with few variations. He perseveres at active as well as quiet games. Having started a bout of chasing or wrestling, he tends to go at it more and more wildly until the game deteriorates. He is a better saturater than shifter. At card games, he likes to keep on playing till he wins.

On all these counts it is clear that the seven-year-old has progressed well beyond the impulsive and episodic tendencies of six-year-old maturity. Although self-centered, he is less completely self-absorbed. His thinking is somewhat more personal-social. It is more prolonged, more serial, more conclusive. It is also more inquiring, even when he withdraws into himself to work over his experiences into feelings of meaning. He is less closely bound to the here and now.

His mental life is embracing the community and the cosmos. He has a more intelligent awareness of the sun, moon, clouds, heat, fire, and the earth's crust. Heaven and earth are uniting. At six he portrayed the sky with a patch of blue; now his drawings fill the void; earth and sky join to make a horizon. The people who inhabit the earth take on more sociological meaning: the policeman, the grocer, the fireman. The seven-year-old has an expanding interest in the community. In all candor, it should be said that he is not too interested in the vanished culture of the American Indian, even when the course of study calls for an Indian life project!

The seven-year-old is attaining orientation in time as well as in space. He can read the clock. He can tell the season of the year and usually the calendar month. Although he can associate a specific time with a specific task, he cannot be depended upon to note the time. His characteristic self-absorption too easily interferes. So he needs warnings in advance. And if he fails, he will plead, "But you didn't remind me." He wants and expects to be reminded.

Although he is interested in fairies, in supermen, and in tales of magic, he is beginning to manifest an almost scientific interest in causes and conditions. Secretly or otherwise he entertains some skepticism of the existence of Santa Claus (but not to the detriment of his Christmas joys and illusions). He betrays a thoughtful interest in God and heaven, and asks concrete questions about them. He has given up the idea that God shoves the clouds around. He is not overcome by the mysteries of death, but shows a marked interest in its possible causes.

However, we would not suggest that the typical seven-year-old is at all times a melancholy Dane who broods excessively on the paradoxes of life and death. He feels life in every limb. He draws his breath lightly as well as heavily. He likes to climb trees, to scuff, tussle and tumble, to play cops and robbers and commandos. He is careless about handkerchief, napkin, and shoelaces. He has his active and silly spells as well as pensive moods.

And yet, in drawing a synthetic portrait of the seven-year-old, it is necessary to reemphasize the inner tensions that are the key to his psychology. He is preeminently in an assimilative stage, in which he develops a working balance between his inner propensities and the demands of the culture. He brings to the task a fund of native intelligence; but the task is not his alone. There are too many artificial and conflicting values in the culture. He is peculiarly in need of a discriminating guidance which does justice to the subtleties of his ruminative inner life. The seven-year-old is too readily misunderstood, too easily imposed upon.

He meets us, however, more than halfway. He is susceptible to praise. He is sensitive to disapproval, to the point of tears. Scolding and physical punishment are too gross for the tender tissue of his personality. His ethical sense is immature only because it is so recent. But in its processes, and even in its early patterns, it suggests sensitivities which he will experience again in the years of adolescence.

Maturity Traits

The following maturity traits are **not** to be regarded as rigid norms, nor as models. They simply illustrate the kinds of behavior—desirable or otherwise—that tend to occur at this age. Every child has his own pattern of growth, and his own timetable. The behavior traits here outlined may be used to interpret his individuality and to consider the maturity level at which he is functioning.

1. MOTOR CHARACTERISTICS

BODILY ACTIVITY

SEVEN appears less brisk than SIX, but he has sudden spurts of very active behavior. A few children are more tensely active than they were at six, and at the other extreme a small number are far more inactive. The tensely active may show choreiform movements of the body, once spoken of as St. Vitus's dance.

SEVEN is more cautious in his approach to new performances. He shows a new awareness of heights and is cautious in climbing and when playing in a tree house.

He repeats a performance over and over to master it. He may have "runs" on one type of activity and then suddenly drop it for another. His interest in piano or dancing lessons has a strong motor component. His motor demands may be a real need but, as with other activities, he may lose his interest suddenly.

SEVEN exhibits extremes in his outdoor play. Sometimes he is tearing about, running and tossing a hand-made paper airplane; at other times he is content to hang around, talking, swapping cards or playing house.

Boys especially are interested in acquiring ability to use a bow and arrow, and to bat a ball, both of which skills require a new orientation to the side position. Carpentry is a favorite occupation and SEVEN likes the tug and pull as he saws a board. Sawing may be preferred to hammering.

Girls are busy with jump rope and hopscotch, but they also find house play or picking flowers enjoyable.

A favorite posture, especially of boys, is to lie prone on the floor, resting on one elbow and activating the legs, while reading, writing, or working.

EYES AND HANDS

SEVEN's posture is more tensed and more unilateral than that of SIX. He maintains a position for a longer period. He sits with head forward and tilted toward the nondominant side, which is the more tensed and closer to the body. He frequently drops his head down on his free arm as he writes or listens; in this position he may occlude one eye.

SEVEN is fond of pencils and erasers and now discards wax for pencil crayons. His grasp, though tight, releases suddenly, and he is apt to drop his pencil repeatedly while working.

He is interested in comparative size, and the height of his capital and of his small letters is becoming more uniform although they taper uniformly as he proceeds across a page. In drawing he represents his human figures in more accurate comparative size than formerly.

SEVEN is less distracted by peripheral movement than is SIX. He becomes absorbed with what he is doing and maintains regard within close range. He is still apt to touch anything he sees, and to manipulate it.

2. PERSONAL HYGIENE

EATING

The seven-year-old's eating patterns have many tag ends reminiscent of the six-year-old's patterns, but the child's relative improvement is summed up in a parent's remark: "He is less aggravating than he used to be."

Appetite. A few girls still show low appetite; they enjoy their food in anticipation more than in reality. A few boys, at the other extreme, have tremendous appetites and are kidded for being "fat." These boys are apt to voice abdominal discomfort, especially if they have eaten too fast or too much.

Refusals and Preferences. SEVEN expresses likes and dislikes, but not as strongly as at six. He is beginning to overcome his aversion by conscientiously eating disliked foods. This is difficult for him, but he makes the task easier for himself by dispatching the disliked food at the start or the end of the meal.

Self-Help. SEVEN handles his implements moderately well and is less apt to finger feed than formerly. He does find it difficult to get some foods on his spoon or fork without using his free fingers as a pusher. Some children will use a piece of toast as a pusher, others will use an actual implement called a pusher, but if given a choice, most would prefer to use their fingers.

Table Behavior. SEVEN is more able to eat with the family. With his general calming down, he is now able to sit better, and may even show an interest in listening to table conversation and in telling some of his own day's experiences. However, he is easily distracted by mention of anything that is going on outside, and frequently has to pop up from his chair to go to the window and see for himself. He often desires to bring to the table with him an object that has just engaged his interest.

He is slow in coming to the table and usually has to be called a second time. He often chooses to eat by himself so that he can continue his reading or TV-watching. Parental judgment is essential here to decide what is best for the occasion. If he is at the table with a younger sibling he may quarrel or become very silly to induce his sibling to laugh at him.

SEVEN does not dawdle as much as SIX. He is now more adept. He is again interested in dessert and can be motivated toward this end. He is also motivated to become a member of the Clean Plate Club. But nothing motivates him quite as strongly as a friend waiting in the backyard for him to come out and play.

SEVEN still needs to be reminded to wash his hands before meals, and may resist with a "Do I have to?" which he overcomes himself if given time and no further pushing. He prefers his napkin beside his plate and actually uses it as needed. He is even equal to the nicety of wiping fingers and face inside the fold of his napkin; frequently he merely rubs food particle from lips to cheek.

SLEEPING

Bedtime. The hour of going to bed remains between 7 and 8 P.M. Some SEVENS are able to get ready for bed by themselves, even bathing alone, but most like the in-and-out companionship of an adult with a few helps and reminders. Those who are independent enough to get ready for bed by themselves still want to call to mother or father to come and tuck them in and say good night. Some like to chat awhile after lights are out, when they divulge secrets about what happened at school, if the parent promises not to tell the teacher.

It is instructive to note the calming effect bed has on the very children who feel jittery and realize that they cannot fall asleep readily. Some sing or talk to themselves as though they were carrying on a conversation between two people. Others listen attentively to catch the conversation of the adults, and to interpret the sounds of stirrings in the house.

Sleep is often delayed till nine or ten o'clock by all this busyness of thought. They themselves report that thoughts go round and round in their heads as though a phonograph record were telling about monsters, robbers, and burglars. Reading or being read to helps to dispel these thoughts for a while. Some see funny pictures in imagery as they fall off to sleep, and others see odd shapes in reflec-

tions, shadows, or the clothes hanging over a chair, interpreting these shapes as ghosts or spies. SEVEN may still want to take a personal treasure to bed with him, whether it be a gun, a panda, or an old bathrobe.

Night. SEVEN has a certain affection for his bed and may even grow sentimental about it. He is a good sleeper. Mothers report that the seven-year-old "sleeps like a log" or that "not even a siren wakes him."

Although he may have disquieting thoughts before he goes to sleep, nightmares are no longer common. Night toileting likewise has almost dropped out. Those who still get up take care of themselves without waking their parents.

Morning. A common waking hour is at 7 A.M., which may fortunately stretch to 8 A.M. or later on Sunday mornings. SEVEN awakens by himself, and may even plan to waken early in order to read or "to have more time." Like SIX, he may get dressed by himself, but he still needs considerable reminding.

ELIMINATION

Bowel. Each child is fairly consistent, with his own individual rhythm of functioning. After lunch or late afternoon are common times. Only a few are able to function easily at school. Typically, the seven-year-old can consciously "wait" until he reaches home.

He expresses control in elimination as well as in many other functions.

Bladder. This is the age when a long span of retention is evident. The child may even have to be reminded to go to the bathroom before he goes to school in the morning, not having gone since the night before. He may put it off so long that he has to make a mad dash. Fewer children need to get up at night, and if they do, they take care of themselves completely.

For the most part, there is not much awareness of and dwelling upon elimination functioning, though a few may express "silly" humor about urinating: "The king of France wet his pants."

If any boy or girl is still wetting the bed, and if no medical reason for this can be found, we strongly recommend use of one of the good conditioning devices now available at moderate cost.*

BATH AND DRESSING

Bath. Some SEVENs still hate to bathe, but as a rule there is much less resistance than there was at six. SEVEN has difficulty in getting started, which is probably why his mother usually draws the water to get him going. Once in the tub, he enjoys it. He can wash himself fairly completely, but for some the whole process is a bit of a chore. He needs checking up after a bath. He is apt to dawdle, to dream, or imaginatively to think that a bar of soap is a boat. This type of child needs considerable reminding and some help. Getting out of the tub when all is done usually is not difficult for him.

SEVEN is reasonably good about washing face and hands before meals if he hears his mother when she reminds him. The mother must make sure that he has heard, and need not be disturbed if his response is "Do I have to?" for he carries out her request in spite of this protest.

Dressing and Care of Clothes. SEVEN is not a poor dresser after he gets started. He has a great tendency to dawdle or to be distracted by things in his room or by thoughts in his head. With one sock on, he may wander around asking about telephone wires, or how many states there are in the union. Some can snap to and concentrate by imagining that they are a fireman in action. Others are motivated best by accepting their father's direct help. If motivation is not secured, parents waste much energy in nagging and emotional tension. A very few children still need to be helped throughout the dressing. Parents can usually anticipate and plan toward self-dependence in another year.

A further difficulty in dressing, be-

---

* Among our favorites are: Dry-O-Matic, 10055 Nadine, Huntington Woods, Mich. 48070; and U-Trol, J. G. Shuman Assoc., Box 306, Scotch Plains, N.J. 07076.

sides the need to tuck in loose ends, is the tying of shoelaces. The seven-year-old can tie his shoelaces tightly, but he usually goes around with them untied. It is the old difficulty of "he can but he doesn't." Therefore, it is wise to demand a little of him, but not too much. A good plan is to provide him with long enough shoelaces so that he can tie a double knot. He can be made responsible for the first tying in the morning, and then he needs help the rest of the day, if his laces come untied or he has taken off his shoes and wants to put them back on again. As with six-year-olds, many SEVENs would prefer to take their shoes off the minute they enter the house.

Seven-year-olds are generally not much interested in clothes. They like to wear old clothes, hate to change to new ones, and girls like to wear the same dress for days in succession. Their pet aversion is the handkerchief (but they will accept a discardable tissue). Very few demand to choose their clothes; they usually accept what mother has laid out for them.

The seven-year-old is apt to "hang his clothes on the floor." With reminding he will put them on a chair, but would prefer to have his mother do so. She, too, may so prefer; otherwise she will have to unscramble an assembly of clothes that he has deposited on the chair.

Rips in clothes are common at this age and are usually not reported unless glaringly evident. Some girls like to shine their shoes (especially if they belong to a Brownie troop).

Boys are becoming more interested in combing their own hair, and girls make a fair attempt.

HEALTH AND SOMATIC COMPLAINTS

Life smooths out at seven, is more reasonable and more understandable to the adult. SEVEN still has a fair share of muscular pains and other difficulties such as he had at six, but these are more obviously related to specific situations and can be more readily brought under control. SEVEN may still complain of muscular pains, especially knee pains, but these are quickly alleviated with rubbing and may even disappear miraculously if the child goes to bed.

He has fewer colds than he had at six. These are less severe and less apt to develop complications. Of the communicable diseases, German measles and mumps are the most common. Chickenpox and measles also occur frequently. Fortunately new immunizations are cutting down on communicable diseases.

SEVEN is more articulate in his complaints than he was at six, and his complaints still have validity. He frequently complains about being tired in general, especially at the close of an afternoon school session. He becomes tired rapidly when asked to do something. Stomachache in relation to school is less frequent. It occurs more often after a heavy meal or before a bowel movement. He is more apt to complain of a headache at seven than he was at six, particularly after too much excitement.

Congestion of the mucous membrane, also noted at six, may occasion the violent rubbing of the eyes at six and a half to seven years of age. Judicious eyewash or drops may alleviate the itching and reduce the rubbing, and thus prevent a possible infection of a tear duct. These symptoms may denote that too much is being demanded of the eyes. Such children should be treated more as six-year-olds than as seven-year-olds. But also visual development coverage by a specialist should be sought.

A common complaint on the part of the mother is that the child seems deaf. But on examination he is found to have good hearing, perhaps even better than he previously had. The apparent deafness is relative to his attention. He hears if he attends, but since he is so deeply engrossed in his activities, he does not readily shift his attention. He will respond better to the signal of a bell, a marked change in the mother's tone of voice, a whisper, a magic word, or a whistle.

TENSIONAL OUTLETS

Being busy with his own activities and inner thoughts, SEVEN now has life under better control. There is less facial grimacing because he has "more control of his facial muscles." He returns to nose-picking and nail-biting especially with a cold or an illness. He may not stutter unless the stimulus is a strong one. If he returns to sucking his thumb—and this may happen especially with a few boys—he himself wants to stop and to have help in devising ways to control this habit. A subtle cue such as the mere mention of the child's name may suffice to remind him to take thumb out of mouth. A better method may be to set up a goal or a nightly reward (as ten cents) for successful control. Having the money to buy one's own baseball cap is more of a stimulus than just working toward a baseball cap.

SEVEN tends to wiggle his loose teeth and to fidget. He may still cling to some of his sleep-inducing stuffed animals or his blanket, but he now can give them up rather readily under some new strong stimulus, such as a favorite relative's spending the weekend at his home. Having given them up for the weekend he may well be able to give them up for good.

3. EMOTIONAL EXPRESSION

By six and a half to seven years of age the child's life takes on a more serious, a more thoughtful tone. He is more inhibited, more controlled, and more aware of other people and of his relationships to them. He may have been worried about heaven and dying at six, or about his mother's welfare and the danger that she might be struck by lightning or locked up in the bathroom. By six and a half, the fathers' health or the children at school, may be on the child's mind; but by seven, he himself is his own chief concern. He worries that second grade will be too hard for him. If he hiccups repeatedly he is fearful that he will die; or if he rubs his eye persistently he fears that something is going to happen to his eyeball (yet he cannot stop rubbing). He is beginning to be able to put himself in the other person's place, or more truly to put the other person's experience into himself. That is why he is so moved by sad stories, television programs, or movies. Some of his tall tales about his adventures turn out to be true happenings to another child, which also have reality for him. Otherwise they would not have evoked a response so vivid.

SEVEN has an initial tendency to withdraw from situations rather than to stay and resist, as SIX does. By this withdrawal, SEVEN is protective of himself. He puts his hands over his ears to keep out loud noises. He actually does not attend enough to hear his mother when she calls him—though he may hear her if she shouts, whispers, or changes her usual approach in some way. When asked questions, he will often say, "I don't know" or "We haven't had that yet." When asked to do something, he may say that he is too tired or that he doesn't "feel like it." He lacks confidence to the point of not wanting even to try.

Though he may attack his mother with a "You're mean," when he is scolded by her or when he gets into some difficulty with her, he is more likely to go off and sulk or to rush to his room and slam the door. If things do not go right in his play with his friends, he may prefer to play by himself, or may stalk off the scene, saying, "I'm quittin'." And if things are not going his way at home, he may say, "No one treats me right. I'm going to run away." He may go as far as to pack his bag and go out of the front door, but usually he does not get beyond the front steps or a few houses up the street. A few SEVENs who seem to be fearful of life in general are actually reluctant to grow up. They withdraw from the new demands growth puts upon them.

SEVEN still has his moments of resistance—his "bad spells"—but these are not simply for the sake of resistance. He may say, "Just try and make me," but more often he seeks a reason: "Why do I have to?" If he has caused a scene over some demand that the parent has pushed through, he thinks it over afterward and wonders why he was so "foolish." His anger is often directed against himself for his actions. He is apt to throw a book if he cannot read it, or to break something if he has hurt himself. He may throw stones at other children as he is leaving a scene of action, but he rarely attacks his parent anymore. He has attained more effective restabilizing mechanisms within himself. If some form of discipline is applied, he usually accepts it, though grudgingly. It troubles him very deeply to be sent to his room or to have to go to bed early.

If he cries, his reasons are more

subjective than formerly. He is disappointed because some gadget of his doesn't work, or because what he was doing did not come out well. He cries because he thinks people don't like him. Although he is better at losing than he formerly was, he likes to win in the end. If life is stacked too much against him, he finally bursts into tears. He also cries when he is physically hurt. Usually he tries to control his crying, especially if he is afraid someone will see him. He may even control it so completely that he merely says, "I feel like crying."

Although he cries less, he screeches more. The general noisiness and gross motor effervescence of the six-year-old have been superseded by high-pitched vocalizations, yells, and occasionally unearthly screams. The seven-year-old shouts his replies to his mother; he shouts his criticisms of life in general with a "That's not fair!" He voices his exuberance in the same high-pitched manner.

SEVEN's chief interpersonal difficulties are with his siblings and with other children. He fights and contradicts, but can be motivated toward self-restraint by the prospect of a reward for better conduct. Planned separation and more opportunity for outdoor play may help him to attain his goal.

SEVEN sets up too high goals for himself. He wants to be perfect, he brings home only his "100" papers. He is deeply concerned about and even ashamed of his mistakes. He may not take correction well, and tries to cover up his errors with "That's what I meant," or "I was just going to."

Though SEVEN has difficulty in starting things, once started he is too persistent, too avid; he must finish, but he does not know when to stop. His mind "wanders on and on." If he is unskillful with his hands but facile in speech, he shows great dependence on conversation; he feels the need of someone to talk to and he talks all day long. He wakes up talking, cannot stop thinking, and persists in asking innumerable questions to support his thinking.

SEVEN is conscientious. He takes his responsibilities seriously even though at times he is not quite sure what he is responsible for. He likes to plan his day, and may enjoy using a chart as a guide to his goal. He is beginning to be thoughtful, to be considerate, and is anxious to please. He is less selfish; can share better; wants and tries to be good. He wants to find his place in the family group, expressing his awareness of himself and his family in pride. He is proud of his abilities, his being good, and of his possessions, home and family. This awareness makes him more critical of himself. Some SEVENs can even laugh at themselves; when they are unable to go to sleep they may say, "I don't know what's the matter with me."

Although life is fairly much under SEVEN's control, he is now sensing forces outside himself as "good luck" and "bad luck," and in general he is inclined to think that he has all the "bad luck." Magic also is looming up as a fascinating unknown. He may imagine a vehicle that transports him home from school when he is tired; he may imagine a musical instrument that plays wonderful music.

4. FEARS AND DREAMS

FEARS

SEVEN's fears focalize upon him-self—his inner self—and his self acting on its own. He has his behavior equipment so much better in hand that he can protect himself as the six-year-old cannot. SIX jumps right in and finds himself over his depth; SEVEN hesitates before acting. His fears and worries are to some extent useful in that they are self-protective.

Although SEVEN has some left-over fears which were not resolved at six, he now handles them differently. He may still want his parents to stay at home in the evening, but he can resign himself to their departure, once he has gotten over the first hurdle.

SEVEN is spoken of as cowardly and brave. These words refer to the lack of or presence of an inner control. Seven is an age when the environment can capitalize on the child's bravery, but bravery also needs environmental support.

Many previously unresolved fears now resolve—the fear of the dentist's chair, the fear of swimming with face under water, or the fear of having hair washed. The seven-year-old has all these situations under better control. He knows what the dentist does

and that he can lift his hand if being hurt. He can now hold his breath under water and no longer "breathes in" as he used to do. He may be able to wash his own hair and can control soap in his eyes and the temperature of the water on his scalp.

But there are a number of things that SEVEN does not have under his control. He does not want to experience new situations by himself. Even his summer may have been miserable because he was afraid to start second grade. He is afraid of his school work because he doesn't know how to begin. He is afraid of being shy, or of being laughed at. He is afraid of physical punishment. And he may even be afraid that his mother will "get down on him" as his teacher has.

Space and time are taking on new meaning for him. He may fear high places and unfamiliar visual impressions. Cellars become inhabited by strange creatures and attics by ghosts. Even his own closet may have a foreign spy in it. Shadows gather form and take on meaning. His clothes on the back of a chair may suddenly appear as a frightening ghost in a half light after he is in bed. He may be timid of his own shadow in his inability to interpret it and its sudden movements. Though he loves hut play with his gang, he may be scared to death of the trap door in the hut.

SEVEN can, however, help to control his fears. He gets his sister to go down into the cellar with him and politely says, "Ladies first." He flashes his flashlight on the burglar in his closet and dissolves him. He calls to his mother to analyze the ghost in his room and enjoys the realization that it was only his clothes on a chair.

The child who is most fearful of being late for school at seven may actually never have had the experience of being late. He is usually the type of child who has his inner timing mechanism under poor control. He has difficulty not only in stopping—he goes on endlessly—but in starting. It is an unsettling experience to be with a seven-year-old who is extremely afraid of being late for school. He may awake at 6 A.M. and shout to his parents, "Is it time to get up yet?" This phrase recurs at intervals. The setting of an alarm may help him temporarily to control his anxiety.

Once he is up he hurries into his clothes, rushes through breakfast, and then waits. Again he plagues his parents with another oft-repeated phrase: "Is it time to go yet?" Even the assurance that his father will drive him to school may not allay his anxiety. During the last ten minutes before departure his whole body is aquiver, he has to go to the bathroom at least three times and may even have a bowel movement. Finally he rushes off in the car, rushes across the playground, and at last crosses the threshold of his room, experiencing immediate calm. He gives his teacher no inkling of what he has gone through in the last two and a half hours.

This type of child under the best of handling may still express some anxiety, but he can be helped to better control. If he does not go by bus, he should not be held to getting to school exactly on time, for his sense of time is still only relative. If the school cannot provide this type of handling, he should be helped to bridge the gap from home to school by one of his interests. Reading a book on electricity may turn the trick, especially during the last ten minutes before starting off for school. Then he might take the book to school, show it to his teacher, and it may be hoped that the teacher will respond with interest.

As with SIX, certain stimuli in comic books or movies may bring on fears—such tales as opening drawers and finding skulls. This is why the child still needs considerable supervision, especially if he is not too self-protective and gets into situations he cannot get out of by himself.

DREAMS

Dreams are diminishing at seven or at least are not reported as much as earlier. Nightmares and dreams about animals are also declining. Only a few children have unpleasant dreams about being chased by persons or beasts.

SEVEN dreams often about himself. He has wonderful dreams when he flies and floats through the air, or dives into the depths of the ocean. Sometimes he dreams he is drowning, but always wakes up before he actually drowns. He may dream of embarrassing situations such as wetting the bed (which may coincide with an actual episode of wetting), or losing his pants on the way to the school bus. A clearly defined shift to the opposite sex may be experienced in a dream. A boy may dream that he is going upstairs without any clothes on and that his nipples have become extraordinarily large.

SEVEN carries on long conversations in his dreams, with spies, policemen, and unfamiliar people. As he talks out loud, one gathers bits of conversation which disclose that he feels himself to be definitely involved. He may say, "It's me" or "I don't think you need a bodyguard."

Certain movies and television programs give him bad dreams. He still needs considerable supervision in making his choices of television and movies.

5. SELF AND SEX

SELF

SEVEN is becoming more aware of himself. By absorbing impressions from what he sees, hears, reads, and by working things over in his own thoughts and feelings, he seems to be strengthening and building up his sense of self. At EIGHT he may take his equipment into the outside world and try it against the environment, but at seven—for all his noisy slapdash exterior, his running through the house slamming doors and shouting—he most characteristically sits quietly by himself, reading, watching TV, planning.

With some SEVENs, self-awareness relates strongly to the physical self. SEVEN is aware of his body and is sensitive about exposing it, especially to the opposite sex. He may refuse to go to the toilet at school if there is no door on it. He does not like to be touched. Girls are especially aware of the style in which their hair is worn, and actually may fear that their identity would be lost or at least that they might not be recognized if it were cut off.

Most SEVENs are concerned about their actions. They are ashamed of their mistakes and their fears, and very much ashamed to be seen crying. They are greatly aware of what others might think, and are careful not to expose themselves to criticism. They cringe when they are laughed at or made fun of.

One of the ways in which SEVEN protects himself best is to withdraw from any scene of action that does not please him. His withdrawal may be combined with a distaste for physical combat. This is not the age to teach the child to "defend himself" by means of boxing lessons. By eight he may spontaneously defend himself. At seven he needs to be helped to withdraw and needs to be protected.

SEVEN is serious about himself, and about any responsibilities that may be given to him—especially if they are responsibilities outside his home, as at school. He thinks and speaks seriously of such concepts as government, civilization, and the like. SEVEN is not only serious, but he also is cautious—

in physical activities, in social situations, and in his approach to a new task. There are beginnings of slight skepticism about Santa Claus, about religion and other matters he has been told of but has not experienced at first hand.

Though he withdraws successfully, he is apt to voice many complaints. He feels that people are mean and unfair. And as he thinks situations over, he worries about what people think of him and fears that they do not like him, or do not think he has done well. He is particularly interested in what his mother and his friends think of him. "Of course the kids will make fun of me," he says. There is a definite minor strain in the feelings of the seven-year-old.

Boys especially may be breaking away from their mother's domination. They may refuse to wear coats, hats, boots. They may ask, "Why should I?" if given a command, and may counter a direction with the response, "I don't feel like it."

SEVEN wants to make a place for himself. This place may be a physical one—his place at the table, in the family car, or a room of his own. But SEVEN is also interested in his place in the social world. He usually has strong family feelings and at the same time may fear he does not really belong to his family, that he has been adopted. SEVEN mulls all these things over in his mind, for even in his thoughts he withdraws. Then he may discuss the fruit of his thought with the adult in relation to such topics as: The

disadvantages of being over five and under sixteen. One particular seven-year-old advanced the following reasoning: "Under five people give you plenty of money, and over sixteen you have plenty of your own. But between those ages they make you work for your money and give you very little for what you do. And between those ages you are changing the fastest, so you need a great many things."

SEX

SEVEN is less likely than SIX to be involved in overt sex play. In fact, he may even withdraw from any possible exposure when he is undressing or going to the bathroom if a younger sibling of the opposite sex is near. If two girls expose themselves, one to the other, they may become interested in the details of the organs and even try to draw what they have seen. A few SEVENs, especially boys, may think that they can magically change themselves into girls by taping up their genitals. These same boys may enjoy playing dolls with a girl.

SEVEN's real interest is in **thinking about** all these things. He shows an intense longing to have a new baby in his family, and almost always a baby of his own sex. One such child, reminded a year later of her seven-year-old desire, which was about to be fulfilled, exclaimed, "Whatever made me say that!" SEVEN realizes that having babies can be repeated. He may ask his mother how many more babies she has in her stomach. He is aware that older women do not still have babies. He may even draw up a plan for his mother to have a baby every five years (because this is the easiest for him to calculate) until she is sixty, when he feels she won't be able to have any more.

Pregnancy is now something that he is beginning to understand. He may be the first to notice that his mother is different. He may ask, "What's the matter with you? You don't act the same." If a baby is coming in his home he is very much excited about it. If permitted the experience, he is thrilled to feel the kicking of the baby against the mother's abdominal wall. He wants to know how big the baby is, how it is fed, will it get sick if the mother becomes ill, and how long it takes before it is ready to be born.

He does not quite understand how the mother knows that the baby has started growing. He is satisfied when he learns that two seeds (or two eggs), one from the father and one from the mother, come together to start the baby. He is not yet concerned about how the seed from the father got into the mother.

He is more concerned about the details of birth. In his own mind he may more or less vaguely figure out that you have to "split the mother open to take the baby out." Or he interprets the bellybutton as the place provided for its exit. He readily accepts the simplified statement that the baby is born between the mother's legs. He wonders whether this takes place with the mother on the floor or on a table,

and whether the baby might fall to the floor. He may even ask to be there so that he can catch the baby when it comes out. It is no wonder that he cannot understand why a baby should cost so much when it grows inside a person.

SEVEN may himself become involved in an elementary love affair. Boy-girl pairs are fairly common, especially at school. The boys who can write and spell may even write simple notes, "Do you like me? Yes or no." with X's for kisses. If the relationship progresses to a specific "engagement" and even to a planned marriage, the boy usually adds that he plans to return to his mother's house after the marriage. The loss of a boyfriend or a girlfriend is usually taken as a matter of course, but some SEVENs are more deeply affected. One seven-year-old who did not have a boyfriend wailed to her parents, "What is the matter with me? I'm not in love."

6. INTERPERSONAL RELATIONS

SEVEN is becoming a real member of the family group, ready to take some of the household responsibilities. Many SEVENs like to help and often take on certain routine chores, especially on Saturday mornings, when they like to empty wastebaskets or garbage pails, fill the potato basket, cut the lawn, make their bed, pick up their room, help with the dishes, prepare the vegetables, run errands. Sometimes this help is spotty. SEVEN also tires of one chore and wishes to shift to another. He works best if the adult works with him. Although the seven-year-old talks about earning money, he is really as interested in doing the work as he is in receiving money for it. Money does not motivate him as much as it may at eight.

SEVEN is less resistant and stubborn than he was earlier. His mother speaks of him as being more easily controlled and influenced. He has lost his six-year-old freshness and is even polite, sympathetic, and capable of genuine affection. His chief trouble comes when he is interrupted in what he is doing, whether he is playing outside or reading a book. You can plan with him, however, on if and how he should be warned, and when and how he will be called.

SEVEN not only gets on well with his mother, for the most part, but he is becoming extremely companionable with his father. Boys especially like to go on long walks with their father and like to have long discussions with him about such masculine matters as sinking oil wells. Girls are more sensitive to reprimands from their father and may be jealous of any attention he shows their mother.

A few SEVENs have real difficulty in adjusting to either parent or home and wish to bolt from a trying situation. As one girl put it, "I don't want to be a member of this family. I'd like to go away!" Or the child may get the notion that he does not actually belong to this family, that his mother and father are not his real parents. Nevertheless, he is proud of his home and his family and often compares them favorably to the homes and families of his friends.

Grandparents are still much loved and admired by most, as well as loving and admiring. Children often still tend to like the grandmother "because she gives us things"; grandfather "because he plays with us and takes us places."

SEVEN wants to make a place for himself in the family group, especially if there is a sibling. If he has been sharing a room with a sibling he may now prefer a room of his own. He is usually very fond of a younger sibling, especially a baby. Then he assumes the part of the big brother or sister, wants to carry him, feed him his bottle, or wheel him in the carriage. If the younger sibling is closer in age, he may play well with him, look after and protect him, particularly if a third child is not added to the group. But frequently he is apt to tease, poke, bicker and fight with his younger sibling. Separation is then indicated. SEVEN is inclined toward jealousy of a sibling and worries that the sibling may put something over on him, or have more privileges. SEVEN admires an older sibling, and is often under the older sibling's influence—which may not always be for the best.

SEVEN does not demand companionship as much as he did at SIX. He spends considerable time by himself watching television, writing lists of things, bouncing a ball, or in other solitary activities. As a rule he plays fairly well with other children. SEVEN often has a gorgeous, silly time with playmates his own age. Some SEVENs play better at home, others play better away from home. Indoor play is more often too stimulating and may make him act pretty wild. Usually, however, SEVEN holds up better than SIX, though he is likely to walk out on his playmates if things go too badly, or to start a fight. Some SEVENs still will not fight and may hide their fearfulness behind big talk.

Several children are likely to gang up against some other child, and many seven-year-old boys have trouble with older boys who bully them. Group play is not well organized and is still carried out mostly for individual ends. The child may worry about his place in the group and fear that he cannot hold his own or that others do not like him, and he particularly does not "want the other kids to laugh" at him. There is usually less direct physical and verbal attack on playmates than at six, although boys indulge in a good deal of half-friendly, half-unfriendly wrestling and scuffling.

Sex lines are not clearly drawn, but some discrimination against the opposite sex is beginning to appear. Boys cannot be bothered with girls, and girls do not think boys are very well behaved. But the opposite sex is still invited to birthday parties though boys may prefer just boys, and boy-girl friendships suggest rudimentary love affairs.

SEVEN is becoming more adept in meeting strangers. He is now able to greet them. He likes to listen to an older group's conversation and he likes to go visiting. A more inept or immature SEVEN may be very much aware of other people and yet be unable to greet them with ease, is apt to push them, rush in front of them, stumble over them, throw a ball treacherously near their noses, contacting them awkwardly in all the wrong ways. Such an awkward SEVEN is greatly benefited if he receives more complete and personal attention from one of the visiting guests.

7. PLAY AND PASTIMES

GENERAL INTERESTS

SEVEN is inclined to be obsessive in his play interests. He is said to have a "mania" for guns, comic books, and coloring. He can spend hours at whatever he is doing, whether it is playing the piano, jumping rope, reading, or working at his workbench. SEVEN has more capacity to play by himself than he did earlier, and therefore can more readily hold to a task without having to adjust to other people's ideas.

SEVEN does not branch out on many novel ventures. But he is better at planning what he is going to do. Boys now have some comprehension of a model and a blueprint. They are inclined to do a little inventing of their own and they like to rig up things, utilizing cereal boxes, electrical wire equipment, and odds and ends. They like to make and to "shoot" paper airplanes as darts. Girls may be inventive in designing dresses for their paper dolls.

There is a strong return to coloring and to cutting things out. Some girls cut out paper dolls endlessly and are content with simply putting the dresses on and off after the cutting. Quantity is the rule in whatever collecting SEVEN may undertake, whether it be stones or bottle tops. Outdoors, girls favor hopscotch, jump rope, and roller skating; boys enjoy tops and marbles.

In his gross motor activities SEVEN is fairly cautious but not fearful. He has become an expert tree climber. Many SEVENs own bicycles and ride them well, but are not yet capable of handling them responsibly off the sidewalk.

SEVEN is really learning to swim. At ball play he is a better batter than catcher. The side stance of bow and arrow play, as well as the cautious release of the arrow, seem to appeal to him. He now has the physical stamina to hold up better during the winter season and is beginning to enjoy sledding, ice skating, and even skiing.

His group play is similar in type to that of the six-year-old, with less ability to pretend and more ability to provide the necessary paraphernalia. He demands more realism. For example, when library is played, he must have library slips and go through the whole formal procedure of lending out books. He equips his tent with a cot, a table and chair, writing material, and a gun. Guns are a prominent feature of his group games. He may become so noisy with his persistent sound of firing that his gun play may need to be restricted to out of doors.

SEVEN is fond of table games and jigsaw puzzles. He can handle games better because he is not quite so intent on winning as he was earlier. He will even tackle complicated games. Magic and "tricks" are greatly favored.

There are marked individual differences in play pursuits, dependent upon talents and temperament. Some boys make simple but serious beginnings in chemistry, telegraphy, and navigation.

Questioned as to their favorite play activities, SEVENs most frequently mention climbing trees, riding bicycles, playing cars. One seven-year-old boy, however, succinctly said, "Color. Everything else stinks."

READING

Many SEVENs are fair readers and enjoy reading what they can by themselves. They can get the sense of a story without knowing all the words. Some SEVENs are even spoken of as "chain readers," for they move directly from one book to another. SEVEN enjoys fairy tales, even though he might be said to prefer his comic books. Boys especially are interested in books on airplanes, electricity, earth, and nature. Girls choose such books as **Heidi** or the A. A. Milne books. Both sexes love riddles. SEVEN is not read to as much as formerly, since he is less demanding, and more preoccupied with his own reading or his television watching.

MUSIC, TELEVISION, AND MOVIES

SEVEN often expresses a strong desire to take piano lessons. The question may be asked whether this craving should be satisfied. It probably is desirable to satisfy this demand if the music teacher will allow the child to take lessons without practicing, which is often the preferred way to learn. Too many home battles are fought over piano practicing before the child is really equal to practicing by himself (nine to ten years).

Television is now a part of the daily routine, and children dislike missing their set programs. Boys claim that they decide which programs they will watch, though girls admit that parents "partly" decide. Amount of watching may need to be curbed, as well as kinds of programs.

Interest in movies is variable with seven-year-olds. Musicals and animal pictures are preferred. Love stories are very much disliked. SEVEN is likely to become overactive and to squeal during a performance. A few SEVENs like shooting pictures. A few attend weekly, but on the whole movies are not much enjoyed before eight years of age.

8. SCHOOL LIFE

SEVEN usually accepts his return to school without protest, but he may anticipate that second grade will be too hard. A few advance visits of the first-grade group to the second-grade room (e.g., a play or picnic at the end of the year) help to forestall and to alleviate such fear. SEVEN may fatigue in spells and this is noticeable at school as well as at home. He has fewer illnesses, but an illness may be of longer duration.

The teacher plays an important part in SEVEN's adjustment. She becomes involved in a more personal relationship with each of her pupils and may be both liked and disliked. Boys are more apt to like their teacher and may form a close attachment to her. Girls may dislike and complain about her. SEVEN continues to bring things to the teacher, but not as much as at SIX, nor does he bring things for the group. However, he enjoys an opportunity to display a new possession.

Home and school are more separated spheres at seven. The child may not like his mother to walk to school with him or to visit school, unless it is for a group performance when other mothers are present. While he is with the group he may ignore her presence.

SEVEN likes to accumulate his papers in his school desk rather than take them home. If they are kept in a notebook he may wish to take this home on occasion. It would then be left at home if his mother did not remind him or put it in his hand as he leaves for school. He is apt also to leave sweaters and belongings at school unless the teacher helps him to remember them. SEVEN is not a good messenger, either for teacher or for parent.

Interviews between parents and teachers may still be more useful than report cards. Two interviews a year may suffice for the majority of second-graders, but in individual instances it is well for the parent and teacher to keep each other informed of any anxieties or fears in relation to the child's adjustments at school (fear of being late, fear of not completing work).

As SEVEN enters the classroom he does not always refer to 'his teacher; he may be noisy and talkative as he makes his entrance, manipulating objects about the room. However, he is interested in a schedule and finally settles into classroom work with absorption. He is quieter while he works than he was at six, talks more to himself. He refers to the work of his neighbor, or makes an impatient demand for the teacher's assistance, often by going directly to her. He is frequently seen with head resting on his forearm while he writes and while classroom discussions are in progress. He shows temporary fatigue with some tasks by shoving at his desk, opening and closing his desktop, or getting up from his chair. These signs indicate that he is ready to change to a different activity.

"What comes next, teacher?" is a typical remark. SEVEN makes abrupt shifts from one situation to the next. He becomes active and talkative. His voice may reach a penetrating, piercing pitch. He whistles or makes different noises and is soon joined by one child after another until the class is in an uproar. The teacher heeds this as a signal to change to a new activity.

SEVEN likes to manipulate objects, so he picks up pencils, erasers, sticks and stones and accumulates them in his desk or pockets. He may attempt to insert one object into another, and manipulates them so forcibly as to break them. It may be helpful to have an emptying of pockets at the end of a morning session, and an occasional desk-cleaning day.

With SEVEN's motor manipulatory pressure, it is no wonder that carpentry is enjoyed, especially by the boys. Although he builds more complicated structures than at six, he is less concerned about his product, which is easily ignored or lost. He likes, however, to make a Christmas gift for one of his parents.

There is less interruption for toileting, as SEVEN has a longer retention span. The majority toilet before and after lunch and after rest period in the afternoon. A few very active boys may have a shorter span. SEVEN prefers the privacy provided by an enclosed toilet and may refuse to use the school toilet if it is without a door.

Classroom work requires the teacher nearby, as she is in almost constant demand. There are many individual differences at seven. Some prefer work at their desks to work presented by the teacher on the blackboard, and others just the opposite. (SEVEN does not combine the two easily; he cannot copy easily from the blackboard because he does not shift easily from far to near and back to far.) Boys like oral better than written arithmetic and girls may prefer concrete to oral or written arithmetic. Some wish widely spaced ruled paper, others prefer narrow. Some respond immediately, others need to be allowed extra time. By eight there will be more uniformity within the group, but such differences need to be respected at seven.

Most SEVENs would prefer to work at the blackboard than at their desk. Ideally there should be more blackboard space. Perhaps someday someone will invent an accordionlike blackboard that can open up and provide space for everyone to work.

In reading, SEVEN recognizes familiar words accurately and rapidly. He is more mechanical in his approach to reading; he reads without stopping for the end of a sentence or a paragraph though in his efforts he is apt to repeat a phrase. He may omit or add familar simple words (and, he, had, but) or a final s or y. He hesitates on new words and prefers to have them supplied so that he can maintain his speed; or he may simply guess, using a word of similar appearance, often one with the beginning and ending letter the same, though the length of the word may now be shortened (green for garden, betful for beautiful). Substitutions of meaning (the for a, was for lived) are prevalent. Vowel errors (pass for puss, some for same) are common. Speed of reading, like other behaviors, shows individual variations.

SEVEN likes to know how far to read; he likes to know how many pages the book has. If he has left a story unfinished he may want to go back to the beginning.

As he improves in the mechanics of reading he may temporarily be less concerned about meaning. He is, however, critical of his reading material and may refuse to reread certain stories. Some SEVENs become inveterate readers, with a special liking for comics. (A favorite time for such reading is in the early morning before breakfast.)

SEVEN's ability to spell usually lags behind his ability to read. He enjoys copying words but he still cannot spell them by heart. He becomes especially confused over vowels and is most apt to use the vowel i (sit for sat). This preference for i is also shown in his pronunciation (cin for can; tin for ten). Though he may dislike and refuse to spell whole words, he does enjoy naming beginning and ending consonants. Thus he grasps the sounds the letters make.

SEVEN likes oral arithmetic and cards with number combinations. He still reverses one or two numbers in writing (usually 2, 6, 7, or 9). He delights in writing long numbers. He likes to continue the same process on a page and may be confused by shifting from addition to subtraction.

Pencils and erasers are almost a passion at seven. SEVEN writes to erase. He manipulates, fingers, drops his pencil, and jabs it into his desk or into an object. He still reverses some letters and numbers, but he usually recognizes his reversal and prefers to erase it. He may say, "Don't be surprised if you find one of my capital J's backward." His pencil grasp is tight at the tip of his pencil with the index finger caved in, and as a rule he exerts less pressure than he did at six. A few children ask to "write" rather than print, but usually just their name.

Pencil and paper work, though a strong interest, makes problems at this age. SEVEN may worry if he cannot finish his written work and even fears being kept after school if his paper is incomplete.

SEVEN has a new awareness of ends. "How far shall I go?" "I can't finish." are typical remarks. He likes to complete, but he wants the teacher to set his end for him, otherwise he is apt to continue too long. He likes to have his paper corrected immediately. "Did I get a hundred?" "Is this right?" He does not compare his with others, but in drawing he may ask the teacher to evaluate who drew the best tree or the best horse.

The thoughtful memory-rumination of the seven-year-old is shown in the following responses to a teacher's question: "What do you see in your mind when you think of autumn?"

"I see the leaves going zigzag."
"I see them going down gently."
"I see pumpkins turning yellow."
"I see milkweeds turning brown."
"I see chestnuts falling down."
"I see the birds going south."
"I see the trees with pretty near all the leaves off."

SEVEN makes a characteristic "explosive" transition from schoolroom to playground at recess time; but on the playground he may be either more, or less, active than he is in the classroom. Entanglements with classmates occur even with the teacher nearby. One child may interfere with another's block structure, one child may want to remain on the swing for the entire period, or monopolize a ball or a jump rope. When several children attempt group play they may become excited and hilarious. This usually ends with destruction of material, or personal altercations. SEVEN needs a variety of outdoor equipment, and even though he is not ready for any directed group play, adult supervision is essential. During the year some become interested in group play set up by the teacher, as long as they are free to join and leave the group at will.

SEVEN wants a place in the group and may be concerned that the other children or the teacher do not like him. He can be separated from the group for special help or to work or play by himself, but he does not like to be singled out for reprimand or praise while he is a part of the group. Group praise, however, is a real spur. The group is slow to include a new member and may even make fun of him.

In play, four or five children may attempt to play together—to build, to shoot airplanes, to play soldier, or simply to talk or wander about together. But there are usually several children who prefer solitary play on swing and Junglegym, or with jump-rope or ball.

9. ETHICAL SENSE

SEVEN is becoming more responsive to the demands of his environment. For the most part, he responds well to directions, especially if he has heard what was said to him. He does, however, forget readily and needs to be reminded. He often requires two chances. He may respond slowly or under protest, but this is reminiscent of the six-year-old. If he is caught in a net of rigid perseverance he must be helped out of it to break its hold upon him.

SEVEN rarely needs punishment because he is a reasoning and by nature a responsible being. You can plan with him and thus avert disaster. Though he may still have some difficulty in making up his mind, especially when a demand is made of him, he is showing greater skill in coming to a decision. He now reasons with his parent, can compromise, and though he may still not wish to change his mind, he may change it when reasoned with. This reasoning with parents is often quite personal, and all his sentences may begin with, "But, Mommy . . ."

SEVEN definitely wants to be good; although he wants to be himself, too. With some SEVENs it is not so much that they are concerned about being good as that they just **are** good. They are proud of a good day and concerned about bad days. They feel sorry for younger children who spoil things by being bad, and they instruct their younger siblings about the disadvantages of being bad. Some SEVENs have good and bad spells, which seem to come in cycles. They are good for a period, and then impossible. Unfortunately this type of child may suddenly turn "bad," even when he means to be "good."

SEVEN's idea of good and bad is beginning to be slightly abstract. It is no longer concerned solely with specific actions allowed or forbidden by his parent, but involves the beginnings of a generalized notion of goodness and badness. One seven-year-old reviewed her day and asked to have listed all the things she had done "Thinking About Myself" and all that she had done "Thinking About Others."

Thinking About Others

1. Telling Susan about a gun for Johnny.
2. Obeying my mother—picking up the living room.
3. Went to bed willingly—fell asleep quickly.
4. Remembered to close the door to keep the bathroom warm.
5. I didn't shout in the library.
6. Came off the ice very quickly when Anne came for me.
7. Put my glasses away in their case.
8. Put my glasses on when I'm reading.
9. Dressing quickly without dawdling.
10. I look before I cross the street.

11. I don't tip my chair as much as
I used to.

Thinking About Myself

1. Eating omelet with my fingers.
2. Saying "Wah!"
3. Speaking rudely to my mother: "Yes you will!"
4. Contradicting.
5. Not washing hands before playing the piano.

SEVEN is less likely than SIX to blame others. He may even act with heroism, when no punishment is involved. Rather than blaming, he may alibi in order to cover up any of his mistakes. He says, "Well, that was what I meant"; "I was just going to." He is now aware of a force outside his control which is influencing him and which he calls "fairness" and "luck." Whenever he gets into trouble, he is likely to say, "That's not fair." Although he may still be a poor loser, he is improving because he realizes that losing along the way does not always mean that you will lose in the end. Winning is often a question of luck to him, not too much under his control. Sometimes he thinks he has "all the bad luck." One SEVEN expressed it this way: "Why do I always have the bad luck? Why do things so often happen to me? I might as well be dead." The bad luck in question was that it was time to go to bed.

SEVEN may be very conscientious about taking things. He may have no use for a stealer or a cheater. But when he is in the schoolroom, he seems to be in the midst of so many things

he wants and can add easily to his desk's store of belongings. He sometimes acquires new things by the more orthodox method of exchanging his possessions with friends. This is usually conducted on the basis of an "even swap" and does not involve real trading.

SEVEN has an increasing sense of possession and of the care of his possessions. He is better about putting things away, he helps his mother pick up his room, or he makes a mad scramble to put it in order at the last minute before it is time to go off to school. The seven-year-old is becoming very much interested in making collections—of such objects as postcards or box tops. The goal at this age seems to be mere quantity, with slight regard for formal arrangement or classification. He also likes to have a pencil case or schoolbag, and in this he carries a veritable collection of pencils, erasers, and rulers.

There is an increasing interest in money. He may be more anxious to earn money than to have an allowance. He is interested in buying specific things—a school magazine, a comic book, a candy bar. Sometimes he puts his money in the bank, which may be a means to saving part of the money for some specific object, such as a bicycle or a typewriter. He is especially enchanted by the appearance of money in the toe of his slipper or under his pillow when he has left a tooth there. The money seems to him to be the proof that fairies do exist.

There is often considerably less lying at seven than in the years that precede and follow. SEVEN, with his rather strong ethical sense, may be very much concerned about the wrongness of lying and cheating. He is particularly concerned if this lying and cheating is done by his friends.

10. PHILOSOPHIC OUTLOOK

DEATH AND DEITY

SEVEN is increasingly concerned about God's place in the world, even as he is concerned about his own place. If he is told that God lives in heaven, he wants to know where heaven is, how God got up there, does He use a ladder, does He live in a house. He wonders how God can see everything and be everywhere, and may answer his own questions in part by thinking that God must, for example, have a magic wand.

SEVEN may have lost his more personal feeling of relationship to God and a certain skepticism about God comes in. As one SEVEN explained, "I have never seen God." He may still wish to go to Sunday school, though many refuse, and he is either likely to refuse to say his prayers on occasion, or to perform antics as he is saying them.

His concept of death is rather similar to that held by the six-year-old, but it is more detailed and realistic, more thoughtful. He is not yet capable of accepting death as a biological process, but is still chiefly interested in it in terms of a specific human ex-

perience. He worries less about his mother's dying, and now is beginning to realize that he himself will die someday, though he usually denies that this could happen.

Chief interest in death is given to funerals and their appurtenances and to burial rites. Children talk about funerals, coffins, graves, being buried. They also take a matter-of-fact interest in visiting cemeteries, looking at tombstones, and noting verses, names, dates and designs on the tombstones. Fortunately most parents no longer exclude children from the funeral ceremonies of those near and dear to them.

Understanding of the various possible causes of death is increasing. Death is no longer entirely blamed on acts of violence or aggression. Disease, old-age, overeating are considered as other possible causes.

TIME AND SPACE

The sense of time is becoming more practical, detailed, and sequential at seven. Most SEVENs, especially boys, can tell time by the clock both by hour and minutes, and SEVEN may demand a wrist watch of his own. SEVEN is aware of the passage of time as one event follows another. He is interested in planning his day. He also is aware of the passage of time from month to month and may ask in September how much longer it is before Christmas. He may know the sequence of months and of seasons. He may even be able to think in terms of years. One seven-year-old who was thinking ahead to the time when she would be sixteen commented, "It's a long time to wait. Nine years. And even one year is a long time. Longer than you think."

SEVEN is especially interested in space as affording him his place in the world. Even God has his place in heaven. SEVEN is especially interested in the various objects in space—the earth's crust, stones, waterfalls, and fire. He is also interested in the use of these elements—oil from the earth, power from water, and heat from fire. He shows improved grasp of the points of the compass. He cannot yet distinguish right and left except in relation to his own body. He does not take an interest in the far places of the earth, but his interest in various parts of his community is definitely expanding.

CHAPTER 8

EIGHT YEARS OLD

Behavior Profile

Four, you will recall, was an expansive age. Five was focal; Six, dispersive; Seven, pensive. Eight again is expansive, but on a higher level of maturity. These adjectives are catchwords; but they serve to remind us of the accents of development and the spiraling trend of psychological growth. The eight-year-old is indeed an elaborated and an elaborating version of the four-year-old. But we can understand him or her best by comparison with the traits of seven-year-oldness.

EIGHT is more of a person by adult standards and in terms of adult-child relationships. One converses with an eight-year-old with lessening condescension. He is growing up and both he and you are aware of it. He is governed by a growing-up impulse which brings him into a positive outgoing contact with his environment, including his elders. He is less brooding and less inwardized than he was at seven. He is more centrifugal. He is also more rapid in his own responses, and more perceptive of the responses of others.

There are three traits that characterize the dynamics of his behavior: speediness, expansiveness, "evaluativeness." He is spreading out into the culture, testing and applying the basic feelings of meaning which were built up in the previous year. There is a new vein of active curiosity; a mounting energy and a certain robustness which is different from the idyllic sweetness of earlier childhood.

Even in physical aspect the eight-year-old begins to look more mature. Subtle changes in body proportions already foretell the more marked changes that will come wth pubescence. His eyes are now more ready to accommodate to both near and far distances.

EIGHT is in general healthier and less fatigable than SEVEN, more fond of rough-and-tumble play and boisterous games. His psycho-motor tempo is heightened. He tends to talk, to read and write, and to practice his piano lesson in high gear. He bolts his food, sitting on the corner of his napkin, ready also to bolt outdoors, without pulling up his socks or tucking in his shirt. He may add a little bravado to his slapdash demeanor to emphasize his masculine tough-ness.

Although we shall continue to use the pronoun "he" in a generic sense, the foregoing characterization applies more particularly to boys. At the age of eight we reach a maturity level where the two sexes are drawing somewhat apart. Boys on occasion like to herd up and to shout derision at a corresponding group of girls. The spon-taneous segregation is not consistent nor prolonged, but it is sympto-matic of the developmental forces that are steadily bringing boys and girls toward adolescence and adulthood.

Not without reason, therefore, does the eight-year-old listen closely when adults talk among themselves. He watches their facial expres-sions; he keeps looking and listening for cues and indicators in the social environment. He recognizes the gap between the world of the adult and his own world and adjusts accordingly. He is not naïvely docile and compliant. Somewhat consciously he shapes and establishes his own position in the circles at home and at school. He is a little sensitive about being told too directly what to do. He prefers a cue or hint. He expects and asks for praise: "This isn't good, is it?" But he does not want to be joked about his shortcom-ings. His sense of self is becoming a sense of status and he is con-stantly redefining his status relationships with comrades, siblings, and elders.

The relationships with mother and with teacher reflect the com-plexity of these interpersonal behavior patterns. Boys and girls alike tend to show strong admiration for their parents, expressing affection in action and words. Both sexes are susceptible to jealousy, particularly in their attachment to the mother. Mothers report that at the age of eight the child is voraciously demanding of maternal attention. "He [she] haunts me, always wanting to walk or to play or to plan with me." This relationship reflects a growth mechanism. Earlier the child mainly wanted his mother's physical presence. Now he wants a closer communion, a psychological interchange, whereby he penetrates deeper into adult life and at the same time achieves increasing detachment from parental and domestic dominations.

At school he has already attained a large measure of detachment. He is not as dependent upon the teacher as he formerly was. The teacher is, in fact, less important and less involved in his emotional life than she was when he was seven. She figures more as a beneficent potentate and regulator. To a considerable degree, he and his schoolmates are beginning to furnish some of their own discipline, and to control their own activity through mutual criticism and assignments of responsibility. He is definitely conscious of the school group as a group to which he belongs and to which he owes something. Teacher does not have to circulate so much to lend her personal support.

However, the eight-year-old is only at the beginning of well-coordinated and sustained group activity. His spontaneous club organizations are sketchy and short-lived. The concept of ballot and franchise is beyond him. He does not grasp complex rules. His ball games are far from orthodox, and often depend upon improvised spot rules. There is much bickering, dickering, and disputation; but the play goes on. Let the seven-year-old secede with his "I'm quitting!" The eight-year-olds generally muddle through, albeit noisily and not altogether without murmurous disgruntlement. Their wrangling is often highly educational.

EIGHT is building up an ethical sense, which consists of an intricate aggregate of attitudes. When he was only a year and a half old he had certain simple feelings of shame. Now he is capable of experiencing this feeling in numerous situations. He can say contritely,

"I will never do it again." He has a lively property sense, reinforced by his urge to make collections and his intense interest in money. He has a growing aversion to falsehood. When he tells tall tales they usually have a grain of truth. He has a germinal sense of justice, based on a regard for "rules" and precedents. This causes him to impute unfairness to others. Frequently he criticizes his sibs severely. He can admit his wrongdoing; but he softens the admission with strong alibiing, which itself denotes an evaluation of ethical issues. The alibiing is not so much to shift the blame as to indicate why under these particular circumstances he did not do what he himself would ordinarily have done! The very refinement of his explanations reveals the complexity of the anatomy of rectitude.

His feelings are easily hurt, particularly when his emotional relationships with his mother are involved. He is sensitive to criticism, whether actual or implied. He looks for the approval of her smile and readily misconstrues her silences and her comments. This is because he has a well-defined image of how he wants her to react in relation to him. He includes her response as well as his own in the total relationship. Tears well up on slight provocation. His mother's passing frown may precipitate a sun-shower cry. She often inadvertently treads on the tender toes of his expectations. But he is not given to prolonged moods of depression, and actively seeks reconciliation. On the playground among his equals he displays a more robust capacity to take and to give criticism. He is learning to lose. He likes to challenge himself. With his abounding energy he enjoys life despite the adult inhibitions he is trying to interpret and to master.

Inhibitions and limitations set by schoolmates and playmates he accepts with increasing reasonableness. He shows a significant readiness to join with three or four companions in setting up a lemonade booth or a roadside stand, with business conducted on a cash basis. There may be conflicts of managerial authority, but the enterprise is carried through. Likewise, eight-year-old boys and girls are able to plan to present with spontaneous flow fairly complete dramatic renderings, historical and otherwise.

This dramatic interest has a double significance. It evidences two of the cardinal traits of the eight-year-old: "evaluativeness" and expansiveness. His ego has a new degree of flexibility; by impersonation he can assume one role after another, *appraising* each role in terms of how he would or ought to feel under the required circumstances. A less mature mind merely mimics roles without this evaluative inflection. Because he is by nature expansive, the eight-year-old likes to put on public shows, and to embark on private imaginative expeditions; he is under a compulsion to *spread himself* into the culture.

As a hungry amoeba thrusts out one pseudopod after another, the hungry eight-year-old mind actively spreads into new territory. This expansive propensity reveals itself in the contents of a boy's pocket or a girl's pocketbook. It reveals itself in the collections and trophies stored in treasure box, drawer, desk, and schoolbag. A mail-order catalogue becomes a magic carpet. The eight-year-old delights in poring over its encyclopedic illustrations, choosing now this, now that item as an imagined extension of his personality. "If I had that, oh, boy, wouldn't I *do* this and that!" Thus he invades both reality and unreality. But each article has a published price; and he has a limiting money allowance. He can spend only so much, no more. This helps to organize his thinking. Everything in the world has a purchase price! If the eight-year-old also has an intense desire for unlimited money, it is not from pure avarice alone. EIGHT likes to barter. When he swaps equivalents he makes a fair trade. When he gets out of his field he can strike some very poor bargains. We have also heard of an eight-year-old girl who became something of a Lady Bountiful in sharing her mother's cosmetic supplies with neighborhood friends.

Boys and girls participate as equals in school and recreational activities. They share many interests; but they are also becoming vividly aware of distinctions that separate them. The expansive trends may lead to experimentations, homosexual and heterosexual. The divisive trends lead to withdrawal and to self-conscious unwillingness to touch each other even in ordinary play. The expansive trends also lead to new curiosities. There is an almost universal interest in babies. There are groping questionings about the origin of life, procreation, and marriage.

Girls explore these family problems through the medium of paper dolls (with sidelights from the comics). Like chessmen on a board, the paper dolls symbolize agents and situations. Father, mother, bride, bridegroom, daughter, son, baby, visitor, etc., are represented in paper effigies which can be freely manipulated with dramatic commentary that serves to organize ideas. Sometimes the dialogue suggests more insight than the eight-year-old mind can actually claim: "My husband would not be unfaithful to me!" said one dramatic eight-year-old girl as she was creating a paper-doll scene. "But he has been already!" replied her more jaded companion.

The eight-year-old has a certain inquisitiveness about all human relationships. But his interest in marital and sexual knowledge normally does not become excessive. Far from being erotic, it is only one manifestation of his many-sided expansiveness. He is extending himself, intellectually and emotionally, in myriad directions, even inquiring into the past history of mankind and into future fate. EIGHT is not a here-and-now age. He is seeking deeper orientations in time and space and piercing beneath surfaces. He wishes to know more about the insides of the earth and the insides of the human body. He asks about the geography of heaven. He is becoming interested in simple maps, Indian trails, and the routes of pioneering covered wagons. He is even interested in the Pilgrim fathers, in primitive man, and Eskimos. He is growing conscious of his own racial status and nationality. But he is by nature so cosmopolitan that this is a favorable time for strengthening sensible attitudes against racial prejudices.

He has an inherent sympathy of insight into other cultures, for he has the native honesty of childhood. This enables him to project his own life interests into the lives of children of foreign lands. He is delighted to hear that Chinese children are like him in so many ways, that they play hopscotch, ball, and hide-and-seek just as he does, that they go to school and read and write even though their word for cow has horns on it and the word for mouth looks like a mouth. He wants to know what the children of China eat for breakfast and what kind of shoes they wear. He hears that they don't have comics to read, but that they have butterfly and dragon kites to fly. He assimilates such information not as bare facts, but as human values. He evaluates as he expands his mental horizon. He is impressed with the realization that one-fifth of the world's children are Chinese.

At his best, the eight-year-old is so glad to be alive, so tolerant in his sympathies, so liberal in his zeal to explore the unfamiliar, that we may regard him as a rather promising preliminary version of adult mentality. He himself already feels more at home with adults. He traffics and talks with them more freely. He likes to confront them with riddles which they cannot answer. When he was more childish, he wanted the adult to give the right answer at once, and precipitately supplied it. Now he enjoys his unilateral advantage. He has begun to doubt the infallibility of his parents and adults in general. He sometimes tells a tall tale with an observant poker face in order to test the listener's capacity to detect the fraud. All this is symptomatic of an embryonic adultishness.

Intellectually he is becoming more expansive. He can express amazement and curiosity. His thinking is less animistic. He is growing aware of the impersonal forces of nature. He knows what makes a sailboat go. He can distinguish fundamental similarities and differences when comparing a baseball and an orange, an airplane and a kite, wood and glass. The origin and growth of plants from seeds begins to intrigue him. He takes a deepening interest in the life and life processes of animals. He is beginning to apprehend the momentous generality that all men are mortal. Yes, he too will die.

But this dawning recognition of death does not unduly depress him. He tends to be superlatively alive and even euphoric. His very speech inclines toward extravagance and hyperbole. And how he *loves* to talk! He comes home from school *bursting* with news. "You *never* saw anything like it!" "Oh, it was *awful*." "I *dread* it!" "He *simply couldn't*." "It was *big dough*." "And *of course* she *would*." "Oh, *Grandma*, you always say such *stupid* things!"

We do not condone any disrespect for grandma. But she probably recognizes the vitality of the growth tensions to which the exuberant eight-year-old is subject. He seems to get a psychological lift from his dramatic exaggerations. By dramatizing himself he stretches out toward maturity. He does not ever like to fail; yet he is very willing to be put on his mettle. When the assigned task proves difficult, he still remains in character. We have seen him clap his brow with histrionic despair: "Hey, what's the matter with me! Am I slipping, or something." "Oh, this has got me crazy. Pretty soon I'll die of this." "I *always* get the easy ones wrong." The adult may well smile at all this. For we see ourselves in the child, in those moments when the child naïvely strives to be ourselves.

The eight-year-old blossoms out in so many directions that it is impossible to sum up his diversity in a phrase. Individual differences are great, sex differences are becoming significant. Not all children are as articulate as those whom we have quoted in our characterization. Nevertheless, the articulate proclaim trends that are basic and typical for their zone of maturity. In subtle changes of physiognomy, in elongating arms and enlarging hands, the eight-year-old faintly foreshadows adolescence. He still has a rich measure of the engaging naïveté and abandon of childhood. But he is no longer a young child.

At five and a half he was already breaking from old moorings. At six he was in transition, capable of contacting a multitude of new facets in the widening world of nature and of man. But he could touch only the beginnings. He saw only in flashes, in opposites, he acted in impulses of avoidance and approach.

By seven, his adjustments and reactions were less piecemeal, his perceptions less sketchy. Patterns more configured began to form in his interior world. They took on a depth of meaning, imparted by memory, experience, and maturation.

At eight, the child begins to see conclusions, contexts, and implications, where before he had seen only in part. His universe becomes less disconnected. He himself is less submerged by the widening world. Above all, he begins to see himself more clearly as a person among persons, acting, participating, and enjoying.

This reorientation marks a tremendous advance in his life history as an individual in a democratic culture. He is now ready for the ninth year and the tenth, with all their rich opportunities for further expansion and evaluation—and consolidation.

Maturity Traits

The following maturity traits are **not** to be regarded as rigid norms, nor as models. They simply illustrate the kinds of behavior—desirable or otherwise— that tend to occur at this age. Every child has his own pattern of growth, and his own timetable. The behavior traits here outlined may be used to interpret his individuality and to consider the maturity level at which he is functioning.

1. MOTOR CHARACTERISTICS

BODILY ACTIVITY

The bodily movements of an eight-year-old are fluid and often graceful and poised. His walk is free. He is aware of his own posture and remembers to sit upright on occasion; he is ready to criticize others who do not. He likes to dramatize and express himself in a variety of postures and gestures. He does stunts and enjoys a game of follow the leader.

EIGHT is on the go. He runs, jumps, chases, wrestles. Hide-and-seek is a favorite pastime, but he is also ready for more organized sports such as soccer and baseball. When he is a part of the activity, he is now a good spectator as well as performer.

Courage and daring are characteristics of EIGHT. If he climbs trees, walks a plank, he steels himself. He may verbalize his fear and may need some encouragement, but he accomplishes the feat.

There is a new enjoyment in his skating, jump rope, and swimming, and he is more receptive to learning new techniques. But he is so spontaneous that he frequently goes his own way after he has tried your way.

EYES AND HANDS

There is an increase of speed and smoothness in fine motor performance. Approach and grasp are rapid, smooth, and even graceful; release is with sure abandon.

EIGHT can change his posture more adaptively. He bends forward, then straightens upright in sitting so that his head is at various distances from his working point. There is more symmetry than at seven and he frequently rests on both elbows or extends both arms out on the table. The variability of posture and overflow shows many of the patterns seen at six and seven, but there is more fluidity.

EIGHT can look before he acts, but he also likes to do things speedily, so the preliminary pause is not a long one. He can sustain regard longer with blinking, but if he wants to talk with someone he shifts his regard in their direction.

EIGHT is somewhat like SIX in his interest in doing many things. He has, however, some idea of a finished product. He does not have the sustaining power of NINE, and may leave many things uncompleted.

In writing, he spaces words and sentences, has a more uniform alignment and slant. His ideas may exceed his ability to write them. He is more aware of body proportions in his drawing of human figures, and particularly likes to draw them in action. He is beginning to draw in perspective, though this comes in more definitely at nine years.

Although EIGHT is an active doer, he is also becoming a good observer. He does not touch what he sees as often as formerly. He can be part of an activity and still watch another child's performance.

2. PERSONAL HYGIENE

EATING

Appetite. Even the poorest eaters begin to pick up a good appetite by eight; they eat steadily and with interest, though not with the speed usually characteristic of this age. EIGHT typically is ravenously hungry. His mother often says, "He eats like a hog; just shovels it in." After completing one round he starts all over again and asks for "everything." He may even request a third helping. Weight curves rise rapidly and the child may suffer teasing about being too fat. This ribbing may produce the desired effect with some control of the food intake, but often a little adult supervision may be needed. Certain foods such as potatoes and desserts can be restricted to one helping; and milk is still relished skimmed.

Refusals and Preferences. EIGHT still has food dislikes. He cannot understand, for instance, why "they had to spoil that beautiful ham with that awful cream sauce." His appraisal of food makes rather candid use of the sense of smell. The smell of peanut butter may repel him (especially if he is allergic to it), or it may produce a beatific suffusion of affectionate delight.

Now that he is eight he is venturously ready to taste almost anything; except that he still does not like fat on his meat and if he has seen a chicken killed, he may not be able to eat chicken for some time to come. He can even inhibit his verbal expressions of dislike, and he obviously musters courage with each spoonful of a disliked food. Parents should be careful not to force foods on a child, because he still may be allergic to some at this age. Nevertheless, the allergic child may most prefer the very foods to which he is allergic.

Self-Help. EIGHT is handling his implements fairly well, though some boys still hold fork and spoon pronately, which results in a pushing rather than a scooping manipulation. Fingers are requisitioned less than formerly. Many EIGHTs are now able to cut their meat with a knife, but a fair number do not attain this skill before nine or ten. Carving a carrot is still easier than cutting meat.

Table Behavior. There is a definite contrast between the table manners of the eight-year-old at home and away from home. When the parent becomes too discouraged with the eight-year-old at home, she needs only to take him out to a restaurant or to invite a friend in for dinner! The stimulus is often sufficient spur to reveal latent possibilities, although it does not follow that the child will easily maintain the higher level.

At home he eats best with the family group, for he does like company. It is well to have him sit next to his mother, where she can unobtrusively keep him in line with slight hints and protect him from father's reprimands.

Bolting and speed of eating are major problems. There is something reminiscent of the ways of Henry VIII when an eight-year-old "goes to it," loosening his or her belt to accommodate the increased intake, and not taking pains to repress a tendency to belch. More than one parent has reported this type of behavior!

Speedy eating makes for further complications; he finds himself ready for his dessert long before the rest of the family. If the outdoors does not call, and if dessert does not immediately follow his main course, he would be happy to leave the table and return when dessert is served. The child may enjoy watching TV during the interval.

Some EIGHTs who are not as speedy are apt to play with the silver, or to mess the food around on their plates. Though EIGHT may remain pretty well settled in his chair, he may suddenly bend his body agilely to take a look under the table. When siblings are present he may get into a dispute, but he may also be able to divert himself without interfering with the adult conversation.

EIGHT still needs to be reminded to wash his hands before a meal, and frequently responds with "All right, if you insist!" He uses a napkin, but still does not know what to do with it when he is not using it. He tries to hold it on his lap, but it frequently falls to the floor. Many eight-year-olds solve their difficulty by sitting on it; others prefer to leave it beside their plate.

SLEEP

Bedtime. There is a definite trend toward a later bedtime hour at eight years of age: 8 P.M., with lights out at eight-thirty or occasionally at nine. Although EIGHT may know how to tell time, he does not utilize this ability to direct himself to bed. He needs to be reminded, and is apt to put off going upstairs as long as possible. To overcome dawdling he needs to be more specifically motivated. If he knows he cannot watch one of his favorite television programs unless he is ready for bed, he sees to it that he is ready. His interest in the clock and his wish to stay up as late as possible make him susceptible to a time stipulation: e.g., if he is not in bed by 8 P.M. he has to go to bed the following night as much earlier as he was tardy. He does not relish this possibility, and musters speed, especially after he has once had to pay the penalty.

Generally he gets ready for bed faster when alone than when he is with his parent. He prefers to read, to be read to, or to listen to a bedside radio. When it is time for lights out, he still prefers to have his mother tuck him in and say good night. This may continue to be a favorable time for chatting and unburdening. But it can be the worst time for talking things over if the child is easily stirred up. This type of child fortunately does not as a rule bring up disturbing subjects on his own initiative, and he is also capable of leaving the room or turning off a television program that frightens him and may produce bad dreams.

As a rule, EIGHT goes to sleep soon after lights are out if he has not been put to bed too early. But there are some children who still regularly need a quieting-down time prior to sleep.

Night. Sleep is usually sound. EIGHT is often described as a "wonderful sleeper." Nightmares rarely disturb his sleep. Even toileting needs are infrequent. His total hours of sleep have dropped to an average of ten.

Morning. Most eight-year-olds awaken between 7 and 7:30 A.M. They are usually dressed by eight o'clock, without much need to be reminded.

ELIMINATION

Bowel. Very few EIGHTs still have a movement following the noon meal. They seem to divide into two groups, one of which functions after breakfast, the other after supper. An increasing number of the after-breakfast group are able to function during the morning at school if they have not already done so at home. EIGHT is susceptible to the same type of rapid onset of a bowel movement that the six-year-old experienced; this, however, is usually in response to a specific stimulus and is more under the child's control. A sudden shift in temperature caused by going in swimming may produce an immediate desire to have a bowel movement. This type of response may be prevented by reminding the child to go to the bathroom in advance.

Bladder. As at seven, the eight-year-old needs to be reminded to go to the bathroom, especially when he comes home from school or before he goes on a trip. Otherwise he handles his needs well by himself. In the midst of or preceding an unpleasant task either at home or at school, he may experience a genuine need of going to the bathroom. The task of drying dishes is certain to be interrupted by a trip to the bathroom, with a little dawdling thrown in.

BATH AND DRESSING

Bath. EIGHT may resist his bath, but he enjoys it very much after he gets under way, especially if it is prolonged into a half hour of play. When the parent suggests a bath, EIGHT may untruthfully reply, "I had a bath last night." An old-fashioned Saturday night bath would suit a number of boys, but for the most part EIGHT adjusts to at least three baths a week.

He has acquired more tolerance of warm water and enjoys seeing how hot he can stand his bath. He truly enjoys the feel of a warm bath. Although he may have bathed himself quite well at seven, he may now prefer to be bathed or at least to be read to as he bathes. He may even do spelling and oral arithmetic in the bath. He will take turns with his mother in washing himself. Boys often enjoy boat play, and may pretend that they are submarines. Now and then they may punctuate their play by drinking out of the faucet. At an earlier age they may have sipped the bath water or sucked the washcloth. EIGHT is not fussy about his face, neck, ears, or back because, as he says, "I can't see them." He can shampoo himself. He can cut his fingernails, but he still needs help with his dominant hand. Keeping fingernails cut is the best way to keep them clean.

A few eight-year-olds spontaneously wash their hands before meals, but most EIGHTs need and accept reminding with only a trace of resistance. They are apt to dash through washing and to wipe most of the dirt on the towel. Therefore a little added instruction of "Soap three times, and remember your wrists" may save some laundry.

Dressing and Care of Clothes. EIGHT dresses with fair ease and speed. He may need prodding and if he is asked why he is so slow he may answer, "I think I'm just lazy." A few would still like to be helped, but they usually accept the challenge "All children dress themselves by eight," and manage quite well, but may ask for help in the finishing touches. They still need to be tucked in, and to be reminded to button the rest of their buttons. Shoelaces are now easily handled and are kept tied; in fact, a new problem arises if a child wishes to remove his shoes without untying them—not too good for the shoes.

EIGHT is again interested in his clothes, and in buying new clothes. He may not only dictate his desires as to style and color, but also help to select his clothes at the store. However, he is usually open to suggestions. Boys often prefer green—pants, plain shirts, or jerseys—all toward the cooler end of the spectrum. Girls are shifting away from red and desire more blues and greens. Some girls refuse slacks or blue jeans and still others prefer them. Changing clothes is no longer a problem; in fact, many children prefer daily changes of everything. Most children can now choose their own clothes each morning, with or without help. If they are still given help, they are highly insulted if their clothes are laid out on the floor instead of on a chair. Some children are left too much on their own and may appear without any underwear and with two different-color socks. Some boys like to use their clothes to show their toughness and purposely keep their socks way down because they do not want to be called sissies.

Girls are more careful of their clothes than boys. Boys are genuinely hard on their clothes, and will now report tears and holes if these make their clothes uncomfortable. When they take them off, they may still drop them on the spot or strew them about, but an increasing number now throw their clothes at a chair or even place them neatly on a chair. EIGHT is able to put his dirty clothes in a hamper, at least if reminded. He is apt to lose detachable pieces of clothing. This is in part related to his greater awareness of how he feels and how much clothing he needs. Teaching him to tie his sweater arms around his waist if he is too warm to wear it may save him from future hunting and often from loss.

A handkerchief as well as a napkin is becoming more meaningful and acceptable. He is beginning to use a handkerchief when he coughs or sneezes as well as when he blows his nose.

HEALTH AND SOMATIC COMPLAINTS

EIGHT's improved school attendance record reflects his better health. If he has a cold, it usually lasts no more than two days. Even though his temperature may shoot up, he tends to recover quickly. This is the first time that some children are said to have an illness "lightly." Occasionally a child may complain of a sore throat and then nothing more materializes. Hay fever and asthma may return; a number of children have not had any attacks since six years of age. EIGHT has fewer communicable diseases than do younger children, and he recovers more rapidly.

The eight-year-old is in general much less fatigable than the seven-year-old. Although he may not fatigue easily, he may have a return of stomach upsets, as at six, if something bothers him. There are eye complaints, as at seven, and a reporting of headaches with overexcitement.

Accidents are a major cause of death at this age: chiefly accidents from automobiles, falls, and drowning. The eight-year-old, like the four-year-old, is out of bounds. He is out for action and is ready to try anything. He has lost the caution he had at seven. He misjudges himself as being better than he really is. EIGHT is not really ready to take his bicycle out on the highway. He is apt to get hit by a passing car. When he falls he tends to land on his feet and may therefore break his leg.

TENSIONAL OUTLETS

The tensional outlets that parents of eight-year-olds report are definitely minimal. The child's whole energy is positively directed toward his social and gross motor activities, which he now has under far better control, or can at least tackle. A few boys pull at their pants in the genital region or scratch their buttocks, especially under rising social tension. This type of behavior is embarrassing for the parent. Looser underwear would help; but often removal of the child from the too demanding social situation is indicated.

The most common tensional outlet at eight is a need to urinate when the child is taxed with something he does not like or is unequal to. Dish-wiping is almost sure to be interrupted after a bare beginning by a trip to the bathroom. A difficult school subject such as reading may produce a distended bladder in a very short time. This reaction is in the nature of "internal perspiration," emotionally induced. It is not an alibi, as shown by the copiousness of the ensuing secretion. Intense laughter may also produce an involuntary release of urine.

Thumb-sucking, especially in boys, has a slight exacerbation at eight. If the child did suck his thumb at six he was careful to hide it from the adult; and he definitely tried to give it up at seven with adult help. But at eight, he may be a bit blatant about it and confess no concern or shame. Sucking tends to occur in relation to reading, television, going to sleep, or waking, but not frequently enough to require specific measures. This is often the last age at which thumb-sucking persists or recurs. It is now time to institute some form of conditioning to help the child stop. The thought of some desired object such as a bike or watch may do the trick. Others need nightly application of some reminding liquid. This may take as long as three months of nightly application. Or children may devise their own means of prevention in a more imaginative way.

3. EMOTIONAL EXPRESSION

EIGHT is more "outside himself" than was SEVEN. He is less sensitive, less apt to withdraw. He is ready to tackle anything—in fact, he likes difficult things. He even shows courage in his attack. He thinks he knows more than he really does and often assumes a know-it-all tone of voice. He anticipates with great eagerness and may even expend his interest in anticipation alone. His interest is short-lived and he shifts rapidly from one thing to the next. This power to shift rapidly makes him more controllable, for he calms down quickly with a little help. It is even possible to control him with a look.

He is full of impatience, especially with himself, and wants to get things done at once. "I can't wait" is a repeated phrase of the eight-year-old, and this may refer to a party next week, next summer's vacation, or the time when he will be ready to go to college. He is constantly in and out of the house. He is so shifting, so little able to sustain his own interests, that he is ceaselessly making demands of his mother. She may say, "He haunts me." He frequently needs someone's complete attention. He needs help to hold better to a task, and he needs support through praise and encouragement. He dramatizes everything, including himself. Even his tall stories catch the drama of a situation, and may, let us hope, elicit the proper response from his audience. For dramatizing always needs an audience.

While demanding so much from his mother, he is at the same time more resistant to her. He may resist her request or suggesion with an outright "No"; but more frequently he gives some excuse: "I'm busy" or "Well, I'll do it later." He should be given his time, for he usually does obey requests if allowed to come around on his own steam.

He bursts into tears for many reasons, especially when he is tired. He may be disappointed because something he wanted very much has been denied him; he may have had his feelings hurt, may have been criticized, or may have done something he knew he should not have done. He cries less from inner confusion than he did earlier, but may cry over a sad dramatic episode in a movie or story.

Occasionally his temper may be aroused. He may become so furious with his mother that he may say with real venom, as his face clouds up, "You're a skunk!" He will rarely strike his mother, but may strike a sibling when he becomes angry after his mother has scolded him. It is wise to point out this mechanism of retaliation to him later, for he will understand it. Other EIGHTs may show their anger more humorously. They may tense up their faces in exasperation, project their lower jaws, and draw back and flex their arms at the elbow as they clench their fists. This same dramatic pose is sure to produce a laugh from other children, especially in a schoolroom situation. EIGHT also dramatizes things verbally: "This always happens to me"; "I never get a chance to do what I want"; "You have asked me eight million questions."

Because EIGHT demands one's complete attention, it is wise for the parent to have very definite planned relief from the child of this age. School plays a large part in this relief. New experiences at school are avidly absorbed and help to widen the scope of the eight-year-old. Competition with other children is spontaneous and helps to hold EIGHT to a task. Although he may be bossy in some situations, he can also, when under supervision, utilize this same urge to direct by helping a child who needs individual attention. His after-school-hours play still needs a certain amount of control. The introduction of an older child often provides a beneficial combination of stimulation and control.

EIGHT is not always the most delightful child to have around. He can be rude especially to his grandmother when she is a part of the household. It would be wise for grandmother to relate herself to the child only through some specific channel such as playing games with him or reading to him. The worst time for her to intervene is when his father and mother are handling him. Then any interference from grandmother is likely to bring forth some very uncomfortable rude remarks from him. He acts quite differently and is very companionable alone with his grandmother when he goes to visit her in her own home.

EIGHT likes to argue. He is most aware of others' mistakes, especially his mother's, but he is also self-critical and may say, "Am I dopey!" He is aware that others may trick him, and he is therefore on the lookout. He expresses his silliness in nonsense rhyming, and when he is tired he may actually go on a laughing jag.

4. FEARS AND DREAMS

FEARS

Though EIGHT has a number of unresolved fears left over from the time when he was seven, and a slight return to some of his six-year-old fears, he for the most part attacks life with courage and is out to conquer. He often will not even admit his fears to himself. But he may still be afraid of fighting, of failing, of others finding fault with him or not liking him, and he may refuse to listen to stories about snakes.

He may have a lingering fear of the dark, and is said to be leery or shy of the dark. Yet he may now demand that the hall light be turned off, and there is nothing that gives him greater joy than to be outdoors with his parent after dark. This is an excellent time to help him to orient himself to the dark, to the coming and going of his shadow according to the direction and strength of the light if there are street lights, and to night noises.

Although fire itself may not be feared, there may be a compulsive interest in everything about fire. Books about fire may be read and reread. Space fears at home are now under his control. He is no longer afraid of the attic; and though he may show no enthusiasm for the cellar, he can handle his fear if sent on a specific errand. Girls especially may fear strange men, though these very men may be trying to be kind and helpful. They may fear that the men are going to kill them or throw them into the water.

Some children instead of having outright fears may be great worriers. In the midst of an enjoyable experience such as a trip, they may worry about repeating the trip. They worry about catching a train or even about mother not being at home when they get there. These are the children who tend to cling to the past and have difficulty in coming into the future smoothly. This is their indirect method of taking the next step. Most eight-year-olds attack directly any feared experience and compulsively repeat it to resolve their fear. Or they perpetrate a fear by scaring a younger child. This may prove very unfortunate for the victim. Eight-year-olds may better frighten each other or a responsive adult. The telling of dramatic blood-and-thunder stories may be a useful method in some cases for satisfying this compulsive interest in the fearful.

DREAMS

EIGHT has apparently not much trouble with dreams. Boys may have a short return of their animal dreams about wolves, foxes, and snakes, or may have dreams of a fantastic nature not necessarily unpleasant. But on the whole, if EIGHT dreams, he dreams of daily happenings and pleasant things. Frightening dreams can usually be traced to some immediate influence from television, movies, or reading.

5. SELF AND SEX

SELF

EIGHT is emerging from his more serious, thoughtful, inward self of SEVEN. Indeed, this new outer self seems to want to be constantly contacting people, going places, and doing things. It is as if the child were trying out against the world the self which he was so busy consolidating at seven. He operates best as a self within the give-and-take of relationships with another person.

EIGHT is increasingly aware of himself as a person. He is becoming an individual, a member of a social world. The adult no longer talks down to him. Rather, he talks with him. The child is becoming enough aware of his "self" to use the term. One eight-year-old, looking at her reflection in the mirror, verbalized, "I don't look like myself." The adult likewise recognizes outward signs of this more distinctive self. One mother remarked of her eight-year-old son, "Even his gestures are like him."

The child now is more conscious of himself in the ways in which he differs from other people. He is conscious of wearing glasses, of being left-handed, of doing not as well as or better than the other members of his class. But as yet he is not greatly disturbed by these discrepancies.

EIGHT loses himself in his very real ability to dramatize. He readily becomes the characters in his books, TV programs, and movies. His ability improves with an audience response. His pretend cry may be so realistic as to deceive.

EIGHT may be torn between his desires to grow up and to remain as he is. Some EIGHTs "cannot wait" to grow up, though some boys hate the thought and frankly state this resistance. EIGHT's idea of growing up may be that he should be treated in a certain way. He has his idea of how he should be spoken to. He does not like the out-and-out reminders he needed at seven. Now he wants suggestive clues in words or looks that give him ideas of what is expected of him. If his mother forgets and returns to a less subtle handling, he may burst into tears because she "gave it away."

EIGHT also wants special privileges. He wants to stay up later or to go to grownup movies. EIGHT needs to have his new demands answered in part, even as he did at four, when on his insistence he was allowed to cross a safe street by himself, but accepted the adult's hand on a crowded thoroughfare.

EIGHT is interested in evaluating his own performance, his relationship with others. At seven he was intent on living up to his own standards. Now he wishes to live up to his notion of the standard that other people have for him. Since his performance is often only mediocre, and his notion of other people's standards extremely high, there is frequently a discrepancy here which leads to tears and temporary unhappiness. Or he may boast and alibi to make up for the difference between what he can do and what he would like to do.

SEX

Some EIGHTs, especially boys, are still searching for some of the facts about babies in relation to their starting, to the period of pregnancy, and to their birth. Many have already thought about these matters at seven. EIGHT may still not be concerned about the father's part in the starting of a baby. Girls are more likely to be knowing, more inquisitive, and more demanding of facts than are boys. Girls may think through far enough to question how the father put the seed into the mother's body. If a girl is not informed by her mother after she has asked such leading questions, she is apt to secure this information from her schoolmates. This second-hand information is often far from clear.

An eight-year-old will usually wait for an appropriate time to ask such questions, preferably at good-night chatting time when lights are out. It is often difficult for a mother to explain in a simple, unemotional way the facts of intercourse to her daughter. But she need not be frightened, for a daughter who is ready to learn can often ask just the right questions. The daughter readily accepts the fact that the father places the male sex organ into the mother's sex organ. This may start an avalanche of questions from the child as to when, where, and between whom the sex act can occur. All these questions can readily be answered according to the child's demands.

It is a wise mother who completes her talk with the suggestion that it is best for her daughter not to discuss these things with her schoolmates or even with her younger siblings. The mother will explain that younger children cannot understand and that other mothers want to explain such things to their own children at the proper time. When the daughter is older and comprehends these things better she may discuss them with her friends.

Boys are less apt to secure their knowledge of the sex act by word of mouth from their mothers. They are more apt to learn about it from observing the mating of animals. However, they may be slow to transfer their accidental knowledge about animals to the human field.

Girls are becoming more aware of sanitary napkins and ask what they are used for. They are no longer satisfied with the information that they are bandages. They may have heard of menstruation or bleeding and if left to their own thought devices they may relate this bleeding to the navel and umbilical cord. Some girls pass through this stage without sufficient awareness to ask questions. Therefore it is important for the parent to choose a suitable time at nine or ten years of age to impart this knowledge, before the child's own menstrual periods begin.

EIGHT is predominantly interested in the girl-boy relationship, even though he may hold it in the margins of his mind. A few boys may still be intending to marry their mothers, even though they may have received proposals from girls their own age. They may even be mulling over ideas about a chemical they are going to invent which will prevent their mother from growing old. The romantic note is creeping into the lives of eight-year-olds. Boys recognize a pretty girl, and girls chase handsome boys, much to the boys' delight. Though a boy may have two or three girls, he knows that he can marry only one of them. Some "engagements" last over from seven. EIGHT can now plan to live in his own new home after marriage. Some EIGHTs sit for hours over a mail-order catalogue choosing furniture for their far future homes. Boys of eight are often very secretive about their girl-friends, especially if they have a new one, because they do not like to be teased or kidded.

There may be some overt sex play between eight-year-old girls and older boys. A few girls at eight are unusually responsive to touch, and readily develop gooseflesh all over the body at the slightest stimulus. They enjoy rolling around on the floor with boys and become quite helpless from laughter. This is the kind of girl who is easily drawn into group sex play with older children; she needs more supervision than the usual eight-year-old. If such groups form, it is an indication that the children involved are not enjoying the more suitable satisfying activities characteristic of their age.

6. INTERPERSONAL RELATIONS

EIGHT may be "easy to get on with" at home, but his best behavior is usually when he is away from home. He is less absorbed in his own activities at home and more dependent upon his mother's suggestions of what to do next. He is not the helper he was at seven. What he does now is dependent upon his mood. He prefers to do jobs he thinks of by himself. He dislikes many of his old jobs, such as drying the dishes, setting the table, or picking up his room. He grumbles and grouches over them. There are, however, certain new and more responsible jobs that he attacks with real interest, and for which he readily accepts any supervision he needs. Boys like to burn trash and repair electric light fixtures and other simple household equipment. Both sexes like to cook and to bake real cakes and cookies.

EIGHT needs considerable help in reorganizing his life. He is likely to spread too much in his thoughts and his activities. Then life gets too much for him and he leaves things in a "mess." His intentions are good and he may return to reorder the mess, but he needs a helping hand. He is, however, aware of orderliness, remarks about a neat kitchen, and enjoys a clean house. He may be very careful of certain things that mean a lot to him—his funny books, guns, and his desk. But otherwise he needs considerable help and planning from his parent.

He likes a reward system of some kind. A point system may suffice, but points are frequently translated into money values. Parents often are disturbed by the "money-madness" of the eight-year-old boy, but they should not underestimate the motivation value of this interest. Here is an excellent opportunity to use a stimulus which at the same time serves to give a child some idea of money values. By his poor bargaining, EIGHT shows that he relates his values chiefly to his own personal needs and desires.

A bulletin board chart of his household tasks helps the eight-year-old to accept some of his responsibilities. Then, as he says, "You won't have to yell at me." Parents need to remember that this and other devices are means of helping the child to organize. The devices are not ends in themselves; therefore one device needs frequently to be supplanted by another.

At eight, the relationship between the mother and child is both complicated and subtle. What the mother does for the child is important, as it was earlier, but more important is what she thinks and feels about him. He is extremely demanding of her— may dog her every footstep throughout the day. He demands not only her time, but her complete attention. He may insist on playing endless games of cards. Even so, her complete attention may not be enough to establish a smooth relationship. Thus he may cry because she didn't do something he thought she might be going to do, such as praise him. EIGHT makes various exactions of his mother: how she should react, what she should do, what she should say. Even an extremely perceptive mother who tries to meet these exactions may find the task a hard one. It is the rare eight-year-old who can promptly forgive his mother when she makes a mistake that directly affects him.

Some EIGHTs who are not too bound up with their mother are capable of showing real devotion and may often tell her how wonderful she is. Physical affection also is expressed. The mother usually continues to be the best-loved parent, although the father is coming in for an increasing share of affection, if he makes a good, adaptive response to the child. Grand-parents are usually still great favorites, though some EIGHTs may now be a little less loving and a bit more critical than when they were younger.

EIGHT does fairly well with younger siblings, but he has rather lost his big-brother attitude. He too readily lowers to the siblings' level of response, gets out of hand, may tease and end by fighting. When EIGHT is responsible in caring for a younger sibling, he is likely to be too strict. He does best when he is helped to a good start, and is warned ahead of time how he is to act. Then he likes to hear later that he has done well, and that he has now been promoted to privileges that a younger sibling does not have. Too often an older sibling is held down to the level of a younger. Simple priv-ileges, such as a later bedtime hour even though he starts to bed with a younger sibling, give him a due sense of prestige and status. He does not have to flaunt these special privileges before his younger sibling. He even enjoys holding them a secret between himself and his parent. If the adjust-ment between two siblings is poor, planned separation is very helpful. Some EIGHTs protect themselves by the simple expedient of shutting a door.

EIGHT is the age when "best" friends begin to play a part in the life of the child. School becomes impor-tant because EIGHT's friends are there. Usually these friends are of the same sex. The relationship between friends may be very close and demanding, something like the mother-child rela-tion, and there is between friends much arguing, disputing, "getting mad" at each other. The quality of the relationship between two children, not simply what they do together, is becoming important in the eyes of the eight-year-old.

Strong friendships are more likely to occur between two children of the same age, but a fair number of EIGHTs play better with older chil-dren. EIGHT is apt to admire an older child of eleven or twelve, and this older child will often in turn protect his admirer from being bullied or mistreated. Some EIGHTs who have previously had real difficulty in ap-proaching children may now make crude approaches in their attempt to attract another child.

The trend is toward longer periods of relatively peaceful play with others, with only minor verbal disagreements, than formerly. However, any unsuper-vised play sesssion often ends in dis-agreement or in the disgruntled de-parture of at least one participant. Nevertheless, EIGHT figures strongly in neighborhood group play, including baseball and hut play. Some EIGHTs are repeatedly picked on by the rest of the group, but others break loose from the group on their own initiative.

EIGHT marks the beginning of a definite change as to preferred sex of playmates. Boys and girls are now beginning to segregate in play. Girls as a rule are the first to separate off from the boys, and to be conscious of this separation, but theirs is usually a mere quiet drawing away. Boys, when they become conscious of a need for separation, are often very rough and boisterous about excluding girls.

EIGHT is beginning to acquire "company manners." He is usually better away from home, and is eager for both visiting and sightseeing, especially in another city. He meets new people with a fair amount of ease and will even talk to strangers in a restaurant. He telephones well and is able to write down simple messages.

7. PLAY AND PASTIMES

GENERAL INTERESTS

EIGHT abhors playing alone. Whatever he does he wants to do either with an adult or with a child, and he demands not only the presence of another person, but also that other person's complete attention and participation. Action is the key characteristic of his play. He has a new sense of the whole, a sense of interplay, of active relationship, and of practical use. His drawings are now full of action. He puts his tools to helpful household uses by fastening hooks, nailing down train tracks, or screwing in loose doorknobs. Girls mix ingredients to make cookies and cakes. Boys mix the contents of their chemistry sets to produce new colors and smells and finally to make what they call "the magic potion."

EIGHT wants to set up his telegraph kit between two rooms or two houses so that he can actually communicate with another person. He may even wish to communicate with the President of the United States about his blueprint book, since he believes the government might be interested in some of his projected contraptions.

EIGHT likes to dramatize. He dramatizes accidents, fights, and car chases with his toys. He impersonates characters in the movies he has seen or in the books he has read. He wants to perform magic tricks. Girls' dramatizing is more verbal and sedentary than that of boys. Girls are likely to arrange performances and to put on "shows." Paper dolls furnish a vehicle for this dramatic urge. They also serve as an outlet for EIGHT's powerful urge to collect. Paper dolls and their dresses can be collected in quantities. Moreover, EIGHT likes to classify, to arrange, and to organize. A collection of varied dolls with their numerous paper appurtenances offers a channel for such organizing activity.

Boys also succumb to a "collecting craze"—in fact, with many it reaches its peak at this age. Children are not only interested in quantity when they collect their stamps or coins; they are becoming interested in quality and in rudimentary classification.

Gross motor activity is characteristic of EIGHT's group play. He needs some restraint, since he readily goes out of bounds. When a group of EIGHTs are left to their own devices, they often revert to abandoned "animal spirits"—wild running, jumping, chasing, wrestling, and tree-climbing. They are, however, capable of organizing simple combat games or hide-and-seek. EIGHT responds well to some supervised control. Both boys and girls enjoy formal baseball and especially soccer or kick ball.

EIGHT spontaneously thinks up reasons for organizing his own clubs, such as the Bottle Collecting Club, the Gadget Club, or the Library Club. These represent a new interest, but are usually loosely organized and very short-lived. Hut play, which may have begun at an earlier age, persists longer and often has the dramatic addition of a secret password.

EIGHT enjoys the different sports in season. He rows in the summer and he skis and skates in the winter. There is nothing more typical of springtime (or of eight-year-oldness) than a group of EIGHTs wrangling over marbles. They seem to enjoy the back-and-forth tug of wrangling and do not wish any adult interference.

Interest in table games—especially cards, parcheesi, checkers, dominoes—reaches an almost passionate height. EIGHT scorns some of the simple earlier games, and enjoys the financial transactions in Monopoly. He is very ingenious in making up his own rules and may even invent new games. Although some EIGHTs can lose at play with fair grace, this is not always true; a good deal of bickering and some accusations of cheating occur.

Kites, marbles, and tops all appear in season, with airplanes becoming a strong rival to kites. Boys make airplane models, draw airplanes, learn to identify different kinds of planes, or indulge in imaginative airplane play. Other objects than airplanes are manufactured as they work at their workbenches. Interest in Erector sets, Legos, and mechanical toys continues strong. Electric trains, chemistry sets, small movie projectors with real films are enjoyed by certain boys of mechanical bent.

READING

Those EIGHTs who are just beginning to read well now enjoy reading spontaneously. Though EIGHT may read well, he may not spend as much time at reading by himself as he did at seven and he again likes very much to be read to. He is beginning to enjoy hearing the classics of childhood. A modern favorite relates the wonderful, magical, and absurd adventures of Mary Poppins. EIGHT is also interested in books of travel, geography, and faraway times and places.

Comic books are still his favorites. This interest reaches a peak at eight and nine years. EIGHT buys, collects, barters, borrows, and hoards his comics. He is more likely to borrow than to barter, since he does not want to part with his own. Though he still likes the animal and slapstick comics, he is branching out into the blood-and-thunder type.

EIGHT likes to look at pictorial magazines. He can pore for hours over catalogues. He plans to send for things, but is more likely to carry this through at nine. Nothing gives him more delight than to receive mail of his own, printed so that he can read it by himself.

MUSIC, TELEVISION, AND MOVIES

The initial seven-year-old flare of interest in music lessons may die out unless someone plays with the child or sits with him while he plays. He enjoys playing duets. Practicing cannot be forced and often it is wise to interrupt lessons for a while until boy or girl is ready to return to them at a later date (nine or ten years).

Television has now become such an important part of his life that he will neglect play for it. This is the one activity he enjoys alone, but he does like to have an adult watch with him and he becomes adept in choosing programs he feels the adult would approve of. He is beginning to choose his own programs more carefully and will even refer to the television page in the newspaper. He listens to the same programs each day or week, and usually knows at what time and on what station his favorite programs occur. He may still cling to cartoons and special children's programs, but he is branching out into domestic comedies and quiz programs, most dislike news.

Some go to the movies, though less than in earlier times. Most like animal movies or mysteries; they do not like romantic movies.

8. SCHOOL LIFE

EIGHT enjoys school and may even dislike staying at home, particularly if it means that he will miss a special event. Even though he may not be doing too well in his work, even though he may not be getting along too well with his teacher, his attitude tends to be one of response toward, of attack, rather than of withdrawal. He fatigues less easily than he did and is more ready to remain for both morning and afternoon sessions. His attendance record is often remarkably good and even when he is out with a cold, his absence is of short duration. When he is absent even for a day he is thinking of the group and what it is doing. He asks to have his school work sent home to him so that he can keep up with the group.

Some EIGHTs, especially boys, may still have difficulty in getting ready for school and in reaching it on time. It is often difficult to motivate them at home, since they are no longer fearful of being late. But they may be motivated by some new school responsibility which challenges them. The eight-year-old's getting to school on time is the responsibility not only of the home, but also of the school. In many communities, buses have solved this problem in an all-or-none way. Either you catch the bus or you don't.

There is now much more interplay between home and school. EIGHT brings to school things that relate to his school projects or to his personal experiences. He also likes to take his products home, but is now willing to leave them with his teacher for a few days' display. Although he remembers to take them home, he may lose them in transit.

Many mothers report that for the first time their child informs them about school activities. Previously they were told more about other children's misconduct or their own child's difficulties. Finally, life in the schoolroom is reported at home by the eight-year-old. The mother enjoys being better informed. She now feels an easier relationship with the school, and is apt to give lavish compliments to the third-grade teacher.

Actually, the teacher is not as important in EIGHT's adjustment as his teacher was in the earlier grades. She may even be taken more or less for granted. EIGHT is most interested in his school group and would like his teacher to become a part of that group. He joyously accepts her, especially when he catches her in some error and when she in turn accepts the criticism and tosses it off humorously. Learning through others' mistakes is often the surest, most rapid way for the eight-year-old.

EIGHTs enter the schoolroom with enthusiasm (unless, of course, it is one of those bad days!) They busy themselves by writing on the blackboard, or by inspecting a globe; they may dawdle in the cloakroom, but are gradually brought together. They smile, touch, hit out at each other as they pass by.

In a classroom situation they are eager to talk and want to answer every question. They may learn self-inhibition long enough for one child to answer, but if he is wrong or too slow they are sure to respond for him. When several become verbal and

noisy the teacher can control them by her own silence. They do, however, enjoy taking turns and are insistent that each one has his turn. They comment on another's response or lack of response. "Oh, you know that"; "That's easy"; "You're too slow, Mary."

Transitions are fairly smooth for EIGHT since he likes to change from one thing to another, but there is some talking and dawdling, and a little extra time needs to be allowed for him to settle down.

EIGHT can shift his eyes more easily from blackboard to desk. He can copy from the board and he also likes to write on it while his classmates attend to his performance. At his desk he sits facing forward with head sometimes at arm's distance from the paper and sometimes quite close; he shifts his positions frequently. He works more independently than at seven and does not need the teacher nearby. He raises his arm with an upward thrust to call the teacher's attention, but he can wait at least briefly for her to come to him. The impatient EIGHT is eager to be given directions and though he seemingly understands them, he may need to have them repeated. Often after he has worked for a while, he stops to speak to his neighbor, telling him what to do, asking what page he is on, etc., but he can return to his own work for a while longer. If his interruptions become excessive, he responds well to a separation to the margin of the group to do his work. It is unfortunate when this need for separation is treated as a means of shaming the child by having him sit in the hall outside his classroom, especially when he improves so nicely after a shift to the margin of the group.

He talks about his own performance and tells another child, "I got three wrong"; "My drawing isn't good. This isn't good, is it?" He may discuss who is best in art. If the class is divided into groups, he is aware of the grouping and may dislike being placed in a lower group. He likes praise and seeks it.

EIGHT enjoys reading. He can tackle new words through context or by phonetics. He is more skillful and only occasionally makes errors similar to those of SIX or SEVEN. He now omits unimportant words, reverses word order in a phrase, but usually maintains the meaning. He has a more uniform speed and can stop and talk about the story and pick it up again. Many now read well enough to prefer silent reading. Exciting and humorous stories are favored and children may express scorn of a story they consider too young for them.

Writing is now less laborious and there is more uniformity in slant and alignment as well as in spacing of words and sentences. There may be an occasional reversal or a substitution of a capital for a small letter. Most are not really ready for manuscript writing till they are nine. Even though careless in writing, EIGHT likes to write neatly. "I'm doing my best writing"; "Is this neat?" Doodling or drawing in notebooks or on scrap paper is a favorite practice. Despite EIGHT's facility, he may not be able to write out a story to full length; he may then wish an opportunity to dictate the unfinished portion, or to continue it later.

EIGHT likes variety. He likes oral or written arithmetic; likes to use the blackboard and to work in a workbook. Most are partial to the new tables they are learning. They like to shift from one process to another. This shifting may even be automatic. In the midst of a multiplication example the child may shift to addition or to subtraction, and something may tell him his mind is playing tricks on him. He likes to take his workbook home to catch up, and is apt to go beyond his assignment. One day he may say he doesn't like arithmetic and the next say it is easy.

EIGHTs are especially oriented to their own group, room, and teacher. They like to have their teacher a part of their activities, to have her play games with them, read with them, and sit with them at table. They like the total group inclusion of a spelling bee. They like to join other grades at an assembly, but on the whole mix less with other ages than they will next year.

There is more grouping at play. All are able to join in a single group activity. Boys and girls separate on occasion; the girls for jump rope and the boys for ball play. They can enjoy taking turns—after some struggle to secure a place—and they watch and comment on each other's performance.

9. ETHICAL SENSE

EIGHT's behavior harks back to that of his six-year-old self, even though he is now less rigid and is not as likely to "explode." When he is asked to do something, he delays his response. He often says, "In a minute" or "I'll do it later," or he may ask, "Why do I have to do it now?" He is likely to argue with his mother or to give excuses: "I'm too tired"; "I'm busy reading"; or "I had a bath last night" (when it was actually three nights ago). He may generalize on a point of view and declare, "But people think differently." Some EIGHTs, as at seven, do not hear what is asked of them because they are so engrossed in what they are doing. EIGHT may look at you as though listening, but after you have finished speaking he queries, "What did you say?" A willing, immediately responding EIGHT is somewhat exceptional. Even when he does respond it may be unwillingly as he says, "All right, if you insist," and often grouches and grumbles along the way.

EIGHT demands that the adult treat him more like a grownup. He wants his instructions to be worded just right, he likes to work from clues, or from secret codes. A look will often be enough to bring him back into line. If he is criticized he may burst into tears. But, as at six, he thrives on praise and likes to be reminded of his improvement. Physical punishment is rarely resorted to with the eight-year-old. Small deprivations, such as being denied a TV program or comic book, or being made to go to bed early, produce the desired effect with most EIGHTs. A few are unimpressed and may answer back, "I didn't want to watch that program anyway." If EIGHT is allowed to determine his own punishment he is often too harsh on himself and may need help to soften his punishment.

EIGHT is more capable at managing his thoughts and of thinking things through. He is fairly rapid about making up his mind about the bigger things of life, although some EIGHTs prefer to have their mothers make up their minds for them. It is usually the little things that set EIGHT into vacillation and deliberation. Maybe the decision involves a choice of cereal, a second helping, a glass of milk, or a valentine. EIGHT does not shift from his decision as readily as he did at seven.

EIGHT wants to be good. He is now more aware of the two opposing forces of good and bad. He feels their operation when he is acting in one way or the other. He may be so concerned about them as absolutes that the parent may need to help him to think relatively in order to explain that "goodness" may be affected by intelligence or age; that one makes allowance for the "badness" of a younger child. EIGHT wants his goodness to be appreciated. He wants to please, to be thought well of, and to get a good report.

Although EIGHT is becoming more responsible for his acts and is willing to take the consequences, his first and usual impulse may be to blame others. He may be laughed out of his blaming, but he is apt to hold to the point that someone else started the trouble and this may have some truth in it. He is more likely to blame others when he is tired or upset. EIGHT is proficent at alibiing. He especially alibis about being late. He says, "I didn't know the time" or "My friends wouldn't let me go." His time sense is often more scrupulous at seven than at eight. Therefore he often needs a little more supervision at eight. Some EIGHTs cannot tolerate making the slightest error and cover up any exposure by saying, "Oh, I knew it all the time. I was just wondering how bright you were!"

The same child who earlier dictated to her mother her list of "Things to Do and Things Not to Do," and "Thinking About Myself and Thinking About Others," at eight asked her mother to write down things that were "Right and Wrong." It is interesting to note that this is a single-column list. Right and Wrong are to some extent brought together into a single standard of conduct and are no longer separated in bipolar opposition. The list follows:

Right and Wrong

1. It's not my fault that they call me a "bad sport" when I want to play a different game after I've played one for a long time. I can't help it if there aren't enough people to start another game. Finally I get up enough strength to play some more. And finally they change to my game.

2. Question of getting to school on time:
   How can I tell the exact time I've got to get up and the exact time to eat breakfast so I can get to school on time? I can't help it if I'm late. It's not my fault. Probably all my guesses about time are all wrong.

3. When some of the people start up a fight, it's not my fault if I want to try and stop the fight even though Miss D. tells us to keep away from fights because the other teachers would think we'd started it. Even if we try to explain to the teachers they think we did start the fight and were just trying to get away from being punished.

4. Something hard comes up and I'm trying to do it.
   I don't think it's fair for other people to come along and call me a "sissy" because I can't do it very well. (Some of these things haven't happened yet but they might.)

5. In the coatroom, even though you're not supposed to talk, I can't help it sometimes because other people ask me questions and tempt me to answer them. Do you blame me?

6. Running in the halls going out to recess:
   I can't help running in the halls going out to recess because I'm

so eager to go out to shout and play.

7. I think I ought to have a little more freedom, more freedom about deciding things—like getting up early in the morning. (I used to plan to, then I'd be too tired when I woke up in the morning.)

8. I think I should have rewards for being good, like candy and books I like very much. But I won't always have to be rewarded. Maybe when I'm about nine and a half or ten I don't think I'll have to be rewarded for being good. Then I'll just be good naturally.

9. If it's a sensible reason and something I can do quite easily and something I feel I can do and want to do, and don't have to force myself to do, then I should obey.

10. I think I should do something more about getting up in the morning. I ought to be able to choose sensible clothes. And if I don't, it serves me right to have to take them off unless they are sensible clothes and the weather is right for them.

11. You shouldn't just force me to do things. I will do them if they are sensible.

12. On the playground it's not my fault if I want to slide on a wonderful sliding place in the back of the school and I'd forgotten at that minute that I wasn't supposed to play in the back .(Oh, it was neat ice, and there was a little bump at the end!)

EIGHT needs considerable help in the care of his possessions. His awareness of order exceeds his ability to keep things in order. This awareness should make the adult feel that there will be better days ahead when the child will become more responsible. EIGHT would happily relinquish the care of his room to his mother.

The one sure motivation to get EIGHT to do things is that of money. His mother says, "He just loves money." He likes to add to his store to get the sum up to "big dough," like one dollar. EIGHT may spend his entire allowance (averaging fifty cents) or his earnings on comic books, but some like to save up for bigger purchases. They pore over catalogues, haunt store windows, and may indulge in a good deal of imaginary spending.

Money may also serve as a collecting medium, for EIGHT has a tremendous urge to acquire. He collects a variety of things such as stamps, postcards, souvenirs, and odds and ends. He hoards, arranges, and gloats over his accumulated belongings, but his interest in acquiring possessions is usually considerably ahead of his interest in taking good care of them.

EIGHT is not prone to take the property of others. However, with his awareness of money and what it can buy, he may be found taking some of the household supply of money. This is usually considered by parents as a far greater offense than taking pencils and erasers at an earlier age. But the child is in each case expressing a need characteristic of his age. Parents should be aware of these needs and should see that they are provided for in suitable ways. Many EIGHTs are quite generous and may use the very money they have taken to treat their friends.

EIGHT is becoming more truthful. He may tell a tall story to impress his audience. The truth he tells may even be to his own detriment, but he does not usually make damaging revelations to anyone but his mother. It is very important to him to have such a relationship of confidence that he feels free to tell her of his misdeeds, failures, or omissions.

10. PHILOSOPHIC OUTLOOK

DEATH AND DEITY

There is often a resurgence of an active interest in religion at eight years of age. There is now new penetration of thought into the concept of deity or death. What EIGHT has worked out in his own mind along with whatever he has been taught to believe at six and seven, he now takes for granted and accepts. He may like to go to Sunday school, may want to be taught passages and psalms from the Bible. He likes to memorize. He may spontaneously read the Bible at home and is very much interested in Bible stories. If he stopped saying his prayers at seven, he may now want to return to

them. He wants his mother to say them with him, and he would often prefer to sing them. EIGHT becomes an active participant without thinking too much about what it all means.

His chief religious interest at this age seems to be in the matter of heaven. This is not so much a concern about God in heaven as it was earlier. Now God's connection with heaven appears to be taken for granted. Heaven is a place where you go after you die.

Death is something he takes pretty much for granted unless, of course, there is a death of someone who is very close to him. Most EIGHTs have accepted unemotionally the fact that all people, even they themselves, will one day die. The earlier interest in coffins, burial, and other appurtenances of death continues, but it is much less intense.

TIME AND SPACE

EIGHT is becoming more responsible in regard to time. His increased speed in action makes him less vulnerable to the demands of time. He can now be expected to arrive at school promptly. Some EIGHTs do not tell time as well as they did at seven. They may read time in reverse so that nine-twenty may be read as twenty minutes to ten. Besides telling time less well, EIGHT is often careless with his wrist watch. It may be wise for EIGHT to put his watch away for a while, if he has one.

Though he may tell time less well,

he is extremely aware of punctuality, that is, of what time he should be here or there. He keeps himself posted by asking others what time it is. If he knows that he is going to arrive home late, he may be responsible enough to telephone.

He is most efficient in telling time when he wishes to tune in on his favorite TV program. He is much less efficient in telling time for bed or school and still needs a certain amount of reminding.

EIGHT is interested in time far past, in ancient times. He likes to hear and to read about things that happened when his own country was new. But his chronology is rudimentary. He may not be able to say certainly whether or not George Washington is mentioned in the Bible.

Personal space is expanding for the eight-year-old. He can now return home by bus from a more distant point and may also travel on a bus by himself on a familiar or prearranged route if he is met. He takes in such a wide walking area within his own neighborhood that it may be difficult to locate him. He is coming to know his own neighborhood so well that he becomes interested in new routes, especially in shortcuts, and may become lost in the process.

He is eager to take trips to new cities, to visit museums, zoos, and places of interest. His spatial world is expanding even further through his interest in geography. He draws maps with keen interest.

EIGHT usually has a fairly clear notion of points of the compass and of different parts of the community in relation to each other. He can now distinguish right and left on others as well as on himself.

CHAPTER 9

NINE YEARS OLD

Behavior Profile

The nine-year-old is no longer a mere child; nor is he yet a youth. Nine is an intermediate age, in the middle zone that lies between kindergarten and junior high school. Significant reorientations take place during this intermediate period. The behavior trends of the eighth year come to clearer issue; the child gets a better hold upon himself; he acquires new forms of self-dependence which greatly modify his relations to his family, to school and classmates, and to the culture in general. The changes come so subtly that parents and teachers often are not sufficiently aware of their import. But they are psychological transformations so important both for the child and for society that they deserve more recognition.

Self-motivation is the cardinal characteristic of the nine-year-old. It is the key to understanding him on his progress toward maturity. He has a growing capacity to put his mind to things, on his own initiative or on only slight cues from the environment. This typically gives him a preoccupied businesslike air, both at home and at school. Indeed, he is so busy that he seems to lack time for routine tasks and he does not relish interruptions. On the other hand, he can interrupt himself. For example, if he is engaged at a paper task he can interrupt it and take a trip to the pencil sharpener and return to his work without loss of momentum and without a reminder. He also is able to fill idle moments with useful activity. He can work two or three hours at a stretch with his Erector set or Legos. He likes to tax his skill, to put *himself* on his own mettle.

In comparison, the eight-year-old is much more dependent on environmental support—on the pressure of the group and the stimulation of the adult. Eight expends a quantum of attention on a difficult task, but soon exhausts his energy. Nine is able to summon reserves of energy and renews his attack for repeated trials. This is due to the greater maturity of his whole behavior equipment. No wonder that he is such an excellent pupil, ready to tackle anything that lies reasonably within his powers. Nine is an optimal age for the perfecting of proficiency in the tool subjects, in the fundamental operations of arithmetic, and in other skills. The nine-year-old is so interested in perfecting skills that he likes to do the same thing over and over again, whether it be throwing darts or dividing by one digit.

Confronted with an unfamiliar task (for example, tracing a maze with a pencil), he may say, "Hm!" with a mature inflection and reflectiveness that remind us that he is no longer a child in his intellectual attitudes. He adds, characteristically, "Let me think about it. I always have to think first." He likes to plan in advance and to see ahead. If a task is complicated he asks to have the successive steps explained to him. Then, when he attacks the problem without immediate success, he reveals a power of self-appraisal. Perhaps he says somewhat self-deprecatingly, "I'm not so hot!" "Gee, I'm just trying to find out what's wrong here." "Sort of sloppy, isn't it?"

Presently we shall note that this power of appraisal is by no means limited to himself, but extends to other persons. He shows considerable ability in social criticism as well as self-criticism. Add to this a sizable capacity of self-motivation, and one can understand why Nine so often makes a good, solid, businesslike impression!

This does not mean that he is a finished product. Although solid at the core, he has a growing margin which is neither fixed nor stable. New emotional patterns are in the making. This is shown in his complainingness, and in variability of mood—now timid, now bold; now cheerful, now grumpy. Shyness may be associated with a new fondness for his teacher. He may "hate" to stand before the class to recite a poem. Sometimes he is said to be "in a daze," "in a fog," "in the clouds." He may need a reminder or he may excuse himself with a remark: "Oh, that's my poor memory." Such benign symptoms of absent-mindedness are probably due to new mental events occurring at his growth margins.

When we say that he is businesslike we do not wish to imply that he is financially minded. He is not as money mad as EIGHT. Frequently he is only feebly motivated by coin and by allowances. He has so many better reasons for being busy. He is fond of making inventories and check lists. He likes to classify and identify, to order his information. He is in character as a baseball fan, familiar with a surprising array of facts and figures. He has a factual interest in seriations and categories—the insignia and ranks of army and navy officers, the distinctions between types of automobile or airplane, the flags of the United Nations, etc. If he has a passion for comics—and he often does—it is their informational content that mainly appeals. He has an eye and an ear for significant details and tidbits that come via radio and television, movies, pictorial magazines, and adult conversations.

We emphasize these intellectual traits of the nine-year-old because they color and direct the manifold patterns of his personal-social behavior. He shows a new discriminativeness in his parent-child and in his pupil-teacher relationships, new refinements in his emotions and attitudes. The deepening of his emotional life (for he is less shallow than he was at age eight) is, of course, due to underlying growth changes in his physiology. Fortunately, however, feeling and insight are in better balance than they were at five and a half and six years. Accordingly, your well-constituted nine-year-old tends to be a relatively well-organized young person, who is taking a measure of himself and who can take a measure of you. He neither likes nor needs to be patronized. Usually he is not overaggressive. And his estimates of his parents and of his teachers can be penetrating and accurate, as well as candid.

In view of his immaturity, he shows an impressive sense of fairness and even reasonableness in his estimates and expectations. He has overcome his more infantile alibiing. He can accept blame; and if several persons—children or adults—are involved in a difficulty, he wants all blame apportioned *fairly*. He lays stress on who *started* the difficulty. He has a keen emotional and intellectual interest in punishments, privileges, rules, and procedures, particularly at school and in his club life. He adjudges the fairness of discipline both by self and group standards. He is very receptive to elementary ideas of justice. The culture can sow seeds of prejudice, but he responds readily to injunctions against racial discrimination.

Naturally, there are innate differences in the depth and patterns of the ethical sense; but under favorable cultural conditions, the nine-year-old is essentially truthful and honest. He can say to himself, "I'll have to be honest," and he will go back to a store to return excess change, as well as to claim short change. Not having as yet reached perfection, he may think it is worse to lie to one's father than to someone else. But all in all, he is dependable and responsible. He likes to be trusted. He likes a little freedom, when he can be "on the town" for an hour or two, without overinquisitive parental supervision. His complainingness need not be taken too seriously. As in the seven-year-old, it may be a symptom that new emotional patterns are in process of growth.

Evidently he is developing a sense of individual status, which needs sympathetic understanding by his elders, above all by his own family. He likes his home; he feels a certain private loyalty to it; he glows with pride at his wonderful father. But he also feels the tensions of pulling away, of achieving a detachment which will place him more on his own. So when he is abroad he does not wish to be obtrusively called "sonny," and she does not wish to be identified as "my little girl"! Above all, the healthy nine-year-old does not want to be babied by a mother who unwittingly treats him as though he were still a young child in need of unremitting protection. Fathers sometimes go to the opposite extreme, and treat a son as though he were a "young man." Actually, the nine-year-old needs help at critical points; and he likes to go to his parents for such help. Skillful management suits the help to the needs; and withdraws the help when it fosters desirable independence.

Parents, therefore, should be gratified when at times the nine-year-old shows more interest in his friends than in the family excursion that has been so benevolently planned for him! Many prefer to gather with their companions for one of those long sessions in which talk and planning may figure more strongly than active play. There is so much that needs comfortable discussion among friends—a kind of exchange that even the family circle cannot afford. NINE is a great talker. Let him talk.

Let him talk with his friends, for thereby he gets at least a rudimentary sense of brotherhood. He does a little social planning. He sharpens his perceptions of others and of himself. He shares confidences and estimates. He discusses future vocations, and frankly tells his pal, "You haven't got the makings of a doctor!" In spite of a little quarreling and disagreement, he gets on well with his playmates. He builds friendships of some depth and duration. He participates actively in the formation and conduct of his short-lived club with its passwords, codes, dress, hideaway, bulletins, and taboos. He is learning to subordinate his own interests to the demands of the group. At school and elsewhere he is more competitive as a member of the group than as an individual.

In school the groups may include both boys and girls, but the spontaneous groupings are nearly always unilateral. Girls have their clubs in which some time is devoted to giggling and whispering, whereas boys indulge in roughhousing and wrestling. The boys have more trouble with bullies their own age or older. Birthday parties are, by choice, usually limited to one sex. Boys tease each other about girlfriends. Girls tease each other about boyfriends. Each sex cordially disdains the other.

This reciprocal disdain is part of the mechanism of development. It has much the same logic as the withdrawal tendencies that cause these same boys and girls to separate themselves to some degree from family ties. Attachment must be counterbalanced by detachment. To grow up, the nine-year-old must achieve a sense of his individual status, in relation not only to his parents but also to the opposite sex.

So each sex expresses a certain contempt for the other. Bragging to each other, spying on and teasing each other serve to define psychological distinctions that are in the making, both with and without the aid of the culture. "Girls don't count," says a superior-minded boy. In rejoinder a perceptive girls says, "Boys are loathsome creatures. I enjoy watching them!"

But significantly enough, with respect to babies, such aversions do not hold. Girls may show a strong and affectionate interest in their younger siblings. And a nine-year-old boy in the capacity of big brother can take over to a remarkable extent the details of infant care when the parents are temporarily absent and entrust him with the responsibility. Such attitudes also are part and parcel of the total sex development which ultimately embraces family life.

There are varied forms of new awareness of the parental and reproductive aspects of sex. Most of the nine-year-old girls have knowledge of the process of menstruation. Many of the boys and girls have some comprehension of the father's part in procreation. They have observed the bearing of young in animals. They show both modesty and inquisitiveness with regard to the elementary physiology and anatomy of sex. The intellectual realism of this age saves it from romantic excesses. The nine-year-old boy is relatively careless as to appearance: but the fact that he does not want to be caught with clean hands shows a negative awareness of what will come later. The reorientations in the sphere of sex, however, are sufficiently marked to indicate that the child of yesteryear has now moved into the preadolescent sector of the life cycle. The girls are nearer to the age of puberty than the boys. This fact and the variations in physiological maturity within each sex account in part for the wide range of individual differences so apparent at this age.

A behavior profile can scarcely do justice to these individual differences, for a profile must be drawn with broad strokes. This compels us to disregard the finer lines and shadings, which are so important for the delineation of a specific boy or girl—the one, for example, in your own household. He is stamped with individuality. He has gestures, ways of laughing and exclaiming; he has humor, sulks and moods, table manners, possessions, modes of speech, demeanors and enthusiasms, which make him unique. Nature will never contrive another like him, for she abhors identity, even in twins derived from a single, selfsame egg.

Nine is above all an age when individuality seeks to reassert and to reorganize itself. An active nine-year-old is not too dependent on praise, and may even show surprise when he gets it; but he accepts approval and benefits from it. In fact, he likes timely praise, and shows much greater capacity than the seven-year-old to assimilate it. If he is of an introverted, withdrawn nature he will, of course, need to be treated with special insight and, at times, with leniency. In case of doubt it is wise to tolerate idiosyncrasies that express forward thrusts of development. He has to find himself.

In spite of the wide diversity of individual differences, we can still recognize general developmental characteristics that typify the nine-year zone of maturity. Recall the eight-year-old. Three traits distinguish the dynamics of his behavior: speediness, expansiveness, evaluativeness. These traits continue to operate at the nine-year level; but with important modifications and a higher degree of integration.

EIGHT seems to work very fast, because he reacts with somewhat abrupt bursts of speed. NINE still is speedy, but his speed is under better control, and therefore less noticeable. Particularly when he puts his mind to a familiar task, he works toward the end and completion of his performance; and he sustains his speed for longer intervals.

He has a greater interest in process and skill; he is more able to analyze his movements both before and during action. He also is more interested and persistent in practicing his skills—an interest and perseverance based on his greater maturity. Sometimes NINE is facile and modulated. Sometimes he seems to overdo something he likes; he repeats it over and over again. He may want to see the same movie again and again. He probably repeats things with slight variations which help him to assimilate and refine a new experience. The extensiveness of NINE likewise shows more purpose, scope, and depth. It is less sketchy, less episodic; it is more channelized, and in the end more organized. Again a maturity difference, enriched by accumulated experience.

The expansiveness of EIGHT was much influenced by his immediate environment. The extensiveness of NINE comes more from within. It is self-motivated. No one needs to tell him to make his expanding lists and inventories; or to add new chemicals to his collection; or to make plans for his future profession. The same inner forces impel him to spread into the remoter worlds of history and biography. This is psychic expansion—an organizing growth process.

As we should expect, the evaluations of NINE are deeper and more discriminating than those of EIGHT. His emotivity, to use an academic word, is more sensitive, more refined. Just as the lens of his eye has greatly gained in capacity to accommodate to small distances, so his total organism has made a notable gain in capacity to feel small values and to accommodate to refined differences. We have already extolled his new powers of self-appraisal and of social judgment. They are bound up with the growth of emotivity which enables the nine-year-old to experience and to express finer shades of feeling. His voice has softened, his tensional outlets are more delicate, his disgusts more dainty. He undoubtedly feels novel emotions and novel variations of old emotions; because emotions grow and change in pattern with each passing age.

Philosophers have not solved the mystery of human conscience. But the nine-year-old might teach them something of its origins. In him, conscience is clearly in the making. He is now so mature that he detects nice shades of wrongdoing in others, and feels the blameworthiness of his own wrongdoing. He wishes to be straight with the world. He comments on an adult's unfairness: "That's a gyp." He is realistic about moral matters. He factually says to his mother, "I know you won't like this, but I'm going to tell you." In such articulate children we glimpse the very mechanisms of conscience. It is heartening to realize that the ethical sense is already so highly developed at this early age.

There is a certain reasonableness in the psychology of the nine-year-old. He is open to instruction; he is factual, forthright. He is not too interested in magic; he has a healthy strain of skepticism. He has put aside the Santa Claus myth, but he is not so ruthless as to destroy it for a younger sibling. He believes in luck and chance; but he also believes in law; otherwise he would not be so anxious to find out how things are done, and why they are what they are. He seeks correction and explanation of his errors. For the time being, he is somewhat less concerned about God, heaven, fate, and prayers. He himself is taking himself in hand, almost in a spirit of rationalism. This is a noteworthy developmental phenomenon.

In portraying the behavior of the nine-year-old we have deliberately emphasized his positive and constructive traits, because they best represent his potentialities in terms of the future and his attainments in relation to his recent developmental past. At times, of course, he still functions like an eight-year-old. But his best traits are authentic indicators of true growth trends.

These traits are his realism, his reasonableness, and his self-motivation. Functioning in favorable balance, they make of him, on a juvenile scale, a businesslike, fair-minded, responsible individual. He is no longer a "mere" child. He is integrating his long past—not finally, but intermediately. He is trending toward the teens.

Maturity Traits

The following maturity traits are **not** to be regarded as rigid norms, nor as models. They simply illustrate the kinds of behavior—desirable or otherwise—that tend to occur at this age. Every child has his own pattern of growth, and his own timetable. The behavior traits here outlined may be used to interpret his individuality and to consider the maturity level at which he is functioning.

1. MOTOR CHARACTERISTICS

BODILY ACTIVITY

NINE works hard and plays hard. He is more skillful in his motor performances and he likes to display his skill. His timing is also under better control. He now shows great interest in competitive sports such as baseball.

Boys are quick to assume an active fighting posture and they strike out at each other and wrestle. They frequently "let off steam" or make a wild rush toward something.

NINE is apt to overdo. He has difficulty calming down after recess or after a strenuous game. He is apt to ride his bicycle too far or to mow the lawn until he is exhausted.

EYES AND HANDS

The eyes and hands are now well differentiated. The two hands can generally be used quite independently. The fingers also show new differentiation. NINE pianos them on a table, picks and fiddles and flicks or fingers the edge of a paper he is reading.

He is now reported to be either good or poor with his hands, or to be a keen observer. Individual skills stand in bold relief at this age.

Movements expressed in so many ways at eight are now more restricted. NINE likes still-life or portrait or poster painting. He sketches lines with short strokes, adds more details to his work. There is a concentrated quality to his quick identification of an airplane in the sky.

NINE has an open-eyed stare which he can maintain for several seconds without blinking. He can consciously see what he is regarding, or he may be focusing without regard. One child said she could look at something without seeing it and thoughts went jumping through her mind.

Sitting posture is now more awkward. The child slouches in his chair and gets into unusual postures. One of his favorite positions is to place one ankle on the thigh of his other leg. He is apt to have his head quite close to his working point at times, although he also leans way back. He thrusts an arm out forward and also back, he stamps his feet, he claps his hand on his head.

NINE can write for a prolonged time. He likes to make extended lists and to catalogue his collections.

2. PERSONAL HYGIENE

EATING

Appetite. NINE has his appetite under better control than he did at eight. The good eaters have less tremendous appetites and the poorer eaters have better appetites than earlier. NINE, however, thinks more about food than formerly. He enjoys reading cookbooks and helping to prepare food. The minute he arrives home from school his first thought may be about something to eat.

Refusals and Preferences. NINE is rather positive in his food likes and dislikes. He states them frankly. Some NINEs do eat "everything," but if not, the adult is inclined to cater to their demands since these are so positive. Plain foods are still preferred. Meat gravies are now accepted. Puréed foods and fat on meat continue to be disliked. Desserts and sweets are in the ascendancy.

Self-Help. NINE is fairly deft with his implements. Although many NINEs cut well with knives, a few continue to need help or tend to saw their meat in their attempt to cut it. Fingers are rarely used. NINE is aware of bad table manners even though he may not be exercising good ones. He may even be enough aware of his own bad manners to keep an eye out for his father, to see if he is going to be reprimanded or not. It is remarkable to see how much better NINE conducts a meal, even in the handling of his implements, when he has the added stimulus of company or of going out to dinner.

Table Behavior. The child's table behavior is evidently improving, because it is less on the parent's mind. NINE may even be complimented for his manners. He chews more skillfully and is less apt to chew with his mouth open. He is also less likely to overload his fork and to bolt his food. He no longer fiddles with his food.

He may be able to combine talking, listening, and eating well, but some NINEs tend to talk too much at the table, while others listen too concentratedly.

NINE may be expected to wash his hands spontaneously before coming to the table, although he at times gets mixed up in thinking that he has washed them when he has not. Actually, he lives up to what is expected of him rather poorly, and most frequently needs to be reminded. He responds willingly. He generally places his napkin on his lap, but it still has a tendency to slide about and may fall to the floor. His eating is so much neater now that he has much less need of a napkin than when he was younger.

SLEEP

Bedtime. Getting ready for bed is no longer a problem unless the child is sent to bed too early and feels that he does not have the privileges of other children. NINE still needs to be reminded that it is bedtime even when his television programs keep him posted on the time. Nine o'clock is a usual bedtime. Some NINEs prefer to read for a while after they are in bed. The majority are asleep by 10 P.M. or earlier. There are still a few who need to be asleep by 8:30 P.M. Such children need to be protected from the influence of their friends who do not go to sleep before 10 P.M. or later. Those NINEs who go to sleep late may need to be protected from themselves by having their lamp or radio removed. They have a tendency to switch their radio or light on again after it is time to go to sleep.

Night. NINE is a good sleeper and on the whole a quiet one. A few awaken screaming from nightmares but are easily quieted. Although NINE often has bad dreams, his sleep is not greatly disturbed by them. As at eight, his total sleep averages around nine or ten hours.

Morning. NINE often controls his waking by setting his alarm clock. He may even set it for an early hour and then go back to sleep, or he may wake up slowly after it has rung. He often plans things to do in the morning on awaking. In fact, he seems to enjoy early-morning activity more than bedtime activity. Seven is a common waking hour and this gives him plenty of time for reading, fooling around, dressing, watching television and even for practicing at the piano before it is time for school.

ELIMINATION

NINE has his elimination functions under his own control. As at eight, the bowel movement is most apt to occur after breakfast or in the late afternoon or evening. One movement is the rule, but there may be two. NINE can function at school, but is more apt to function at home. He rarely gets up in the night to urinate. He rarely needs to be reminded to go to the bathroom, for he now possesses both an inner and outer control.

BATH AND DRESSING

Bath. The bath is neither resisted nor especially enjoyed. NINE does not wish to bathe more than two or three times a week. He accepts the adult's suggestion that he bathe and usually manages the tub by himself, but he still needs some supervision and likes to have an adult around. When he is once in the tub, he rather enjoys soaking in quite warm water. On the whole, he carries through the entire bath procedure rather well and fairly independently.

He still needs to be reminded to brush his teeth and to brush them well. He may also have to be reminded to wash his hands before meals. But he usually takes suggestions good-naturedly and as though he had been planning to do all these things by himself but had forgotten.

Dressing and Care of Clothes. NINE is better than he was about finishing the loose ends of dressing. He finishes buttoning, ties his shoelaces, and tucks in his shirt. He is not too much interested in clothes and would prefer to have his mother lay them out for him. He is apt to throw his clothing around the room, but can be taught to put it neatly on a chair. He is not very consistent about putting his dirty clothes in the hamper unless he has a daily change. In fact, he is not very proficient at judging whether clothes are dirty or not and is apt to put on yesterday's clothes because they are handy. Boys especially prefer old clothes. Most NINEs are fairly good about reporting tears and holes in their clothes and may even be insistent about their being mended.

NINE is as negligent about hanging up his outer as his other clothes. The minute he gets home he is inclined to dump all his belongings on the nearest chair or to fling them about. He responds well to being reminded, but he responds even better to some device such as having to pay a fine for each piece of clothing he has neglected to hang up. Untied shoelaces also respond well to a fine system.

Boys and girls alike are becoming interested in combing their own hair.

SOMATIC COMPLAINTS

On the whole, NINE enjoys excellent health. He continues to throw off colds rather quickly. Children who have previously had ear, lung, or kidney complications may have a recurrence between the eighth and ninth year and may suffer a rather prolonged illness. A few children show marked fatigue and need to be protected from doing too much. Many complain a good deal, especially about headaches and stomachaches, and these complaints often occur when the parent has requested the child to do some task that is disagreeable to him.

TENSIONAL OUTLETS

There is a marked decrease in the more obvious tensional outlets at NINE. A very few children continue to suck their thumbs, but only at infrequent intervals. These children respond well to parental reminding, or better yet, a dentist's warning. In some cases, placing a pronged plastic in the roof of the mouth provides an adequate reminder.

Boys especially seem to need to "let off steam." They often wrestle around and cannot seem to keep their hands off each other. NINE is apt to growl, mutter, sulk, or find fault in relation to specific happenings.

NINE's most characteristic tension release is through fine motor movements. He fiddles, picks at his cuticle, runs his hand through his hair, or shuffles his feet.

3. EMOTIONAL EXPRESSION

NINE is finally becoming what his parents have been striving for. He deserves and receives outright compliments such as: "He takes more responsibility"; "He is both more independent and more dependable"; "He is easier to get on with"; "He can be trusted"; "He obeys well."

Something very real is happening to NINE in relation to his self-organization. He is coming within the realm of the more positive emotions. He may say that he hates certain subjects, but he tries to do them anyway. If, however, he is apprehensive about a certain subject, such as arithmetic, it is important that he does not become more apprehensive to the point of "going to pieces" and refusing to go to school. Apprehensive children need more concrete material, so that they may succeed at one level and then gradually work up to a higher level, knowing the exact process through which they must go.

NINE may be impatient and quick-tempered, and may flare up, but all these responses tend to be very short-lived. He may cry, but only if he gets mad enough or is really hurt. NINE is more likely to be upset and apprehensive about his own actions.

NINE is actually the opposite of impatient. He plans his separate activities and even his whole day. He is persistent and wants to complete what he has planned to do. He can, however, be interrupted by a request from his mother, obeys with good grace, and returns to continue with his activity. His one difficulty may be that he is so absorbed that he does not hear his mother when she speaks. Some NINEs are still distractible, but they can be very persistent with the few things they set their minds to. NINE, like SEVEN, is capable of developing passions for certain activities. As his mother says, "He could watch television all day long."

NINE is ashamed of some of his past acts in fields he now has under better control. He may show embarrassment at being criticized, at exposing his body, or when he is in a social situation with the opposite sex. Both his parents' and his siblings' acts are subject to his disgust. He applies his own measuring stick to them; he wants them to act "properly."

NINE is a loyal and devoted friend. He can always be sought by his friends for protection and is upset when his friends are browbeaten. He is prone to admire members of his own sex, his own age or often a few years older. This is the beginning of hero-worship.

It is surprising to see how little needs to be done to tip the scales in the right direction for NINE. One experi-

ence may set off a spark that needs no replenishing. The sight of a person with bad table manners may be a powerful stimulus for NINE to improve his own ways. The redecoration and rearrangement of his room may shift him from a persistent pattern of disorder to one of pride in the care of his room. The present of a small fossil may set him on an encyclopedic search for all the knowledge he can secure about prehistoric life.

This is an age when the child becomes impressed with whatever he is told. Prejudices, which often start at eight, need to be explained to the nine-year-old so that he will not become mired in them.

NINE is an age when a strong feeling tone prevails. We see here definite signs of empathy; for instance, the child may say that when he sees anybody else hurt, he hurts in the same place. Some of his established emotional reactions, like other characteristics, are variable, however, and he may swing quickly from one extreme to another, as for instance from marked shyness to extreme boldness. Another extreme is shown in his alternation between a "don't care" attitude and an extreme sensitivity to criticism and a desire to please.

4. FEARS AND DREAMS

FEARS

NINE says about himself, "I don't frighten very easy." Indeed, he has very few fears. Some NINEs, however, are still resolving tag ends of earlier fears of storms, cellars, blood, or swimming with the face under water. These fears have a specific personality reference by this age and have usually had a prolonged and intense course.

Though NINE has few fears, he is a great worrier. He is upset by little mistakes he makes. He may be apprehensive about crossing a street at a traffic light. He worries about failing in his studies; about doing the wrong thing in a social situation, such as extending his left hand instead of his right; or not measuring up to the other children. He needs reassurance, or praise, to be informed where he stands. Sometimes competition makes him worry more and if it does it should be minimized or avoided.

DREAMS

The sleep of the nine-year-old, though uninterrrupted and quiet on the surface, is often ruffled underneath by many scary, horrid dreams. A few NINEs awake screaming, sit up, or get out of bed, usually to go to their mother's bedside, but for the most part they may appear to be sleepwalking. They know they have been dreaming and quiet quickly. When they do realize that they have been dreaming, they may not be able to remember their dreams.

Horrid dreams are reported most commonly, and these can often be explained in the light of what has happened during the day. Reading, movies, television, and circus performances all leave their imprint. NINE is chased by animals or people. He may be hurt, shot, or kidnapped. Murder plays a prominent role. His best friend or his mother may be killed. His mother may be running away. Fire and tornadoes may come to destroy trucks and houses.

NINE knows that there is a relationship between his daily activities and his dream life. He may know that a certain repeated rhythm will produce one of his awful dreams of standing on his head and whirling round and round. The thought of it makes him shudder. That is why he tries to protect himself from stimuli that might produce certain bad dreams. He reads scary books during the daytime only, and may be selective about television-viewing.

NINE has some pleasant dreams, but these seem to be in the minority and more difficult to remember. He often enjoys dreaming in the morning and may want to go back to sleep to continue his dreaming.

5. SELF AND SEX

SELF

NINE is rightly spoken of as "self-sufficient" and "on his own." His independence is something he can now manage. He can think for himself, reason by himself. You can usually depend upon him: if he says he has done something, he really has. He can be trusted.

NINE has himself under better self-control. He withdraws from his surroundings enough to gather up his sense of self and put it to good use, but he does not retreat far into himself, as he did at seven. He does not feel impelled to boast and to attack to protect himself as he did at eight. Now he thinks in terms of fighting with his brain as well as with his body. For instance, he plans his time so that he can get off to school easily to protect himself from being pestered on the way if he is walking.

NINE has a new capacity to set his mind to a task and see it through. He is even ambitious in his demands of himself. He wants to succeed not only in a single task but also in general.

A good relationship with others is important to NINE. He is anxious to please, he wants to be liked, and he loves to be chosen. He will work for a favor and he thrives on praise. But he still is sensitive to correction and may be embarrassed by it. This is the first year he has himself well enough in hand to do things in a spirit of service. These episodes of doing "wonderful things" are infrequent, but they are stimulated by the child's feeling that so much has been done for him.

Not all NINEs are as well organized as this. A number of boys at this age are wrapped up in themselves, very busy with their own activities, and very thoughtless of others; they are aggravated and can indeed be aggravating when their preoccupations are broken into. One gets on better with this type by planning ahead with him or leaving orders on a bulletin board.

Some NINEs are anxious and apprehensive about their work and their health. They may underrate themselves as persons, lack confidence, and remark, "Oh, am I stupid" or "I'm the dumbest." "It is very important to make sure that NINE is not overplaced in regard to his school work, for if he is, he will receive both his own condemnation and that of others.

One has to be careful, however, of taking NINE too seriously in regard to what he says. He tosses off self-critical remarks, such as "I would do that"; "Oh, that's my poor memory"; or "Oh, you know me and my dirt." He complains about many things, but may forget what he was complaining about the minute he has stopped. One naturally rides over much of NINE's complaining, but it is important to judge whether or not any specific complaint has real meaning to him.

SEX

There is less interest in reproduction on the part of many NINEs, if their desire for information has been satisfied at eight. Nevertheless, there may be much more continuing discussion of this subject with friends than parents realize. If sufficient information has not been given, the child usually shows his dissatisfaction. A mother can no longer stop with the explanation that a mother and a father marry and decide to have a baby. An alert nine-year-old will comment, "But you can't just decide."

Nine-year-old girls may relate themselves to their role in the process of reproduction. They may ask, "Have I got a seed inside of me?" Or if they notice that the mother is growing "fatter" they may ask, "Will I be that fat someday, too?"

Some NINEs continue to think that the baby is born by Caesarian section. This is often easier for them to understand than the process of normal birth. However, birth of animals is taken quite naturally by the nine-year-old who has had familiarizing experience with animals.

NINE may be self-conscious about exposing his body. This awareness may be related only to those outside the family group, but NINE may not wish to have the parent of the opposite sex see him nude. If he is with a friend of his own sex, he may exclude a younger sibling of the opposite sex while he is changing his clothes, even though he might bathe with that same sibling on occasion.

His interest is more in the details of his own organs and functions than in those of the opposite sex. He may even seek out information, especially pictorial, in an encyclopedia or reference book. Girls have usually been told about menstruation.

Swearing is now shifting from the earlier elimination type of vocabulary to sex allusions. Rhymes that children pick up at play have more pointed sex implications. They may repeat them at home to shock mother. Neighbors may complain about the kind of language used by boys.

The girl-boy interest may persist with NINE even though there is now a marked separation of the sexes in play. The sexes are rarely mixed at a birthday party, and if they are, kissing games may result. NINEs tease each other about girl and boy friends and about getting married. There may be some writing of terse notes: "I hate So-and-so"; "So-and-so really likes you"; "I love you." Boys try to kiss their girlfriend, with one success as the final goal. But all this playfulness has an impersonal, matter-of-fact quality without any feeling of jealousy even though you share your friend with a member of your own sex. A few NINEs show obvious embarrassment about the opposite sex and try to avoid situations that expose their embarrassment.

6. INTERPERSONAL RELATIONS

Most of the child-mother embroilment of eight has quite disappeared by nine. Even episodes of "arguing back" now may be infrequent. NINE is so busy with his own life that he makes many fewer demands upon his parent. Yet when his parent makes demands upon him, he usually responds willingly and may even interrupt what he is doing without any resentment. But at times, when he is very much absorbed in what he is doing, he may not hear his mother's request. Therefore it is important to secure some response from him to make sure he has heard your voice.

NINE needs a great deal of reminding. He may forget to wash his hands before meals, to brush his teeth, or to hang up his clothes. He accepts reminding willingly and usually acts on it at once.

NINE is now less involved with routine chores, and accomplishes more tasks of the moment, both when asked and spontaneously. He wants to please his mother. He enjoys running errands and likes a commission to go to a place far enough away to require his taking a bus. He prepares a simple meal when someone is sick or when he wants to help his mother. Some boys are even protective toward their mothers and will not allow them to do certain difficult tasks, especially when they are pregnant.

NINE does not need the assurance of a reward for his helping. He is far less motivated by money than formerly. He may forget to ask for his allowance, and may be careless with it after he has secured it. NINE really wants to perform a personal service and may prefer a pat on the back for a job well done to a material reward, or even to praise. There are some jobs for which he may be interested to receive pay, but for other jobs, like caring for the baby, he may refuse to accept remuneration.

The mother no longer needs to be there when NINE comes home from school, although a few NINEs still need a note telling them where their mother is. Many can have a key left for them and can take over the household for a short span before their mother's return.

It usually is not difficult to discipline NINE. Often he is controlled merely by a look from his mother. At times he may need a short isolation period, especially from other children. He accepts it, and soon returns a better child. NINE responds well to a warning or to an actual deprivation.

Father is not as actively demanded as he was earlier. NINE is so busy with his own activities and his friends that he does less with his father except when they go on special trips together. NINE is often very fond of his father, enjoys discussing various things with him, and may be especially sensitive to any paternal criticism.

NINE does not as a rule present a problem with younger or older siblings. Usually he gets on well with them and shows a real feeling of loyalty, standing up for them as needed. NINE is especially good when he is made responsible for younger siblings for brief periods. He is then extremely understanding and without the strictness and sternness he exhibited at eight.

The tendency to have special friends, seen to be forming at eight, is stronger at nine. NINE chooses only a member of his own sex for a special friend. There is now overt criticism of the opposite sex. Girls may remark, "Boys stink"; "too fresh"; "too tough." Boys also have their say—"Can't be bothered with girls"—and accept them only as a necessary evil.

Boy-girl attractions persist, but there is not much playing together. Often two boys have the same girl, or vice versa, without any feeling of jealousy.

The boy's goal of conquest is to kiss the girl, and this becomes an episode to talk about.

NINEs love to talk among themselves. This desire to chat even breaks into their more active types of play. Favorite topics of conversation are the bedtime hour and television programs.

NINE enjoys group play that shows a fair amount of organization. Informal clubs may last as long as two weeks or so. These clubs start out with a very real purpose—press club, scrapbook club, paper club, sewing club. They are more elaborately set up than they were the year before and may include hideouts, codes, a secret language, and club bulletins. But these clubs do not last. Many NINEs enjoy the formal clubs such as Cubs and Brownies, under adult leadership.

Ball play of some sort is a sure organizer of groups and may take precedence over the earlier absorbing interest in television programs.

NINE is quite natural in his manners. He excuses himself from the table, greets a newcomer, often with a handshake, and thanks his hostess very easily and feelingly for the good time he has had. Parents may now enjoy watching their children perform rather than having to coach them from the sidelines.

7. PLAY AND PASTIMES

GENERAL INTERESTS

NINE demands little of his mother's time. He is extremely busy in his chosen recreations. Much of his time is spent in solitary activities such as reading and watching television. NINE wants to do endlessly what he enjoys doing. Boys play football until they are black and blue, or they sled until they are soaked to the hips. Girls play dolls or paper dolls the whole day through, reenacting an entire day's routine including scoldings, visits to the doctor, and fairly complex interpersonal situations.

Baseball is a favorite outdoor sport for both boys and girls. Bicycling, roller and ice skating, swimming, sledding, and skiing are enjoyed by both sexes. NINE is setting his mind to the task of improving his skills. Though he worked more spontaneously at eight, he is now acting more purposefully. But he does not yet work with the ease and facility that he will show at ten. After bicycling he complains that his legs are tired. Boys enjoy roughhousing and lifting heavy objects.

The indoor life of the nine-year-old is fairly well planned. He has certain absorbing interests such as television, reading, or constructing with a Lego set. Some NINEs enjoy making scrapbooks. Others pore over maps and often draw them. NINE continues to enjoy card games.

READING

NINE is a great reader. He may even appear to be living in a book world. He plans to rise early in the morning just to read. He rarely reads fairy tales now. He is too much of a realist and may say about fairy tales, "They're fantastic; they aren't true."

The books he likes, he likes so much that he reads them over and over again. He is very fond of animal stories. The junior classics are now coming within his own reading scope. Repeated favorites are **Tom Sawyer, Treasure Island, King Arthur,** and **Bambi.** Biographies, mysteries, and the encyclopedia for reference all interest him.

Although he enjoys the classics, he still may be very fond of his comic books, which he enjoys trading with his friends. With many NINEs, however, the interest in comic books is beginning to wane, and can be broken into. They will accept the fact that any comic books outside their own rooms will be confiscated. When the interest becomes so absorbing that it interferes with school work, sharp measures may have to be taken, for science fiction paperbacks or comic books can have the attributes of a drug. This more drastic handling, however, is seldom necessary and even when indicated, the books should not be entirely forbidden. NINE gets what he wants and becomes proficient at sneaking them into the house or reading them out of sight of his parents if he is not allowed to read them in his room.

MUSIC, TELEVISION, AND MOVIES

If a child at this age persists in his interest in taking music lessons, one may expect that he will really apply himself. Many NINEs can practice by themselves, although they still need to be reminded. The child is becoming interested in correct fingering. His touch is lighter and staccato, which gives him better control over the sounds he produces. He is beginning to enjoy his accomplishment of playing and fortunately his playing has improved so that his family can enjoy his music. Biographies of composers interest him.

NINE knows the time and channel of his TV programs by heart. Detective stories are becoming more important to him, though he still may cling to a selected few of the children's adventure stories, and he continues to enjoy the situation comedies aimed at children, quiz programs, and adult comedies. A few NINEs watch the news. Happily, the child is not as rigid and intent on his programs as he was earlier. He can even miss an occasional program if some more interesting activity offers. NINE is becoming more aware of the commercials, and though he has been warned, he may finally beg his parents to buy the product advertised.

Television programs provide one of the topics of conversation for the nine-year-old.

There are marked individual differences among NINEs as to interest in movies.

8. SCHOOL LIFE

NINE usually enjoys school. The morning routine has smoothed out; he has better control of time and is now responsible for getting to school on time. He has trouble, however, in remembering to take his school material even though he has planned ahead and put his things in a convenient place. He still needs to be reminded. Parents should not be aggravated by this lag. They should remember how well he is getting himself ready and allotting his time. If he takes a gun or a ball to school he will readily respond to his teacher's request to leave it in the coatroom.

NINE reports more about home and outside activities at school than about school happenings at home. He tells a long, detailed, strung-out story at school about his television programs or some movie he has seen. At home he is most apt to report on his subjects—which he is best in; who is ahead of him, etc. He will also tell about a school play or some special event. He does not talk much about his teacher, but may describe some of her mannerisms, such as how she talks or how she does a certain thing.

Teachers report that fourth is a difficult grade to teach. The teacher needs to realize that NINE is an individualist, with rather positive likes and dislikes. NINE wants to be independent of his teacher, but in dealings with her wants her to be reasonable and resents any decisions he considers unfair. The teacher soon recognizes that she should delay helping him until he really needs her. NINE is actually more related to his subjects than to his teacher. Dislike of a teacher may be linked to a dislike of a subject, especially if the child has more than one teacher. He may even blame the teacher for a lowered grade.

Because of these more emotional responses it is very important to be sure that he can handle the more self-demanding tasks of fourth grade. NINE is afraid of failing and is also ashamed of having failed. Need for repetition of a grade or going at a slower pace is best taken care of within the first three grades, when the child does not become as emotionally involved and usually improves by the removal of too high demands. He is happier with the group that will allow him to operate at his optimal level rather than his minimal level. Parents are the ones who feel the emotional pangs of failure within the first three grades and wrongly ascribe their own emotions to the child.

The change from third to fourth grade is a crucial one. Many who have been developing on the slower side, with some support to hold a place (such as a reading or arithmetic "disability"), may now have a real spurt of improvement. Some who have previously done well may now need individual help.

In the classroom NINE appears to be more orderly and performs with greater dispatch. Each child has an individual manner of entering the room. One child tosses his book on his desk, another slams it down, and a third places it carefully. A few may need a word from the teacher to stir them on their way, but once the class is started they take out a book, make a comment or two about the task, and set to work. NINE has a greater capacity for working independently both of children and of teacher. He is challenged by a task.

He sits with trunk bent forward, resting on his elbows, hands propping his chin as he brings his face near the book on his desk. At times he throws himself way back, extends his whole body, and holds the book at full arms' length. He flings his arm forward or backward to call the teacher's attention, usually without calling her name, and awaits his turn. He may look at his neighbor's work, but prefers the teacher's assistance.

He has less need than EIGHT to verbalize and also can talk more quietly. The classroom is therefore quieter. When he drops his desktop down with a bang, he may give his neighbor a glance as though expecting a complaint. On occasion he sits with wide-open eyes, stares forward, apparently fixating without regard, and seems to be in a daze. At the end of a period there is a general stir; some children rush to leave their papers on the teacher's desk, while others remain at work until they have finished. On some occasions the whole class becomes so interested that it remains overtime to continue with a discussion or lesson.

NINE is interested in achieving in his school subjects, and likes to be graded. He is anxious for good marks and works for them. He can be discouraged by failure. There is considerable competition with others and he may show resentment if surpassed by one who is close to him in achievement, or he may be impatient with a duller classmate. When failing, he usually needs individual attention rather than isolation. He also often competes better as a member of a group than as an individual.

NINE has a better critical evaluation of his own abilities. He can describe his preferred method of working. He knows he can do a problem better if he writes it down; that he can do arithmetic combinations better with flash cards than orally. Some say they cannot maintain meaning when they read aloud. Some tasks are better performed at home than at school.

Complaining comments may precede any task, but soon fade out. NINE has a certain amount of self-discipline. Faced with an unpleasant task, if told how much he is required to do and about how long it will take he proceeds without further ado. He is speedy in his work, and given a goal, he rushes to get there.

"I haven't a good memory" is one of NINE's favorite complaints. Immediate recall is not always easy. He may remember better if he writes an item down or if it is written down for him. Once his mind is made up, however, he is not easily influenced to change it. He can evaluate his performance: "This one I'm not too sure. This one I am sure."

In reading, he may prefer to read silently and may dislike to read orally before the group though he still needs to be checked by oral reading. He tackles any word and is not too concerned if he does not know the meaning, unless it is important to the story. Reading is now associated with several subjects. Those who have been slow in learning to read can now join the group in their favored subject. NINE especially likes to read for facts and information.

Handwriting is now put to practical use. Perhaps he keeps a diary. He writes lists, cataloguing his collections. He likes to order things by mail. "Business" letters hold more interest than do social ones. One nine-year-old made out a form letter which she used to acknowledge her Christmas gifts. NINE likes to copy. This is his way of supporting a "poor memory." When he looks up a subject to write about, he is truly a plagiarist.

Penmanship, particularly in girls, is smaller, neater, and done with less pressure. Boys usually still write with heavy strokes. Most use finger movement with tension of the forearm. The nine-year-old ordinarily sustains his writing long enough to complete a given task. However, some children may continue to avoid writing any more than is necessary. NINE is also critical of his writing: "Sort of sloppy, isn't it?" "That's my most careless thing." He may even copy his own paper to make it more legible.

Arithmetic is perhaps the most talked-of subject in fourth grade. It is "loved" or "hated," but despite the latter emotional response, NINE may do well in this subject. He may fluctuate in his like and dislike from day to day according to his accomplishment and grasp. He now knows many number combinations by heart and is aware of the ones that cause him difficulty. He writes these down and wants to master them by having someone call them off to him. He usually prefers written to oral work. Though he likes to prove his long division, he does not yet check his own error spontaneously. He wants to know how he made his error and enjoys analyzing his process with his teacher to determine how he made his mistake. The teacher in turn needs to know how his mind works than to think just about correct or incorrect answers. He may be close to or far from a correct answer.

NINE often has more spontaneous interest in problem-solving than his school work affords. He becomes interested in the prices of things and figures out many practical problems related to numbers which he encounters in reading or conversation.

Although individual differences appear to be strong, NINE uses the pronoun "we" to identify himself with the classroom group. A comment such as "I wish we could do reading workbooks all day" may bring an echo in unison from the rest of the class. At times the whole class will muster a sudden spurt in order to finish a task.

Friendships are being formed. NINE chooses a best friend to work or play with. He protects and defends him on occasion. There may now be a definite shift in twosomes. Some who have played together off and on during the earlier grades may form completely new friendships. Also, two children who have had difficulties getting along together now suddenly become friends. Boys form stronger twosomes and also act as a group more than girls. Girls are more varied in their groups, and two-, three-, and four-somes often exist. Boys and girls now play separately for the most part, and there is exclusion of the opposite sex in play; the adult is rarely included or referred to. However, they do enjoy a group game supervised by an adult.

9. ETHICAL SENSE

NINE is, as a rule, responsive to any demand put upon him if he has heard it. His hearing may be related to his absorption of what he is doing, but it also may be related to his interest in and willingness to do the task required. His response often has the quality of a rapid flash. If he acts upon it immediately he "clicks" in the demanded direction. But if he delays he is apt to forget and then needs to be reminded. He takes reminding with good grace. NINE's intentions are often higher than his acts. He really wants to be helpful, to relieve his mother, but he lacks spontaneity in doing things. He is, however, feeling the demands of his age, which bring him more privileges and more responsibilities. Although there are fewer battles over chores now, if too much is demanded of NINE (especially a boy), he resents it and speaks out his mind. Most NINEs are so busy that they have little time for chores. Fortunately NINE responds well to immediate little demands and these usually take the place of chores.

The drag and uncertainty in making up his mind which he experienced earlier are no longer evident. NINE makes up his mind rapidly, definitely, and often to his parents' satisfaction. His decisions often are easily made and almost automatic. He also shows a considerable degree of forethought, for he can set his mind to a task and can thus carry it through to completion.

NINE accepts blame fairly well when it is due him, but he becomes very much upset if blamed for something he has not done. At times he becomes involved in some group activity he did not start, but circumstantial evidence points to him as the responsible party. Evidence should then be sifted by an adult so that each child may take a just share of blame, and not leave him "holding the bag." Fairness is NINE's credo. He can always be appealed to through fairness. He may even be so realistic about it that he will not accept praise that he thinks is not his due even though he likes praise very much. One nine-year-old refused an award in a public-speaking contest because he felt it should go to his mother, since she had helped him to learn the poem he recited.

The rudiments of a conscience are developing. This does not, however, mean that NINE never blames or alibis. If he is in a tight spot he is capable of making quite plausible excuses. He would often alibi if permitted, but usually can be held to the evidence of the truth.

NINE has less need to want to be good than he did when younger, for now he is good more naturally. He may be more concerned about the things he has not done than the things he has done. He thinks in terms of right and wrong. He says he is ashamed that he is failing in school or that he does not eat well. He may even say that he "feels guilty" because he has neglected to return something.

His are becoming the errors of omission as well as of commission. If he has committed some wrong he feels the need to confess to his mother. He does not come straight to the point but approaches her considerately. He watches his mother's face. He does not want to offend her, so he breaks things to her easily. But if he does not confess, his conscience, young as it is, may bother him.

NINE is relatively easy to discipline. He does have to be reminded a good deal. Hanging up his coat and his pajamas, and tying his shoelaces, should no longer require reminders. A fine for each forgetting brings him into line with amazing speed. Isolation is needed at times, and denials of favored activities such as favorite TV programs produce the desired result. Often a mere threat of denial or some very small denial is sufficient. One does not have to be drastic with NINE. Most NINEs accept punishment with good grace, though a few become extremely resentful and express their feeling with "That's a gyp." A few NINEs, who are obviously riding for a fall and cannot be helped to bypass their difficulty, respond well to a retrial. In the midst of their tears they are eager to start all over again and do it right on the second trial.

NINE is beginning to be neater about his room. He may even be particular about his own things and spends hours sorting out his numerous possessions. He responds well to his mother's reminders and can carry through a task on his own.

The words "honest" and "truth" are now becoming a part of NINE's vocabulary. Even when he exaggerates on occasion he rapidly sets things right by saying, "Oh, Mom, you know it isn't real." NINE rarely takes things not belonging to him, and if he does he wants to return them and set things right. He is now developing a sense of ethical standards and means to live up to them.

Most NINEs are no longer as intrigued by money as they were at eight. Some handle money very well, even budget it, lend it, and carry around a fair sum in their wallets. Some do work in return for their allowance, others have a basic allowance and supplement it with pay for tasks. Yet it is surprising to see how many NINEs forget to to ask for their allowance and leave it lying around after they have received it. Many would prefer to receive money as they need it, for their needs are often small and immediate.

10. PHILOSOPHIC OUTLOOK

DEATH AND DEITY

NINE, the realist, often shows a marked lack of interest in God and religion. He also no longer believes in Santa Claus and does not enjoy fairy tales. He may refuse to go to Sunday school and to say his prayers. Church schools may anticipate a marked reduction in the attendance of nine- and ten-year-olds. The choir attracts some, and if they are paid they are more certain to attend. With some the social aspect of Sunday school still holds interest. And with others a true religious feeling persists and grows. NINE may even pray spontaneously if he is in great need. He may have the rudiments of faith and an ethical feeling that it is important for him to do certain things.

Although a few NINEs may be concerned about the soul and its separation from the body, death is usually thought of more closely in connection with the process of dying. NINE is interested in how you "stop breathing" and have no pulse, and in the fact that you are "not living." NINE may say, "Oh, I wish I'd never been born" or "I wish I were dead," but he does not mean these remarks seriously. As with so many of NINE's complaints, one has a justified tendency to treat them lightly, because for the most part they are very transient.

TIME AND SPACE

NINE is controlled by time more than he controls it. His day is filled to the brim with things to do. He is going here and there and has difficulty in finding time to do extra things that may be requested of him. Everything he does is important and therefore anything is difficult to give up.

NINE does control time, however, in that he plans his day and knows what follows what. In his race with time he may set his alarm clock for early morning, either to gain time for reading or to enjoy the leisure of an extra hour's sleep.

His handling of space involves the same type of restriction and specificity as his response to time. He goes to a special place by himself: to the doctor's or the dentist's office or for his music lesson. He handles this well even though his destination can be reached only by some public conveyance. But one does not divert him by demanding an extra errand on such an occasion. One thing at a time fully accomplished is NINE's set goal.

CHAPTER 10

TEN YEARS OLD

Behavior Profile*

Five years of age is in many children a time of glorious equilibrium and contentment. The child enjoys himself and he also enjoys other people. TEN is equally glorious and content, well balanced and comfortable, both with himself and with those around him.

Both ages bring to partial fulfillment the trends of immediately preceding development, but TEN much more than FIVE suggests the future. A typical five-year-old is so self-contained and self-adjusted that he might almost seem to be a finished product. The environment scarcely has any separate existence for him. It is virtually an extension of his own well-ballasted self. A typical ten-year-old, likewise, is in good equilibrium, but he is so adaptively and diversely in touch with the adult enviroment that he seems rather to be an adult in the making, or at least a preadolescent.

The five-year-old may make little distinction between the sexes. At ten, sex differences are pronounced. The psychology of a ten-year-old girl is clearly distinguishable from that of a ten-year-old boy of equivalent background and experience. The girl has more poise, more folk wisdom, and more interest in matters pertaining

---

* For a fuller description of behavior to be expected at ten years of age, including gradients, readers are referred to a companion volume, *Youth: The Years from Ten to Sixteen,* by Gesell, Ilg, and Ames (Harper & Row).

to marriage and family. This difference appears to be fundamental.

The distinctive characteristics of the ten-year-old level are seen very clearly when compared to the maturity traits of the nine-year-old. NINE, as we have seen, is earnestly engaged in mastering skills; he works with channelized intentness and is not too easily diverted from activity to another. He is in a more or less constant state of urgency, as though in contest with time.

In comparison, TEN is relaxed and casual, yet alert. He has himself and his skills in hand; he takes things in his stride; he works with executive speed and likes the challenge of mental arithmetic. He may even show a genuine capacity to budget his time and his energy. His general behavior, his demeanors, his orientation to the household, are more modulated.

This greater self-possession shows itself in many ways. NINE may have to stop at a task in order to talk. TEN can talk and work at the same time. TEN is more capable of little courteous amenities that have a motor basis. Since his whole organization is less channelized, his attitudes are more flexible and he is more responsive to slight cues.

This relative fluidity makes the ten-year-old peculiarly receptive to social information, to broadening ideas and to prejudices, good and bad. It is relatively easy to appeal to his reason. He is ready to participate in elementary discussions of social problems—racial minorities, crime, the relationships of management and labor. Parents often fail to sense the social intelligence of the ten-year-old child. Sometimes they treat him as though he were less aware than he actually is.

Perceptive teachers are conscious of the great power they can wield through suggestion and through the social science studies of the fifth grade, studies that touch the fundamentals of the conditions of human welfare. Social workers also are aware of the critical importance of this age period in the lives of neglected children. The channelized characteristics of the nine-year-old and the fluidity of the ten-year-old readily lead to bullying and delinquent forms of behavior in an adverse environment. A gang simply organizes these traits for better or for worse.

It is said that the ten-year-old sometimes esteems his gang or his club more than his family. This may be partly true; but on the whole, he has a fairly critical sense of justice and frequently surprises you with the judiciousness of his observations. He sizes up his parents and compares them freely with those of his playmates, usually to the advantage of his own. In fact, he tends to be well satisfied with and admiring of his parents and his family. Compliments to parents are given freely. A girl may tell you, "My father is the most wonderful man in all the world. He is a doctor, and he's so busy, but he just sits there and drinks his coffee as if he had all the time in the world."

Or a boy may say, "My father is a wonderful man, though if he gets angry, he hits you. But that's a father's privilege."

This satisfaction with parents may extend to the complete family. Thus a ten-year-old may report with great enthusiasm, "Every Sunday our whole family goes for a ride."

He accepts with calm parental edicts about behavior: "Yes, Mummy lets me stay all night at my friend's house" or "No, my mother says I'm not old enough to go downtown alone at night." Not for him the snippy eleven-year-old's complaint: "No, I can't. My mother won't let me!"

Many of his comparative judgments about grownups are kept secret. Others are freely expressed. Ask him to describe his teacher and you may get a candid portrait: "Miss A, she's reasonable. She yells a lot but she's really nice." "Miss B doesn't like some kids. One kid she doesn't like at all." "Miss C, she's pretty big and has sort of yellow-blondish hair. She never stands up straight. She walks like this." The ten-year-old is clearly aware of individuality in others as well as in himself.

Individual differences in children themselves, apparent earlier, become even more manifest at ten. The ten-year-old gives a fair indication of the person to be. Talents now declare themselves, particularly in the realm of creative arts. Giftedness in personal-social behavior also reveals itself, if we take pains to read the subtler emotional patterns of the child. He may show fineness of character, graces of deportment, executive ability, perceptiveness of interpersonal relationships, and a wide range of personality traits which have great predictive value as to potential vocation and career. In the management of interpersonal relationships boy or girl may already show a kind of skill and a sense of justice which signify capacity for leadership. Ask these very children who show this capacity for leadership how the various members of their class are doing. They may be shy to give their opinion because they don't want to hurt anyone's feelings. But they know the children who are not up to grade level, not only from an academic but also from a maturity point of view. When a school is geared to developmental placement, teachers can sense those who may be below the group average. The transition from fifth to sixth grade is very important. A child may have seemingly come along from grade to grade not doing too badly. But in fifth grade, with puberty just around the corner, he or she may seem very young and not at all ready for the coming greater demands of sixth grade.

A democratic culture will ideally place a premium on all kinds of skill. The schools continue to bestow excessive emphasis on academic skills. But the nonverbal child with mechanical skills should also have full opportunity to exercise these skills and to have them appreciated. The exercise of skills with social approval serves a valuable double purpose: it strengthens that self-respect and self-confidence which is so important in meeting the perturbing demands of adolescence; simultaneously, society thereby protects itself against the delinquencies of adolescence. Cultural planning for the teens should begin at ten.

The ten-year-old will respond to such planning. He takes kindly to liberalizing ideas of social justice and social welfare. Although critical, both of self and of others, the ten-year-old is capable of loyalties and of hero-worship, and he himself can inspire it in schoolmates. He can be readily prompted to group loyalties in his club organizations. He likes the sense of solidarity that comes from keeping a group secret.

Girls and boys alike have a certain fondness for secrets. A shared secret intensifies both the private sense of self and the identification with another self. So in television, movies, comic strips, and paper-backs, we find that ten-year-olds like mysteries, conspiracy, practical magic, and hero-worship. Comics still hold sway with some children but are losing it with others.

Romance and love in cinema or on television are spurned, at least by the boys. There is usually not much companionship between the sexes. They keep pretty much apart in play, though some enjoy group games of one sex against the other and possibly the formal situation of dancing school. Boys express their camaraderie with other boys in wrestling, shoving, and punching each other. Girl pals walk with arms about each other. There is much gossiping in and out of school, among schoolmates, with writing and exchange of more or less complimentary notes. Girls write notes to other girls. True to the secretive in-group tendency characteristic of the age, the notes are often phrased in cryptic terms understood only by those "in the know."

When two or three girls get together with their assorted paper dolls, they dramatize many life situations, in whispered secrets or in spoken dialogue. By using the dolls as concrete symbols, or by staging plays, they explore the whole family structure, including en-gagements, brides, weddings, and the rearing of children.

Girls are more aware of interpersonal relationships than boys are. They are more aware of their own persons, their clothes and ap-pearance. At the same time they are more discerning of their in-dividual relationships with others. If a younger child giggles at the movies, her companionship may be spurned. More than boys, girls are interested in family life, and they are most perceptive of dif-ferences in family living. A less favored child may inspire sympathy.

By such signs girls, and to a lesser degree boys, of ten give evi-dence of the years of adolescence that lie ahead. The mechanisms of development during those years remain the same. The increments will come slowly and often painfully. Endocrine changes will bring about new physical and mental manifestations. But the patterning of behavior will remain a gradual process of growth.

Just as the equilibrium of age five gave way to the impulsiveness of five and a half and the creative thrusts of six, and as these in their turn gave way to the inwardized subjectiveness of seven, the expansiveness of eight, the self-motivation of nine, and the reorientation of ten, so the eleventh through the sixteenth years will lawfully manifest themselves in distinctive shapes of behavior. Each year of the teens and the early twenties will bring forth its own characteristic behavior shapes.

The culture cannot do justice to the psychological needs of the adolescent without a realistic knowledge of development as a patterning process, a process that produces lawful shapes and configurations of all behavior—motor, adaptive, and personal-social.

The changes are in essence comparable to those that we have described for infancy and childhood. The foundation and most of the framework of the human action system are laid down in the first decade. The consolidations of those first ten years will not be sloughed off. They will remain an integral part of the action system of the maturing youth. The teens do not transform the child. They continue him. Herein lies the preventive and the hygienic significance of infancy, the preschool years, and the years from five to ten.

PART THREE

THE GROWTH COMPLEX

There was a child went forth every day,
And the first object he look'd upon, that object he became,
And that object became part of him for the day or a certain part of
    the day,
Or for many years or stretching cycles of years.

The early lilacs became part of this child,
And grass and white and red morning-glories, and white and red
    clover, and the song of the phoebe-bird,
And the third-month lambs and the sow's pink-faint litter, and the
    mare's foal and the cow's calf,
And the noisy brood of the barnyard or by the mire of the pond
    side,
And the fish suspending themselves so curiously below there, and
    the beautiful curious liquid,
And the water-plants with their graceful flat heads, all became part
    of him. . . .

His own parents, he that had father'd him and she that had conceiv'd
    him in her womb, and birth'd him,
They gave this child more of themselves than that,
They gave him afterward every day, they became part of him.

The mother at home quietly placing the dishes on the supper-table,
The mother with mild words, clean her cap and gown, a wholesome
   odor falling off her person and clothes as she walks by,
The father, strong, self-sufficient, manly, mean, anger'd, unjust,
The blow, the quick loud word, the tight bargain, the crafty lure,
The family usages, the language, the company, the furniture, the
   yearning and swelling heart . . .

The strata of color'd clouds, the long bar of maroon-tint away solitary
   by itself, the spread of purity it lies motionless in,
The horizon's edge, the flying sea-crow, the fragrance of salt marsh
   and shore mud,
These became part of that child who went forth every day, and who
   now goes, and will aways go forth every day.

WALT WHITMAN

Orientation*

The Behavior Profiles assembled in Part Two furnish cross-sectional views of the ascending stages of maturity from five to ten years. Part Three assembles the Growth Gradients, which are implicit in these stages. But the life career of the child does not begin at the age of five years, and to get a clear view of the trends of

---

* Further details on the period from birth to five may be secured from the following volumes: Gesell, Ilg, and Ames, *Infant and Child in the Culture of Today*, rev. ed. (Harper & Row); Gesell et al, *The First Five Years of Life* (Harper & Row).

growth, the gradients must begin with infancy. The following ten chapters therefore group the growth gradients from birth to ten years in ten major fields of behavior. Special attention is, of course, given to the period from five to ten, but the earlier period is treated in sufficient detail to show the development continuities.

For convenience, each gradient consists of a series of levels arranged by weeks, months, or years. This does *not* mean that the itemized gradient levels should be regarded as statistical age norms.

The parent who reads a gradient should never say, My child *ought* to be at this particular level of the gradient because he is old enough. The child may well be younger or older than the chronological age assigned by the gradient. It is more important to find the gradient level that approximately describes the stage of maturity he has actually attained. The gradients are intended to show the overall developmental *sequences* of behavior rather than rigid standards of expectancy. Individual differences are too great to permit rigid standards rigidly applied. Generous allowances should be made for age variations.

Nevertheless, the gradient levels are *location points* which help to give us bearings. They indicate, suggestively, the kinds of behavior that precede; and still better, they indicate the kinds of behavior that are likely to follow in due course. This orientation, this *forward* look, provides perspective and usually affords cause for optimism. The gradients are not designed to *rate* the child; they are designed as tools to aid interpretation. They are rough charts to sail by.

Each of the chapters of Part Three concludes with a group of gradients in tabular form for ready consultation. The introductory discussion interprets the general significance of these gradients in terms of child development and of child guidance.

CHAPTER 11

MOTOR CHARACTERISTICS

Most of the readers of this book, to say nothing of the authors, are especially interested in problems of child personality. But one cannot make a frontal attack upon the psychology of personality; because personality is really the sum and resultant of all possible forms of behavior. So one must approach the subject from several angles, which are represented by the titles of the ten chapters in Part Three. Naturally, we begin with the child's motor characteristics, because the very core of his physical and practical self is muscular.

All told he has over six hundred distinguishable muscles. Most of them are firmly attached in symmetrical pairs to the skeleton, with its elaborate apparatus of joints and levers. Anyone who has tussled with a lively preschool child knows the versatility of that apparatus. The complexity of the muscular system is beyond imagination, because a child has some forty million muscle fibers, each of which, in turn, is made up of an immense number of microscopic fibrils, and they in their turn are linked up with nerve fibrils which receive impulses via a veritable jungle of nerve cells in the brain and spinal cord. Because of the myriad of nerve connections, the muscular system is really a neuromuscular system.

Considering its vast complexity, is it strange that it takes literally a score of years to organize this system? Most of the organization takes place in the first ten years of life, and proceeds with an orderly sequence suggested by the gradients of growth. The process of organization really begins before birth, when the deep spinal muscles of the trunk come into action. These muscles are very ancient in the evolutionary history of the race. They antedate even the muscles that move the fore limbs and the hind limbs. In general, the development of the massive fundamental muscles is basic to that of the finer accessory muscles, such as those that wag the tongue and fingers, purse the lips and move the eyeballs.

But nature cannot wait until the birth of the child to lay down the primary networks for the coordination of the neuromuscular system. Accordingly, as we have already seen, even the unborn baby is capable of making movements and of striking attitudes. Some of the movements involve the gross muscles, many involve the fine. The total amount of activity that takes place during the fetal period is considerable; and if we had the requisite information we should find that this activity is already predictive of certain motor characteristics the child will display in later life.

Soon after the baby is born he assumes active postures that involve eyes, head, arms, legs, and trunk. His eyes, which moved intermittently under closed lids while he was still in utero, now assume a fixed posture as he stares at some object. He holds the posture by means of his twelve oculomotor muscles. These are so tiny that they could go into a thimble, but they are in many ways the most important muscles in his entire body. They have extremely extensive connections with millions of nerve cells (neurons) in the brain. Through these cells the eyes are brought under voluntary control, and they are also brought into association with countless muscle fibers in other muscles.

The eyes acquire their own skills; they also acquire directional skills which are built into the skills of other muscle groups. Having "learned" to hold a posture, the eyes learn to move right and left, up and down, and obliquely; they learn to converge, to follow a moving object, and to rove in exploratory inspection. In a few years they make hop-skip excursions across the printed page of a book that the reader holds in his tight hands.

This remarkable feat, which needs the coordination of eye, head, hands, and body postures, had its humble developmental beginnings in the tonic-neck-reflex (t-n-r) of early infancy. In its most typical form the baby lies supine, head turned to the right, right arm extended, left arm flexed. In general outline this activity bears resemblance to the stances assumed in fencing, boxing, creeping, walking, throwing, golfing, and violin-playing! In all these motor skills, the action system must strike asymmetric as well as symmetric attitudes in order to maintain poise and make progressive movements.

At first the infant gazes rather vaguely in the direction of the extended arm; but in two or three months his eyes "pick up" his moving fist, and he begins to look regardfully at his hands—an event that marks an epoch in his mental growth. Later he looks at an object held in his hand; he seizes an object on sight and inspects it. All this preparatory to the supreme achievement of holding a book simultaneously with eyes and hands—and perhaps even lifting the head a moment to smile at the teacher. But if the teacher is wise she will not expect that amenity too early.

The complexities of postural control are well borne out in the development of throwing, a motor skill which was of life-and-death importance to primitive ancestors, and which figures prominently in the play activities of child and adult. Well defined casting begins at about fifteen months, when the baby is perfecting his capacity to let-go-of-a-hold. Safely seated in his highchair, he takes great delight in casting one object after another overboard. His oculomotor muscles are alert enough to follow through as the objects fall—a very important visual skill, basic to the eye movements of reading.

At eighteen months he can cast while standing; but his throw is a crude forward thrust, and he toddles both before and after the throw. He is nearly four years old before he acquires a definite standing stance for delivery. His legwork, however, is still immature. He tends to use his right foot as fulcrum, and to twist and lean awkwardly with his trunk. At five years he advances with the left foot, shifts weight to the left foot on delivery, releasing the ball when the arm is in full extension. As in so many other behaviors, the five-year-old prefigures the adult. He shows many of the elements of mature throwing. Boys throw much farther and more accurately than girls, and are obviously more masculine in their style of delivery. Here is a constitutional sex difference in behavior which can scarcely be ascribed to cultural factors. The sex difference becomes evident well before the age of four.

Primitive man not only hurled missiles; he also struck blows with a cudgel. After toss ball comes bat and ball. Batting requires a higher order of coordination on the part of the eyes, hands, fingers, body posture, and feet. Nimble shift of stance, instantaneous perception, accurate timing, and flash-flood release of energy are demanded. The six-year-old makes swatlike strokes at the ball from a rather stiff stance; the ten-year-old makes a creditable swing with promising footwork. Batting form during the years from five to ten improves perceptibly, not merely because practice makes perfect, but because the total neuromuscular system of the child undergoes progressive growth changes. Similar changes affect numerous motor aspects of his school work.

Crayon and pencil require more delicate handling than bat and ball. The manipulation of pen, pencil, and crayon is highly dependent upon motor maturity. Details will be given in Chapter 18, School Life, in connection with the growth gradient for writing. Here again the general form of the motor activity varies with age and with inborn ability, rather than with exercise per se. This accounts for the fact that children at one stage will prefer bold and free flowing strokes with crude crayon; and at another stage, the will enjoy circumscribed finer strokes with pencil. Speed and accuracy also show a tendency to vary with the current maturity of the neuromuscular system. The seven-year-old doodles, the eight year-old likes to be timed for speed of performance, the nine-year-old tends to write at top speed without special regard for neatness. Such variations are entirely normal; and if we understood them better, we would not place as much stress on straight-line progress in the acquisition of motor skills.

Inasmuch as maturity is such a fundamental factor in determining the motor traits of growing children, we should expect distinguishable differences in the general motor deportment of the various grades of an elementary schoolroom. To be sure, much depends upon the freedom of movement allowed the pupils. If they are restricted to fixed positions at fixed desks, we should have to observe the tensional outlets of the children—the ways in which they wiggle, squirm, tap, grimace, etc. Such tensional behavior affords good clues to the motor maturity of a child. But if the atmosphere and the equipment of the room allow a normal degree of freedom, we get a truer picture of the motor characteristics of the children.

Most, if permitted a reasonable amount of freedom of movement, do fairly well. A few, because of either diet or disposition and in spite of freedom to move about the classroom in a reasonable way, must still be classified as hyperactive. Hyperactivity—that is, overactivity which cannot be controlled by reasonable and usual means—is a medical or behavior problem which should be treated by the specialist. But a kindergarten or primary-school child should not be labeled hyperactive simply because, as some teachers put it, he is "always up and down from his seat."

In the *kindergarten*, the typical five-year-old may move from one place of interest to another, making a transitional contact with the teacher. But when he gets to an area of choice, he stays there for a prolonged period, working smoothly. He is moderately aware of the whole room in his play, relates readily to his teacher, is not disturbed by a visitor.

The motor demeanors of the *first grade* are significantly different. The setup and the atmosphere of the room are more fluid. Materials are less in evidence. The typical six-year-old frequently moves from one place to another. Indeed, he seems always to be in motion. Even when he settles down he keeps on settling, continually shifting his posture and sketchily manipulating the material with which he is engaged. He does not build a tower or wind thread on a bobbin as smoothly as he did a year ago. He seems to be overaware of the contexts of his task, and too ready to move to the next task.

There is less moving about in the *second grade*. SEVEN settles down for longer periods, narrows down to the task in hand, and shows persistence even in the finer use of pencil and scissors. When restless, he may push his desk, but he can remain on location better than more mercurial Six. He is interested in finishing his task; if he moves about, it is more typically for a round trip to his teacher.

EIGHT is still more sedentary. There tends to be even less moving about in a *third grade* room. Performance is more even, group cohesion more evident. The room looks neater, and if it gets out of order from group activity, it is quickly put back in shape by group action. The individual children are more poised and self-dependent. There is less opening and closing of desks and fewer round trips for teacher contact; and more communication by an eager raising of the hand in a modified and agitated t-n-r attitude.

The *fourth* and *fifth grades* are more businesslike. The pupils remain seated for a much longer period; but for some developmental reason or other, postural proprieties have slumped. A typical nine-year-old raises his hand at the end of a flail-like arm which is so flaccid that it is often supported by the free hand! Perhaps, for temporary developmental reasons, his energies are draining from the proximal spine to the distal precinct of the fingers; for he has a new interest in speedy but skillful performances which require fine coordination. At any rate, if an immature nine-year-old should be in the group, he might give symptoms of his immaturity in his motor demeanors and motor deportment, and also by dependence on his teacher.

The motor characteristics of a child are worthy of observation because they are indicators both of individuality and of maturity status. By the age of nine a child acts like himself. He reveals his psycho-motor make-up in the way he comes into the schoolroom, and in the gestures he makes under tension or excitement. Nutritional and environmental factors should always be weighed; but we may also look for the core of individuality which expresses itself in postural and physiognomic demeanors.

Dr. William Sheldon, however, holds that "postural preferences are unquestionably innate." He speaks in terms of three temperament types which are associated with three body types: (1) endomorph: round, soft body, short neck, small hands and feet; (2) mesomorph: square, firm body with rugged muscles; (3) ectomorph: spindly body, delicate in construction. The extreme endomorph has a good digestive tract. He is good-natured, relaxed, sociable, communicative. The pronounced mesomorph is active, energetic, assertive, noisy, and aggressive. The fragile ectomorph is restrained, inhibited, tense; he may prefer solitude to noise and company, ". . . and," continues Sheldon, "it is probably as natural and desirable for an ectomorph to sit round-shouldered on the middle of his back as for a mesomorph to sit square-shouldered on the end of his back." Mary Lyon, founder of Holyoke, was a dynamic individual. With characteristic zeal, she used to exhort the girls in her Female Seminary with the injunction: "Sit with energy!"

Posture remains a key concept for the adequate interpretation of child development. But the concept must be enlarged to include the fine muscles as well as the gross—the tiny muscles of the eyes, the slender fascicles of the fingers, as well as the massive muscles of the trunk. Motor health depends upon a harmonization of the heavy fundamental and of the delicate accessory muscles. To establish that harmony, nature accents now one or the other group: now the flexors, now the extensors; now symmetry, now asymmetry; now the *go* muscles and now the *stop* muscles. School and home may consider the meaning and the trend of these accents. The varying accents come to the surface in all sorts of activity: tossing the ball, batting the ball, molding clay, painting, scrawling, printing, writing, reading. Even manners and morals have a motor basis. We may well look for a motor ingredient in all the gradients of growth.

Growth Gradients

1. BODILY ACTIVITY

15 months—Walks a few step and falls by collapse.
Creeps up steps.
18 months—Walks; seldom falls. Runs stiffly.
Walks into rather than kicks a ball.
Likes to move large toys by pulling, pushing, carrying.
Explores rooms and closets in the house.
Seats self by backing into a small chair.

2 years—Runs without falling, and squats in play.

Rhythmical responses, as bending knees in bouncing, swaying, swinging arms, nodding head, and tapping feet.

2½ years—Walks on tiptoe; jumps on two feet.

Runs ahead or lags when walking on street.

Pushes toy with good steering.

Runs, gallops, and swings to music.

Can carrry breakable object.

3 years—Walks erect and is sure and nimble on his feet.

Walks rather than runs. Can stand on one foot momentarily.

Throws a ball without losing balance.

Gallops, jumps, walks, and runs to music.

3½ years—Increased tension and may stumble or fall.

Hands may tremble, as in building with blocks.

4 years—Very active, covering more ground. Races up and down stairs. Dashes on tricycle.

Enjoys activities requiring balance. Can carry cup of liquid without spilling.

Prefers large blocks and makes more complicated structures.

Throws a ball overhand.

In rhythms, interprets and demonstrates own response.

5 years—There is greater ease and control of general bodily activity, and economy of movement.

Posture is predominantly symmetrical and closely knit. May walk with feet pronate.

Control over large muscles is still more advanced than control over small ones.

Plays in one location for longer periods, but changes posture from standing, sitting, squatting.

Likes to climb fences and go from one thing to another. Jumps from table height.

Likes to activate a story. Runs, climbs onto and under chairs and tables.

Throws, including mud and snow, and is beginning to use hands more than arms in catching a small ball, but frequently fails to catch.

Can skip.

Attemps to roller skate, jump rope, and to walk on stilts.

Likes to march to music.

Wants to hold adult's hand when unsure of self, as in descending stairs.

5½ years—There is demond to discard tricycle for bicycle, and many enjoy a few experiences on a bicycle.

6 years—Flings out arms and legs as he walks.

Very active; in almost constant motion.

Activity is sometimes clumsy as he overdoes and falls in a tumble.

Body is in active balance as he swings, plays active games with singing, or skips to music.

Enjoys wrestling, tumbling, crawling on all fours and pawing at another child, and playing tag.

Large blocks and furniture are pushed and pulled around as he makes houses, climbs on and in them.

Balls are bounced and tossed and sometimes successfully caught.

Tries skates, running broad jump, and stunts on bars.

Some boys spend much time digging.

Enjoys walking and balancing on fences.

7 years—Shows more caution in many gross motor activities.

Activity is variable; is sometimes very active and at other times inactive.

Repeats performances persistently.

Has "runs" on certain activities, such as roller skating, jump rope, "catch" with a soft ball, or hopscotch.

There is a great desire for a bicycle, which he can ride for some distance, though is only ready to handle it within limits.

Beginning to be interested in learning to bat and to pitch.

Boys especially like to run and shoot paper airplanes through the air.

Likes to gallop and to do a simple running step to music.

Many have a desire for dancing lessons, girls especially.

8 years—Bodily movement is more rhythmical and graceful.

Now aware of posture in self and others. Likes to play follow the leader.

Learning to play soccer and baseball with a soft ball and enjoys the shifts of activity within the game.

Girls are learning to run into the moving rope and can run out when beginning to fail, but cannot vary step while jumping.

Stance and movement free while painting.

Very dramatic in activities, with characteristic and descriptive gestures.

Enjoys folk dances but does not like rhythms unless of a spontaneous dramatic nature.

May enjoy piano lessons if doesn't have to practice.

9 years—Works and plays hard. Apt to do one thing until exhausted, such as riding bicycle, running, hiking, sliding, or playing ball.

Better control of own speed, but shows some timidity of an automobile's speed, of sliding, and of fast snow when skiing.

Interest in own strength and in lifting things.

Frequently assumes awkward postures.

Boys like to wrestle and may be interested in boxing lessons.

Great interest in team games and in learning to perform skillfully.

2. EYES AND HANDS*

4 years—Draws object with few details. Can imitate the picture of a square. (Copies at 4½.)

In painting, works with precision for some time, but shifts ideas. Makes crude designs and letters.

Enjoys having name printed on his drawings and begins to copy. May sense number of letters in name and may print first two letters, making marks for the remainder. Identifies several letters.

Uses scissors and attempts to cut on a straight line.

Builds extensive complicated structure with blocks, combining many shapes in symmetrical form.

Laces shoes and buttons front buttons.

Fingers piano with both hands.

5 years—Coordination has reached a new maturity. Approaches an object directly, prehends it precisely, and releases it with dispatch.

Builds with blocks, usually on the floor—graduated towers or low rambling structures with roads and small enclosures.

Manipulates sand, making roads and houses. Molds objects with clay.

If cannot do puzzle with precision and dispatch, will ask for help or abandon it.

Likes to color within lines, to cut and paste simple things, but is not adept.

Makes an outline drawing, usually one on a page, and recognizes that it is "funny."

Paints at an easel or on the floor with large brushes and large sheets of paper. May enjoy making letters in this manner.

Can "sew" wool through a perforated card.

Can manipulate buttons he can see, and can lace shoes.

Places fingers on piano keys and may experiment with chords.

This is a focal age visually. Child tends to sit with trunk upright, with work directly before him. Is aware of the totality of space, but does not take it in all at once. Rather, moves from one somewhat restricted spot to the next.

May get stuck visually on a focal point, so may need specific instructions to complete any eye-hand activity.

Ocular fixation is superior to ocular pursuit: child is better at looking than at following.

Can pay attention to something without looking directly at it—may look through it or even look in a different direction.

5½ years—Awkward in many manipulations.

---

* Here and in many of the gradients that follow, we start with 4 years of age since many immature 5-year-olds may still be behaving at a 4-year-old level.

Boys interested in tools, in Tinker Toys, and in watching an electric or wind-up train. Girls like to dress and undress dolls.

Many show interest in learning to print own first name and in underlining capitals and words in a familiar book.

Can copy, recognizably, the inside of divided rectangle.

More experimental visually than at 5. But can easily lose visual orientation and thus may often reverse numbers or letters.

May experimentally cross eyes; may do this just to be "funny."

6 years—Makes good start in many performances but needs some assistance and direction to complete tasks.

Is more deliberate and sometimes clumsy, but handles and attempts to utilize tools and material.

Cuts and pastes paper, making books and boxes; likes to use tape to fix things.

Hammers vigorously, but often holds hammer near the head. Can join boards and make simple structures.

Is beginning to use pencil crayons as well as wax crayons for coloring and drawing.

Can print capital letters, commonly reversing them. Likes to write on the blackboard as well as to use crayons and pencils.

Can usually print first name.

Attempts to sew, using a large needle; makes large stitches.

Is experimental visually; likes to try out new visual combinations.

Monocular behavior may be giving way to a new binocularity.

Better at following than at looking directly at something. May need to use finger to keep place in reading.

7 years—Manipulation of tools is somewhat more tense, but there is more persistence than earlier.

Pencils are tightly gripped and often held close to the point. Pressure is variable, but is apt to be heavy. As print becomes smaller, pressure grows lighter.

Can now print several sentences, with letters getting smaller toward end of line. Individual differences in size of printing: some print very small, but others continue to make large letters.

Boys especially interested in carpentry, and many can now saw a straight line.

Girls prefer to color and to cut out paper dolls.

Some show marked interest in the piano. Usually both hands are used, with unequal pressure.

Can copy a diamond.

Tends to pull in close to things he can't see well.

Many restrict visually, choosing smaller units than formerly.

Because of difficulty in shifting from near to far, should either work at the blackboard or at seat, not sit at seat and copy things from board.

Most are less distracted by peripheral movement than at six.

One eye leads, but the partner eye participates; a more formative evolving binocularity is on the way.

Tends to fatigue visually.

8 years—Increase in speed and smoothness of eye-hand performance, and an easy release.

Holds pencil, brush, and tools somewhat less tensely.

Enjoys having a performance timed, but does not compete with time.

Gap likely between what he wants to do with his hands and what he can do.

Writes or prints all letters and numbers accurately, maintaining fairly uniform alignment, slant, and spacing. Likes to work neatly, but sometimes is in too much of a hurry.

Beginning to get perspective in drawing. Draws action figures in good proportion.

Girls can now hem a straight edge in sewing.

Most can now shift from near to far much better than earlier, thus can sit at seat and copy from blackboard.

May actually lose things at near point, as when a ball thrown to child comes directly at him.

To escape difficult situations, child may turn eyes away. May definitely be more interested in looking out window than in looking at book.

Does not have to touch what he sees as much as earlier. Binocular visual activity now much smoother.

9 years—Individual variation in skills.

Can hold and swing a hammer well. Saws easily and accurately and uses knee to hold board. Makes finished products.

Garden tools used and handled appropriately.

Builds complex structures with Erector or Lego set.

Handwriting is now a tool.

Beginning to sketch in drawing. Drawings are often detailed. Especially likes to draw still life, maps, and designs.

Girls can cut out and sew a simple garment. Both boys and girls can knit.

Can dress rapidly. Some interest in combing own hair.

Interest in watching games played by others.

CHAPTER 12

PERSONAL HYGIENE

Eating

By the time a child reaches the age of five, one might well suppose that "he should know how to eat!" In a happy-go-lucky household perhaps he does know. But in a household with exacting standards, he may fall far short of expectations! He dawdles, he talks too much, and he may even ask to be fed. He wiggles in his chair, and his napkin must be tucked in at the neck to stay anywhere at all! Well, perhaps he will improve in another year.

But at the age of six things may be even worse! He stuffs his mouth, he spills, he masticates grossly, grabs for his food, knocks things over, teeters back in his chair. Besides, he is reputed to talk altogether too much, and to kick the table legs. Well, well, perhaps he will improve in another year.

At seven he may talk less at meals; but his mouth is still likely to be full to capacity when he does talk. He may bolt his food, but he is "quieting down." His napkin is variably below his chin, on the floor, or it lies neglected beside his plate.

At eight and nine he is not impeccable, but the napkin gradient registers an advance. The napkin has moved from its earlier position at the chin to the lap or its vicinity. The eight-year-old anchors his napkin by sitting on a corner of it.

And so each year brings its achievements and its promise. Meanwhile year in, year out, parents punctuate the meals with admonitions, reminders, frownings, and disciplinary dismissals from the table. An incredible amount of emotional tension disturbs the mealtimes of many American homes. All because of an exaggerated emphasis on table manners for their own sake.

In most instances the child is not truly ill-mannered. He is inept, immature. The demands made upon him are often out of all proportion to his skill. It takes not only motor skill but a certain degree of maturity to coordinate smoothly and with precision the following components of faultless table manners: (a) poised sedentary posture; (b) immobilization of napkin; (c) cutting, spearing, and loading with one or two feeding utensils; (d) graceful transit of the load to the mouth; (e) timing of the next load; (f) agreeable conversation; (g) timing conversation to mastication and to the conversation of others; (h) swallowing; (i) social deference to elders; (j) inhibition of kicking table legs (and nearby sibling!); (k) satiety; (l) and the conventional requestion to be excused.

It is safe to say that the eating behavior of children would tend to improve and not deteriorate if less stress were placed upon the formal aspect of manners. A friendly atmosphere at mealtimes is of importance, because enjoyment (rather than strict discipline) is still the best aid to appetite.

From a developmental standpoint, graceful table manners constitute a minor problem. They depend primarily upon the maturity of the child's motor skills and his tensional controls. Under ordinary conditions "manners" improve with age (rather than with scoldings). Even at the age of eight, the child eats tolerably well in public; and by ten he usually eats acceptably both at home and abroad. Viewed in this developmental perspective, the sternness and exasperation of the supervising adults seem wasteful and misplaced. (The family life does not need to be ruined after all.) The chief guidance rule is preventive. Make gradual rather than excessive demands; avoid complexities; make concessions; simplify the mealtime situations; rely on favorable atmosphere and attitudes. When parents themselves have highly emotional attitudes with respect to good manners, the problem has shifted from child to adult.

Many feeding problems vanish as soon as parents relax and place more faith in the lawful fluctuations and the favorable trends of development. The *level of appetite,* for example, fluctuates from year to year, but shows a tendency toward overall improvement. It may be low at eighteen months and at four years, but there is usually a steady rise from five years on. By nine years nearly all children have a vigorous and generous appetite. Nor is it wise to expect uniform levels of appetite throughout the day. Breakfast is often "the poorest" meal, even though one might wish to insist that it be otherwise. At many ages there is marked variability from meal to meal. But again, such variability tends to decrease with increasing age.

Closely related is the question of *speed in eating,* which in turn is "manners," because parents become impatient with dawdling and equally impatient with bolting. There are marked individual differences, based on constitutions and on maturity. Speed, however, tends to pick up with appetite, and accordingly varies with age. The five-year-old may eat very slowly. The eight-year-old likes to eat with dispatch and directness, and without deferment of dessert. One must not expect an orderly and uniform progression in eating behavior between the ages of five and ten. There is a constantly changing ratio between appetite, motor skill, social amenity, and tensional control. This results in unavoidable fluctuations in the general pattern of eating behavior. We should be more tolerant and optimistic with respect to table manners.

A closing word about *preferences and refusals.* They cause no end of worry and vexation. The cultural elevation of spinach, for. example, betrays a tendency toward induced feeding, which is not warranted by the science of nutrition. Parents should avoid strenuous efforts to overcome honest aversions to certain kinds of food. To be sure, we cannot always determine whether the refusal is whimsical or due to imitation, custom, or some other environmental factor. But if it is based on biochemical incompatibility, it should be respected. The phenomenon of allergy has shown that some supposedly wholesome foods are positively harmful to the organism.

We know a great deal more about allergy than we did a few decades ago. Thanks to Drs. Cott, Crook, Feingold, Smith, Wunderlich, and others, we have come to appreciate that not only much physical illness and discomfort, but also many supposed "behavior problems" are caused by food, drink, or other substances to which a child may be allergic. In fact, Feingold goes so far as to propose that the so-called hyperactivity and other learning disorders a number of children now suffer from is in many cases due to the artificial coloring and flavoring present in many foods. Such additives, he claims, may cause allergy or other physical difficulties which express themselves in all sorts of undesirable behavior. Sometimes a parent and child may have very similar allergic symptoms, suggesting the hereditary transmission of biochemical constitution.

Preferences and refusals often become less marked and less frequent after the age of eight years. In the preceding years there are significant fluctuations. A food preferred at one age is often discarded at a subsequent age. There are temporary periods of passions for certain foods. The five-year-old may manifest a strong dislike for stringy and lumpy foods. This may coincide with a special susceptibility to throat difficulties at this time. The six-year-old tends to emotional reactions in relation to the taste of food. He makes rather fine taste discriminations, and behaves somewhat ritualistically in regard to them. The eight-year-old likewise has emotional reactions to the smell of food. Such reactions, however puzzling and unwarranted they may seem, suggest the presence of physiological factors.

From this brief survey it is clear that eating, in our modern culture is a curious mixture of simple and complex, primitive and cultivated patterns of behavior. The whole child eats. Emotional and physical factors are intimately blended. And it is difficult to separate environmental from intrinsic origins. Consider the authenticated story of the two-year-old, who survived many weeks at sea in a lifeboat that escaped a torpedoing. After long experience, he cried for sharks to make their appearance, and he cried when he did not receive his anticipated ration of hardtack!

Differences in cultural experience and differences in race and individual constitution are reflected in the patterns of eating behavior. Sheldon writes almost a paean describing the alimentation of the endomorph, who attends and exercises in order to eat (while the ectomorph eats and exercises in order to attend, and the mesomorph eats and attends in order to exercise). The endomorph has a love of food and a warm appreciation of the process of eating for its own sake, which is not to be confused with mere voracity of appetite. "Digestion is excellent and is a primary pleasure."

But not all children are endomorphic so we may end on a broader note; based on the famous self-selection study already cited: "The joys of eating bulk large beyond our adult power to remember; they are our best ally in getting children to eat heartily, and it would seem that some latitude should be allowed in the matter of the conventions of eating in the interest of that enjoyment which is after all the best sauce for appetite."

Sleep

The gradients that follow give ample indication that sleep is not a simple function. It is a growing function which undergoes many changes from year to year. Sleep is not simply a clever trick, which can be learned with practice. It is a complex behavior which was built up through long ages of racial evolution. Every child must rebuild his sleep structures as he matures. The culture helps him as best it can.

The term "sleep structure" is not altogether figurative. To begin with, sleep depends upon certain structural arrangements in the central nervous system. Sleep is not merely a cessation of activity, a turning off of a switch. It is a positive method of inhibitory control, which must be adaptively related to other functions of the organism, especially those of nutrition, movement, and of mental activity. And the structure of the sleep mechanisms inevitably changes as all these related functions change. Sleep is not an isolated function which grows by itself.

The newborn baby is sometimes characterized as an expert sleeper. In a restricted sense this is true. He surely shows marked ability to stay asleep; but should he be considered less competent because as he grows older he becomes more wakeful? Sleep is an intricate behavior complex, which comprises four distinguishable phases: (1) going to sleep; (2) staying asleep; (3) waking; (4) staying awake.

All skills are relative. The newborn infant is most skillful in phase 2. He shows a simple kind of ability in phase 1, often falling asleep in the very midst of nursing. He is likely to cry as he wakens and may continue crying until the next feeding. He has not made a clear-cut differentiation between feeding and sleeping.

By the age of sixteen weeks the pattern of his sleeping behavior undergoes remarkable changes. He displays increased competence in all four phases of the sleep cycle. He is likely to finish his meal before he sleeps (phase 1); he stays asleep for a long but not over-long stretch (phase 2). He may awake without crying from hunger; and he stays awake talking to himself and playing with his hands until the next feeding. He has two or three naps during the day, and a corresponding number of periods of awakeness. This remarkable gain in phases 3 and 4 is based upon structural changes in his nervous system. The brain cells in his "waking center" have reached a new stage of maturity. Consequently he can be more easily awakened; and he also wakes himself up more often and more easily. He is really a much more highly talented sleeper than he was as a newborn.

If sleep were an independent faculty, this would be the end of our story. But as the child's action system changes his sleep problems change. Awakeness becomes more and more demanding, and it is more difficult to operate those brain cell controls which govern release into sleep. Nature's problem and the culture's problem is to keep phases 1 and 2 in equilibrium with phases 3 and 4. Now one, now another phase is apparently over accentuated. For example, at fifteen and at twenty-one months the child often wakes up spontaneously during the night, and in an apparently capricious manner remains awake for an hour or two.

During the second and third years release into sleep proves to be a complex process, because it entails a voluntary inhibition of the wakeful cerebral cortex. Going to sleep from choice is a release act comparable to prehensory release. The child first learns to seize an object and then he learns to let it go. At the age of two and a half years he is in a peculiarly unsettled developmental stage. He not only shows difficulty in going into sleep, but he may have difficulty in getting out of sleep! He temporarily loses some of his knack in waking up.

This brief review suggests that we need to make a similar analysis when confronted with the sleeping problems of the years from five to ten. It is the whole child who sleeps; but it does not follow that his entire organism slumbers homogeneously, with simultaneous equality of depth. He stirs, he dreams, he smiles, laughs, frowns, grimaces, talks in his sleep. He is rarely completely quiet. Fears disturb his sleep, taking the form of nightmares and night terrors. Whether pleasant and wistful dreams should be considered guardians of sleep must be left in doubt. It is true that at about the age of eight or nine a child may even protest on being awakened in the midst of an enjoyable dream.

Many of the management problems of the middle years (from five to ten) have to do with bedtime preliminaries. Here, as elsewhere, there are great individual differences, but also there are developmental trends in the demands made by the child upon the parent. The demands are variable from age to age; but they are definite and they usually denote a real need at the time. The nature of the need is not always apparent. One child makes a quick jump into bed so that the man under the bed won't get him. Another child shakes his head to shake out the bad thoughts before going to sleep!

The fall of night, the impending separation from the parent, and the prospect of the blackout of sleep itself all combine to weaken daytime morale and open the way to apprehensions, imaginings, and clinging behavior. The five-and-a-half-year-old likes to be read to or talked to before going to sleep. He seeks reassurance. He even finds comfort in the companionship of a toy animal as bedfellow.

Such props and preliminaries do not necessarily become habitual, because with the expansion of personality the presleep demands take on a more constructive character. The bedtime hour, once known as the "children's hour," may transform into a kind of social hour during which the household is, admittedly, in danger of overstimulating the child. But it may also become a more quiet witching hour, when the rapport between parent and child is sensitized by a heightened feeling of interdependency. The competitive strivings of the day abate. The child becomes more receptive, and emotionally more aware. It is a favorable time for confidences and for organizing mental processes by questions, answers, discussions, and hints. Routine prayers have a function; but the more mundane intercommunication also serves a spiritual purpose.

No set rules can be offered. All depends on good timing, which means finding the psychological moment, which in turn depends on recognizing a developmental stage.

Although the seven-year-old may show a certain fondness for his bed, the child is quite likely at eight to exhibit increased ingenuity and energy in an effort to stave off bedtime. Often this is legitimate because the need for sleep is decreasing. Given some leeway, the eight-year-old helps to settle this problem satisfactorily. He tends to adjust if granted the privilege of some pleasant self-regulated pre-bed occupation. This is a fair tribute to his self-dependence.

But as his self-dependence grows, his self-assertiveness may also increase. Unless carefully managed, this may precipitate a sharp resistance to going to bed at the expected time. The problems of sleep and personality again reveal their close union. The rebellion is not so much against sleep as against the domination of a parent-imposed task. If the parent meets the challenge wisely he will widen the area of his strategy.

And this principle holds for the management of sleep throughout the whole period of childhood. Sleep difficulties cannot be handled by direct assault. The whole child sleeps—and wakes. Sleep is a complex of four phases: release into sleep—staying asleep—waking —staying awake. It took ages of evolution to produce these phases. The child needs a befitting allotment of time to organize them into his own developing personality.

Elimination

A physiologist would include under the heading of Elimination the excretory functions of perspiration, respiration, urination, and evacuation. These functions are seemingly so automatic that one might wonder whether they need to be included in a volume on child behavior. The first two mentioned do indeed take care of themselves to a marked degree, although they always retain a significant relationship with the psychological states of the individual.

The functions of bladder and bowel, however, are not allowed to take care of themselves. They are so heavily complicated by superimposed cultural controls that they undergo a tortuous course of organization and of reorganization throughout the periods of infancy and childhood. The controls are not fully established even during the first five years of life.

These excretory functions are governed by a combination of voluntary and involuntary mechanisms. When bladder and bowel are empty or partially filled, the urethral and anal sphincters (ringlike muscles) are kept in tonic contraction by the sympathetic nervous system. This mechanism takes care of itself; it is involuntary. When the contents of bowel and bladder reach a certain level (which varies greatly with conditions and individuals), the sphincters relax; the smooth muscles of the containing walls contract; the contents are expelled. Here again the basic mechanism is involuntary.

As the child grows older, a higher mechanism is gradually superimposed upon the lower. Increasingly complex connections are made with nerve fibers that go to and from the brain. Voluntary control becomes possible only as these nerve conections take shape. Sphincter control, as we sometimes call it, therefore depends not upon "will power" but upon nerve cell structures, which have to grow. All toilet training must defer to the maturity of the child's central nervous system.

This principle holds even during the middle years. The lapses that come at the age of six, for example, are readily explained in terms of current developmental changes which affect the entire organism and therefore involve the sphincters.

Parents do not have to be neurologists in order to appreciate the difficulties that confront the child in the acquisition of sphincter control; but a brief tabulation of the progressive steps toward mature control will throw light on problems of guidance and prevention:

(a) In the newborn infant the excretory acts are numerous and apparently irregular.

(b) They decrease in number and tend to occur during periods when the child is awake.

(c) Being awake, he attends to the accompanying internal sensations.

(d) He associates the act with a particular place and with customary events in his daily routines.

(e) He "learns" to delay, as inhibitory neural mechanisms mature. He delays by inhibiting the otherwise spontaneous relaxation of the sphincters.

(f) Lengthens the period of his delay.

(g) Learns to terminate the inhibition at will. This is true voluntary release; but the occasions when he can exert that will are few and limited in scope.

(h) Uses gestures, vocal signs, general names, and later distinguishing names for the products of bladder and bowel, *after* excretion.

(i) Uses such words *during* excretion.

(j) Uses the words *prior to* excretion, "tells," at first not soon enough; but eventually he tells in good time.

(k) Dry all night.

(l) Wakes by himself and asks to be taken to the toilet.

(m) Develops a curiosity about the excretory functions of others. He takes a special interest in strange bathrooms. He experiences a sense of privacy and of modesty.

(n) Lengthens the span of retention and facilitates voluntary release.

(o) Foresees urgencies long in advance and plans accordingly.

(p) Adjusts and controls despite changes of scene and the hurly-burly of school life.

(q) "Accidents" decline almost to the vanishing point.

It requires nearly all the letters of the alphabet to list the progressive stages of organization in bladder and bowel control for the first ten years of life. Even so, our listing greatly oversimplifies the underlying developmental processes. Progress does not proceed in a straight and steady line. There are many fluctuations and apparent lapses, due chiefly to the ever-changing accents and patterns of growth. Sphincter control does not develop independently, but must always be incorporated into the total action system.

Moreover, the interweaving of opposite skills (e.g., inhibition versus release) is going on all the time. At times inhibition takes the upper hand: the child withholds valiantly for a long period but is unable to release at will. Later the release mechanism dominates: inhibition is overpowered and release becomes expulsive. These are normal growth fluctuations. They are not due to perversities. They are expressions of physiological awkwardness.

Similar awkwardnesses beset the child even after he is old enough to go to school. In spite of a sharp strengthening of cultural inhibitions, the organism seems to lose some of its previous inhibitory capacity. Accidents of bowel as well as bladder increase during the sixth year, when the organism is undergoing profound transformation. Sphincter controls are affected.

Needless to add, individual differences in this field of personal-social behavior should be recognized both at home and at school. The tonus of the sphincters is highly susceptible to reflex stimulations. Psychic activity tends to increase their tone; but in temperamentally susceptible individuals the bowel and bladder organ systems react as tensional outlets. We must, therefore, think in terms of physiological status and maturity, as well as in terms of cultural propriety.

Parents are unduly mortified by lapses in children of school age. The lapses are most likely to occur following an afternoon session at school. It is not so much the child as the adult who needs to foresee these midafternoon urgencies. Similar urgencies and instabilities reappear among eight-year-olds. Many teachers aggravate these difficulties by unnecessarily rigid restrictions. School toilets should be readily available to all primary- and elementary-school pupils.

Bath and Dressing

Birds and four-footed animals frequently exhibit forms of behavior that are ascribed to instincts of cleanliness and adornment. The human species may be credited with comparable instinctive tendencies; but under the conditions of modern culture these tendencies in the young do not always come to spontaneous and clear-cut expression! Sometimes the infant displays a positive aversion to clothes; and although he may enjoy the aquatic aspects of bathing, he may soon resist the sanitary. At any rate, the tugging, the pulling, the dawdling, the bribing, the exhorting, and the scolding that, at varying ages, are occasioned by the demands of bath and dressing are sufficiently impressive to warrant a brief examination of underlying causes.

The causes are primarily developmental, and they are exaggerated whenever parents and caretakers become too exacting. The child's failure to meet expectations must always be considered in relation to his sense of time and timing, and the maturity of his attention patterns. The ultimate goal is self-dependence, but it must be reached by gradual stages.

For a baby the bath has many facets of interest—social, tactile, athletic, and playful. He delights in the water play and the gross motor activity. At the age of one he plays exploitively with washcloth, soap, and floating toys. Needless to say, he has no appreciation of the more practical purposes of the bath. At eighteen months he may show resistance for brief periods because of the strength of new gross motor drives. At two years he takes a positive interest in helping to wash himself; he especially likes to wash his hands at a bowl— but not from motives of cleanliness. At two and a half years he is likely to be in a ritualistic phase of development. He does not entertain an image of the objective of the bath. He imposes more or less elaborate and irrelevant rituals upon the whole situation. If his caretaker thinks solely of the relevant objectives and not of the ritualisms, child troubles ensue. By three the rituals abate. By four and five the bath is an easy routine; and often so pleasant that it is difficult to terminate. By eight years some children can take over completely.

The five-year-old washes his hands before meals, if reminded. Reminders are necessary for the next two or three years. The eight-year-old, however, prefers a very mild reminder in the form of a faint and tactful hint.

Children between the ages of five and nine still need some assistance in the niceties of cleanliness, neatness, and manicuring. There are individual differences in the degree of docility shown. Some children react with extreme resistance to help about the ears, and even to combing and brushing of hair. In some instances this extraordinary resistance is based not on personality negativism, but on a temporary hypersensitiveness of skin, which probably has a developmental basis and is exaggerated in certain individuals.

The development of self-dependence in dressing is roughly parallel to that of self-dependence in cleanliness. It depends first of all on motor abilities, and secondly on consciousness of social approval. Interest in adornment and display serve to motivate the child at certain ages, even though earlier he may have shown a preference for no clothes at all. Individual and sex differences become apparent in the perschool period, and pronounced during the elementary-school period. Adolescence brings a host of elaborating manifestations.

The five-year-old usually can dress himself almost completely;

but he is somewhat careless or indifferent about attire. His mother daily selects the clothes to be worn and lays them out in advance. The six- and seven-year-olds need similar assistance. The six-year-old, characteristically enough, presents special problems, due to the transitional phases of his current development. He is more clothes-conscious than at five, but he does not readily accept the help he needs. By nature he dawdles. He is very easily distracted from the task of dressing. He needs management (and forbearance) more than direct pressure. Time brings changes. SEVEN likewise dawdles; but is more likely to end with an effective spurt. EIGHT is more efficient in dressing, even though boys may affect disdain of neat and tidy clothes once they have them on. From eight to ten there is a marked increase of responsibility in selection of clothes, disposal of soiled clothes, and adaptation of garments to weather and occasion.

Although culture plays a powerful role in the shaping of customs and costumes, the spontaneous child is likely to disclose certain trends of natural man. Even in the removal of clothes we glimpse, at least darkly, a developmental gradient! FIVE AND A HALF casts his garments all over the room. SIX drops them on the spot or flings them aside. SEVEN drops them more decorously. EIGHT puts them on a chair (where they may accumulate from day to day in some households). NINE may even hang them up neatly.

And for the record it should be added that the boy who *never* would comb his hair is reputed to give it altogether too much attention when he is in his teens.

Somatic Conditions

Under this heading we shall sketchily consider some of the somatic or bodily, conditions, that are intimately related to the development of the child's behavior characteristics. The subject is much too vast and complicated for full treatment. We simply wish to suggest, somewhat concretely, how the maturity of the child reacts upon his physical and mental well-being.

From an anatomical and physiological standpoint, the child's organism consists of a collection of organ systems—skeletal, muscular, gastrointestinal, urogenital, pulmonary, circulatory, etc. The various organs are, of course, closely interrelated; indeed, they are knit into a single living unit through the nervous system and the humoral system—that is, the blood and body fluids. When all these organ systems function in ideal harmony, the child is ideally healthy. When the harmony is disturbed by disease, injury, or excessive strain, the child reacts with illness, with somatic "complaints," with tensional symptoms of varying severity. Sometimes the symptoms are signals of danger; very often they are methods by which nature attempts to compensate or to restore an optimal working balance. Sometimes, also, the symptoms are passing, normal indicators of growth changes. These latter symptoms are very interesting. We wish that we knew more about them.

It is certain that the child's body chemistry undergoes alterations with age. This is demonstrated by shifting allergies, by fluctuating appetites and food preferences, by changing susceptibilities and immunities to disease. There are certain diseases seen in infancy and childhood which are seldom or never seen after adolescence. The severity of a given disease also varies with age. Contagious diseases are, in general, more dangerous before rather than after five years of age. This is partly due to differences in the "immunologic maturity" of the tissues. Fatigue, psychologic stress and shock, malnutrition, and other factors may precipitate illness, but the primary susceptibilities of the organism are determined by biochemical defenses, which are closely correlated with age and constitutional type.

With modern medical techniques, the incidence of infectious diseases is reduced by protective inoculations. Nevertheless, conservative opinion holds that hereditary factors, influenced by the age of the host, may be of importance in determining whether an individual is capable of forming antibodies when stimulated by infectious agents. The marked individual and age differences in allergy reactions lend support to this point of view. Some writers use the term "serological maturation" in much the same way that we speak of behavior maturation.

Although the organism may be described as an interdependent collection of organ systems, this does not mean that the several systems mature at a uniform rate. On the contrary, each system has a more or less unique and independent curve of growth. Now one system or function is in the ascendancy, and now another. It is these very deviations from lock step that produce both commonly observed and commonly unrecognized irregularities of child development.

Four-year-old children often prove to be peculiarly susceptible to colds. A child may have one cold after another throughout the winter. At five he may show excellent health, escaping, perhaps, with one cold. In the period approximately from five-and-a-half to six-and-a-half years there is marked increase of susceptibility to infectious diseases, and the child is sicker with illness when it strikes. The mucous membranes of throat, bronchi, and ears appear to be peculiarly vulnerable at this age. This is not surprising, because much other evidence corroborates that the six-year-old is in an active stage of developmental transition. At seven and eight years illnesses are fewer. The total death rate is lower in the age period from five to ten years than in the years under five, and it is lowest of all in the half decade from ten through fifteen years.

The statistics for injuries and fatalities from *accidents* also show significant age trends. These trends again are based on maturity factors. Parents and educators should realize that the incidence of accidents is determined by three sets of interacting factors: (1) the child's physique; (2) his behavior traits; and (3) exposure to risk. Even the preferred site of injury may be affected by the child's body build and motor characteristics (factors 1 and 2). For example, the two-year-old still leans forward when he runs. Should he fall he is likely to bruise his forehead. As he grows older his running stance becomes more erect; at two and a half years he is more likely to hit his nose; at three or four years his teeth; at four and a half years his collarbone. A six-year-old may break his fall with his arm (and his arm with his fall); the eight-year-old is more likely to jeopardize his legs.

A report of the Children's Bureau has shown that accidents represent the leading cause of death among school children, and therefore constitute a public health problem of the first rank. Sex difference is marked for the two principal accidents, motor vehicle fatalities and drowning. Boys are more daring and reckless. Girls are more cautious, and age for age, are physically and psychologically more mature. Girls, accordingly, incur fewer risks, with one outstanding exception: the rate of fatalities for accidental burns is more than twice that of boys for the five-to-ten-year age group.

These trends must not be taken too literally, because many accidents unfortunately contain unpredictable elements of physical place and circumstance. The most predictable areas lie in the field of behavior. Among preschool children the amount of exposure to risk (factor 3) is largely determined by their immature behavior traits and lack of parental foresight. It is not surprising that fatalities and injuries from burns, scalding, poisons, knives, etc., are excessive for the household age from infancy to five years. Automobile, bicycle, and street accidents, on the other hand, play a leading role in the period from five to ten years. Six and Eight are notoriously "careless" ages, not because the children are willfully heedless, but because they lack the capacity to take adaptive heed. In fact, a six-year-old may take very conscious heed before he runs across the street to meet his mother, who is waiting for him. He may close his eyes, clench his fists, and dash; but he may fail to make adequate allowance for an oncoming car. Perhaps the parent did not make adequate allowance for the limitations of the child's psychology. Here are two sets of behavior factors which can be recognized and brought under preventive control. A similar control should be extended to the eight-year-old. He is in an expansive hurry-up, dash-away age. He does not look far enough ahead. Frequently he is given altogether too much freedom in the use of his bicycle. He needs more delimitations and supervision to reduce exposure to risk.

This entails planning and management. Parents and teachers are inclined to place too much reliance on admonition and explanation. Children need help in acquiring attitudes of caution; but mere words, even emphatic words, do not suffice. Sometimes the repetitive, worrisome, scolding insistence on caution is only a form of relief for the mother, expressing her subchronic state of anxiety. Often there is excessive appeal to fear. Caution has elements of fortitude as well as fear. If the child is unduly afraid he cannot be duly cautious, that is, duly prudent and wary. The parent-child relation should not be fearsome in either direction; there should be mutual confidence, so that children will freely and promptly report home even apparently minor accidents or injuries regardless of the "guilty" circumstances under which they may have occurred.

The organism of the child rarely remains in smooth equilibrium for a prolonged period. Even in the absence of accidents and frank disease the child is subject to tensions, which express themselves outwardly in different forms of *tensional activity*. These tensional manifestations are varied in kind and degree. Some are transient and benign; they may even be part of the mechanisms of adjustment. It is difficult in many instances to determine the origin and basis of any given tensional activity. There are enormous individual differences based on temperamental characteristics. Poorly organized children show marked, frequent, and even multiple symptoms.

The classic tensional activity of the pre-school period is thumb-sucking. In the years since this book was originally published, the public attitude toward thumb-sucking and other customary tensional outlets has changed considerably. In the 1930s and 1940s parents used to ask the child specialist, "How can I stop my child from sucking his thumb?'" In the 1950s the question became: "*Should* I stop him from sucking his thumb or does he perhaps need this tensional outlet?" And now, with the publication of such children's books as *Danny and His Thumb*, by Kathryn Ernst, we have reached the place where at least some grownups assure their boys and girls that thumb-sucking is *all right* while they are still young, and that "pretty soon" they won't need to do it or have time to do it anymore. That is, today we respect the fact that children as well as adults do sometimes feel tensions, which they need to relieve.

Temper tantrums, which might also be listed among preschool tensional outlets, vary in nature and severity with age and temperamental type. They are extremely prevalent up to the age of two and a half years. Their later manifestations will be considered in the following chapter, which deals with the expressional aspects of emotional behavior, including crying, anger, and aggression.

Rocking, head-banging, head-rolling, various forms of rhythmic and premasturbatory and masturbatory movements, stuttering, fingernail-biting, and psychic tics like repetitive eye-blinking may occur before the age of five, with resolution usual during the middle years after five.

Tensional behavior is at a relatively low ebb at five years, and is ordinarily limited in scope; but it shows a marked increase in the period from five-and-a-half to seven years. School entrance is frequently accompanied by temporary speech tensions, nail-biting, an exaggeration of thumb-sucking, hand-to-mouth gestures, pencil-chewing, hair-chewing, tongue protrusion, pulling of mouth corner, pursing of both lips and biting the lower one! This cataloguing of the various patterns conveys a reminder of the tensions under which the school beginner is laboring. Many of these tensions escape by the mouth outlet in the form of clicking, blowing through the lips, heavy breathing, gasping with excitement, and throat-clearing. But the tensions also involve the eyes, which dart with horizontal thrusts; the legs, which shift and jiggle; the knees, which knock; and the feet, which tap restlessly. For no apparent reason a child may make somewhat peculiar throat noises and may even repeat them so often as to suggest a convulsive tic. But usually such a "nervous habit" proves to be a temporary manifestation, on a par with his general restlessness and the clumsiness which, so it is said, causes him to trip over a piece of string.

The tensional behavior of the seven-year-old is less pronounced throughout. If thumb-sucking, nail-biting, or stuttering persist from earlier years, he now makes a voluntary effort to bring them under control. The outlet activities of hand to mouth are less emphatic, but lip-pursing, whistling, and throat noises may become very persistent. Fingers and hands are perhaps more restlessly active than feet. Some SEVENS show a marked sensitivity and tensional overflow into the hand. They may not like to be touched, but they themselves like to touch objects in an exploratory manner. A characteristic tensional expression of the seven-year-old at school is a mildly pensive sigh, head resting in hand, elbow propped on desk, eyes averted obliquely.

The eight-year-old, true to his expansive, highly geared nature, displays a larger variety of tensional outlets. Many earlier patterns reappear, but with a fluidity of shift which makes them less noticeable. His tensional behavior is more diffuse, and much of it is channelized in chatter, gestures, and mimetic expressions. There is grimacing, scowling, raising of eyebrows, humming, and smacking of lips. The eyes not only dart, but roll. No part of the body seems to be free from tensions. He plays with a gadget, he jiggles his legs, he shoves his body; he may feel an urgency to urinate when confronted with an unpleasant task. It is as though every one of his organ systems were permeable to the inner tensions which ordinarily are a relatively normal feature of his behavior day. The diffuseness and diversity of his reactions are in character with his bodily make-up, his physiological maturity.

At nine and ten there is often a quieting down of tensional manifestations. They are less diffuse and are more closely associated with specific situations, and they tend to reflect the idiosyncrasies of the individual. Several reactions are rather characteristic of this age period: pianoing of the fingers, fiddling at a button, blowing of lips and cheeks, picking at fingernails and cuticles, tiny gestures of plucking at eyelid, and a sweeping gesture of clapping the hand on the head in pseudo dismay. Equally characteristic are the emotional refinements of worry and anxiety; for the fields of tensional behavior and of expressional behavior inevitably overlap. The nine- or ten-year-old can grimace with mock deprecation of his failures; he can smile and laugh at situations and at himself. Thereby he registers his increased maturity.

Growth Gradients

EATING

4 years—Appetite. Fair. Drinks milk rapidly and well.

REFUSALS AND PREFERENCES. Food jags or food strikes indicate marked and definite preferences for certain foods and dislike of others.

SELF-HELP. Beginning to help plan meals. Helps set the table. May dawdle if eats alone, though does not need to be fed.

TABLE MANNERS. May be able to eat several meals a week with family—often breakfast, or Sunday dinner. However, talking may interfere with eating and child usually has to interrupt meal to go to the bathroom. Much leaving the table.

5 years—Appetite. Usually good, though varies markedly from meal to meal, with breakfast often the poorest. Child cleans plate.

REFUSALS AND PREFERENCES. Refusals definite: cooked root vegetables, gravies, casseroles, puddings. Prefers meat, potatoes, raw vegetable, milk, and fruit.

SELF-HELP. Feeds slowly but per- sistently and with fair amount of ability. May need help toward end of meal or with certain foods. Beginning to use a knife for spreading.

TABLE MANNERS. May eat most meals with family, but may have supper early in the kitchen. Talking interferes with eating. Napkin tucked in at neck.

6 years—Appetite. Usually large (said to be a "wonderful" eater); but may eat more between meals than at meals. Likes a snack before bed. Takes more than can handle. Wants the biggest piece. Breakfast often continues to be the poorest meal.

REFUSALS AND PREFERENCES. Refuses foods by spells; dislikes certain foods because of texture. Likes and is willing to try new foods. Dislikes cooked desserts and cooked vegetables. Prefers meat, potatoes, milk, raw vegetables, peanut butter, ice cream, candy.

SELF-HELP. Many prefer to finger feed, though some will not touch food with their fingers. May prefer fork to spoon. May be awkward in spreading.

TABLE MANNERS. Manners are poor. Child talks too much, spills, stuffs mouth, chews with mouth open. Grabs for food, knocks things over, wriggles or teeters back in chair. Kicks table legs. Criticizes behavior of siblings and adults. Dawdles. May refuse napkin or bib, or may have it tucked in at neck.

7 years—Appetite. Moderate. Extremes of poor and excessive appetite in different children.

REFUSALS AND PREFERENCES. Beginning to accept disliked foods, though dislikes strongly flavored cooked vegetables or cheeses. Likes milk, meat, ice cream, and sandwiches, especially peanut butter.

SELF-HELP. Very little difficulty with implements. Pushes food onto fork or spoon with free fingers.

TABLE MANNERS. Improving, though may spill, bolt food, stuff mouth, talk with mouth full. May want to bring his last activity to the table with him. Leaves the table with any distraction. At times may be interested in table conversation. May quarrel or fool with siblings. Sometimes prefers to eat alone so as to continue watching TV or reading. Prefers napkin beside the plate and uses when needed.

8 years—Appetite. Excellent. Poor eaters for the first time have a good appetite. Increase in intake as well as increase in weight. Some may need to have intake restricted.

REFUSALS AND PREFERENCES. Fewer refusals. Preferences about as at seven years. Will attack new foods. Judges food by the odor. Expresses "love" for certain foods.

SELF-HELP. Less frequently needs to use fingers. Beginning to cut meat with a knife, but not skillful. Can "fix" own baked potato.

TABLE MANNERS. Variable. Definite contrast between poor table manners at home and good ones in company. At home, bolts food, spills it, pushes it around on plate, takes large mouthfuls, talks with mouth full. Plays with silver. Aware of good table manners, but unable to put them into practice. Wants to have his turn to talk and tends to interrupt adult conversation. May anchor napkin by sitting on it.

9 years—Appetite. Under better control. Now eats approximately an adult meal and even poorer eaters settle into more balanced intake according to needs.

REFUSALS AND PREFERENCES. Frankly refuses certain foods. May refuse an old food cooked in a new way. Usually prefers and looks forward to dessert.

SELF-HELP. Good control of implements. Tends to saw meat with a knife and cut too large pieces; therefore may need help.

TABLE MANNERS. Generally improved, but may still be better away from home. May become too absorbed in listening or in talking.

10 years—Appetite. Majority "love food—eat tons—eat constantly," though many express this quite casually: "Sometimes I like to eat, sometimes I don't." Even poor eaters have usually improved. They eat more, will try some new foods, will eat cooking other than mother's. Many do not eat big breakfast.

REFUSALS AND PREFERENCES. Related with enthusiasm—eyes sparkle as they tell of likes, gesture of vomiting as they describe disliked foods. Greater variety of likes than of dislikes.

FAVORITES: "Any kind of meat," "any kind of potatoes," raw vegetables, cooked peas, cake, ice cream.

REFUSALS: Liver (almost universally), fish, eggs, many cooked vegetables, "mixed things like stew"; some dislike desserts, and some turn against that old favorite, peanut butter.

SNACKS AND SWEETS. Majority do eat between meals, and even the self-styled abstainers may eat a little. "I can have all the cider I want between meals—it's good for me, my mother says." Favorite between-meal snacks are soft drinks, cookies, fruit. Marked individual differences in liking sweets. Some crave them, have a "terrific sweet tooth." Some not interested. Others like them but try to cut down because of teeth or weight or parents' limitations. Ice cream is among the favorites; candy, dessert, pie may not be.

TABLE MANNERS. About half of our group are described as having adequate table manners, and they themselves say their manners are "not mentioned" by parents. Of the rest, some are described as "bad" or even "terrible." Poor posture is greatest complaint. Also criticizing food, holding fork incorrectly, talking too much. Some children criticize table manners of parents. Mother may let up on them when father not present. Children try to do better when father is there.

COOKING. Considerable enthusiasm about cooking, in boys as well as girls. About a quarter of our subjects do some cooking. Bacon, eggs, hamburgers, or hot dogs are chief foods cooked. Some even try cakes or pancakes.

SLEEP

4 years—Nap. Usually enjoys "play nap" alone in room, with books or toys, 1–3 P.M.

BEDTIME. May go to bed willingly at 7 P.M.; enjoys hearing a bedtime story. May then enjoy half an hour alone in bed with books or crayoning. Takes dolls or teddy to bed.

NIGHT—Wakens only for toileting; usually needs only a little help from adult.

MORNING—Wakens between 7 and 7:30 A.M. Gets up and plays alone till time to go to parents' room.

5 years—Nap. Many nap once or twice a week for an hour or more. A few, especially boys, may nap several days a week.

BEDTIME. Variable from 7 to 8 P.M., dependent on nap and activity of the day. Now may go to bed without presleep activity, though some "read" or crayon for a while. Less taking of toys to bed.

NIGHT. Some sleep through, but many waken for toileting, usually after midnight and may have difficulty returning to sleep. May have frightening dreams and wake screaming.

MORNING. Most waken at 7–8 A.M. and can busy themselves with play materials until time to get up.

6 years—Nap. A few have half-hour nap on occasion at five and a half years. At six years an hour's "play nap" may be desirable.

BEDTIME. At five-and-a-half rarely resists bedtime hour, usually between 7 and 8 P.M. May prefer supper in bed, followed by play. May want mother to talk or read story. Return to taking toy to bed. May enjoy prayers. At six years

most usual bedtime is at 7, though most wait till 7:30 or 8. Enjoys some activity with adult. May tell day's experiences.

NIGHT. More can sleep through night. Child disturbed by bad dreams and gets into bed with mother, or mother goes to him. Several still waken for toileting and usually manage by themselves.

MORNING. At five and a half, two extreme groups: one wakens very early (5–6 A.M.), the other has to be awakened (8 A.M.). By six years, usual time is 7–7:30 A.M. Gets right up and can then dress self if clothes are laid out, but apt to dawdle.

7 years—Bedtime. From 7 to 8 P.M. Gets ready with little adult help. May like to be read to. Two extreme groups: one group falls asleep rapidly; the other sings, listens to noises in house, or sees shadow objects in room before sleep. A few take toys to bed.

NIGHT. Usually sleeps soundly, with less waking with nightmares or for toileting.

MORNING. Wakens about 7 A.M., but may sleep later on Sunday mornings. Some like to waken early on occasion to read or do some special thing. Needs some reminding to get dressed.

8 years—Bedtime. Later, usually 8–8:30, occasionally 9 P.M. Getting to bed now more difficult. Wants to put off, stay up later, read one more chapter, etc. Can get ready unaided, but needs motivation. Mother tucks child in. May need quieting-down time of reading or music before ready to fall asleep. NIGHT. Usually undisturbed. MORNING. Awakens 7–7:30 A.M. and dresses self.

9 years—Bedtime. Knows bed hour, which is usually 8 P.M. or later; but may need to be reminded. Gets ready by self. Reads, listens to radio or watches television until 9 P.M. May continue this too long and need reminding. A few need to be asleep by 7:30 P.M. NIGHT. Usually quiet, though some waken screaming from nightmares.

10 years—Bedtime. Average bedtime 8:30, with range from 7 to 9:30. Bedtime may be different on school nights and weekends. Most have to be reminded of bedtime. Many resist and have to be urged. The majority delay and "stall"; one more bike ride, homework not finished, etc. Listen to radio, watch television, read, think, worry, or daydream before falling asleep. Boys may go to sleep quickly. Girls may lie awake an hour or so. Girls asleep by 9:30 on the average; boys closer to 8:30. NIGHT. Most sleep through the night without waking, but nightmares are frequent and (at this age only) equal the number of good dreams. At least a third of our

subjects report nightmares—about "bad guys", robbers, animals, dragons, being chased or killed. A few wake or call out. MORNING. Average hour of waking is 7. Most get up right away or within half hour. Girls average nine and a half hours of sleep a night; boys, ten and a half. Rising causes much less trouble than bedtime. But there are marked differences between those who wake early and get up as soon as allowed, and those who need much help in getting up.

ELIMINATION

2 years—Bowel. Trainable. Parent may remove child's pants and leave to own devices near toilet facilities. Some children do best if divested of all clothes. BLADDER. Better control. No resistance to routines. Some tell in advance. May go into bathroom and pull own pants down. May express verbal pride in achievement: "Good boy" [girl]. May call puddle "Bad boy" [girl].

2½ years—Bowel. Extremes and exaggeration. May skip a day between movements. BLADDER. Retention span lenghtening: may be as much as five hours. Child can stop and then resume act of urination. May have difficulty initiating release. Some already dry; others just beginning to achieve daytime dryness.

3 years—Bowel. Tendency to withhold and postpone. Daily movement may occur in afternoon. Child asks for and accepts help.

BLADDER. Most are well-routinized. Accepts assistance if needed. Few accidents. May be dry all night; may wake by self and ask to be taken to the toilet.

4 years—Bowel. This function has become a private affair. But there is curiosity about the functioning of others. A few boys still not routinized.

BLADDER. May insist on taking over routine. Curiosity about strange bathrooms.

5 years—Bowel. One movement a day, usually after a meal, most commonly after lunch but may be after supper. When irregular, may show increased constipation. Many still need help with wiping.

BLADDER. Takes fair responsibility, but may need reminding during day. Few daytime accidents. Some dry at night, some not. Less reporting to mother. A few girls have reddened genitals. Many waken for night toileting and report to parent.

6 years—Bowel. Time of occurrence variable. Many have one movement a day, usually after lunch, though may be earlier. Some now have it in early morning or at night. Some may be unable to complete it at one time. Function-

ing may be rapid. Occasional accidents. Use words suggestive of function, such as "stinker."

BLADDER. Mostly takes responsibility, though may have to dash. Accidents rare; child disturbed by them. May need reminder before going out to play. Some giggling at sound of urine stream; may mention this function in a humorous or angry attack. Some require night toileting, but these can attend to themselves. Some still wet at night in spite of late-night pickup.

7 years—Bowel. One regular movement a day, consistent with individual timing, usually after lunch or dinner. A very few have a movement at school; many wait until they reach home in afternoon.

BLADDER. Definite increase in span. Accidents rare. May forget to go to bathroom at times, such as before school in morning, but accepts suggestion. Only a few now need to get up at night and these can care for themselves. Most now dry all night.

8 years—Bowel. Two groups: one functions after breakfast, the other after supper. May now be able to function at school if necessary. On occasion may have a rapid release.

BLADDER. Manages by self with occasional reminder before going out or on a trip. May have to urinate before or during an unpleasant task.

9 years—Both functions are well under child's own control. One or two movements a day, usually after breakfast or late in day. Rarely needs to be reminded to go to the bathroom.

BATH AND DRESSING

4 years—Bath. Now an easy routine. Child can wash, though mother needs to supervise lest he get marooned on one part of body. Can dry self in part.

DRESSING. Dresses and undresses with little assistance, especially if clothes laid out.

Can distinguish front from back, lace shoes; may button front buttons.

5 years—Bath. Can with encouragement and reminder wash face and hands before meals.

Cannot bathe self, though tries to participate. Likes to wash parts of body—hands and knees.

Can scrub fingernails with a brush, but cannot cut or file them.

DRESS AND CARE OF CLOTHES. Dresses self completely, lacing shoes, buttoning front buttons. Cannot button back buttons or tie shoelaces.

Motivation may be lacking. "He can but doesn't." Mother responsible for selecting clothes, laying them

out, picking them up after they have been removed.

Careless about clothes.

6 years—Bath. A few can bathe selves if mother gets tub ready. Many need to be bathed entirely. Some wash own arms and legs.

Many do not like bath—or other routines.

Dawdling; may refuse to leave till all water has gone down drain.

Most wash faces and hands before meals, if reminded.

DRESS AND CARE OF CLOTHES. Can dress self except for tying shoelaces and buttoning very difficult buttons. May tie shoelaces, but too loosely.

May need some help and is unwilling to accept this help. Mother needs to be nearby to give some assistance.

Dawdling.

Boys brush hair; girls need to have it combed.

Careless about clothes even though may be clothes-conscious.

Drop clothes off as they remove them, or fling them about.

Not responsible for keeping clothes clean and tidy, except for a few girls.

Mother needs to select clothes, and may need to lay them out.

Accessories frequently lost.

7 years—Bath. Washes face and hands before meals if he hears mother's reminder, though may protest.

Some bathe without help and with

only a little supervision. Others still need considerable direct help or may prefer to be bathed.

Dawdle in tub.

Girls still like to be clean and neat; some boys prefer not to be.

DRESS AND CARE OF CLOTHES. Many can dress without help if clothes selected for them. Others dawdle, lack interest, need help. May dawdle till ready to dress, then actually dress quickly.

Variable in appearance. Often neater than at eight; some girls like to look neat, some boys to look sloppy.

Still careless about clothes: drop them as they remove them; do not report tears. A few put away clothes after removing them; hang up pajamas.

Can tie shoelaces, but does not like to bother.

Slow and distractible about dressing. May suddenly speed up and finish.

8 years—Bath. Washes face and hands less thoroughly than when younger, because in a hurry. Does not yet wash spontaneously. Needs to be reminded but insists on mother wording reminder in a certain way, just a hint.

Can keep fingernails clean and may be able to cut nails on one hand.

More than half now bathe themselves, may even fill own tub; others need help. Dawdle in tub, playing with soapsuds, sliding back and forth. May be slow to get to bath but like it once in

tub. Like warmer water and feeling of water on skin.

DRESS AND CARE OF CLOTHES. Can dress without assistance. Can choose what to wear and may be able to select outdoor clothing suitable to the weather.

Some children (mostly girls) can take good care of clothes, hanging them up or piling on a chair on removal. Some take full responsibility: select clothes, hang them up, put dirty garments in hamper, report on tears or missing buttons.

Many are completely careless. Clothes may be dirty and torn, and not tucked in.

May hang up clothes at night, but not hang up outdoor clothes in daytime.

No longer allow mother to lay out clothes, and may insist on selecting outer wearing apparel.

Can and do keep shoelaces tied without reminder.

9 years—Bathing. Is not resistant to a bath. Bathes two or three times a week.

Is fairly independent, but likes to have an adult around. Still needs reminding to brush teeth well and wash hands thoroughly.

DRESS AND CARE OF CLOTHES. Does complete job of dressing.

Boys and girls interested in doing own hair.

Careless with clothes, apt to throw them around. Not concerned about how clean they are. Fairly good at reporting tears and holes.

10 years—Bathing. Most bathe about once a week—under protest, since they dislike bathing, washing hands or face, brushing teeth. Most prefer being dirty to washing; have to be reminded, urged, even forced to bathe.

Mother may need to fill, empty, and wash out tub, lay out clothes.

Many have to be reminded to wash before meals and even sent back to do so.

Most are not much concerned about appearance of their hair. Shampoo usually given by mother once a week, and is reasonably well accepted.

COSMETICS. Use of cosmetics is not yet a problem.

DRESS AND CARE OF CLOTHES. Mother and child shop together. Though to some extent consulting child's taste, mother decides which clothes to buy, and most children accept this. Some hate trying on clothes in the store. But in general not too many arguments.

Most select own clothes for wear in the morning, but mother usually checks, and may even lay clothes out. Some battles over what is "suitable" clothing. Several hate idea of wearing new clothes or dressing up. Though some mention that they are fat or thin, most not particularly concerned about appearance.

Majority extremely careless about care of clothes. Outer garments flung down anywhere; other clothes dropped where they are removed, "just slung around," or at best piled on a chair. Most don't notice or mind if their clothes are dirty; and do not report tears.

ROOMS. On the whole, very messy. Clothes all over everything, shoes on the bed, desk piled high. Many say they prefer rooms this way.

Spasmodic cleaning, parent-instigated.

Some pennants or pictures on walls, but most rooms not "fixed up" very specially.

HEALTH AND SOMATIC COMPLAINTS

4 years—May have one cold right after another, all winter.

Stomachache in social situations.

Needs to urinate in difficult situations or at mealtimes.

May have "accidents" in emotional situations.

May knock out front teeth if falls.

May break collarbone if falls (4½ years).

5 years—Good, even excellent health is characteristic.

Many have only one or two colds all winter.

Some increase in whooping cough, chicken pox.

Occasional stomachaches or vomiting in relation to disliked foods, or stomachaches just prior to elimination.

Constipation in girls.

5½ years—Complains that feet "hurt." Some have frequent colds.

Headaches or earaches beginning.

Stomachaches with some nausea and vomiting in connection with school.

Somatic symptoms may appear after a week or two of school.

Whooping cough, chicken pox the most common communicable diseases.

Hypersensitivity of face, head, neck region to washing, hair-combing, etc.

Child may endure large pains yet fuss about a splinter or nose drops.

6 years—More susceptible to diseases and sicker with illness than earlier.

Frequent sore throats, colds, with complications (lung and ears); increase in allergies.

Chicken pox and whooping cough; diphtheria and scarlet fever; German measles and mumps.

Stomachaches and vomiting in connection with going to school.

Toilet "accidents" with overexcitement.

May break arm if falls.

Hypersensitivity of face, neck regions if washed or touched. (Some become hysterical with laughter if tickled.)

Increased redness of genitals in girls.

7 years—Fewer illnesses than at six, but colds of longer duration.

German measles and mumps frequent. Chicken pox and measles may occur.

Complaint of headache with fatigue or excitement; complaints of muscular pain.

Minor accidents to eyes, but fewer gross accidents; eye-rubbing.

Extreme fatigue.

8 years—Improving health. Fewer illnesses and of shorter duration. Less absence from school because of illness.

Increase in allergies and otitis media.

Headaches, stomachaches, and need to urinate in connection with disagreeable tasks.

Accidents frequent; from falls, drowning, and in relation to automobiles and bicycles.

May break leg if falls.

9 years—Improving health and few illnesses, but marked individual differences.

Some have a prolonged illness or show marked fatigue.

Very few general somatic complaints, but innumerable minute ones related to the task at hand (eyes hurt when tested; hands hurt when gripping); often say, "It makes me feel dizzy."

10 years—Health generally quite good; greatly improved in many who had poor health earlier, especially around six years. Some stomachaches and headaches and a little hypochondria, but usually less than at nine.

TENSIONAL OUTLETS

4 years—Thumb-sucking only as he goes to sleep. Many still masturbate.

Out-of-bounds behavior:

Motor—runs away, kicks, spits, bites fingernails, picks nose, grimaces.

Verbal—calls names, boasts and brags, silly use of language.

Nightmares and fears.

Needs to urinate in moments of emotional excitement.

Pain in stomach and may vomit at time of stress.

5 years—Home. Not much tensional overflow. Often not more than one type in any one child.

No total facial grimace; broken up into segments.

Hand to face: nose-picking, nail-biting.

Thumb-sucking, before sleep or with fatigue, often without accessory object.

Eye-blinking, head-shaking, throat-clearing at meals.

Sniffing and twitching nose.

SCHOOL OR EXAMINATION. Little tensional overflow: hand goes briefly to various parts of face and body.

Grasps thighs or scratches arm or leg. Pulls at clothes.

General restlessness; lifts buttocks from chair.

Nasal discharge; needs to blow nose.

5½ years—Home. Number and severity increasing. One child may show several types of overflow.

Hand to mouth, nose-picking, nail-biting increasing.

Some throat-clearing, sometimes tic-like.

Mouthing of tongue and lips, tongue projection.

Less presleep thumb-sucking.

School entrance may cause increase in stuttering, nail-biting, and thumb-sucking.

SCHOOL OR EXAMINATION. Many hand-to-face gestures, especially hand-to-mouth.

Some tongue protrusion, pulling mouth at corners, mouth pursing, biting lower lip.

Chews, bites, or taps pencil. Chews hair.

6 years—Home. Numerous and quite constant (increase begins at 5½).

Total body wriggling with thrusting of legs and kicking at table legs and piano, swinging arms and striking out or pushing.

Clumsiness, "falls over a piece of string," also falling off chairs.

Facial grimacing, throaty noises, gasping, sighing, and tongue-mouthing.

Hands in almost constant activity, especially about the face: chewing fingers, hair, pencils; picking nose; biting fingernails.

Also an occasional outburst of

screaming and temper tantrums.

May be an increase in stuttering.

SCHOOL OR EXAMINATION. Overflow in mouth region: tongue extension and mouthing, clicking, blowing through lips, biting lips. Throat-clearing and throaty noises.

Biting, chewing, or tapping pencil.

Gasps with excitement.

Hand to mouth lessening.

Shifts legs: jiggling, knocking knees together, tapping feet.

Throwing and kicking.

Eyes shift horizontally.

7 years—Home. Very few tensional outlets reported. Old ones dropping out.

With fatigue or absorption, may still suck thumb, pick nose, bite nails, or stutter, but attempting control.

Touches and manipulates objects: rubbing, tapping, jabbing, raking.

A few show tensional chorea-like movements.

Eye-rubbing, scowling, some blinking.

Makes throaty noises such as grunting, whistling.

Gross bodily outlet: hangs from doorway, tilts chair back, athletic stunts.

SCHOOL OR EXAMINATION. Less hand-to-mouth, though some fingering of teeth.

Less tongue protrusion, but mouth movements, lip pursing, whistling.

Hands finger pencil, roll it over mouth, rub or tap it on table, and usually drop it. Hands rub over desk. Touching anything seen.

May rest head on hand, elbow propped on desk, or put head down on arm.

Throaty noises, grunting, whistling.

Jiggling of legs but less kicking, though may kick people.

Oblique or horizontal eye thrusts.

8 years—Home. Very diffuse. Any of the earlier patterns may appear: blinking, nail-biting, eye-rubbing, but all less persistent.

A few persistent thumb-suckers still suck during reading or TV-watching or during illness or fatigue.

Crying with fatigue.

Making faces when given unwelcomed command.

Stomachache and headache. Need to urinate before unpleasant task.

SCHOOL OR EXAMINATION. All five-to-seven-year patterns of overflow are seen, and many in one child during some one situation.

Now more expression through verbalization and gesture.

Grimacing, scowling, raising eyebrows, eye-rolling, humming, smacking lips.

Leg jiggling prominent, though may be controlled by pressing feet against furniture or crossing knees.

Fiddling with gadgets. Shoving.

9 years—Home. Marked individual differences. Some boys "let off steam" by wrestling around. Girls may wander around house, restless and moody. Fiddle around, can't sit still.

Some growl, mutter, sulk, find fault, stamp feet, or may actually destroy things.

Specific personal habits fewer—cry, pick at self, suck tongue, pick at hangnails.

SCHOOL OR EXAMINATION. Pianoing of fingers; fine distal activity.

Draws in breath, blows lips and cheeks; or hums, sings, whistles, whispers.

External rotation of leg and crossing ankle to knee; jiggles and swings legs.

Grimaces with failure; smiles and laughs at material and at self.

Large gesture of clapping hand on head; or tiny gesture of plucking at eyelid.

10 years

Stomachaches and headaches are the chief tensional outlets, followed in frequency by nail-biting and oral outlets—drawing in lips, stuttering, muttering. Hand-to-mouth behaviors, hair-twisting, fiddling with things. A few still suck thumbs.

Eating seems to be a tensional outlet for many. Some sudden, short-lived anger outbursts. Some seem to be in constant physical motion.

CHAPTER 13

EMOTIONAL EXPRESSION

A child cannot tell us exactly how he feels, even after he has learned to talk. For that matter, the adult may have difficulty in describing his own emotions. Emotions are elusive. They are not entities which can be neatly classified and labeled. The dictionary does not have labels enough to do justice to their infinite variety.

Nevertheless, the emotional life of the child is not altogether hidden from view. It comes to expression in numerous tokens of visible behavior. If we read these outward signs aright we gain a glimpse of his inward states of feeling. In this sense his expressional behavior is a form of communication. It constitutes a kind of radar screen which reflects his inner electronic storms and tensions!

If the outward activity consists of a blinking of the eyes, chewing of the lips, or jiggling of the feet, we may think of it as a kind of tensional outlet, an overflow escape. In the previous chapter we have shown how these simple forms of tensional behavior reflect the "somatic conditions" of the organism. One cannot always draw a sharp line between tensional behavior and emotional expression.

Emotion is not an entity; it is a process. From the standpoint of child guidance, we must consider the total sequence of the process. The preliminary phases of the emotional sequence are often more significant than the end products. They are more subtle and pliable, making preventive measures possible. On the other hand, we may also be thankful, within limits, that the child declares himself, now and then, with an outburst of emotional expression, which after all constitutes his most basic language. As he grows older his expressional behavior becomes more refined; he uses words as well as gestures, not only for communication, but also as controls, symbols, and embodiments of his emotional life. And thus his "emotions" grow. They take on pattern and texture, through dynamic relationships with his ideas and intellectual orientations. Emotions are not independent forces which in some mysterious way take possession of the child. They are structured modes of reaction which, like perceptions, yield to the organizing influences of experience and education. They have had an awesome evolution in the history of the race. They have a biographic development in the history of the individual.

The following growth gradients of affective attitudes, crying, anger, and aggression will strongly suggest the ancient racial background of the emotions. But we should point out that our discussion of the child's "emotions" is not confined to the present chapter. Emotional processes pervade all his life, private and social, genial and elevating, as well as violent and disturbing. For full perspective we must consider in later chapters the emotional formations that pertain to fears and dreams, to the child's play life, to his interpersonal relationships at home and school, his ethical and philosophic reactions to good and evil, and to the true and the beautiful. But inasmuch as emotions are not self-subsisting entities, we shall focus our attention throughout on the processes and the patterns of development.

Crying

Life begins with a cry. During the newborn baby's stay in a hospital nursery, he cries, on the average, about two hours of each day. This is his most eloquent expressional behavior. We know that babies do not cry without reason. They cry from hunger, pain, discomfort—and also from denials which are not too well understood. If we arrange a baby's day so that he spends more time with his mother and less time in the nursery, crying decreases in amount and insistence. Such a hospital rooming-in arrangement (as described in *Infant and Child*) shortens the interval between distress and attention; and if the baby is reared on an individualized self regulation schedule throughout the first year, his various cries become more meaningful to his mother. He does not need to assert himself too violently and too frequently. He is permitted to "oversleep"; his hunger cries are answered promptly. Many experiences of satisfied expectation give a sense of security, a simple kind of faith in the universe. This sense of security is comparable to a felt "emotion," even though it is not as dramatic as a fit of rage.

Crying tends to arouse so much emotion in the adult that it is easily misconstrued. In earlier centuries it was regarded as one of the major signs of the imperfection, "the pettishness," of childhood. It figured in the discussions of infant damnation. St. Augustine believed in "hereditary guilt," but held that the crying of a baby is *not* sinful. Susannah Wesley took matters into her own efficient hands. She relates of her numerous offspring, "When turned a year old (and some before) they were taught to fear the rod and to cry softly . . . and that most odious noise of the crying of children was rarely heard in the house. . . ."

But this was over two hundred years ago. A more rationalistic view is slowly gaining ground, because the liberating concept of organic evolution has made us conscious not of hereditary guilt, but of the biological basis of the frailties of the child's nature. In the light of that liberating knowledge it is almost incredible that so many children should still be severely punished *because they cry*!

Crying is expressional behavior. It is a symptom, not a vice, and it can be understood only if interpreted in terms of its developmental determinations. Individual differences of temperament, fatigue, and physiological irritability will naturally influence the incidence of crying episodes; but maturity factors are primary. In the first few months the infant cries on slight provocation; a mere startle may evoke a screaming cry. The infant may wake with a hunger cry;

in time he also cries or fusses before he goes to sleep, as though actively perfecting his growing ability to stay awake. At about the age of sixteen weeks there is a quieting down; there are fewer crying episodes and they are shorter. Why? Because the infant is now in a state of relative equilibrium, as shown by many other aspects of his behavior. He is under less stress and tension. With new growth increments, equilibrium again becomes less stable. Such developmental fluctuations occur throughout the first ten years of life, with an overall trend toward diminution of frank crying as a mode of emotional expression. The nine-year-old usually does not cry unless extremely tired, or severely hurt, physically or mentally.

The characteristics of the act of crying and of the associated behavior also undergo some developmental changes. At first the cry is tearless and the vocal component of call is prominent. Later come tears, sobs, a lump in the throat, and a large variety of body attitudes and motor activities. The physiological reactions are similar to those that accompany the rejection of food. The mechanism of weeping deeply involves the digestive apparatus, whether it registers pain, displeasure, sorrow, helplessness, resignation, or self-abasement. In the crying act, the child tends to use the motor and verbal equipment available to him at his stage of maturity. A very premature infant may exhibit all the facial contortions of weeping, which culminate, however, in a perfectly soundless cry or a faint bleat. The lusty neonate cries with a scream and thrashing of legs and arms. The eight-month-old infant may shift precariously from crying to laughter. Ten months later he uses his gross postural muscles tantrum-wise to supplement his cry. The three-year-old is more equable. The four-year-old cries rather freely, and supplements with whining verbalization.

The five-year-old already has himself much better in hand. His cries are typically sun showers. Moods are fleeting. He can consciously hold back tears. At six years we witness again the phenomenon of paradoxical regression. The child "reverts" to tearful tantrums and outright bursts of loud crying; not because he is sinking to a lower level, but because he is in transit toward a higher. This is no time to shame him for being a crybaby. (Crying itself is not the vice, but an outward sign.) And, of course, he should not be punished *because* he cries.

At seven years most are able to pull themselves together; but he is in a sensitive phase which results in overtones and moods of sadness, and sometime in broken-hearted sobs. There can be no doubt that he has problems of emotion organization, for he is variably sweet and good, or cross and tearful. He even declares, "I feel like crying," an infallible sign of increasing control. The eight-year-old further extends the control by dramatizing emotions, and curbing tears after they well up. By ten years the child, though not a stoic, is still nearer to an adult level of self-control.

Throughout the period of infancy and early childhood the causes of crying are diverse. Sometimes they seem very trivial and apparently superficial because the infant readily changes from crying to laughter. But this should rather remind us of the underlying immaturity of the child's nervous system.

Assertion and Anger

Self-preservation is the first law of life. The second law is self-expansion. When an infant declares himself on one or both counts with a vigorous burst of crying, we are likely to say, "Baby is showing his temper." Some babies, of course, show a larger amount of this so-called temper than do others; but no normal child is altogether devoid of it. Temperaments and tempers differ. Ages likewise differ. As a child grows older, he displays his temper in new modes of expressional behavior, by violent and then less violent bodily attitudes, by facial contortions, by gestures, words, and muted words! With maturity he advances from one order of self-assertion to another. If at a later school age he persists unduly in using the expressional channels of the nursery, his behavior is properly regarded as infantile. Whatever his mode of expression, he behaves as he does not because he has a "temper," but because he has organized his personal-social reactions in a given manner.

The infant in a fit of rage thrashes arms and legs and arches his back; at fifteen months he pulls himself forcibly free from a thwarting adult; at eighteen months he cries, stamps, casts himself on the floor. In a tantrum of the first magnitude he hits, kicks, and struggles furiously. Fortunately even such hopeless behavior is not beyond the reach of psychotechnology! The recalcitrant eighteen-month-old is responsive to gross motor humor: his struggle dissolves if you pick him up like a bag of rags with a light-hearted, executive maneuver. He cannot be controlled by hypnotism or solemn injunctions. The whole episode might have been avoided in the first place by utilizing methods of gradual transition—for his rebellion was against a too sudden change. That was the critical maturity factor in his management.

At twenty-one months the anger pattern is already somewhat different. He is disappointed by an unwitting omission in his accustomed bedtime routine; he reacts by freezing into resistance or by "howling." The reason is so obscure that the parents are sorely perplexed. But from the child's standpoint there *is* a reason: You don't brush your teeth unless you are in your pajamas.

At two and a half years he may resent interference with his activity or with his possessions. His tantrum reactions are more aggressive, especially when precipitated by his mother. He may be destructive with objects and surroundings, not excluding wall and wallpaper. In disputes over toys he may attack other children with rather indiscriminate hitting, biting, kicking. (We are describing his conduct, without condoning it. Our readers will grant that such things can happen, and they will agree with the gentle Darwin when he says: "Everyone who has had much to do with young children must have seen how naturally they take to biting, when in a passion. It seems as instinctive in them as in young crocodiles who snap their little jaws as soon as they emerge from the egg.")

The age of three, being a period of relative equilibrium, shows a temporary decline in physical aggressiveness. Interference with plans and belongings still arouses anger; but by and large the three-year-old displays much more self-control than he did several months earlier. He also uses language to a greater degree to solve his personal emotional problems. At five years and at seven, eight, and nine there is a similar constructive or substitute use of language with a diminution of frank physical aggressiveness. The stimuli that arouse the child's anger are becoming more social in context and vary with the development of his personality.

The relationships between language and aggressiveness are rather complex. Words should not be taken at their face value when first used by children: The three-and-a-half-year-old, flourishing his new-found verbal sword, says, "I'll cut you in pieces." To be sure, he may be angry at the moment; but that he is truly sadistic may be honestly doubted. Indeed, there is a strange, shallow matter-of-factness about young children which often causes them to use words glibly at the very time when they least appreciate the social import of the words. For example, a child may talk blithely about his mother's death, until he begins to comprehend. Then he denies that his mother will die, or he worries in silence. Children's silences are often more eloquent than their words.

At five and a half and at six years, aggressiveness takes both physical and verbal forms: "You're a dope"; "I'll shoot you"; "Get out of there!"; "I wish you were dead." These illustrate the winged missiles that are directed toward friend and foe. Some of these missiles may even be hurled at grandmother. Even so, the roof of a peaceful household should not fall. Now, if ever, one should calmly consider the true and, in essence, temporary psychology of the crisis.

It is temporary in the sense that the seven-year-old already shows less crude and less frequent aggressive behavior. He has, or should have, very few tantrums, and he offers less resistance to his mother's commands. He is not equally pacific with his siblings; and on occasion he may even throw a stone, which is indeed an ancient behavior, probably antedating the stone age. But the seven-year-old is more in character when he mutters an aspersion and withdraws from the scene of irritation. Withdrawal is, to be sure, the opposite of aggression; it partakes less of courage and more of fear; but it has a useful function in the economy of development, to say nothing of the perfection of morals.

The typical eight-year-old is inquistitive rather than boldly aggressive. He illustrates the second rather more than the first law of life. He accomplishes his self-expansion by fluid, multiple contacts with his social environment. He invades his environment not to dominate, but to gain new experiences, new insights. There is a quality of aggression in his argumentativeness, his alibis, and his occasional epithets and disagreeable remarks. But when he is eagerly and loudly confabulating with his confreres he does not wish to quiet down on command. There is little animus in his heated discussion. He is really rising above brute levels. He and the nine- and the ten-year-olds at their best give encouraging evidence of human capacities that make for peace and mutual understanding instead of war and bloodshed.

The Structuralization of Emotion

Emotions are not self-subsistent entities which in some mysterious manner suffuse or attach to patterned states of consciousness. They are themselves patterned; they are structures that grow in the same manner in which percepts, concepts, motor skills, or any other configured behavior takes shape. An *emotional attitude* is simply a more or less habitual tendency to react and feel in a particular manner in a given situation. When the attitude is excessively emotional or unreasonable, we call it a *prejudice*. When the attitude tends to occur time and time again in much the same way under varying circumstances, we call it a *stereotype*. Racial antagonism readily becomes a prejudice or even a stereotype. *Racism* is a systematized, dogmatic attitude—"the dogma that one ethnic group is condemned by nature to congenital inferiority and another group is destined to congenital superiority."

These simple definitions suggest the far-flung extent of the problem of so-called emotional education. We are dealing with structured modes of behavior which have their developmental basis in the instinctive constitution of the child, and which are only secondarily transformed or redirected by the sanctions and taboos of culture. For this reason we greatly need more knowledge of the innate determinants, racial and constitutional, of all emotional or affective traits—particularly the traits of sociability, affection, pride, jealousy, sympathy, curiosity, competitiveness, and creativeness, anger, fear, and humor, which have such an important influence on the health or well-being of society.

A discussion of emotions in the abstract would serve no useful purpose in the present volume. We shall therefore portray the emotional life of the growing child in terms of his specific reactions to other children, to parents, to teacher, to school groups—to the conjoined world of things and persons.

Anger and fear, however, are so basic that they call for special consideration. Crying and laughter likewise. We cannot close the present chapter without a brief reference to the saving sense of humor, which not only is an affective response in its own right, but plays an important role in the hygiene of the emotions—those of parents as well as of child.

In smiling, laughter, and humor we are dealing with fundamental elements in the pleasurable aspects of emotional life. If crying had evolutionary roots in the lack of food, primitive laughter was associated with the enjoyment and digestion of the feast. The well-fed infant tends to smile from sheer satisfaction; he smiles socially at the sight of his caretaker at the age of eight weeks; at twelve weeks he chuckles; at sixteen weeks he definitely laughs aloud, and throughout infancy he participates in various grades of nursery humor, from rollicking roughhouse to many kinds of peek-a-boo and mock-scare games, addressed to his eyes, ears, skin, or his total physical (and mental) self. But be it noted that both the child and his opposite must be in a playful attitude, or the nursery game comes to grief and tears, rather than to fun and laughter. Laughter, humor, relaxation reflexes, and tensional behavior are all closely allied.

Children would not indulge in so much spontaneous and (apparently to us) meaningless laughter if it did not have a wholesome effect upon their behavior and mental growth. Some of this laughter might be set down as private or physiological; but it tends to spread and to increase in social situations. Even at the age of one year the child likes to repeat performances laughed at by his elders. At two years he can initiate humor and "carry on" with his playmates. At three years an abundance of laughter accompanies his play. At two and a half all is not well with the world and he does not laugh quite so freely. He is caught in the rigidities of ritualism, perseveration, and negativism. One might wish he were not so humorless. If the responsible adult meets this behavior with an equivalent insistent rigidity, matters go from bad to worse.

Here is the ideal time to utilize the biological function of humor—namely, to dissolve tension and to increase the pliancy of the mind and to keep it from overstretching. Here humor becomes a technique in child management—a technique that either prevents or atomizes an impasse.

The early plays of Shakespeare were full of low comedy, buffoonery, mistaken identity, broad punning, and rustic horseplay. Later plays show a ripening and the jester becomes an exalted humorist. A similar trend toward maturity is reflected in the humor of childhood. The three-year-old is already refining the gross motor humor of the two-year-old. His humor is becoming more verbalized. He enjoys the verbal play of tossing a word (like "golly") back and forth with someone who will play with him. At five years he enjoys slapstick humor, more or less verbalized, which he himself initiates. Six is not notably a humor age, for reasons already indicated. SEVEN somewhat ineptly perpetrates hackneyed jokes. He seems to sense the social aspect of humor and will deliberately do something ludicrous in order to get a laugh; but he is still somewhat bound by his subjectivity. He will make a better show and use of humor in another year.

The typical EIGHT has a high humor sense. He loves humorous stories and relishes the way certain wily animals (or people) fool a victim. By the same token, he rather likes to catch a teacher in a mistake. But the emotional fabric of the self is complicated. Particularly at home, where he has a status and prestige to protect, he still dislikes humorous references to himself.

At nine and ten the humor sense, if it matures, becomes more robust. The child is not only able to perpetrate a more or less practical joke, but he can take one on himself. He may even be able to laugh off teasing, which is an excellent achievement. Some philosophers have located the origins of humor and laughter in the domain of derision, superiority, and degradation!

If, then, the sense of humor is subject to the laws of growth, it will in some measure yield to training. Education in humor must come through suggestion, atmosphere, and experience. At home the child has innumerable social experiences that call for impromptu humorous handling. An institutionally reared child misses out sadly because he does not have the unscheduled experiences that normal family life yields.

At school nearly everything depends upon the teacher, because humor is not an official subject of the curriculum. A vital teacher naturally and also deliberately establishes an atmosphere of cheerful give-and-take. In such an atmosphere humor comes somewhat by contagion. Many unpredictable social situations arise that can be exploited to release humor. There is hardly an art that does not have a place for the expression of humor in the schoolroom: drawing, music, sculpture, dancing, dramatics, broadcasting and television, but above all literature.

By literature we do not, of course, mean the *funnies*. The so-called comics deal rather, for the most part, in anger, fear, and adventure. They tend, if anything, to give their readers an undue, untrammeled sense of power. Whatever their merits, they usually do not introduce the child to that fine territory where humor verges on philosophy.

English and foreign literatures contain materials for this enriching type of humor. But much remains to be done to create new humor materials based on the developmental characteristics of the child and his developmental needs, both moral and philosophic. The techniques of humor applied by himself and others are needed to safeguard sanity. This has always been a function of laughter and of humor.

Growth Gradients

AFFECTIVE ATTITUDES

4 Years—Out of bounds. Quarrelsome. Argumentative.

May be selfish, rough, impatient with younger siblings.

Expresses affection at bedtime: good-night kiss and strong hug.

May be jealous of mother and father together.

Proud of own products and creations.

Silly, boisterous humor. Wild laughter accompanies play.

Enjoys silly rhyming—"mitsy, witsy, bitsy"—and play on words.

Likes to call silly names; exaggerations amuse him. Silly showing-off.

Out-of-bounds verbalization: Tattles a great deal, exaggerates, boasts, tells tall tales, calls names, threatens, is profane or mildly obscene.

5 years—Serious, businesslike, realistic, literal. Well-equilibrated, poised, but may be resistant.

Dependent on adult company and support. Cooperative.

Likes and invites supervision.

Friendly, sympathetic, affectionate, helpful.

Strong feeling for family. Likes to be with family. May be very proud of mother.

Proud of his own appearance, nice clothes, etc.

General curiosity and eagerness for information.

Enjoys slapstick humor, which he initiates.

Mother reports that he "loves" to be read to.

Likes to talk and will talk to anyone. Some talk "constantly."

Excited in anticipation of future. Knows own mind and sticks to it.

Calling names: "skunk"; "rat"; "I'll kill you."

6 Years—Highly emotional. Marked disequilibrium between child and others.

Expansive and undifferentiated. Good or bad; sweet or horrid; adoring or cruel.

Knows "everything;" boasts, brags.

Likes praise and approval; resents correction and is easily hurt by a cross word.

Loves or hates mother.

Rapidly explosive with crying, strikes out physically or verbally, or has temper tantrums.

Quarrelsome, argumentative, explosive, rebellious, rude, "fresh," stubborn, brash.

Noisy, boisterous and easily excitable.

Silly, giggling, grimacing, showing off.

Resents direction, but is also over-conforming.

Domineers, blames, and criticizes others, alibis.

Glowers and glows; has fire or a twinkle in his eye.

At times angelic, generous, companionable.

Jealous of possessions of other children.

May not be too responsive to humor at this age.

Uses language aggressively: calls names, threatens, contradicts, argues, uses mild profanity.

7 years—A "feeling" age. Gets on better with others, though disequilibrium within own feelings.

Serious, absorbed, thoughtful, inhibited, empathic.

Sets too high a goal for self.

Self-protection by withdrawal from situation. "Deaf" ear.

Anger directed toward self. Throws or breaks something if he cannot perform.

Often moody, sulky, and unhappy.

Sensitive to praise and blame. Cannot take compliments, but can be reassured.

May not be able to accept affection, though he gives it.

Anxious to please and considerate of others.

Jealous of privileges or abilities of siblings.

Little sense of humor and cannot be handled with humor.

Worries about place in family or school group.

Uses language complainingly: nobody likes him, people are mean and unfair, he has nothing to play with. If angry, may retreat into silence instead of, as earlier, into angry verbalization. May be given to "screeching." Complains of headache.

8 years—Tendency to disequilibrium between self and others.

Attacks life with some courage, also feels he is being attacked.

Thinks he knows "everything," but beginning to recognize that others may know more.

Impatient especially with self. "Snippy," cares less.

Dramatizes anything. Tall tales are dramatic, but usually with a grain of truth.

Demanding of mother; fresh and rude, or strongly affectionate.

Some jealousy of mother and father being together.

Critical of others and also of self. Selfish and demands much attention. Bossy or helpful. Quarrelsome.

Bursts into tears; has laughing jags.

Often gay and cheerful.

Very curious about personal activities of others: phone calls, conversations.

Feelings of guilt.

High humor sense. Enjoys humor in stories, especially when one person is fooled by another, making someone uncomfortable.

Likes to catch teacher in a mistake. At home dislikes humorous references or jokes about himself.

Out of bounds verbally: talks a great deal, exaggerates, boasts. Raises voice when angry or tired.

9 years—Becoming more independent. Better equilibrium.

Quick extreme emotional shifts, short-lived.

Impressionable, reasonable, explosive, empathic.

More responsible, independent, cooperative, dependable.

Evaluates own performance, may be disgusted or apprehensive about own actions. May be ashamed of past behavior.

Wants things to be proper. Disgusted with others who deviate even slightly from his standards.

Gets mad at parents, but is also proud of them, brags about them, affectionate toward them.

Enjoys competition.

Protective and loyal to friend or to younger sibling.

Responds well to compliment.

Has passions for certain activities. Often overdoes to point of fatigue.

Many complain a good deal—headaches, eyes hurt, hand hurts, etc. —while doing a task, but continue to do required task.

Enjoys humor—if he thinks something is funny, repeats it over and over. Likes surprises in a story. Beginning to accept jokes about self.

Uses language to express subtle and refined emotions: disgust, self-criticism, pity, envy.

10 years—Seen by his parents as direct, matter-of-fact, simple, clear-cut, childish. Generally easy-going and balanced.

Some fears persist, but less anxious, exacting, and demanding than at nine. Seldom cries, and reports he is "real happy."

Anger not frequent, but violent, immediate, expressed physically, soon resolved. Humor is broad, labored, not generally funny to adults.

One of the happiest ages. Majority describe themselves as "happy as anything." Sources of happiness are simple: "If after supper I go out and play"; "If I was going someplace nice"; "If the girls are nice to me at school"; "If we can take the dogs with us on our summer vacation."

Asked if ever sad, may reply, "Occasionally" or "Seldom."

Humor mostly obvious, often heavy and labored, and not usually funny from an adult point of view. Cannot understand why no one laughs. Asks, "Get it?" Explains joke.

Most cannot take a joke on themselves, or any kidding; are afraid someone will make fun of them.

Practical jokes. Jokes about one another's names. Considerable punning. Riddles.

When repeating jokes of others, apt to tell them badly, omit salient parts, miss the point. May repeat "dirty" jokes to mother, usually not understanding them.

CRYING AND RELATED BEHAVIORS

4 years—Much crying. May whine if wants are not met or he has nothing interesting to play with.

5 years—Less crying, though may cry if angry, tired, cannot have own way. Crying now of shorter duration and can sometimes be controlled, tears held back.
Little moodiness. "Gets right over" crying.
Some whining, though less than at four years.

5½ years—Abrupt onset of temper tantrums, with loud angry crying.
Much crying at routines. Also excitement and fatigue bring on crying.
Some moodiness, whining, expression of resentment.

6 years—Tears and tantrums. Tantrums involve loud crying. Adult can often get child to laugh when he is crying.
Called a "crybaby"; cries at "any little thing."
Some whining and fussing, but more outright crying.

Brave about real injuries, but cries at small hurts.

7 years—Less crying. Becomes moody, sulky, "in the dumps."
If cries, sobs broken-heartedly, but can control crying and can pull self together.
Sensitive about crying and ashamed to be seen crying.
May merely say, "I feel like crying."
Moods very variable: sweet and good, then cross and tearful.
May cry if spanked or spoken to sharply; or unhappy or cannot make up mind. Less because of routine requirements or small disturbances.

8 years—Less crying, but sensitive, feelings hurt, and tears well up.
Feelings easily hurt by careless remarks or by criticism.
Less temper and less moodiness. But may say, "I'm not in the mood to do so-and-so."
Dramatization of own emotions.

9 years—Cries only when emotions are overtaxed. May then cry if angry, overtired, feelings hurt, or if wrongly accused.
Complaints of "That's no fair."

10 years—One of the least tearful ages. At least half as many are said not to cry as are reported to cry. Most, however, say they "might" cry. Main cause of crying is anger; next is physical hurt.

ASSERTION AND ANGER

3½ years—Verbal threats, such as "I'll cut you in pieces."

4 years—Physically aggressive: bites, hits, kicks, throws.
Verbally aggressive: calls names, brags, boasts.
Rough and careless with toys.
May aggressively exclude others from group.

5 years—Not characteristically aggressive.
May stamp feet, slam door. An occasional tantrum.
Verbal aggressiveness: "I'll kill you."

5½ years—Transition from calmness of five to aggressiveness of six years.
Calls names: "Stinker"; "You're a dope."
Verbal threats: "I'll hit you"; "I'll shoot you."
Resists directions "I won't"; "Get out of here."
Temper tantrums. Slams doors. Strikes parents or other children.
Destructive in play.

6 years—Extremely aggressive, both physically and verbally.
Tantrums: throws self to floor, hits, kicks. If sent to room, may not stay there unless door is locked. Then may destroy furniture.
Says that he is "mad."
Calls names.
Verbal threats: "I'll kill you."

Contradicts, argues, resists: "No, I won't"; "Try and make me."
Hits and kicks—adults or playmates.
May exhibit considerable cruelty toward animals, insects, children.
Destructive with objects.

7 years—Less aggressive behavior. Few tantrums and less resistance to mother's commands.
May be considerable fighting with siblings.
May threaten to "beat somebody up."
May kick or throw stones.
Verbal objection: "That isn't fair"; "It's a gyp."
If angry may leave the room or the playground.

8 years—Contacts environment curiously rather than aggressively.
Responds to attack and criticism with hurt feelings rather than with aggression.
Aggression seldom physical, chiefly verbal. Argues, alibis, calls names, or makes disagreeable remarks.

9 years—Fighting and "beating somebody up" common (with boys), but may be in the nature of play.
Aggression chiefly verbal. Objects to what people say and do. Criticizes.
Verbally expresses indifference to adult commands or adult standards.

10 years—Competition. Majority state they are not competitive, though typical comment "Sometimes I am, sometimes I'm not." More aware than at other ages that it is "hard on the other kids" if they win; some say winning makes them "feel funny."

Some like to excel in certain situations only, as "in sports, not in lessons."

JEALOUSY. About half admit to being occasionally jealous or envious mainly of other children's possessions. Some envy attributes of others; some envy children—especially siblings— "treated better" by mother or teacher.

As at most ages, some say they envy others but would not change places with them. Some say they are not envious of anyone—that they have everything in the world.

PRIDE. Few are self-centered enough to think in terms of pride.

REVENGE. Getting even and spiting others often occur as strong motives.

ANGER. Not a characteristically angry age. Many say they try to keep their tempers, and more than at following ages say they don't get mad, or don't do anything about it when angry.

Response to anger, when it comes, is violent and immediate. Most commonly expressed physically: "Beat them up"; "Sock them"; "Kick the place around." Less common is some kind of emotional violence: "Blow up"; "Explode"; "Get so mad I could kill people." More cry in anger than at any following age.

A few leave the room or go away by themselves when angry, though usually preceded by some token of violence: "Stamp my foot and go to my room." Merely verbal response also occurs, but less often than at following ages—and nonetheless violent. They yell, screech, call names, shout back if sent from the room.

Many plot revenge, though they seldom remember to carry it out.

Response depends on whom they are mad at. If parents, some can't do much, some boil over. If friends or siblings, there is usually physical violence. If teachers, they "can't do anything," or "just tell the other kids."

CHAPTER 14

FEARS AND DREAMS

Emotions are so pervasive and at the same time so fluid and elusive that it is difficult even to enumerate them. But all listings give a leading position to fear. One convenient classification recognizes seven primary emotions: fear, disgust, wonder, anger, subjection, elation, and tenderness. The child manifests these emotions in various patterns of behavior: he seeks, he avoids; he desires, he rejects; he is inquisitive, aggressive, joyous, affectionate, fearsome.

The baby is born with a capacity to startle, to feel pain, to feel pleasure. This threefold capacity lies at the basis of emotion, because in all emotion there is an element of shock or excitement issuing in feelings of the agreeable or disagreeable. The startle pattern is very fundamental, very primitive. It is exhibited by adults as well as children (to say nothing of the lower animals). Eyes blink, head bends sharply, mouth opens, abdomen contracts, elbows, fingers, and knees flex into a startled attitude. The organism thus assumes a preparatory postural set, and if in a moment it also feels distress or anticipates pain or danger, we call the reaction fear. At the same time the heart may begin to pound, blood pressure to rise; the spleen releases red corpuscles, the liver releases glycogen into the bloodstream. Many other physiological changes take place. The reaction may be mild and temporary; it may be violent and prolonged. It may result in cries of terror, in efforts of flight and escape; or it may assume a more chronic and refined form of timidity, anxiety, and worry. Fear is constantly present. In yet other developments it contributes to the exalted sentiments of awe and reverence; and to the homespun virtues of caution and vigilance.

From the standpoint of child guidance, fear should not be too much feared. Fear is normal. Fearing is natural. Often it has a wholesome influence on the life of the growing child. Fear, like fire, is useful in the right place at the right time; harmful if misplaced and out of control.

The early fears of childhood change with age. These changes depend on the maturity of the child. Some of the fears seem entirely reasonable, and others, which seem irrational, may have a deep developmental justification. Possibly we should look for a rationale even in inexplicable night terrors and nightmares. Significantly enough, they too diminish with increasing age.

The organism reacts with fear (or with fancies) whenever it senses insecurity or the threat of insecurity. A baby hears a door slam; he startles, cries. Likewise, if he sees an abrupt movement or feels a sudden loss of support he cries. At sixteen weeks he may cry time and time again, whenever he hears the kitchen clock strike. At twenty-four weeks he listens unafraid to the selfsame clock; but he cries at the sight of an approaching stranger. At thirty-two weeks he is afraid of his own mother when she dons a new hat. Similar changes in the content of fears take place throughout the whole span of childhood. The child sheds old fears because experience teaches him true meanings. The child acquires new fears because he detects novelty and portent, which formerly he was too immature to apprehend. The new perceptiveness actually denotes a growth advance. Significantly, the word "apprehension" means grasping with the intellect as well as distrusting with dread!

Our gradient of fears therefore shows a progressive trend toward increasing sophistication. An infant fears many sounds—his father's deep voice, the roar of the vacuum cleaner. As a preschool child he may fear the wrinkled visage of a withered old woman, or a Halloween mask. Later he is awed or even terrified by the ominous roll of thunder or the vague obscurity of attics and cellars. Still later he fears the burglar or spy who hides there; or who comes over the air in a too thrilling television program. By the age of ten he can laugh retrospectively at these "childish" fears, which he has outgrown. But his mental structure has probably been enriched and strengthened by some of these very fears. As he matures he does not banish fear altogether; he refines and organizes its patterns.

A further glance at our gradient reveals developmental fluctuations in types and degrees of fear susceptibility. During periods of relative equilibrium, fears are not as prominent as at the ages when the organism is actively crossing frontiers into strange new territories. Susceptibility also changes in type: there is a trend of emphasis from *auditory* (two–two and a half years) to *spatial,* to *visual* (three years), to *auditory* (four–five and a half), to *personal* (seven years).

Even within any one type of fear, significant developmental changes take place. For example, consider fears of sounds. At first the child fears especially loud or sudden sounds or those outside his natural range (one–six months); then sounds of mechanical gadgets (eighteen months); sounds of trains, trucks, flushing toilets, barking dogs (two–two and a half years); fire engines (four years); rain and thunder (five years); doorbell, telephone, static, ugly voices, bird and insect noises (five and a half–six years). A similarly elaborating development, based on the child's increasing perceptiveness, is apparent in his visual fears and fears about his mother.

All these trends are, of course, highly subject to individual differences in temperament, and environmental conditions and experiential association. Fears are notable for their individuality. (We know of a three-year-old who had a highly organized fear of rubber boots; and an older child who was obsessed by the fear that our government could not pay its national debt!) When fears reach an overpowering intensity, or when they take the form of protracted anxiety, special aggravating factors must be looked for.

The basic variations in ordinary fears, however, are attributable to maturity factors. Growth processes determine in a broad way what and when a child will fear. They determine also the what and the when of his reveries, his imaginary companions, his daydreams, his night dreams, his nightmares. There are profound parallels and interactions between these various modes of behavior in normal child development. All afford a sidelight on the formation of personality.

For example, at about the age of two years the child begins to play imaginatively with objects. Month by month his dramatic fantasy elaborates, because his nervous system is a growing structure: (a) he animates a material object; (b) he plays the role of a baby; (c) he plays with an imaginary object; (d) he plays with an imaginary animal (thirty to forty-two months); (e) he impersonates an animal; (f) he has an imaginary human companion; (g) he personalizes an object (thirty-six to forty-eight months); (h) he impersonates another person; (i) he has an alter-ego type of imaginary companion (five–ten years).

The daydreams of the child reflect a similar sequence. And so do his fears and night dreams, which show a trend from wild animals to domestic animals, to separation from mother, to bogymen, to witches and ghosts, to burglars, and finally to personal and to private worries.

Vast areas of the child's dream world are never reported; but when he is old enough to report reliably, we find that while the content of his dreams is influenced by his personal experiences, their general format has a deeper determination. In the deepmost sequences we dimly see the impress of millions of years of racial evolution when the elemental fears of man took shape, in his struggle with nature, with beasts, and with his own kind.

Far from being banished with civilization, fear remains an important factor in child behavior. It figures prominently in the dreams of infants and children. Fear dreams greatly outnumber anger dreams. Indeed, we have found few purely aggressive dreams in the five-to-ten-year age group. A typical dream is a fear dream in which the child is chased. He flees, he runs, he pedals his bicycle, he flies toward safety. Or he is frozen to the spot. But he does not fight to conquer. If his dream is blissful, it is not because he victoriously destroys or annihilates. It is rather because he enjoys a full release from the clutch of fear and revels in the free use of his dreamed activity. Many of his dreams are pleasant not because they fulfill a wish, but because they activate an unimpeded power. Such dreams we would not rudely interrupt.

All of which suggests that in fears and dreams we are dealing with a natural function, which in moderation is harmless if not actually useful. Perhaps the dreams themselves may prove to be a natural device for organizing and resolving fears. Even the milder forms of nightmare may serve as a tensional outlet and facilitate a fuller development of ultimate inhibitory control. Conceivably a nightmare takes the place of more serious and more chronic somatic complaints.

A night terror is a more extreme sleep experience than a nightmare. The child sits up in bed; or jumps out and clutches at the furniture or at a person. His face is terror-stricken. He stares with wide-open eyes but without recognizing his caretakers or surroundings. He cries; he hallucinates; he perspires. The episode may last fifteen minutes. It terminates sharply. He returns to bed without memory or recall of the event. Peaceful sleep ensues immediately.

An ordinary nightmare is much less dramatic. The episode lasts only a minute or two. It is preceded by brief crying or moaning and body stirring. The child wakes up without perspiration; he recognizes his surroundings and is fully oriented to them. But there is often a long period of waking and a verbalized going over of the frightening dream before the child goes back to sleep. Peaceful sleep is delayed.

Ordinary night dreams are milder, more comprehensive, and better modulated, despite their grotesqueness and despite the fact that the cortex is sleeping on the job. We incline to the belief that the cortex is not entirely asleep, and that its lackadaisical participation is constructive and puts method in the apparent madness of the dream. This participation is at once a physiological and a developmental device. We need not worry too much about either the luxurious or the dreadful dreams of normal children. Dreams are telling us something about the child in his growth process, and about his method of coping. A wise parent may jot down the dreams a child reports. Often in retrospect the meaning may become more apparent. Some dreams all children have. They are part of the human experience. Others are more personalized. And if they are written down, the child shares his experiences and recognizes a dream as a usual phenomenon.

But what about daytime fears, when the cortex is wide awake? Here the cortex of the adult must supply controls that the immature cortex of the fearing child lacks. Many childhood fears seem inconsequential and amusingly absurd. They should, however, always be taken seriously by the adult. They should never be laughed out of court. Nor should the child be shamed for cowardice. Valiant fathers, in particular, are likely to get too tough with their fledglings in the supposed interest of the nation's morale. "What, is this boy afraid of the water? Even with water wings? I'll toss him in and he will swim!"

We may well wonder whether the child's fear of water should not be respected. It is an ancient fear in the history of the race. The child may tremble at its impersonal vagueness, its darkness and the vast expanse that spreads before him. At any rate, before the age of seven, under certain conditions of temperament and experience, it may take a year or two before a young child overcomes his terrified screaming and his timorousness at the water's edge. The fear seems to us entirely irrational. But we might well hesitate to cast it out altogether even if we could; because there should always remain a residue of controlled fear in the form of self-protective caution. We would not set up a completely fearless child as a paragon. Water is a danger as well as a delight.

The same philosophy applies to all forms of safety education. The everyday dangers of the home (falling, burning, scalding, injury from sharp and pointed objects, etc.) call for concrete training and insight. The dangers of street and traffic likewise call for calm training in the art as well as attitude of caution. Caution also has a place in moral education. Children should not be kept too innocent of evils, which, after all, are comparable to physical dangers.

The preventive hygiene of fear, therefore, is many-sided. A happy and secure home life is the best general safeguard against unreasonable fears. A sense of humor combined with sympathetic common sense helps to forestall the misgivings that lie at the root of exaggerated fears. Fatigue, also, may undermine fortitude. A warm bath and a glass of milk may help to banish an unaccountable fear.

Do not unnecessarily expose the child to manufactured fears. Keep him from movies, radio, comics, and television programs that are absurdly terrifying. Good stories, however, may provide fear experiences that enlarge the child's imagination. Literature, like life, introduces him to pain and evil and helps him in the task of surmounting both.

A final word about the dynamics of fear and the resolution of fear. To understand fear we must also understand anger. The preceding chapter dealt with aggression and anger reactions. Anger is in some respects the counterpart of fear. In fear the organism avoids; in anger it attacks a danger. The dilemma is fight or flight. Life calls for a working balance between these opposed tendencies. When they are not well coordinated the result is indecision, confusion, or a conflict emotion like jealousy. Jealousy seems to be a subtle mixture of anger and fear.

Of the two opposing impulses, fear is by far the more complex and the more fertile in its end results for human behavior. It is more subjective, more flexible and tentative, and therefore more consequential in the organization of personality. Certainly it needs more insight and subtle management on the part of parents and educators. The regulation of anger is by comparison simpler in scope. Anger leads to drastic, definitive responses—some of them destructive and irreparable. Fear leads to withdrawal, and to avoidance responses, but withdrawal does not preclude a return to the scene of danger and a final resolution in terms of conquered and compensated fear.

What are the dynamics of fear in such instances of resolution? Let us assume that an angry dog barks at a timid child as though to devour him. The child is so afraid of the sound and the sight that he runs away. On a later day he runs away at the mere sight and sound of a dog. During this period of withdrawal an injudicious parent forces the child to touch and pet a harmless dog. The withdrawal is thereby intensified. Left to himself and aided by more subtle reassurances, the once affrighted child begins to feel impelled by curiosity and tenderness. Inner forces reverse: he approaches the dog almost compulsively. Now he is actually drawn toward the dog. The intensity of this reversed behavior probably varies with the intensity of the original withdrawal behavior. If the latter was pronounced, the child may overdo his reconciliation. The child whose withdrawal was exaggerated by ill-timed interference is most likely to react with marked and prolonged compulsion. Whether the fear be normal or abnormal, its dynamic course tends to follow the same sequence: "shock"→withdrawal→compulsive return→and then, finally, resolution.

Growth Gradients

FEARS

3½ years—Children at this age can be afraid of almost anything, or of everything. This is a highly fearful, anxious age.

4 years—Auditory fears: especially of fire engines. Fears people of a different color, old people, bogeymen; the dark; animals; mother leaving, especially at night.
Uses word "afraid" or "scared" and then is afraid.
Enjoys being mildly frightened by the adult in play.

5 years—Not a fearful age.
Less fear of animals, bad people, bogeymen.
Concrete down-to-earth fears: bodily harm, falling, dogs.

Fears the dark; sounds: thunder, rain, siren, especially at night; that mother will not return home, or be at home when he gets there.

5½ years—Very fearful, especially of sounds: doorbell, telephone, static, ugly voice tones, flushing of toilet, insect and bird noises.
Spatial fear of being lost, of the woods; of the dark; of sleeping alone in a room or of being alone upstairs.
Domestic animals.
Deprivation of mother: that she will not be at home when he gets home.

6 years—Marked increase in fears, especially auditory and spatial.
May stem from one experience.
Fear of supernatural: ghosts and witches; of large wild animals

and large dogs; of woods and tiny insects.

Fears the elements: thunder, rain, wind, fire, especially sounds. May cover ears or comfort another.

Sounds of sirens, static, telephone, flushing of toilet.

Fears that mother may die, or that something will happen to her.

Fear of man under bed, or hiding in woods (especially girls).

Injury to self: splinters, little cuts, blood, administration of nose drops.

Afraid of being late to school.

7 years—Deeper, worrisome fears.

Many visual and spatial fears: shadows, ghosts, and creatures in attic or cellar; heights.

Fears war, spies, burglars, people hiding in closet or under bed.

Beginning to resolve fears by getting someone to precede him into feared place, or by using flashlight.

Worries about not being liked by parents, teacher, playmates.

Fears he is adopted.

Fears new situations: starting second grade, new school work.

Worries about being late for school, or of not finishing school work.

Fears now stimulated by reading, television, movies.

8 years—Fewer fears, less worrying.

May still have fear of fighting, of failure, of not being liked.

Less fear of elements and fewer visual and auditory fears.

Now shy of dark, but likes to be out at night with parents.

Girls may fear strange men.

Enjoys frightening others with "Boo!" or by telling frightening tales.

Compulsively repeats fear situations to resolve them.

May worry in the midst of an experience: that he won't catch train, that he will be punished, etc.

9 years—Few fears, very variable from child to child.

Worry mostly about school failure. Some trouble at home. Worry that they cannot meet demands of a competitive situation, about report cards. Upset by own mistakes.

Enjoy frightening each other: spying, hiding.

Spontaneously report that they were "frightened to death" of something. Seem to enjoy this and feel proud of it. Also say, "I don't frighten very easy."

10 years—Fewer worries than fears. Main worries from ten to sixteen concern school, and center around homework, lessons, and being late. A few worry about family finances and the cost of food—a concern which drops out in later adolescence.

Many different kinds of fears reported, but fewer than in ages that follow. Animals, especially wild ones and snakes, mentioned most; the dark feared by many. Also high places, fires, criminals, "killers," burglars.

Some mention things they are not afraid of—chiefly the dark, dogs, and being left alone.

DREAMS

4 years—Less wakefulness caused by dreams; more reporting, probably fairly reliable.

Reports of dreams may be confused with fanciful tales.

Dreams of parents, playmates, play.

4½ years—Considerable dreaming and can report dreams.

Dreams of animals, especially of wolves.

5 years—Nightmares awaken and frighten child. Child often cannot tell dream. Has difficulty going back to sleep.

Animals, especially wolves and bears, chase the child.

Strange or bad people—may be of odd color or appearance.

Activity in regard to elements: fire, water.

Child may still confuse dreams and own waking imagination.

A few dream of ordinary daily events.

5½ years—Dreams things in his bed. Wakens and goes to mother. Can usually tell dream. Less disturbed than earlier.

Wild animals (wolves, bears, foxes, snakes) chase or bite child.

Domestic animals, especially dogs, hurt him or his dog.

Some pleasant dreams of everyday events.

Talking in sleep: "Mommy," or names of siblings.

6 years—Dreams are funny or ghostly; nice or bad; few nightmares.

Fewer animal dreams. Foxes, bears, lions, or snakes chase, bite, etc.

Domestic animals often in "nice" dreams.

Fire, thunder and lightning, war.

Ghosts, skeletons, angels.

Bad men trying to get into room (girls especially).

Mother killed or injured, or abandoning him.

Pleasant dreams of everyday people, siblings; playmates; may laugh and talk.

Can usually go to mother's bedside if disturbed, and also usually able to tell what dream was about.

7 years—Less dreaming; fewer unpleasant dreams.

Some still dream of animals; of being chased or threatened and unable to move or speak.

Dreams mostly about himself, the central figure.

Flies, swims, dives into ocean, floats through air, walks above ground.

Daily events, often embarrassing situations.

Ghosts and supernatural; burglars and war.

Movies and television affect dreams.

8 years—Very little dreaming reported.

Varies from child to child. Some like to dream and tell about dream.

Chiefly pleasant dreams about experiences, possessions, playmates. Some about personal difficulties or worries.

Some boys have returned to animal dreams or the fantastic.

May have frightening dreams from TV, movies, radio, reading.

Does not want to be awakened during dream.

9 **years**—Many have horrid, scary dreams of being hurt, shot, or kidnapped. Not only child himself, but his mother or friend may be the victim.

Motion dreams: whirling, swimming, flying.

Daily experiences and personal worries.

Dreams of natural events (storms, fire) or of being chased or threatened.

Aware that dream is stimulated by radio, TV or movie.

Some like to dream, especially in early morning, and may want to go back to sleep to finish a dream. Like to tell dreams.

CHAPTER 15

SELF AND SEX

When asked to give the very shortest definition of life, Claude Bernard, a great physiologist, answered, "Life is creation." A newborn baby is the consummate product of such creation. And he in turn is endowed with capacities for continuing creation. These capacities are expressed not only in the growth of his physique, but in the simultaneous growth of a psychological self. From the sheer standpoint of creation, this psychological self must be regarded as his masterpiece. It will take a lifetime to finish, and in the first ten years he will need a great deal of help, but it will be his own product.

What is the self made of? And how is it made? Basically, of course, it is made of the attributes and potentialities that were inherited from the baby's ancestors. But a baby does not come into his inheritance all at once, not even on his birthday. He comes into it gradually, over a long period of years, through the impulses and organizing processes of growth and through his responses to the world around him. He has impulses to look and listen, to touch and to explore the physical world. He has equally irrepressible impulses to explore the world of persons and to respond to their approaches. Paradoxically, the development of his self depends upon the impact of other selves.

At first he is so closely bound up with the milk that nourishes him, the bassinet that contains him, and the internal sensations that suffuse him, that his embryonic self is virtually in a state of Nirvana.

With the growth of the waking center of his brain (referred to in the earlier section on Sleep), he emerges out of this beatific absorption. He begins to take notice of the hands that minister to him, and a little later he stares intently at his own hands, as though he had made an important discovery. And so he has. Through sight, and active and passive touch, through ceaseless experimental contacts with the external physical world of things, he steadily builds up a fund of experience which becomes the core of his sense of bodily self-identity. It is a long process. We recently saw a bright but totally blind infant who, at the age of one year, was still in a state of confusion with respect to his relationship to his hands and to his feet. The seeing child has many advantages in arriving at a knowledge of his physical self. A looking glass is one advantage. Yet he will chase his own mirror image before he becomes wiser. And even as late as the age of three years, he cannot qualify for a hide-and-seek game because, ostrichlike, he thinks he can conceal himself by simply covering his eyes with his hands! Picture him as he stands there, to the amusement of an older sibling. His naïveté in this interpersonal situation reveals the developmental complexity of the psychology of the self and its dependence upon social insight.

The social insight grows and patterns through a countless succession of interactions between Baby and Someone Else. Nursery games illustrate the mechanism, and actually help Baby to find himself. Peek-a-boo sets up an acute expectancy, which is realized. How-big-is-the-baby? produces self-approval. Give-it-to-me! stimulates response to someone else. Rolling a ball to and fro sets up reciprocity. Such situations are simple, but they reveal universal dynamisms of development which continue to operate throughout childhood and youth. Sometimes the dynamism accentuates the ego; sometimes it accentuates the social group or some member of the group. The accents vary with age, with individual temperament, and with the specific situation. A child may behave as a "socialized" being in one situation, but react as an infant in another because of a specific immaturity. These variations are extremely interesting (rather than irritating) to the perceptive parent.

The fifteen-month-old infant provides an example. He no longer plays the give-it-to-me game as of yore. He intensifies his hold on an object, because he has a new sense of possession, which, by the way, is an important component of the sense of self. Conversely, he may even refuse to take a cracker from his mother's hand. He will accept it only if the cracker is proffered on a plate! Is he individualizing himself at the moment by emphasizing his detachment from her? Many of his quirks of resistance and his assertive "Me do it myself" are symptoms of reorganizations going on in the territory of his ever-changing self.

Baby also has moments and spells of accentuated dependence. These are not necessarily regressions to a lower level of behavior. He has to strike a balance between two opposite tendencies: attachment to apron strings and detachment therefrom.

The adult offers his hand to a child. Note the fluctuating course of the resultant behavior patterns between the first and the tenth year. The one-year-old accepts the adult hand as an aid to walking. At eighteen months he spurns the hand but accepts a runabout harness. At twenty-one months he takes the initiative himself, comes to the adult and takes his hand and leads him to a point of interest. At two and a half years he refuses or pulls away; at three years he accepts; at four he won't; at five he will (he also shakes hands on request). At six he is refractory or unready to shake hands; at seven he does so responsively, but not with ease. At nine he shakes hands spontaneously. Not until ten is he certain to extend the "right" hand!

Language is a cultural tool which works in a reciprocal way. It helps, by communication, to keep the social group together; it helps the individual to define his own status and to do his own thinking. Words are useful labels. They also are indicators to the observant parent. A child who overuses the pronoun "you" may be lagging in the concept "I." At two-and a half years his speech may be imperious, because he has difficult self problems to solve.

Many of his thinkings and feelings in regard to himself never come to utterance. He likes his name before he can speak it. He could scarcely realize himself if he didn't have a name. In the beginning was his name. He hears it so often that he finally identifies it with himself. Step by step he interprets other names and makes significant distinctions between pronouns in the first, second, and third persons, and in nominative and accusative cases.

The first differentiations have to do with the *me* and the *not me.* But very early the child has to reckon also with the distinctions of sex; at the age of two he distinguishes boys from girls by clothes and style of haircut. Soon he detects more fundamental physical differences. All this helps him to understand what he himself is. His early interests in sex are by no means purely sexual; they are part of a wide-ranging curiosity which comprehends his whole environment. He cannot get his bearings unless he makes certain elementary observations and inferences, concerning mommies and daddies, boys and girls, animals and persons, men and women.

Of great psychological significance is his gradual realization that he has a *historical* self as well as a *present* self. *He* was once a *baby!* A little recapture of that babyhood by questioning or even by dramatic revival helps to impart a new dimension to his enlarging self. At four or six his interest expands into the family tree from which he himself stemmed, and so he inquires about his relationships to parents, grandparents and great-grandparents. A seven-year-old observing his newborn brother taking a first meal at the breast asked with astonishment, "Did I do that? And, Mommy, did you do that, too; and you, too, Daddy?" He was in the throes of assimilating a tremendous fact. His questions reveal how closely the development of the self is intermeshed with the phenomenon of sex.

"Are you a boy or a girl?" is a question Binet made famous. One addresses it to a child about the age of three years. Usually the response is correct, though some respond in terms of an emphatic negative: "Not a girl!" or "Not a boy!" (as the case may be).

Having made a correct intellectual discrimination as to sex, the child will still take years to define and establish a proper role as girl or boy. Nothing follows automatically. Some even hold that it is the culture which imposes the role. In fact, the question is raised increasingly as to whether we *create* sex differences by our expectations, or whether society merely reinforces innate sex differences by its expectations.

Our own experience over the past fifty years leads us to believe very strongly that society reinforces but does not create the differences we commonly see (or expect to see) in the behavior of girls and boys. Our studies indicate that there are differences in temperamental predisposition, in psychomotor demeanor, and in developmental timing which are intrinsic in nature. The differences may not be great, but they can be decisive and they cast doubt on any hypothesis that ascribes sex differences in personality solely to environmental or cultural factors.

The child, however, must actively find and adapt himself to his sex role, and this is not a simple matter, because each individual of each sex has a distinctive equipment of innumerable qualities of maleness and femaleness. The two-year-old begins to identify his own sex by making elementary distinctions based on dress, haircut, and possibly voice. A few months later he becomes interested in the differences between boys and girls in their mode of urination. Still later each sex may imitate the other in an effort to understand this special difference, and a great many other differences as well.

A young child, when confronted by two rival alternatives, tends to try out both when he is relatively unfamiliar with the behavior in question. And so during the formative preschool years, before the so-called sex role is well established, the child shifts rather readily from one sex role to another. Our guidance nursery staff is frequently interested to see how often the domestic corner of the nursery is used by boys age two and a half to three years. This corner is equipped with nothing but dolls, beds, brooms, ironing boards, and general housekeeping facilities; and it may be the boys who are doing the housekeeping, including the laundry.

The problem of parents is to help the child, boy or girl, to find his or her role in the broader family setting. The child needs guidance all along the way. Parents sometimes think they will wait until the child can understand, and then they will tell him or her the whole story of sex, sex differences, and reproduction. But it is never so simple and decisive.

Even before the age of four, questions about sex differences and babies and marriage begin. The four-year-old may ask questions about how a specific baby arrived into the family. He may not accept too factual information. He may think the baby is born through the navel. Or he may prefer to think it was purchased. At five years his curiosity is less intense than at six. At six his questions become more specific and he may show some interest in the mechanics of mating in animals.

Especially at four and at six years of age, children may attempt to satisfy curiosities through sex play. At seven, sex interests are usually less openly expressed; but the child reflects and muses on sex relationships as he does about many other aspects of life. If he has heard about "seeds" he thinks about one or two seeds. At eight, his interest in the father's functions in procreation becomes more realistic. He is more aware of the marital relationship of his mother and father; and perhaps more susceptible to jealousy. At nine and ten he feels a deepening identification with his family. He displays it by a heightened sense of shame at any shortcomings on the part of the household. He is now tragically sensitive to disharmonies and antagonisms between his mother and his father.

The period from five to ten years is not a dormant or a latent sexual period, as some have insisted. It is a period of progressive organization. Unremitting elaborations of the self and sex attitudes are laying the foundation for the more acute developments of puberty. Guidance during this precritical period should consist in progressive orientation. Information must be skillfully imparted. It should be graduated to suit the occasion and the child's maturity. The same story needs to be told and retold in changing versions. Some facts need to be given in advance as a buffer against misinformation. The chief goal, however, should be to preserve easy, mutual confidence and communication between mother and child, father and child.

If sex exploration or an adventure in nudity is reported or discovered, the parent should so far as possible rationalize it calmly in his or her own mind as well as in that of the child. The two extremes to be avoided are overprotection through silence and evasion; and overreliance on excessively candid information.

There are enormous individual differences with respect to the strength of sexual expression and interest among adults as well as children. (Sheldon, for example, states that the endomorph is "notably greedy for routine outward affection by members of his family.") Intelligent, outgoing, factual children want and comprehend many sexual facts early. Other children are so slow or naïve that they must be told a little at a time, with much repetition, and sometimes even a little skillful prodding. Still others assimilate best by making their own deductions from a realistic knowledge of reproduction in animals.

A few children of both sexes seem blind to the implication of sex until a relatively advanced age. Boys are more likely than girls to get sex "information" from nonparental sources. They are more active and persistent in experimental play and exploration. They bring home tales they have heard, new "bad" words they have learned. They ask for specific explanations. Parents can be of service in helping the boy to a suitable vocabulary. Comparing boys and girls as groups, girls tend to show a more precocious interest in sex than boys. Their questions are more comprehensive, and less dependent upon the stimulus of information picked up from other children. The questions seem to come from a more integrated curiosity.

It is evident, then, that the acquisition of a mature sense of self is an extremely intricate process in which the sphere of sex figures importantly. The younger the child, the less developed the self, even though the vigor of self-assertion may be strong. With increasing age and social experience, this self becomes less shallow; it grows in depth; it consolidates the past; it orients the future.

The child's awareness of self expands with deepening awareness of others. Gradually he acquires a sense of hierarchy. He senses his seniority over his baby sister, but tends to defer to an older boy. At six he has been known to say, "I hope they won't ask me to do baby things in school." By the age of ten he is so aware of standards that he is capable of hero-worship.

The child begins to use the word person in a new way. The word is coming to represent a new concept, a new relationship to self and others. Boy or girl may even ask, "Am I the type of person who could [who would] . . . ?" An inarticulate child does not formulate the question, but virtually asks it in numerous ways in confronting the various situations of life. Increasing interest in the far-off future indicates that an irrepressible impulse to grow up is part of the irrepressible self.

One of the major cultural changes we have observed in the past twenty years is an increased concern on the part of society for the young child's sense of self and feelings about self. In times not long past, the chief adult concern has been with the child's behavior—that he behave in a way that will reflect credit on himself and on his family.

Today adult concern is perhaps less in what the child does and more with the way he feels about what he does. This concern is especially extended to those children who may be deprived or different in any major way that may cause the child anxiety or undermine his self-esteem. As a society we are becoming increasingly compassionate and concerned.

Growth Gradients

SELF

4 years—Expanding sense of self indicated by bragging, boasting, and out-of-bounds behavior.

Tendency in play groups for a division along sex lines.

Beginning of strong feeling for and boasting about family and home.

Exhibits some self-criticism.

Begins to realize that other children are separate entities, like him in some ways but different in some ways; that they, too, have mothers and fathers, and thoughts and feelings of their own.

Is interested in growing older.

5 years—Rather impersonal age. Self and others taken for granted.

Not as interested in own name or in names of others. "I am five" may be more important than "I am Johnny."

Close and secure relationship with mother (or another adult); even blames mother for what he does. Mother center of the child's universe.

Believes that self and mother are "eternal." Likes to hear of mother's babyhood.

Self-contained, serious about self, impressed with ability to imitate grownup behavior.

Needs, invites, and accepts some supervision. Likes to ask permission and to help.

Likes to have things go smoothly.

Interest in immediate experiences. Realistic. Undertakes only what he can do.

6 years—Child is center of own universe. Is expansive, undiscriminating.

Interest in own babyhood, stories—anything—pertaining to self. May act like a baby.

Conceives of himself as always living, past and future.

Knows everything, wants everything, wants to do everything own way.

Possessive of belongings and likes to display them.

Own name important: likes to be called by it and write it on all his products.

Relationship with mother most difficult. May behave worst with her. Resists with "No, I won't"; acts like a baby, is rude and argumentative. Also fears that she may

die, or may not be at home when he returns.

Mother describes child as "changed for the worse."

Does not know when to ask for assistance. May not accept help when he needs it. Is domineering, stubborn, aggressive.

Wants and needs to be first, to be loved, to be praised, to win.

Does not know what to do, but resists direction of others; accepts direction only when it coincides with own idea of what he is doing.

Emotionally excitable, defiant.

Physically and verbally aggressive; belligerent and resistant when attacked.

Interest in good and bad behavior in self and playmates.

7 years—More aware of and withdrawn into self. Absorbs impressions from what he sees, hears and does. Seems to be in "another world." May not hear commands.

Self-conscious about own body. Sensitive about exposing body. Does not like to be touched. Modest about toileting.

A definite minor strain: believes others are mean and unfair.

Ashamed of fears, mistakes, or to be seen crying.

Protects self by withdrawal. Spends more time alone. May be unwilling to expose knowledge, for fear of being laughed at or criticized; or suddenly responds and withdraws. Leaves a scene when things are going badly.

Fear of losing identity. May dislike new clothes, having hair cut. Begins to suspect that he will one day die. Denies this.

May believe he is adopted, does not belong to his family.

Loses or hoards products. Forgets to put name on them.

Child's world is broadening, and he is trying to place himself in the social and physical world.

Worries that mother, teacher, or playmates do not like him.

Wants own place in family group and in school group. Wants own place at table, in a car; wants own desk, own room.

Cautious in approach to anything new.

Less responsive to mother's demands. May say, "Why should I?" "I don't feel like it."

Wants responsibility, especially at school, but concerned that he may not do well.

Slight skepticism about religion and Santa Claus.

Senses a goal but has little evaluation of it. Wants to complete a task if he starts it, but does not judge own capacity to do so. Apt to expect too much of self.

8 years—More outgoing, contacting people and places. Cannot stay out of contact with any part of environment. Seems to be trying "self" against the environment. Conscious of self as a person. Rec-

ognizes some differences from others and voices them. Talks more freely about self. Thinks about "self."

Interested in own inner anatomy.

Personality more expressive. Facial expressions and gestures are "like him."

Dramatizes. May seem to consider self the center of the stage.

Belittles self, expecting or hoping for praise.

Wants adult to be part of his world. Makes many demands of mother and wants her to act in certain ways.

Chief interest is relationships with others—children and adults.

Resents being treated as a child. Wants to be like adult. Begins to recognize that adult may know more than he does. Can't wait to grow up.

Can make up mind easily and respond to reason. May respond with "Oh, all right, if you insist," if instruction is given in a way that suits.

May have sudden shower of tears at "undeserved" criticism.

Give-and-take with another person needs to be in balance.

Tries to live up to standards of others; may feel guilty if thinks he doesn't.

Concerned not only by what others do to him but what they do to others.

Expanding information and experience lead to knowledge that standards differ. Increasing identification with social, political groups, and exclusion of those who are different.

Increased interest in distant and long-ago people and places.

9 years—A "change for the better" at nine. Many earlier tangles smooth out. Less tension. Life simpler. Child more independent, self-suf- ficient, dependable, trustworthy. Frequent spurts of better be- havior.

More responsible: can have key and let self into house, get a meal, go downtown, make simple pur- chases, phone if going to be late.

Very busy with own concerns. Doesn't have time for routines or parents' demands. Many are be- coming "workers" and may pre- fer work to play.

Active and interested in many things: school work, succeeding at any task, the future, history, mechan- ical things, electricity, making things.

Much planning, in great and prac- tical detail: for the immediate future or about going to college and what he or she will do when grows up. Making of lists.

"Don't care" attitude, bold front; at other times anxious to please, wants to be liked. Loves to be chosen.

Increasingly self-conscious: about own activities, body, home, par- ents' and siblings' behavior.

Self-criticism: "I **would** do that"; "Oh, that's my poor memory."

May be overambitious in demands of self.

May be apprehensive about work and health.

Short-lived but innumerable com- plaints about many aspects of life.

Wants to succeed. Will work for a reward.

Sensitive and embarrassed by cor- rection.

Some self-projection in beginning of crushes on others, or hero-wor- ship.

Child now oriented more toward contemporaries than toward par- ents. May experience some con- flict between adult code and the code of his contemporaries.

Beginning of marked individual dif- ferences from child to child in all fields. Child's own individuality and personality making itself clearly apparent.

10 years—Shows no great concern about self, tends to take self (and life) as it comes. Parents report he or she much happier and easier to get along with than at nine.

Easygoing and matter-of-fact. Very specific; doesn't generalize.

Shrugs off responsibility; can usually toss off criticism and bad grades. If asked a question, replies easily: "Sometimes I do, sometimes I don't."

Much interested in future parent- hood and in how he will treat own children.

Still describes self as "a pretty good boy [girl]."

SEX

3 years—Sex Interest and Differentiation. Expresses affection by "I like" (3½ years: "I love").

Affirms own sex if questioned: "I am a boy [girl]."

Verbally expresses interest in physiological differences between sexes and in different posture for urinating. Girls attempt to urinate standing up.

Desire to look at or touch adults, especially mother's breasts.

Interest in marriage and marrying; proposes to either parent and others; thinks you can marry either sex.

No distinction between sexes in play.

Temporary and shifting attachment to some "friend" of the opposite sex (3½ years).

BABIES. Beginning of interest in babies, wants family to have one.

Asks questions: "What can the baby do when it comes?" "Where does it come from?"

Most do not understand mother when she answers that the baby grows inside her.

4 years—Sex Interest and Differentiation. Extremely conscious of the navel.

Under social stress grasps genitals and may need to urinate.

May play the game of "show"; verbal play and name calling

about eliminating.

Interest in other people's bathrooms; may demand privacy for self, but extremely interested in bathroom activities of others.

Some segregation along sex lines.

BABIES. Questions about where babies come from. May believe mother's answer that baby grows inside mother's "tummy," but may cling to notion that baby is purchased.

Questions about how baby gets out of mother's "tummy." May spontaneously think baby born through navel.

5 years—Sex Interest and Differentiation. Familiar with, but not much interested in physical differences between sexes.

Decrease in sex play and game of "show."

More modest and less self-exposing.

Less bathroom play, less interest in strange bathrooms than earlier.

Aware of sex organs when adult seen undressed and may wonder why father doesn't have breasts or sister a penis.

Boy may reject girls' toys such as dolls, although he may make a doll's bed in carpentry, or take part in house play.

Takes opposite sex largely for granted; little distinction between sexes in play. Frequent boy-girl pairs.

BABIES. Interest in baby and in having a baby of own; may dramatize this.

Some boys as well as girls may relate back to when in mother's abdomen, or to future when they will have own baby.

Reasks, "Where do babies come from?" and accepts "mother's tummy" as an answer.

Some cling to the idea that you buy the baby at a hospital.

Make little connection between size of pregnant woman and presence of a baby.

6 years—Sex Interest and Differentiation. Marked awareness of and interest in differences in body structure between sexes. Questioning.

Mutual investigation by both sexes reveals practical answers to questions about sex differences.

Mild sex play or exhibitionism in play or in school toilets. Game of "show."

Some children subjected to sex play by older children.

May play hospital and take rectal temperatures.

Calling names, remarking or giggling involving words dealing with elimination functions.

Some confusion in differentiation of male and female. May dress in attire of opposite sex.

Interest in marriage to someone of opposite sex, often to a relative.

Strong interest of older boy for younger girl.

BABIES. Interest in origin of babies, pregnancy, and birth.

Vague idea that babies follow marriage.

Interest in how baby comes out of mother and if it hurts.

Some interest in knowing how baby started. Accepts idea that baby grows in mother's stomach and started from a seed.

If told of intercourse by older playmates, child may be disturbed and usually questions mother.

Wants a new baby in the family.

Wants to hold baby after it is born.

7 years—Sex Interest and Differentiation. Many have long since satisfied interest in differences in physique between the sexes. Less interest in sex.

Some mutual exploration, experimentation, and sex play, but less than earlier.

Interest in sex role and characteristics of boys and girls.

May be last age when boys and girls play together regardless of sex lines.

Strong and persistent boy-girl love affairs with the idea of marriage usually strong.

BABIES. Intense longing for a new baby in family, usually of own sex.

Knows that having babies can be repeated and that older women do not have them.

Interested in mother's pregnancy. Excited about baby's growth. Wants to know how it is fed, how big it is, how much it costs.

Interest in literature, such as "The Story of a Baby," by Marie Ets.

Associates size of pregnant woman with presence of baby.

Satisfied to know that baby came from two seeds (or eggs), one from mother and one from father.

May ask details of birth: just where mother will be, how baby will get out.

8 years—Sex Interest and Differentiation. Interest in sex rather high, though sex exploration and play less common than at six. Girls may be unusually responsive to touch and rough play with boys.

Interest in peeping, smutty jokes, provocative giggling; whisper, write, or spell "elimination" and "sex" words.

Girls begin to question about menstruation.

Boys recognize pretty girls, and girls, handsome boys.

A boy may have several girls, but he knows he is going to marry only one of them. But fewer boy-girl twosomes.

Plan to have own home when married.

Sexes begin spontaneously to draw apart in play.

BABIES. Warm and loving interest in babies.

Understands slow process of growth of baby within mother; connects appearance of pregnant woman with a baby.

Wants more exact information as to where baby is in mother's abdomen. Confused by use of word "stomach."

Some girls may ask about father's part in procreation.

9 years—Sex Interest and Differentiation. May talk about sex information with friends of same sex.

Interest in details of own organs and function; seeks pictorial information in books.

May be self-conscious about exposing body.

May not wish parent of opposite sex to see him nude.

Sex swearing; sex poems.

Division of sexes in play; if mixed, may stimulate kissing games; teasing about "girl" or "boy" friends.

BABIES. May relate selves to process of reproduction: "Have I a seed in me?"

Some may still think babies born by Caesarian section.

10 years—Girls. Many, by ten, have experienced some sort of sex play, usually of an incidental, transitory nature.

The majority, though not all, have heard about menstruation. Some show mild interest in father's part in reproduction. A few show no interest in sex and ask no questions. If not, this is an ideal age to give sex information.

Some interest in smutty jokes, usually related to the buttocks rather than to sex. Often report these to mother.

Some interest in boys, in marrying, in having children someday, but quite matter-of-fact and unromantic.

Boys. Many have been involved in childhood sex play. Most do little questioning about sex. Most not shy about being seen nude within family.

Most aware that mother is origin of babies, and most have heard of intercourse and the father's role. Interested in the father's "planting the seed," but may comment, "I think that would be embarrassing."

Some use of "bad" words, interest in "dirty" jokes, especially about elimination. May report these jokes to mother, often not knowing their meaning. May have little sense of which jokes can be told in mixed company.

Some talk of their own (future) children—what they will save for them or how they will treat them.

Most are not much interested in the opposite sex. May say things like "I'm just too young for all that" or "I'm only in fifth grade." Others may say, "They're all great" or "I love them all."

CHAPTER 16

INTERPERSONAL RELATIONS

The roots of the growth of a child's personality reach into other personalities. The detailed make-up of personality depends upon the interpersonal relationships one experiences from day to day, from age to age. If boys or girls did not come into contact with other human beings from the moment of birth, they could scarcely acquire a distinctive personality recognizable either to themselves or to others.

The personal self, however, as shown in the previous chapter, is subject to the laws of growth. These laws place limitations on the *kinds* of contacts and the *depth* and *scope* of the contacts the person can make with other persons, young or old. Even a cursory reading of the growth gradients at the end of this chapter will demonstrate the presence of maturity factors and the resulting involvedness of the "anatomy" of the child's personality.

We need not shun the connotations of the word "anatomy," because the child's personality assuredly is a living structure, made up of attitudes, predispositions, and potentialities. Personality is not a pure essence which in some obscure way absorbs the influences of abstract good and evil. It is a patterned and a patterning fabric which takes form and gives form within countless interpersonal relationships.

These relationships are highly diversified. They include interpersonal forces which impinge upon the child at home, at school, and in the community.

Home includes father, mother, siblings, visitors, and guests (young and old), and sometimes grandparents and other relatives. *School* includes teachers, classmates, principal, janitor, supervisors, playmates, and pupils from the various grades. *Community* includes a host of persons and institutions, regularly or occasionally encountered on street, road, and byway; in shops, at church or theater, in club room, park, and public places. The community includes also the intangible and yet personal forces that are embodied in laws, manners, and customs, the local mores and the prevailing attitudes toward racial and minority groups.

Other persons react upon the child; but the child also reacts upon the other persons. The gradients that follow show the growth trends of these interactions. They show how unprofitable it is to consider the social nature of the child in generalized terms. Social characteristics consist of concrete tendencies and orientations, and far from remaining static, these orientations are constantly changing, with circumstance and with age.

Home and Family

Great changes have taken place in family living since the first edition of this book was published. Children themselves have not changed appreciably. But the families in which they are being brought up are in many instances quite different from what they would have been thirty years ago.

To begin with, families are smaller. The average American family in 1972 included an average of only 2.025 children, in contrast to the average of 3.67 in 1940. This means, of course, not only that more children born into the world are *wanted*, but also that family resources and parental attention do not need to stretch as far as they used to.

Also, a higher percentage of babies born today are strong and healthy. The new science of fetology has helped parents to produce healthier babies.

On the other hand, fewer children today than in the past enjoy the care and protection of a full-time mother at home. That many mothers who want to work outside the home now do so is unquestionably a good thing for these mothers. In most instances it makes them happier and more fulfilled as individuals. And it does not necessarily deprive their children. Though some people don't go along with the statement, we heartily agree that it is the quality and not the quantity of mothering that counts.

So long as a child is provided with a warm, loving, and reliable caretaker, preferably in his own or in the caretaker's home, there is no sound reason to assume that the child will suffer from the fact that his mother is not always present.

In fact, Jessie Bernard (in *The Future of Motherhood*) believes that the isolation of the mother of small children and the overintense relationship that often exists between mother and preschooler may not necessarily be beneficial to either.

Nor has the Freudian threat that an infant requires the constant presence of his mother in the home if he is to be emotionally healthy ever been proved true. It is to be hoped that any mother employed or not, will if possible breast feed her baby. But we have no reason to suppose that so long as a baby is in the care of a warm, loving, motherly person who will provide the daily security and comfort he needs, he will necessarily suffer from the fact that mother is not at home all day long every day.

(In fact, perhaps the greatest harm that can derive from a mother's working outside the household comes in the form of the guilt which some child specialists have wrongly made her feel because she does work. Admittedly almost any young child, if given the choice, would prefer to have his mother right with him all day every day. But it may be that the separation necessitated by a mother's working outside the home *may* be a good thing for all concerned.)

Another thing that is different in many households today from the way things used to be in the past is that, especially in families in which the mother is a strong adherent of women's liberation, the father may be taking more of a part in the care of household and children than used to be the case. In most instances, it seems to us, the more father the better.

In contrast to those families in which the child receives more of father's time and attention than in the past are those in which there is available much *less* fatherly attention. Today there is a substantial increase in the number of so-called single-parent families.

With the increase of divorce or separation, more single parents— usually mothers—are now bringing up their children alone. In fact, in certain instances single parents are allowed to adopt. Some unmarried women are intentionally producing children of their own.

Though the double burden faced by the single parent is un- questionably somewhat of a hardship for many, some very strong individuals are up to the responsibility involved. And as for divorce itself, the general feeling today is that it is not a good thing for warring marriage partners to stay together "for the sake of the children."

Excellent books have been written to help families faced with the problems of divorce. Counseling is becoming increasingly available both for parents in marital difficulty and for those faced with the problems of divorce. And family therapy can be sought for whole families in trouble.

Many families, today as always, with or without natural-born children of their own, choose to add to their family by adoption. We have always urged that when considering adoption, any parents see to it that they receive a behavior evaluation as well as a check on the physical health of the child to be adopted. This precaution is not always followed, especially by those agencies that believe that how the child turns out depends on how you treat him rather than on his biological endowment. Evaluation is still our recommenda- tion.

Even should you be willing to adopt a child of low intelligence, poor health, or difficult or abnormal personality, it is our feeling that the adoption agency owes it to you to give you in advance all pertinent information about any negative factors.

But whatever the decade or whatever the exact make-up of any given family, much that we said about family living when this book first came out is not too different today. Thus we may tell you now, as we told you then:

At the age of two years the child may actually be overtaxed when both parents are present at the same time. Boy or girl can adjust to each one individually, but not to both simultaneously. At later ages the child has comparable difficulties in apportioning affection evenly. Parents will find it wise to shift their roles from time to time. When necessary they may even permit unilateral confidences, if the child so demands. At the ages of six and eight, children are rather deeply embroiled with their mothers. The eight-year-old is often so deeply sensitive toward his mother that he betrays impatience if she deviates even a moment from the consuming demands he makes upon her. This intensity can show itself in qualms of jealousy when mother and father are together. At the age of six the same child may have expressed both deep affection and contradictory hate. At seven relations, though still variable, tended to be more smooth and companionable. At six he probably feared and admired his father more than his mother. At nine the father-child bonds strengthen, particularly if the father is companionable and respects the child's increased maturity. The child has reached the age when he is beginning to evaluate (intellectually and morally) his parents' actions and standards of conduct.

It is idle, of course, to exact affection, or to stipulate its occasions. Parents and their children must grow up together, and work out their several compatibilities in terms of temperament and maturity. Parents are likely to overlook the maturity factors and to be unduly sensitive in regard to the unforeseen fluctuations in the child's attitudes. Many of these fluctuations have a natural developmental basis. One need not worry. When the child himself reaches maturity, his fundamental regard for his parents will prove to be the summation of an overall trend of development throughout a long stretch of years.

During the years from five to ten the parent-child relationship demands a high degree of flexibility. If there is more than one child in the family the principle of impartiality should not be applied too artificially. Each relationship is unique, and parents need not treat all children alike. With varying accent a child may display several stages of response: dependence, demandingness, indifference, worship, companionship. Comparable developmental variations reveal themselves in the relationships between siblings, even when every effort is made to avoid envy and jealousy. Often the frictions are temporary; many could be avoided if the household permitted the children to spend more time apart. The amicability span, like the attention span, tends to be shorter for younger children.

The family unit is a complex institution. It needs more planning and deliberate self-appraisal than it ordinarily receives. This is particularly true when the household has to reckon not only with children, but with uncles, aunts, grandmothers, and grandfathers. Inasmuch as we cannot cover the whole gamut of these complicated relationships, let us venture a few special comments concerning grandparents.

The recording angel alone can do justice to the many practical services and to the words of counsel that understanding grandparents can supply. Their presence and contacts greatly enrich the experiences of their growing grandchildren. Most grandparents adore their grandchildren, and this adoration tends to be mutual. Adults even late in life often remark, "Nobody was ever as good to me as my grandmother!" Not till the teens, in many instances, does the growing child's need to criticize his elders include even his formerly beloved grandma and grandpa.

The five-to-six-year-old's love of his or her grandparents may be somewhat mercenary—"She gives us things." But by seven or eight the relationship is becoming more companionable. "They play with us"; "They take us places." By ten, children say they like their grandparents because "She loves me" or "He is nice to me."

Grandparents as a rule have a special brand of tolerance and patience or insight not to be found elsewhere.. The emotional bond with them is naturally different from the parent-child relationship and these extra bonds may exert a broadening beneficial influence on the developing personality of the child. But there are hazards in this very relationship if the grandparents, unwittingly or otherwise, overstep their prerogatives. For better or for worse, the *mother and father* should be responsible for the government and management of the home. *They,* as parents (and not as children of their own parents!), should determine the goals of the family's life. On matters of so-called discipline, the judgment of the parents ought to prevail. Grandparents can claim no natural authority in these matters, although their consultative wisdom may often prove invaluable.

If a grandmother becomes too exacting, her misplaced strictness can easily disturb the domestic tranquillity. Perhaps she becomes too severe with the nine-year-old who is growing up, and who has a symptomatic aversion to being "treated like a little child." She may grievously misunderstand the six-year-old when he bursts out with one of his aggressive verbal threats. Granted that a six-year-old can, on occasion, be very "rude," his shocking behavior must be managed philosophically. He has even been heard to say, with probably more echo than comprehension: "If Grandma wants to be a burden, let her be a burden!"

The family is clearly a closely knit body politic. Psychologically it consists of a veritable network of interpersonal relationships, subject to normal tensions and sometimes to abnormal frictions. The child's developing image of family life is chiefly the outgrowth of the experiences he undergoes in his own home circle. If harmony prevails, it will help to integrate his orientations and to direct his affections. Maladjustment between husband and wife obviously has far-reaching effects upon the emotional life of perceptive children.

Perceptiveness, of course, varies with maturity as well as with inborn sensitiveness. It is interesting to note the stages by which the ordinary child achieves a progressive insight into the meaning of family life. At eighteen months he likes the run of the house, is interested in household activities such as sweeping and dusting, and will soon participate in putting away the groceries. By three years he is helpful in little tasks and errands. By four years his identification with his home has become personal and self-conscious, even to the extent of boastfulness. At five years he may use the word "family" in a manner that suggests that he has attained an elementary concept of the family as a social group.

During the sixth year he gives many evidences of forging to a higher level of relationships, even though at times he seems self-centered, resistant, or overly mother-centered. He takes a new kind of interest in family outings, family secrets, and paternal and maternal relatives. SEVEN in his little serious way has a deepened sense of the family as an institution; he is proud of his home and family possessions; even his negative behavior betrays an emotional strengthening of the family ties. EIGHT is somewhat less subjective; he is interested in the family as a going concern, and at a festival gathering he is especially anxious that everyone should be having a full share in the good time. NINE likes to be on his own, likes to be with his friends and away from his family. It gives him a growing sense of self-sufficiency. But at the same time he shows increased awareness of family standards and of differences between his family and the families of his friends. His greater sensitivity denotes a deepening personal identification with his family. The steady processes of growth have wrought extraordinary changes in his family relationships since the innocence of age five. During the teens there will be another series of significant transformations; but the basic orientations are well-nigh complete by the age of ten.

School

The school is a larger social unit than the home; but it is much less complex, and in many ways less decisive in the organization of the child's personality. It brings about, however, important extensions in the network of his interpersonal relationships.

The school beginner is confronted with a whole host of problems of social adjustment. Even if he has acquired some background wisdom as a member of a nursery school, he is obliged to make many readjustments; moreover, he is no longer a nursery-school child. He has the new impulses and the new uncertainties that come with being six years old. The smoothness of his school entrance will hinge largely upon his emotional maturity. The school world may seem so different from his home world that he may tend to retreat into the latter. In cases of acute conflict he may even react with a temporary stomachache, or other symptoms of immature morale.

Usually, however, he weathers his transitional difficulties, and will soon regard that strange new adult, his teacher, with various degrees of tolerance, awe, and affection. He comes to consider her word law. He likes to please her, likes to be commended by her, but he is related to her not so much in emotional terms as through the activities and physical materials of the school program. When these activities appeal to him, he makes a so-called good adjustment to the first grade. At seven years the teacher-child interdependence is more personal; and adjustment to school is more dependent on an interpersonal relationship.

The pattern of that relationship, however, is, or should be, different from that between parent and child. Teachers should not take over the mother role, and parents, for similar reasons, should give all possible support to the role of the teacher. The amount of interplay of these two roles will vary enormously with the age of the child and other factors. In complex situations the aid of a third intermediary in the form of a visiting teacher or guidance worker is very beneficial. Parent-teacher complications are avoided if the psychological needs of the child are always considered paramount.

The teacher-child relationship undergoes natural developmental changes as the child progresses through the elementary grades. In the kindergarten he responds best to a homey, friendly teacher who is chiefly concerned with releasing the spontaneous interests of the children. The successful first-grade teacher typically likes to work with materials herself; she manages a fluent group as a whole, through skillful manipulation of her activity program. The second-grade teacher depends rather more on perceptive personal contacts with individual children. The third-grade children like a comradely, factual, businesslike teacher who, in their eyes, can be a good sport and keep the show running. Personality factors continue to count in the fourth and fifth grades; but the pupils are now less submerged by the school group. The nine-year-old and the ten-year-old have attained a measure of detachment. They understand themselves better; and they have some capacity to step aside and make an objective appraisal of the teacher. They respect a teacher who knows, and who can satisfy their critical interest in why? and how? They are anxious to perfect their skills in the tool subjects, so they can launch out into the new fields they are eager to conquer. If now and then they play a mild practical joke on the teacher, it is probably because they are sensing a new kind of confidence in themselves. An understanding teacher will know what it is all about in terms of social psychology, to say nothing of the psychology of her own self.

The Community

It is difficult to draw any sharp precinct lines separating various areas of the community. Electrons keep to their orbits, but in the vast domain of interpersonal relationships, private, domestic, and public circles are forever cutting across and into each other. When we say that radio and television have brought the outside world into the home (and the school), we are scarcely using a metaphor; because the essence of the community is a psychological compound of awarenesses, ideas, and attitudes. Developmentally, therefore, we can see the sketchy beginnings of the "community" in the early experiences that take the child beyond the confines of the family. Visitors from the outside come into the home; he greets the postman or the grocery boy; he takes a trip to the market; he joins a play group in the neighbor's yard.

It takes him many years to master the elementary structures of the community. He must become acquainted with it in terms of time and space, and its physical technology. Step by step he becomes aware of houses other than his own, of doors, windows, streets, curbstones, elevators, traffic lights, automobiles, airplanes. As physical phenomena these many impacts come without much order or sequence; but the child assimilates them in terms of his interpersonal experiences. His social self alone can give meaning and order to the physical community. He becomes community wise through other persons, particularly playmates.

He has to adapt to them and thereby learns what a community is. At eighteen months he has scarcely made a distinction between persons and things; at twenty-one months he hits or hugs a playmate without discretion, without modulation; at two years his constant refrain is "It's mine." But at three years, as noted before, he shows a germinating capacity for cooperative play and can even wait his turn. This capacity increases through the years that follow. But the complexity of the social situations also increases. Accordingly there are many manifestations of self-assertion and self-aggrandizement along the way. Normally the social and the selfish forces balance each other so that the overall trend is favorable in spite of tattling, exclusions, cheating, sulking, ganging up, secret passwords, wrangling, and combat. However, if the adverse behavior is not kept in bounds, and if it is not resolved *in its immediate contexts* by the child with the legitimate help of an adult, the overall trend can be decidedly unfavorable. The years from five to ten can breed delinquency and can lay the foundations for poor citizenship.

The spontaneous groupings that take place on the playground are primarily determined by maturity factors. In the preschool years there is a discernible progression from solitary to parallel, to occasional cooperation, and to sustained cooperation and imaginative play. At seven there is an interesting developmental phase in which group and individual tendencies oscillate as though competing for dominance. The eight-year-old has a keen zest for group activity. At nine years his group consciousness is so strong that boy or girl likes to organize and to belong to a club, to accept a role in a group, to contend as a member of a group. The group solidarity is so strong that if a feud starts on the playground it is likely to carry over into the schoolroom—an early example of how group loyalties overlap, even in juvenile years.

The spontaneous sex groupings, likewise reveal the presence of innate maturity factors. The three-year-old can affirm his sex; but he makes no sex distinctions in playmates until about a year later. At four years there is a tendency toward division along sex lines in group play. At seven years a boy and girl may pair off as playmates for a period of weeks or months, but the larger play groupings generally ignore sex lines. In another year boys and girls begin to separate in their play; and from nine years to ten there tends to be a definite period of segregation. The segregation is marked variably by self-consciousness, sexual modesty, shyness, passing hostilities, giggling, teasing, spying, feuds, and derisions. However temporary these diverse manifestations prove to be, they indicate the complexity of the growth processes that underlie the social nature of man.

Racial Attitudes

The problem of racial antagonisms has become so important in our American culture that it deserves consideration here. Interracial tensions involve complex political, economic, and religious factors, but for children the problems are mainly psychological and concern interpersonal adjustments.

Strictly speaking, a race or a racial group is based on community ancestry. Every true race doubtless has certain innate physical and mental characteristics which distinguish it. Races, like individuals, are not born alike. Many so-called racial differences, however, are not due to ancestry or heredity, but to cultural differences—differences of language, nationality, tradition, manners, and customs. And so far as behavior goes, it seems probable that one can find almost the entire range of almost any behavior in almost any group. In the last analysis, we have to reckon with problems of the individual.

Prior to the teens, children tend to be catholic and cosmopolitan in their interracial contacts. A preschool child may be as fond of a black doll as of a white. Most three-year-old children are scarcely aware of differences of color, or for that matter of sex and other individualizing characteristics. Polyglot groups fraternize and intermingle harmoniously.

At about four years of age an exclusive in-group feeling definitely asserts itself. Children still play together cooperatively; but every once in a while several children will separate and organize into an in-group which actively and noisily excludes other children. The exclusion is more likely to be on sex than on color lines. The seceding group, for example, sets up a post office and with brave words ("You can't play with us!") repels the minority group. The exclusion may be temporary. It may last for fifteen minutes or a forenoon. But it may recur next day in new circumstances and with new groupings.

It recurs because it is a mechanism of development. The exclusions may seem very arbitrary, but they have a developmental logic. By banding themselves together for negative as well as positive reasons, the children spontaneously practice group action and intensify group consciousness. They are exercising their powers of social behavior. The behavior is relatively innocent. We do not need to take these transient bravadoes and intolerances too seriously.

In moments of verbal aggressiveness the six-year-old may indulge in vigorous anthropological name-callings; at seven he may shout a folk-rhyme derision and even gang up on a victim. At eight and nine years clubs may be organized with exclusion as their primary purpose. The exclusion occasionally follows racial lines. Under unfavorable environmental conditions such exclusions may prepare the way for unintelligent and stereotyped racial attitudes. Left to themselves, ordinary American children are not inclined to develop serious interracial tensions and conflicts. But children, of course, are not left to themselves. They are constantly subject to the attitudes, the preferences, and the antipathies of their elders. Through deliberate imitation, and still more through subconscious suggestion, the children acquire the likes and dislikes expressed by their elders.

This suggests how cultural controls can be strengthened. Home, school, and community should avoid the contagion of prejudice which comes from slighting remarks and uncritical generalizations. *Races and nations should not be slurred as groups. All persons should be appraised in terms of their merits as individuals.*

A sociologist recognizes a legitimate kind of attitude which is not colored by prejudice or antagonism, but which can be called a race feeling, namely "the ancient and deep-seated preference of practically every individual for his own kind of people." Individuals then adjudge each other as individuals on the basis of proven and potential qualities. Justice between persons becomes a more significant and difficult virtue than undiscriminating benevolence in the planning and practice of social living.

An attitude is a habitual tendency to react in a characteristic manner in a given situation. The refinement of interpersonal attitudes accordingly constitutes one of the major tasks of elementary education. We know that adolescence is the period when all social attitudes, racial and otherwise, come to their final stages of development. This is the optimal period for educational control; but the basic groundwork should be prepared in the first decade of life. Children from five to ten have more insight into their mental processes than we may give them credit for. We do not listen closely enough to what they say and how they say it. With shrewd suggestion and skillful spot guidance, while the occasion still tingles with its emotional realities, it is possible to help children toward more concrete self-control. We rely too much on abstract, remote, idealistic goals. Fortunately we improve our own interpersonal relationships when we become more perceptive and alert to the concrete interpersonal relations of our children.

Growth Gradients

MOTHER-CHILD

3 years—Gets on well with mother. Mother usually the favored parent at this age.

Child may be of real help to mother around the house.

Child relives babyhood, talking it over with mother.

May want to get into parents' bed during the night.

3½ years—Mother-child relationship can be very difficult at this age. Child tends to be very demanding with mother and very bossy, but at the same time may resist almost any demand she makes of him. Child may refuse to eat, dress, nap, or take part in any daily routines in the way his mother wants him to. May do much better with almost anyone other than his mother.

4 years—Great pride in mother. Boasts about her away from home, and quotes her as an authority.

Frequently resists mother's authority, both physically and verbally.

May threaten mother with "Wait till I'm your mother."

5 years—Mother seems to be center of child's world. Relationship smooth, pleasant, and not overintense.

Likes to do things correctly, as mother desires. Likes to obey.

Likes to help mother, be near her, play or work near her. Tells her what he is doing.

Does not require all mother's attention though likes her presence.

Expresses affection for mother: "I like you, Mummy."

Sympathetic and helpful if mother is ill.

Likes to have mother at home on return from school; disturbed if she is not there.

Accepts punishment from mother, though it glides right off.

May say, "You're a mean Mommy." Blames mother, saying, "Look at what you made me do."

Boys may talk of marrying mother.

Again relives babyhood and likes to hear of mother's babyhood.

Needs, invites, and accepts mother's supervision in learning.

6 years—Mother no longer center of child's world; child himself or herself now holds this position.

This shift, this separation of child from mother, has not yet been achieved; is merely being achieved. Leads to much difficulty and dissension; child and mother are embroiled.

As at 2½ years, child behaves best and worst with mother.

Very sensitive to mother's moods, emotions, tensions.

Contradictory responses toward

mother: says he loves her, then says he hates her; says he wishes she were dead, but worries that she may die.

Unwilling to accept help needed from mother.

Child is rude, resistant, and argumentative toward mother. Speaks rudely to her; says, "No, I won't"; "Try and make me." Strikes her.

What mother does is important—not, as later, what she thinks.

Not good about accepting directions, and is hard to punish.

Tantrum response.

Child "takes things out" on mother. Threatens "I'll get another mother."

7 years—On the whole child gets on well with mother, likes to do things with her at times. A "we" age for mother and child.

Relationship more companionable and less intense than earlier.

Child variable in this as in other things: may become moody and sulky, "mad" at mother.

Likes to argue with mother: "But Mommy . . ." But mother can begin to use reason and appeal to child ethically.

Easier to discipline, as sensitive to praise and blame. Obeys mother quite well if he hears what she says.

May be extremely proud of mother and self-conscious about her in public.

Occasional strong battle of wills between child and mother.

8 years—Child "all mixed up" with mother; haunts her; wants all her attention.

Strong physical and verbal expressions of admiration and affection for mother.

Tries to live up to what he believes is mother's standard for him; often feels that he fails.

Child has definite standards of how mother should speak and act. Unhappy if she fails to respond in the expected manner.

What mother thinks as well as what she does about child is important to him.

Obeys mother if she words directions in way that pleases.

Very sensitive toward mother: tears likely to well up. May be sensitive even to a change in facial expression. An emotional relationship.

Likes to please mother and very responsive to praise.

May be jealous of mother and father when they are together.

9 years—Child wants to be on his own and, busy and self-centered, makes less demand of time and attention from mother. The relationship smoother, provided that mother treats child with respect for increased maturity.

Child may at times be demonstrative, affectionate, and anxious to please.

Boys especially react against mother's demands that they be neat and clean. They are becoming more independent about large matters: mothers react by exercising authority in little matters.

Some quite indifferent to mother's directions, admonitions, scoldings; have a "deaf ear" at home.

Some sulky, "growling," fault-finding with mother. Others bold and argumentative.

Best relation with parent in regard to some activity that interests both: girls and mothers share interest in cooking, clothes, etc.

Does not like to be reminded, by mother, of self as a young child. Some boys may be embarrassed at being bathed by mother.

Beginning to "put things over" on mother.

Opinion of contemporaries may be much more important than that of parents.

10 years—Relationship with mother tends to be straightforward, uncomplicated, sincere, trusting. Child throws self wholeheartedly and positively into this relationship. Many say they like mother (and father) the best of anything in world—"My mother's just about right!"

Mother important as a final authority: "Mommy says . . ."; "Mommy doesn't like me to . . ."

Girls very confidential with mother, like to confess not only bad deeds but bad thoughts. Boys and girls extremely affectionate and physically demonstrative, sometimes embarrassingly so. Boys like to

snuggle and have mother tuck them in at night.

Several boys described as having a "mother attachment"—"trails mother everywhere, depends on her." But boys also seem more ambivalent than girls: "Trails mother, but you don't dare give him an inch"; "Wants to give mother things, but much turmoil —shouts and loses his temper."

Aware of mother's criticism, and may try to improve. But some—boys more than girls—feel that mother is always trying to improve them.

The beginning of some eleven-year-old resistance and "yelling" appears in some.

FATHER-CHILD

3 Years—Mother is commonly the favored parent at this age, but father can take over in many situations.

Child clings less at bedtime and may go to sleep more quickly for father.

Each parent should have authority over certain kinds of situations; should not try to divide authority, or child will play one against the other.

3½ years—Girls propose to fathers; say, "I love you."

4 years—Child boasts about father outside home. Quotes him as an authority.

Excursions and times alone with

father greatly prized, though father may need to use techniques.

Some say they hate father, especially if his being at home cuts them off from mother.

5 years—Some now for first time accept father when mother is ill.

Relations with father smooth, pleasant, undisturbed.

Enjoys special occasions (excursions) with father.

Boys, especially, may prefer father to mother, but this is exceptional.

Takes punishment better from mother than from father.

Fond and proud of father, and may obey father better than mother.

6 years—Both fears and admires father more than mother.

Usually respects father's word as law and does not question it.

Is not rude and resistant to father as to mother.

Feelings hurt by a cross word from father.

Child may believe that father—in his office—knows everything that happens.

Many situations can be carried through more successfully and with less friction by father.

Child enjoys playtime with father and may demand every minute of father's time while he is home.

7 years—Variable from child to child and from time to time.

Father's role may be slight at this age, as child is occupied with own activities.

Some, especially boys, "worship" father, think he is wonderful. Have long, confidential talks with him. Confide their worries, troubles, even sometimes their misdeeds.

Girls more sensitive to any reprimand from father and may be jealous of his attention to mother.

8 years—Relationship with father less intense but smoother than that with mother.

Less ardent expressions of affection toward father, but less demanding of him. Can allow him to make a mistake.

Likes father's company but does not insist on his complete attention.

Respects father's opinion and authority and (usually) obeys his commands.

Father frequently needs to step in to settle disputes between mother and child.

Child's best responses may come with father at this age.

9 years—Relationship smooth when father respects child's increased maturity.

Boys often come into new relationship with fathers, sharing real interests. Child shows respect for father's technical knowledge. Father-son may group together against female interference.

Very sensitive of criticism from

father. Thinks highly of his good regard.

Relationship with father largely through things they do together.

Most "approve" of father except for occasional specific criticism of his actions, as that he drives too fast, or too slowly; or that he smokes.

May feel superiority in pride over father's occupation.

10 years—Boys and girls said to get on extremely well with their fathers. Girls described as "adoring" their fathers, being "wonderful pals." Many boys described as "admiring" or "idolizing" father. Children themselves spontaneously report: "We have fun"; "I think he's the best father in the whole world."

Many girls believe they are more like father than mother. Several mothers say they leave the disciplining of daughters to the father, since he is more effective.

A few boys do not get on well with father—he loses his temper with them.

Some, of both sexes, complain that father doesn't have time to do things with them. But most spend a good deal of time alone with father—at ball games, on walks, or playing games.

SIBLINGS

4 years—Relationship not very good. Out of bounds with siblings as with other people.

Old enough now to be a definite nuisance to older siblings.

Likely to be selfish, rough, impatient with younger siblings.

Much quarrelling over toys and physical fighting.

5 years—Usually good with younger siblings. Girls especially protective and kind, like to take care of them. Helpful rather than domineering.

May be good when someone else is present, but when alone with younger sibling may take things from him or tease. May be better outdoors than indoors.

Should not be given too much responsibility over younger siblings, as not dependable.

Often plays well with older siblings, accepting the "baby" role in domestic play.

6 years—Not usually as good with siblings as at five.

Likes to teach younger siblings, but also may "egg them on"; likes to see them scolded; bosses them, hurts them, fights with them, tattles on them.

Gets on better with siblings outdoors than indoors.

Some are good with siblings except for the "usual spats."

Much quarreling with older siblings.

7 years—Chiefly good with siblings.

Plays "big brother [sister]" to younger siblings and likes to protect them.

Boasts about older siblings and is proud of them.

Variable, however, from time to time: "Bickers with sister but thinks she's cute"; "Protects sister but teases her." A few are consistently bad: "Fight like cats and dogs."

Frequently jealous: wants to do things siblings cannot or are not allowed to do; fears that sibling will "put something over on him."

8 years—Less good with siblings.

Some consistently bad, teasing and being selfish and quarrelsome about possessions.

Others variable: sometimes protective and thoughtful; at other times getting down to sibling's level and teasing and fighting.

Some are "kind, though they scrap around."

9 years—Frequently get on well with siblings. May be thoughtful and protective if siblings are younger; proud of and try to emulate older siblings.

Some trouble if near same age: may argue, fight, compete, accuse. But often show considerable loyalty to siblings, uphold them.

May in presence of contemporaries be much embarrassed or disgusted by actions of siblings. May dislike their "messiness."

Boys often wrestle and "fool around" with siblings.

10 years—Majority fight with brothers and sisters—at least younger ones (except infants), at least part of the time. Most say they would not want to be an only child, but several comment, "Once in a while I wish he'd just disappear."

Minority express stronger antagonism: "That spoiled brat! Sometimes I feel I hate the sight of her"; "I'd like to smash her face in!" Whether or not there is real rivalry and jealousy seems to be more a matter of individuality and situation than of age.

Fighting most frequent with younger siblings. Younger one will tease, "needle," taunt, or pester until TEN retaliates physically. Younger one calls for help, or parents step in spontaneously; then TEN thinks parent is unfair. Most feel that younger siblings are favored, and also that they "get away with a lot of stuff I never got away with."

With younger siblings closer in age, though there is much good-natured playing together, fighting and bickering very common. Fighting involves name-calling, "wrassling," and real physical fighting intended to hurt—pushing, kicking, hitting, biting. Good-natured "wrassling" becomes real fighting when someone is hurt. Much fighting occurs over possessions.

Younger siblings feel ten-year-olds too bossy and try too hard to keep them in line. TENs do at times play nicely with younger siblings; younger ones often tease TENs to play with them. And many very good about caring for or helping with siblings under five, who are often reported to "adore" ten-year-old.

Some know they are not good to younger siblings: "If I want to play with him I'm nice, but if I want to be alone he's a goner!"

Get on better with older than with younger siblings, and report that older ones sometimes play with them or take them places, but that there is still a lot of fighting. Many think older siblings consider them a nuisance or tattletales, because they seek protection from parents.

FAMILY AND GRANDPARENTS

4 years—Developing a strong sense of family and home.

Quotes parents as authorities; boasts about them.

Compares outside world to the home, to home's advantage. Family's way of doing things is the right and only way.

Family, as earlier, continues to be all-important, though child has not too clear a structured concept of family.

Likes family picnics and other outings.

Looks forward to visiting relatives; to trips on train or by car.

Likes to be taken on nature trips. Excursions alone with father especially prized.

5 years—May have strong feeling for family. Likes idea of the "family," likes to talk about it, to use the word.

Enjoys family picnics and other outings; likes details of family celebration of holidays.

May be very proud of mother and father.

Likes to hang around mother and help her in the house, go downtown with her.

Seems to assume that self and parents eternal, that parents also omniscient and all-powerful.

Usually very fond of grandparents; likes to visit them; likes grandmother's stories of his or his parents' babyhood.

Says that best thing about grandmother is that she makes good food. Girls say that best thing about grandfather is that he loves them; boys say that he makes good food and give them things.

Tends to describe grandparents in terms of the color or type (curly, straight, gray) of their hair.

Girls say the best thing about visiting grandparents is that they "give us things" and "give us good food." Boys like visiting because of things they can do, as going to the beach.

Believes that parents and grandparents in agreement concerning child's discipline.

As at nearly all the early ages, most children say they like (or love) their grandparents.

6 years—Likes family outings though behavior frequently does not hold up well. Teases for things he cannot have, is restless to get home, gets into trouble.

Enjoys family secrets, as about Christmas presents.

May cooperate in family matters, but not as naturally as at five.

Boasts about home.

Likes to go downtown with mother to make some small purchase for self.

Child begins to suspect that mother will one day die and thus destroy present family setup and someone else will have to take care of him. Thinks about what might happen in this case. May think in a long, orderly succession of ancestors and parents dying, then he will grow up and reproduce.

Likes to have mother at home when gets home from school.

Argues with parents and likes to prove them wrong.

Wants to hear about parents' baby-hood.

Interest in extended family—back in time and outward to cousins, uncles, and aunts.

Likes to talk about attributes, activities, and possessions of aunts, uncles, cousins.

May be very rude ("bratty") to grandparents, especially to grandmother, and may act badly on visits to grandparents, though sometimes better if parents not there.

7 years—Interest in and feeling for family very strong.

Serious about such concepts as "home," "family," "government."

Very proud of home and family possessions. May think own family is rich because they have such nice things.

Compares own home and family to others, to the detriment of others. (One child loved home so much she hoped that mother and father would move out when she married so that she could have their home.)

Proud of family, parents, and especially of older siblings.

With characteristic variability, fluctuates between love for family and anxiety that he does not belong.

May threaten to run away "from this family." May think family does not like him, or that he is adopted (and is actually of more rich and powerful parentage). May say he doesn't want to be "a member of this family."

Interested in place in the family, and in relation to all members of the family.

Interested in own and everyone's place at the table, in the car, etc.

May prefer to stay at home and play rather than go outdoors.

Variable about helping: sweet and helpful, then very disobedient. May inquire why he should help parents.

May like to have house orderly and attractive but does not contribute much toward this.

May be interested in doing own share of work: "That's my job."

Enjoys family outings. More interested in what goes on and behaves better than he did at earlier ages.

Likes to play games with mother or grandmother.

Wants the "family" to have a baby.

May realize that oldest die first and that just as grandparents may have died, later parents will die and then finally himself.

Continues to say best thing about grandmother is that she "gives me things." Likes grandfather because he plays with him and takes him places.

Describes grandparents in terms of hair, color of eyes, whether or not they wear glasses, or age.

Boys still think that parents and grandparents agree about their discipline, but majority of girls now report they do not.

Nearly all children still say they like (or love) their grandparents.

8 years—Interest at this age seems to be more for mother than for family as a whole. Relationship with mother very close and exacting. Child "haunts" mother.

Very insistent about both parents doing and saying things "just so." Quick to point out a fault or error on part of parents.

At seven, was building up a concept of family; now tries to make it really work. Very much aware of people's reactions and anxious to have things "go right" in family: at Christmas, wants everyone to get gifts and be pleased.

Had seemed to assume, unless there was overt evidence to contrary, that all was well between parents. Now worries about this relationship along with other relationships. May express some jealousy of mother and father's being together.

May be curious about telephone calls, mail, people's conversation.

Through this age may think own home is perfect.

May be the last age for wholehearted enthusiasm about family outings.

Wants to have house neat and tidy, though does not keep own room neat.

May do home tasks if rewarded or some goal or prize offered, but not anxious to help around home for the sake of helping or for the sake of the home.

Interest in family background, relatives on both sides.

Very strong demand for mother's time and attention. Likes to have her present when practicing music lesson. Likes to play games with her.

Wants her there when gets home from school, as at six.

As at six, may be rude and impatient with grandmother, but may greatly enjoy long play periods with her, who may have more patience than his mother for the absorbing detailed play child requires.

Grandparents liked because they "give me things and play with me and take me places."

Girls describe grandmothers in terms of their hair, or say they are "nice." They describe grandfathers in terms of hair or lack of hair, or in terms of activities, as "He reads the paper and watches TV."

Boys describe grandmothers in terms of hair, age, glasses; grandfathers in terms of age, hair, type of work, or, more maturely, say he is "nice" or "fun."

9 years—Concept of family important to most, though in practice they like to be away from family, on their own, with own friends.

May be very sensitive as to how family and family possessions compare with those of others. May want a better house. But some still feel that anything of their own (city, house, father's occupation) is superior.

May be shamed in public by behavior of siblings or even of parents.

Some are indifferent, self-centered, irresponsible so far as family life is concerned. "Taking part in the home" doesn't mean a thing to them. Prefer not to go on family excursions.

Others have "strong feeling for family." Feel need of parents' care and happy to be cared for.

Many are more helpful than formerly with younger siblings.

Girls say the best thing about their grandmother is that she is nice (or kind). Boys' chief reasons for liking grandmother are still that she makes good food, gives them things, takes them places, "is nice to us."

Boys and girls give same descriptions as formerly: boys add that grandmothers are generous, helpful, friendly; grandfathers tell jokes.

Best thing about visiting grandparents is that they get to play with their friends (or cousins).

Children feel that parents and grandparents agree about disciplining them "Yes, no, or sometimes."

10 years—Feels a much closer relationship with family. Accepts and enjoys family and usually participates willingly in any kind of family activity—picnics, rides, movies, trips.

Most are not critical of parents and do not like older siblings to criticize them.

Quarreling with siblings may upset family harmony: "We're not a very harmonious family. Every meal something happens. We eat and scream mostly."

Girls commonly say they like grandmother because she is nice (or kind). Some boys still say best thing about their grandmother is that she makes good food or gives them things, but most are becoming more abstract: they like her because "She loves us" or because "She is generous and understanding."

Like to visit grandparents in order to see their friends, or "Because I like them" or "It's nice to see them."

Most say parents and grandparents get on about their discipline sometimes, or they do not get along.

MANNERS

4 years—Very little spontaneous and unprompted use of conventional phrases of politeness.

Shows off and acts very badly before company.

5 years—Some are able to greet friends, let them into the house, etc.

A few, if reminded, can say "Please" and "Thank you."

Some may be able to shake hands with adults and say, "How do you do," but this is a learned response and does not seem natural to the child. Many are unable to make a conventional social greeting without undue embarrassment.

Usually docile before company, though may retreat to four-year-old showing off and noisy, conspicuous behavior. Likes to be present.

5½ years—A verbal child may be able to say that you should keep quiet, answer people when they are talking to you, always say "Please" and "Thank you," always remember to say "Good morning," "Good afternoon," "Good evening." This knowledge may exceed the child's performance ability.

6 years—Marked difficulty in formal social situations, though with people he knows and likes he can open the door and with enthusiasm say, "Come on in."

Not yet good at shaking hands with strangers and saying "How do you do" or "Goodbye." Has difficulty in responding to the query "How are you?"

Forgets to say "Please" and "Thank you." "Goodbye, I had a nice time" is especially difficult.

Most can at least look squarely at people who greet them. No longer hang their heads.

May behave very badly before company, though some are better away than at home. Very bad, however, at social gatherings such as birthday parties.

May be very rude in company without meaning to be: "Oh, this soup is terrible!"

Many can entertain contemporaries (if not too many at a time), offering and receiving hospitality.

Uses telephone. Some can dial.

If parent gives exact words to use in social situation, child may be able to repeat them.

7 years—Many can greet people with "Hello," looking straight at them, better than saying "Goodbye."

Very likely to rush in front of others to secure his "place."

Behaves quite well in the presence of company for a while, then withdraws to own activity.

Considers it important to say "Excuse me," or "I didn't mean to," if things go wrong.

Social telephoning to friends.

Can listen courteously in an audience situation for short periods (about twenty minutes).

Can talk about experiences in a pleasant manner.

May shake hands responsively though not with ease.

8 years—Can verbalize "proper" greetings and "proper" goodbyes.

Some carry on real social conversation with adult.

May monopolize mother's attention if company is present.

May be very rude, as to grandparents.

Table "manners" now considerably improving in a new situation.

Many have excellent company manners away from home.

Marked individual differences between those who love formalized things and those for whom artificial steps are difficult.

Much social telephoning to friends.

9 years—May be ready to shake hands spontaneously and with ease. May enjoy this formality. Can manage adequate formalized greetings if he takes time for them. "Manners not deliberately bad, just never thinks. No consideration for others, no gracious courtesies." Child often simply ignores adults.

Marked individual differences here; some being "naturally polite."

May behave with extremely good manners in public, as at a restaurant.

10 years—About half of group studied described as having adequate manners, and they themselves say their manners are "not mentioned" by parents. Of the rest, some are described as "bad" or even "terrible."

Poor posture is greatest complaint. Also criticizing food, holding fork incorrectly, talking too much. Some children criticize table manners of parents.

Mother may let up on them when father not present. Children try to do better when father is there.

TEACHER-CHILD

4 years—Greets teacher, but more interested in talking to other children.

Responsive to verbal suggestion or direction from teacher.

Teacher needs to provide ahead plenty of play materials.

Teacher needs a wealth of information at her fingertips to answer questions.

Child can often be handled through silly language.

Child enjoys taking on a teacher or mother role with new or shy children.

5 years—Child likes teacher. Relationship is matter-of-fact and pleasant.

Child obeys teacher as a matter of course. Quotes her as an authority.

Relationship less personal than it will be later.

Child may complain: "The teacher makes me do things"; "The teacher makes me stay in line."

Needs immediate attention from teacher.

Refers to teacher for materials, to tell experiences, and to show own products.

Seeks teacher for approval and for affection.

6 years—Child related to teacher through materials and activities.

Likes to conform to teacher's demands. May even like discipline.

Usually likes teacher, and likes to please her.

Wants and likes to be commended. Wants praise, attention, and help from teacher.

In awe of teacher. Her word is law.

May need teacher to sit next to him and to work closely with him for a period.

Apt not to know when to ask for help from teacher.

Likes teacher to talk with him about what he is doing.

Looks for teacher immediately on arrival, wants to be assured that she is there. Brings things to school for her.

Does not like to have teacher laugh at him.

7 years—More personal relationship. Crushes. Boys especially like to stand by teacher and hold her hand, to bring her presents.

Teacher really paramount in school. Child depends on her. If teacher upholds child's behavior, all goes well.

Because of personal relationship, child, girls especially, may think teacher is mean and unfair, or may act silly toward teacher.

Poor transitioners may remain loyal to first-grade teacher and prefer her.

Child often depends on a word from teacher to start the simplest task.

May be interested in doing something forbidden when teacher is out of room.

Wants own teacher and does not like a substitute. Likes to be with her, to sit with her.

Makes an impatient demand for teacher's attention and assistance.

Asks teacher, "Who did the best drawing?" "Did I get a hundred?"

May be concerned that teacher does not like him.

8 years—Teacher less personally important. Child wants her to be a part of group.

Child usually likes teacher. May evaluate: "She looks sour, but she isn't."

Fewer complaints about teacher as well as less ardent liking.

Children like a teacher who is factual, businesslike, comradely, a good sport.

Pleased at idea of teacher making a mistake.

Likes to have some individual contact with teacher relative to tasks to be done, but better able to wait for teacher's attention than at seven.

May be concerned about how teacher treats a friend.

Likes to help teacher, to pass papers, etc.

Likes to do things in order, in certain ways, and tells teacher if she deviates.

Wants teacher to enjoy activity with him, to have a turn.

Tells teacher what another child is doing.

Teacher can handle with humor and can control by her silence.

9 years—Most seem to like teacher well or even be devoted to her.

Often a very strong feeling one way or other: teacher is "terrible" or "wonderful."

Great stress on whether teacher is fair or unfair.

Tendency toward crushes and this makes child shy with teacher.

Perhaps less talk at home about teacher than earlier.

Teacher needs to be aware of individual intellectual difference in children, and to help them perfect their individual intellectual implements for later use.

Child wants to be independent of teacher both in work and in play.

Still prefers teacher's assistance when needed in work.

Critical of teacher in relation to a specific subject. May blame her for a lowered grade.

Wants teacher to be reasonable.

May report on her mannerisms or conduct in a specific situation.

10 years—Most like and respect teachers. May pay even more attention to teacher than to parents; "Teacher is God," one parent reports.

Critical analysis of teachers is just beginning. Most describe teacher as "nice" or "okay." Describe in terms of physical characteristics: "A little bit fat and not too tall"; "Small and dyes her hair." Like to compare one teacher to another. Main demand is that teacher be fair. Beginning criticism of methods of teaching: "Monotonous" or "Makes sense."

Express affection for and accept affection from teacher. Can be easily hurt and upset by criticism. However, respond well to firmness, seem to appreciate it. If there is to be punishment, they want it to be on the spot; can't stand long-term punishments.

CHILD-CHILD

4 years—Will share or play cooperatively with special friends.

Very conversational with friends. Good imaginative play.

But much excluding, tattling, disputing, quarreling, verbal and physical.

More interested in children than in adults.

May spontaneously take charge of younger or shy child.

May have special friends of same sex.

5 years—Plays well with other children, especially groups kept small.

Does not insist on having own way and does not worry about behavior of others.

Prefers playmates of own age.

Some are too rough, too bossy, or cry too readily to get on well in unsupervised play.

May play better with another child outside rather than indoors.

6 years—Marked interest in making friends, having friends, being with friends. Uses term "school friend" or "playmate."

Seems able to get along with friends, but play does not hold up long if unsupervised. Quarreling, physical combat. Each wants own way.

A good deal of tattletaling.

May be very dominating and bossy with some playmates.

Much exclusion of a third child: "Are you playing with So-and-so? Then I'm not playing with you."

Cannot bear to lose at games and will cheat if necessary to win. Also thinks friends cheat or do things the wrong way.

Many are said to be a "bad influence" on playmates or are thought to play with someone who is a "bad influence."

May prefer slightly older playmates.

7 years—Much fighting with playmates, though less than at six. May leave the scene if things go wrong.

Less domineering, less set on having own way, less worry about how others do things.

Tattletaling and some worry about goodness and badness in others.

Learning to lose, but must win in the end.

Begins to be aware of friends' attitudes as well as of their actions.

Needs to be happy himself in a two-way relationship, but does not worry much about friend.

Prefers older playmates.

Boys may have trouble with older boys who are bullies.

8 years—Group play better: more cooperation, less insistence on having own way, less worry about behavior of others. But any unsupervised period of play may end in dissension.

Effort to work out a relationship with "best friend." Friend's attitudes important. Child wants to be happy and wants friend also to be happy. Much arguing, disputing, getting "mad" caused by this.

Can take part in competitive games and can sometimes lose with grace.

"Enemy" is a word frequently used.

May again prefer same-age friends.

Subverbal appraisal of selves and others; controlled somewhat by criticism of others.

9 years—Most have a special friend

of same age and sex, as well as a group of friends.

Gets on well with playmates in spite of some quarreling and disagreement. Interested less in relationship with friend and more in what they do together. The activity or goal is important. Real cooperative activity.

The gang or club is important. May subordinate own interests and demands to getting along in the group. Try to live up to group standards and criticize those who do not.

Girls beginning to like to spend the night with each other.

Beginning of crushes on older child or adult.

Evaluation, not just judging, behavior of others.

Much good-natured roughhousing and wrestling among boys. Boys have considerable trouble with "bullies" of own age or older.

Boys dash about shouting; girls giggle and whisper.

10 years—Same-Sex Friends.

Girls: Most have a best friend, often several. Relationships among these friends extremely complex and intense—much getting mad and not speaking.

Much anger, jealousy, and fighting if friends associate with other, disliked girls. Very possessive of friends and very demanding.

Apt to be very cliquey and purposely say things to put girls against other girls.

Much emphasis on secrets and whom they can trust. A few describe personality of friend, but most emphasize mainly trustworthiness.

Considerable spending the night with each other.

Boys: Some have one or two "best" or "trusted" friends. Others have a whole "gang" whom they seem to like about equally.

Groups may be fluid. Or one boy may have two definite groups which do not mix. Some, though they have many friends, often prefer to play with one at a time.

Not as much fighting and getting mad and not speaking among girls. However, some ganging up of two against one.

Girls: Majority are "not interested in boys yet" or are against boys. Complain that boys pull their hair, chase them, push them down, act rough, and throw food at parties.

Some girls are willing to play with boys, but are not personally interested in them.

Some express positive, personal interest in boys or in some one special boy.

Most consider that girls who kiss boys are extremely forward.

Boys: The majority express either disinterest in or active dislike of girls.

Some say they used to have a girl but now she likes someone else and they "haven't bothered to get another." Some still let girls play baseball or other games with them. A few express friendship, but nothing warmer, for girls.

Typical comment: "We haven't gotten to girls yet. All we're interested in is shoving them down on the ice."

GROUPINGS IN PLAY

4 years—Cooperative and imaginative group play—sustained dramatic or imaginative play.

Tendency in group play for division along sex lines. Play groupings fluid. Some chanting at other sex, in an excluding way.

Some have special friends of same sex.

Racial attitudes: Exclusion from play groups may be along sex lines; usually not along race lines.

5 Years—Children mostly play in groups of two: seldom more than five in in a group.

Personnel of any group is rapidly shifting.

Little solitary play, but often parallel play.

Imaginative play gives appearance of being cooperative though actually involves little real cooperation. Each child carries out his individual ends and has little concern for the group as a whole.

Children symmetrically organized in play, ready for all relationships. Largely ignore sex in choosing a playmate or a group of playmates.

Most frequent grouping is of two children of same sex. These pairs of friends may be shifting.

Racial attitudes: Usually no concern about racial differences.

6 years—Much group play, especially in imaginative play of house, store. Groupings so flexible that any one child may leave or join the group without being noticed.

Little organization to group play, though can choose sides and may accept direction of a domineering older child or teacher.

Little concern for welfare of group; interest still primarily self-expressive.

Leaders are leaders of small group only (in school).

Little solitary play.

Considerable time spent in play with constant friend.

As at five, may group for games ignoring sex lines.

Some constant friendships begin to persist.

Parties: behavior diffuse, child is "all over the place," all want to have presents and win prizes.

Racial attitudes: There may be some verbalization of racial differences, but usually no exclusion in play. In anger, some name-calling stressing any distinctive characteristic, race among others. Child is beginning to be aware of own race.

7 years—Play in pairs (same or opposite sex); but also much group play.

Group play not well organized and still primarily for individual ends. But beginning of real cooperation.

Several children "gang up" against some other child.

Child worries about place in the group, afraid he will not hold his own.

Girls are eligible for Brownies, boys are eligible for Cub Scouts.

Largely ignore sex lines in play groupings. But if by chance children have separated along sex lines they may verbalize this in exclusion chanting.

8 years—Child enjoys group activity. Accepts fact that role in group is to some extent determined by abilities and limitations.

Real cooperative play and carrying out of simple projects.

Not ready for complex rules, but can accept very simple ones, or directions.

Organization of simple same-sex clubs with names and passwords, of temporary duration.

Beginning to have a "best friend" of same sex.

Boys and girls separate off in play. Prefer play with same sex. Girls conscious of this sooner, but boys probably the first to actively exclude child of other sex from play.

Children will not play long in a group in which they are only one of their sex.

Racial attitudes: Ganging up against a child may be along race lines. Calling names may stress race differences.

9 years—Informal clubs, still short-lived and very varied, though a little longer duration and more structure than earlier. May be for some definite purpose: press club, scrapbook club, sewing club.

Clubs are mostly secret, with passwords, initiations, hideaways, codes, secret language, dues, club bulletins. Rigid exclusion of nonmembers. But clubs "don't last."

More formal clubs under adult leadership: Cubs or Brownies.

Children like to act as a group and compete as a group. Accept own role in group and can evaluate contributions of others. May be more interested in success of group than in own enjoyment. In games or for projects, organization is complex and detailed, cooperation excellent.

Birthday parties: usually one sex. Rather complex entertainment, as magician, treasure hunt, athletic event, and refreshments.

Racial attitudes: Very little interest or comment.

10 years—Many now belong to some kind of club, either a "secret" club or a more structured organization such as Scouts. Boys' groupings tend to be fluid and flexible and based quite as much on shared interests as (except in secret clubs) on the basis of strong personal friendship. Girls' groupings are more rigid and often involve the specific excluding of certain nonfavored girls.

CHAPTER 17

PLAY AND PASTIMES

Children reveal themselves most clearly in their play life. They play not from outer compulsion, but from inner necessity—the same kind of necessity that causes a kitten to chase a rolling ball, and to play cat and mouse with it. The kitten is not a cat, and the ball is not a mouse; but in all this playful pouncing we see a preliminary exercise of serious adult activities. The kitten's play is also reminiscent because it involves a rehearsal of activities inherited from the ancestral generations. It is indeed a zestful merging of past, present, and future.

A child's play possesses similar qualities. It rises spontaneously out of instinctive promptings which represent developmental needs. It prepares for maturity. It is a natural enjoyable exercise of growing powers.

No one needs to teach a child to play. Even a young infant knows how. What does a twelve-week-old baby do with his "idle" time? He practices all his budding abilities in the four major fields of human behavior—motor, adaptive, language, and personal-social behavior. He flings his arms and flexes his legs (motor); he fixates his eyes regardfully upon his fisted hand (adaptive); he coos and chuckles (language); he vocalizes on his mother's approach (personal-social). He is ceaselessly active during his waking hours, playing in one form or another. Play is his work, his business.

Play never ceases to be a major business throughout childhood. Nature plants strong play instincts in every normal child to make sure that certain basic needs of development will be satisfied. The culture directs, restrains, and redirects these play impulses into approved channels, but always at the risk that the child will not get an optimal measure of the kind of play life that is best suited to his stage of maturity. All things considered, the modern child has too many set tasks, and not a sufficient amount of untrammeled leisure and self-activity.

Needless to say, a child does not play because he is too lazy to work. Often he puts forth his most strenuous energies in moments of play. He concentrates with his whole being and acquires emotional satisfactions he cannot get from other forms of activity. Deeply absorbing play seems to be essential for full mental growth. Children who are capable of such intense play are most likely to give a good account of themselves when they are grown up.

The gradations of play interest are part and parcel of the very process of growing up. Take, for example, such ancient play materials as sand and mud. They must have figured very early in the playful manipulations and workmanship of our remote ancestors while they idled at a sea or lake shore. Sand appeals even to the eighteen-month-old. Although he is naturally a runabout, he is so intrigued by the tractability of sand he will sit for a long period filling and dumping, refilling and redumping endlessly. In this self-perpetuated play he is getting a delectable mixture of visual, tactile, and motor experience, and a sense of mastery which feeds his mental growth. His later exploitations will be more sophisticated, but they will have a similar developmental function.

Already at two years his play is more elaborate; he mixes stones with his sand; he fills a pail and lugs it back and forth; he plays with water, too, filling and emptying dishes. In another year he makes mud, combining the basic elements of earth and water. He even fashions them to his devices, molding, patting, and smoothing his plastic mud into cakes and pies.

By five years he does not like to be confined by the sandbox; he prefers a generous heap of sand which he can dramatically use as a stockpile for filling his truck, which will transport and retransport its load to distant points. The six-year-old operates on a more imaginative scale; and combines sand and water to build definite structures. The seven-year-old elaborates still further. He likes to combine fantasy play with his digging and construction. He builds streets and houses, lakes and river beds out of sand and mud; and as he builds he chatters, soliloquizes or ruminates. And so he weaves new threads into his growing mental structures. Perhaps he is already preparing to become an engineer. There is an element of anticipation in all play; and if he is by inborn aptitude an engineer, he may already be revealing talent in the accents of his play.

By eight years the sandbox has graduated from the backyard into the schoolroom. Here, under the influence of curriculum and culture, the desert sand may blossom into an Indian village or an Arab camp. The distinction between play and work dissolves into an educational project. And the project in turn is reinforced by the pressure of the schoolroom group and by the teacher. The child's play impulses thus are socialized.

But there still is scope for the more aboriginal type of undirected play, and we hope that the eight-year-old boy will not be prevented from going to some hillside to dig himself a cave, or erect himself a hut planted upon mother earth. These private ventures and contacts with nature go deeper than a schoolroom project.

What a nine- to ten-year-old will do in this particular gradient of play cannot be predicted. As a child grows older, the culture tends more and more to intervene, and determines even his extracurricular activities. He may dig a tunnel, a trench, or a canal. He still likes to dig and to feel the earth yield to his hands. With his like-minded companions he builds a well-drilling machine—a wooden derrick, a pulley, a sash cord and iron weight, and perhaps a wheel and axle to operate the rhythmic drop of the drill. With what triumph he sinks a shaft and pulls up the moistened earth in his tomato-can bucket! The play sequence of sand and mud and water which began before the age of two has come to higher issues.

In many fields of play, one could trace a similar developmental sequence, the patterns of play always conforming to the advancing patterns of maturity. A child's play often appears to casual observation to be so haphazard, so determined by chance environmental factors—what playmates are available, what toys are at hand, what play space is provided—that it is easy to underestimate the strong developmental factors that underlie his choice of activity. Closer observation will disclose that deeply determined developmental trends often underlie this choice. Again and again, from child to child, do we find the same sequence repeated with increasing maturity: sand and water; doll and teddy bear; cars and wagons; tricycle and domestic doll play; dramatic play of store, hospital, and school; reading; games; radio; TV; bicycle; paper dolls; comic books.

There are variations based on individual and sex differences, and on cultural influences, but age is the basic factor. Children of high intelligence, accelerated beyond their years as measured by an intelligence quotient, nevertheless tend to remain true to their chronological age in many of their spontaneous play interests. This fact itself testifies to the basic significance of play in the dynamics of development.

In a more utopian child world we would doubtless make more room for free, unregimented play activities. There would also be more organized outdoor play, in which children might make spirited and rhythmical use of their large, fundamental muscles, through the medium of folk games, dancing, music, pantomime, and dramatic games. Such group activity taps the deeper springs of personality, which are not reached by sedentary and restricted indoor schooling. Such expressional play can bring about much-needed improvements in body posture and motor control. It would have a beneficial effect upon the organization of the emotions. It surely would be preferable to the aimless physical activities of unsupervised and chaotic recess periods.

As our culture becomes more technological, the psychological health and growth of children need increased protection. This protection requires a deeper understanding of the play interests of children, particularly in the age period from five to ten. For this is the period when we are in danger of introducing children too rapidly into our adult culture. We should have more faith in the simple, unsophisticated forms of play life, which keep the child closer to nature.

Technology tends to use more and more technology in order to catch up with the pace technology itself sets. Hence television, comics, movies for children. These devices have come to play a tremendous role in the recreation and pastime of the school child. They do indeed induct him into the civilization into which he is born, and they inevitably stir his elemental emotions as well as his fantasy. To that extent they serve the true functions of play. But they are a poor substitute for the more basic types of play, which come from inner urges and which express the initiative and resourcefulness of the growing mind. Carried to excess at the expense of natural, old-fashioned (!) play, these recreational facilities lead to superficiality. Television will aggravate the present imbalance in play diet, if not offset by more active forms of self-expression.

So much for the general philosophy of play and its underlying principles. These principles suggest that we should give considerable scope to the child's own spontaneous play enterprises. His play has a developmental logic which does not necessarily fit into our preconceptions. We must be tolerant toward some of his apparently illogical reactions. For example, you may enthusiastically give your girl a new and shining toy. There are so many different things that she could do with it. You can think of all of them; but if the timing of your gift was poor she may disappoint you with a very meager response. It may, however, be just the response that befits her and her maturity. Perhaps if the toy is put aside, she will come back to it with a wider range of response when she is older. Children themselves like to come back for a new contact with previously discarded playthings, when they can use them again at a higher level. The sand-mill toy which had superficial attention at three or four years may be revived at six years with a mounting of new interest. Then there is the common error of giving too many toys all on one occasion, when spacing would work to everyone's advantage. With pets as with toys, good timing is important. Many a child has been given a dog when he was scarcely ready to take care of a goldfish, and might, in fact, have had more pleasure in the latter.

Parents are sometimes worried about obsessive preoccupation with a single toy or with one kind of play, to the exclusion of others.

Such obsessive interest is more common in boys. Girls are more balanced and diversified in their play preferences. At the age of five and a half years a boy may be obsessed with the motion of his toy trains. At six years he may be obsessed with climbing. At seven years, characteristically enough, he shows a succession of intensified interests. At nine years he can hardly wait for school to close, so he may get back to his building set. These obsessions have their own logic in the scheme of development. They are benign and probably beneficial seizures.

At another extreme, a child's play is sketchy rather than obsessive; exploratory rather than conclusive. He starts something—a lemonade stand, a post card collection, or a play hut; but he does not carry through and finish the job. A father, unfamiliar with the ways of child development, detects a weakness in such behavior, and sternly expresses his disapproval. It is usually wiser to be patient with such beginnings. They are embryonic. They will come to fuller fruition at a later stage. One must also be patient with a certain amount of disorderliness. Unaided, the child may not be interested in completing what he has begun, he does not have the maturity of perception to see the whole. We can make concessions to his request that we do not molest his unfinished construction.

We can also make concessions to so-called destructiveness, which may well be a form of constructiveness in reverse. Oftentimes a child shows interest in taking a toy apart long before he is able to put the toy together. A baby spills the contents of a wastebasket before he is able to replace them. He delights in demolishing a tower of blocks before he can re-erect the tower himself. An older child may show a readiness to dismantle a block building well before he has the capacity to reassemble its parts. A wise father or older brother will encourage this kind of mechanical interest, because it actually represents a positive as well as negative form of workmanship. It is a preparatory stage.

However, unreasonable or destructive behavior does not necessarily denote either sadism or real destructiveness. Even when a child jabs a doll in the stomach and tears out its eyes, it does not automatically follow that these acts are symbolic. Among normal and relatively normal children play tends to be practical and experimental in its essence. Even in the play of fantasy, the child projects his private mental images in a practical spirit. He manipulates them in order to organize his concepts of reality, and not to deepen his self-illusion. Even his imaginary companions are amazingly serviceable devices and so he uses them pragmatically—until he is old enough to dispense with them. This is one more evidence that play has a positive role in the drama of development.

This role is many-sided. Play is an outlet for obstructed and overflowing energy. It manifests exuberance in laughter, rollick, and euphoria. Play is imitative, repetitive, or rhythmical in skipping, dancing, and dramatic expression. Play is psychomotor exercise in running, jumping, tossing, hustling, balancing, and a host of gross and fine muscular activities. Play harks back to the past, in the emotional stirrings that accompany games of hunt, hide-and-seek, combat and chase, and in the quieter pastimes of exploring, collecting, hoarding, camping, and caring for flowers, plants, and animals. Play penetrates into the future, spurred by impulses of curiosity, experimentation, exploitiveness, and workmanship. In highly gifted children, this workmanship declares itself in resourcefulness, originality, or even in genius. In all children play has a creative function. It serves to organize the abilities with which the child is endowed. In its supreme moments it reveals his individuality and his potentialities.

Growth Gradients

GENERAL INTERESTS

4 years—Prefers to play with other children. Dramatic play of house, store, train, hospital involves costumes and "props." Combination of real and imaginative.

Rides tricycle, climbs, does "tricks."
Plays with imaginary companions.
Draws, paints, colors.
Admires own products, whether of clay, paint, paper, blocks.
Blocks: makes detailed constructions. Combines with furniture for dra-

matic play. Builds cooperatively with others.

Christmas: Asks for specific presents, then brags about size and amount. Strong interest in Santa Claus.

5 years—More independent play, indoors or out according to season or weather. Likes to have an adult nearby.

Much play centers around a house.

Builds house with large blocks or with draped furniture. Plays house, imitating adult activities.

Plays with dolls, using them as babies.

Child runs, climbs, swings, skips, jumps, dances.

Rides tricycle, pushes cart.

Tries roller skates, jump rope, even stilts.

Uses sand in making roads, transporting it in cars.

Imitative play: house, store, hospital.

Paints, draws, colors, cuts and pastes, does puzzles.

Copies letters and numbers.

Games of matching pictures and forms.

Builds with blocks, large and small.

Likes to copy designs with blocks.

Christmas: Asks for specific presents. May request things by letter to Santa Claus. Anxious to tell what he has received. Strong belief and interest in details about Santa Claus and in visiting him.

Girls: Doll play, playing house, dressing up.

Boys: Blocks, tools, cars and trucks, war games, mechanical toys.

6 years—Elaborates and expands five-year play interests.

Mud, sand, and water play.

Games of tag, hide-and-seek; stunts on trapeze, on rope, and on tricycle.

Ball play: tossing, bouncing, throwing.

Rough-and-tumble play, climbing, swinging.

Interest in roller skates, double-runner ice skates.

Simple carpentry: hammering, sawing.

Table games with cards ("Go Fish"), anagrams, dominoes, and puzzles.

Paints, colors, draws, and uses clay. Cuts and pastes.

Collecting odds and ends.

Printing letters to spell real words.

Games of oral spelling or oral numbers.

Imaginative play: pretending to be a horse; pretending furniture is a boat, etc.

Blocks used imaginatively and constructively.

Christmas: May want specific toy (doll or train) and be disappointed if it is not received, but also wants many presents. Boasts about how many received. Strong interest and belief in Santa Claus.

Girls: Doll play elaborated with dolls' accessories: clothes, suitcase, furniture.

Dressing up in adult clothes.

Playing school, house, library.

Boys: Tinker Toys and simple Lego sets.

War games, cowboys, cops and robbers.

Digging holes and tunnels and simple activity in garden.

Interest in transportation using wagon, trains, trucks, airplanes, boats.

7 years—More intense interest in some activities, fewer new ventures.

Has "mania" for certain activities.

More solitary play.

Some play with mud, and digging; some interest in garden tools.

Tricycle usually discarded; some ride bicycles.

Magic and tricks. Jigsaw puzzles.

Collecting and swapping cards, bottle tops, and stowing away stones and bits of this and that.

Interest in swimming often strong.

Plays library, train, post office with elaborate paraphernalia.

Rudiments of ball play: catch, batting with soft ball.

Christmas: Very great disappointment now if does not receive a requested toy. Writes letter to Santa Claus with list of desired toys.

Girls: Cutting out paper dolls and their clothes. Doll play may decrease. May "invent" dresses for dolls.

Playing house, which includes dressing up in elaborate adult costumes.

Playing school, with emphasis on teacher role.

Hopscotch and jump rope, roller skating, ball bouncing.

Boys: Active outdoor play of running, wrestling, climbing trees.

Carpentry, especially sawing. Like to make Christmas presents.

Rigging things from cereal boxes, etc.

Make model airplanes.

Cops and robbers, gun play.

Building and playing in tree houses, forts, and tents.

Beginning interest in chemistry, telegraphy, navigation.

8 years—Variety of play interests. Prefers companionship in play (adult or child).

Games of all kinds played indoors or out. Differentiates work from play.

Table games of parcheesi, checkers, dominoes, cards. Jigsaw puzzles and map puzzles. Scorns too simple games. May make up own game with own rules.

Dramatic play; arranges and produces shows.

"Gadget" age. Likes to have variety of things and tries to make something of them.

Collecting, and arranging of collections.

Beginning interest in group games such as soccer or baseball, with supervision.

Unorganized group play of wild running, chasing, wrestling.

Beginning of secret clubs, usually short-lived.

Seasonal interests: Rowing and swimming in summer: skating, sliding, skiing in winter; playing with kites and tops in spring.

Boys and girls beginning to separate in play.

Christmas: Has innumerable ideas of what would like for Christmas and wants are now intense. Interest in how many presents received. Does not want useful things. More interest than earlier in giving presents.

Girls: Doll play and "house," stressing more complex adult relationships.

In make-believe play, child requires complete attention of companion.

Paper-doll play: Collect large number of dolls and doll clothes. Cut out and try on dresses. Like to have them admired. Simple dramatic play with dolls, involving much verbalization. Like books with many different dolls.

Boys: Beginning to utilize tools to fix things around house; make mixtures with chemistry set. Uses telegraph to communicate.

Continue to work with airplane, car, and boat models.

War games, cops and robbers.

Electric trains and movie projectors.

9 years—Plays and works hard and is apt to overdo to point of fatigue.

Busy with own activities. Plans what he is going to do.

Individual differences stronger: some read and listen to radio more; others play outdoors more.

Some former interests may be dropped, others intensified.

Sledding a favorite outdoor sport, but also marked interest in baseball, skating, swimming, etc.

Interest in organized clubs such as Cubs and Brownies.

Spontaneous clubs are short-lived. Stress special interest in clubhouse or hideaway.

Collecting of stamps, minerals, etc.

Hikes and goes for walks in woods.

Drawing maps, making lists of collections. Writing "business" letters in response to magazine advertisements or catalogues.

Playing more complicated table games.

Some have animals to care for.

Christmas: Makes long lists of presents, not expecting to receive all. May understand that cost of presents may be too high or that they may not be procurable. Interest in number of presents and may classify them by size or type.

Interest in trimming own tree and in making ornaments for it. May do own Christmas shopping, buying presents for family and friends. Interest in what they give others and how much they spend for each.

Girls: Paper dolls used in dramatic play. Identify with dolls, playing out elaborate dramas. Like books with fewer dolls and more different costumes. Or may enact entire day's routine in doll play.

May show interest in manipulating puppets.

Put simple abilities in sewing and cooking to practical use.

Boys: Constructing wth Lego, Mechano and Erector sets and in workshop. May work with material for long period on a planned project.

Roughhousing and wrestling. Some

are interested in boxing or gym lessons.

Beginning interest in bowling and horseshoes.

10 years—Indoor Activities. Collecting stamps, coins, china animals, dolls, post cards, trading cards, model airplanes, stones, shells, nature specimens.

Card and table games. Jigsaw puzzles. Scrapbooks.

Entertaining, especially reading to, younger siblings.

Pets.

Secret clubs.

Girls: Doll play: playing house, sewing for dolls. Creating paper dolls.

Dressing, painting, ceramics. Writing stories or plays, then dressing up and acting them.

Boys: Drawing, designing, creating, or imagining gadgets and inventions, secret rooms, jet rockets or planes, boats, etc.

Constructing model planes.

Lego sets. Electric trains.

Chemistry sets. Beginning interest in photography.

Disdain is expressed for outgrown activities.

Outdoor Activities. Bike riding very strong. Horseback riding (girls more than boys).

Baseball, catch, throwing ball against house.

Sledding, skating, swimming.

Building or playing in "secret huts." Climbing trees.

"Pretend" games—may involve activity or just be verbal.

Running and hiding games.

Playing with and caring for pets and younger siblings.

Nature interests (in a few).

Girls: Jump rope, roller skates, hopscotch.

Boys: Racing—plain, bicycle, three-legged.

Cowboys, guns (some are outgrowing this).

"Just fooling around," "wrassling."

READING

4 years—Listens to long stories and poems.

Likes nonsense rhymes—**Nonsense ABC**; humorous stories—**Junket Is Nice**; exaggeration—**Millions of Cats**; alphabet books—**The Jingling ABC's**; stories of function or growth of things—**Mike Mulligan and His Steam Shovel**, or **Tim Tadpole and the Great Bullfrog**; information books—**I want to Paint My Bathroom Blue** by Ruth Kraus; **The Silly Book** by Stoo Hempel.

5 years—"Loves" to be read to and shows preference for certain stories, which he likes to hear over and over.

Likes poetry, stories of animals who behave like human beings, holiday and seasonal stories. (E.g. **Winnie the Pooh; The Country Bunny.**)

Likes to have first-grade primer about children in play activities read to him.

Comics: May puzzle out pictures in

newspaper comics. May like to have some comics read to him. Slight interest in comic books.

6 Years—Likes to be read to. May read familiar stories from memory. Likes to hear stories about himself.

Beginning to recognize words.

Less selective in choice of stories and may be disturbed by unpleasant event in story.

Likes poetry (as of A. A. Milne), stories about activities of children.

Comics: Rudimentary interest in newspaper comics and comic books. Tries to read them or likes to have them read to him. Interest general, but some have particular favorites.

7 years—Some become inveterate readers and even want to bring books to the table and read as they eat. Others like to be read to while at play.

More individual reading interests: books about children, animals, nature, the elements. Boys like books about space, airplanes, and electricity.

Likes fairy tales, myths, and legends, poetry. (E.g., **Alice in Wonderland; The Hobbit**.)

An interest in going to the library for books.

May enjoy a children's magazine which suggests activities which they may carry out.

Comics: Reads these himself. Become a "passion" with some. Child buys, collects, barters them.

Has definite favorites: adventures of animals, ordinary people, or supermen.

8 years—Variable enjoyment in reading. Girls may read more than boys.

Interest in reading stories such as childhood classics. Books of travel, adventure, geography, primitive times, and Bible stories.

Still enjoys books about children, animals, the elements, fairies.

Expanding interest in books about faraway or long-ago people.

Delights in the humor of people put in the wrong position. (E.g., Mary Poppins.)

Enjoys looking at catalogues and at adult magazines as well as own literature.

Comics: Continued interest; now buys, collects, barters, borrows, hoards. Likes animal, adventure, and some "blood and thunder" comics.

9 years—Individual differences: some are omnivorous readers who secure books from the library weekly; others do not read at all.

Reads junior classics. Rereads favorite books.

Many like a book with several stories in it. Like mysteries and biographies.

Increasing interest in magazines.

May still enjoy being read to on occasion.

Comics: Interest reaches a peak with some, beginning to wane in others.

10 years—Great personal variation in interest in reading. Some are "not much for reading." Others "love" it.

Amount read varies from less than a book a week to five or more, and for many reading time equals time spent watching TV.

May get books from library, school, or may own them.

Quite a number are good about reading to younger siblings.

Prefer animal (especially horse or dog) stories, mysteries, girls' and boys' adventure series, biographies.

Comics: Most read comics, many avidly, and some still collect them avidly, though there is somewhat less collecting, swapping, and borrowing than earlier. Mothers mostly object and some forbid.

Magazines: Very little magazine reading, except for looking at pictures and cartoons in family's magazines. May subscribe to special children's magazines.

Newspapers: Minimal. Funnies and headlines are read most. Many just skim through.

MUSIC, RADIO, TELEVISION, AND MOVIES

5 years—Some may pick out tunes on the piano. Prefer phonograph records to radio, but prefer television to either. Some listen to scattered radio programs, liking a combination of music and talking.

Most, when asked, say they watch television "a lot." Most claim that their parents do not object to the amount of viewing they do, though may object to certain programs they would like to watch.

Girls say they themselves decide which programs to view. Boys say that they and their parents decide together.

Favorite programs (1976) are **Bugs Bunny, The Flintstones, Mister Rogers' Neighborhood, Sesame Street**, and Saturday cartoons. Most dislike the news, soap operas, and "scary" programs.

6 years—Now enjoy own phonograph records.

Radio is becoming a great favorite with most. Girls prefer songs; boys like news and music. Nearly all prefer television to radio.

Most, when asked, say they watch television "a lot." Both boys and girls now admit that their parents sometimes object both to the amount of time they spend watching and certain programs they would like to watch.

As at five, nearly all girls claim that they themselves decide what they will view, but about half the boys say they and their parents decide together.

Most have one or two preferred programs which they watch regularly. Favorite programs (1976) include **Bugs Bunny, The Flintstones**, and Saturday cartoons. Both sexes dislike the news and old movies. Boys especially like **Lost in Space**, but that is the program most disliked by girls.

Children like short home movies about nature, animals, or their own early life.

Go to the movies occasionally, but may become restless, close eyes, or cry.

7 years—Craving for piano or dancing lessons. Like to use various percussion instruments.

Radio and television now part of daily diet. Dislike missing set programs.

Both sexes, when asked, still say they watch television "a lot," but cannot give specific amounts of time. Divided about equally on whether or not they have trouble with parents about amount of watching. Majority admit their parents object to some of the kinds of programs they view.

Boys now say they themselves decide what programs they will watch, but nearly half the girls say they and their parents decide together.

Favorite programs are similar to six-year-olds.

Girls say they like "songs" on the radio; boys like music.

Some enjoy the movies. If so, they like musicals and animal pictures. Some like adventure movies; others are disturbed by them. They dislike love stories.

8 years—Less desire to practice on piano. May like to change a passage in a piece to one of their own invention. Like to have an audience. Enjoys duets.

Marked interest in radio, though prefer television. Most listen to several regular T.V. programs each day and do not like to miss these. Both admit they watch television "a lot." This is the last age at which about half the children say their parents object to the amount of time they spend watching. Some girls and the majority of boys say their parents also object to certain programs they like to watch.

The majority of girls claim that they themselves decide which programs to watch. About half the boys still say they and their parents decide together.

Favorite programs for both sexes include **The Flintstones, The Brady Bunch, Lost in Space,** and the Saturday cartoons. Boys also like **Emergency,** and sports programs. Boys and girls express strong dislike of the news. Frightening programs may influence their dreams.

Both sexes listen to radio "sometimes," and prefer music programs.

Children in general do not attend movies as much as some years ago, but interest may be high at this age. Boys like action pictures; girls like musicals. Both like animal and adventure stories and any about children. All dislike love stories. If a movie is too exciting they may close their eyes, hide their heads, or go to back of theater.

9 years—Child may really apply self in practicing music. Touch is lighter with girls but surer with boys. Enjoy executing staccato or legato notes.

Beginning to be interested in different composers.

Listening to radio or watching television may be almost constant from late afternoon to bedtime in some. Boys still say they watch television "a lot." Girls are more specific and admit to two to three hours a day.

The majority claim that their parents do not object to the amount of time they spend watching though some girls and the majority of boys admit that parents still object to some of their program choices.

Though most claim they themselves decide what programs to watch, a substantial number say that they and their parents still decide together.

There is now a wider variety of preference than earlier, and more marked sex differences. Girls like best **The Brady Bunch, Lucy, Lost in Space**, and the Saturday cartoons. Boys prefer **The Six Million Dollar Man**, game shows, **Lost in Space, Planet of the Apes**, movies, and Saturday cartoons.

As usual, children listen to radio "sometimes," though much prefer T.V. Girls like music best. Boys specify they prefer rock music.

Individual differences with movies. Some go regularly; others only sporadically. Girls like musicals. Boys like action, war, westerns. Both like animal stories and still dislike love stories.

10 years—Radio and television still strong with many. In fact, their whole lives may be regulated by the timing of their special programs. As at earlier ages, both sexes listen to radio "sometimes," but much prefer TV.

Both sexes now like rock music best, though girls also say they enjoy "songs." Boys now like the news. Boys, but not girls, say they like sports and some boys choose their programs by the station rather than by the type of program.

Now both boys and girls can specify the number of hours they spend on television—two hours a day on weekdays and two to three hours a day on weekends.

For the first time, by far the majority say their parents do not object to either the time they spend watching or the kind of programs watched. The majority also claim that they make their own decisions about what to view.

Both sexes enjoy **The Six Million Dollar Man, All in the Family, Good Times**, and the Saturday cartoons. Girls also like **The Brady Bunch, Lucy**, and **Scooby-Do**. Boys also like sports, Planet of the Apes, and movies. There is more variety in boys preferences.

Much less interest now in music lessons and in practicing.

CHAPTER 18

SCHOOL LIFE

Why do children go to school? Because our civilization has grown so complex that the home alone cannot transmit to the child the culture that the race has prepared for him. The home is still the primary cultural workshop in which he learns the alphabet of civilized living; it remains an extremely important workshop even in the years from five to ten. But the accumulated inheritance from past and present is so vast that teachers and schools and pencils and books have become a social necessity.

Schools Are Changing

Many changes in our schools as well as in our homes have been introduced in the thirty years since this book was first published. Many of them, whether successful or not, represent substantial efforts toward the individualization of instruction. Nongraded primaries, whether entirely effective or not, have as their aim the commendable purpose of permitting every child in school to proceed at his own pace. Their effort is to see to it that every child at all times should be taught in a way and at a level that is suitable to his own level of development.

Similarly, the "open classroom," however effective or ineffective it may be, attempts to remove the regimentation from teaching. In actual practice it has turned out to be much better suited to some children, and to some teachers, than to others. Many feel that it requires much more skill on the part of the individual teacher than had been anticipated, and that the results have been less glorious than had been hoped for.

In a time when, as Midge Decter puts it, liberated parents produced a generation of radical children, and many school systems attempted to take off the lid, so to speak, and do away not only with walls (and windows) and grade distinctions, they also did away with report cards and many other formal rules and regulations.

The obvious failure of much of this liberation has resulted recently in a rather abrupt return, at least in some communities, to self-contained classrooms, a more formalized curriculum and, once again, an objective type of grading.

The serious problem of providing a better education, especially for so-called underprivileged and minority groups, has produced a wild flurry of educational efforts, not all of them particularly effective. The trouble-racked story of forced busing to solve the educational problems that face us has not yet been finally told. It is considered by many a naïve and inadequate effort to provide good schooling for all our children.

Admitting that adequate educational opportunities have not always been provided for all children, we must also admit that not all educational failures are due to poor teaching. Some children, whatever their racial or geographical or social background, are less intelligent and/or less academically motivated than others.

It is not always the teacher's fault when a child does not learn. Doing away with intelligence testing or developmental evaluation does not increase a child's intelligence and maturity level. But evaluating intelligence and maturity level can help us to properly place children in that kind of class or at that grade level where they can learn most successfully.

We particularly believe that special classes should be provided for the 80–90 IQ boy or girl, by no means dull enough for placement in a class for the retarded but by no means bright enough for the "regular" classroom.

And just a word or two about the many children now classed as suffering from so-called learning disabilities. Some feel that interest in and concern about these children and the legislation in their behalf has far outstripped any real understanding of their problems or our ability to really help them. Certainly the term has been overused.

It is unquestionably dangerous to lump together all children who have trouble in school. But if we can provide adequate diagnostic facilities to help us determine whether problems in learning are due to low intelligence, immaturity, visual or perceptual or emotional problems, or some other of the dozens of reasons why children find learning difficult, then one hopes the current vast national concern about children who cannot learn can be turned to their advantage.

A recent study by Samuel A. Kirk and John Elkins checked on three thousand boys and girls labeled as suffering from learning disabilities and enrolled in Child Service Demonstration Centers for Learning Disabilities in twenty-one states. It showed that most of these children were *general* underachievers to a moderate degree in reading, spelling *and* arithmetic. In addition, many tested below an IQ of 90, and thus, before the American Association of Mental Deficiency changed its definition of retardation from IQ 84 to IQ 68 or below, would have been classed as retarded. It might be fairer, therefore, to consider and teach many of these children as slow learners or mentally deficient, rather than as suffering from more *specific* learning disability.

A further possibility of helping young people do better in school than some of them may now be doing is suggested by Dr. Lendon H. Smith, in line with current concerns about physical ill health and improper nutrition as a source of poor behavior function.

If your child is doing badly in school, assuming that he is properly placed and his reading is not too bad, his difficulties may result from an inadequate diet, both prenatally and postnatally. Since it is too late to go back and feed any mother an adequate protein diet so her unborn baby can be assured his normal brain potential, we have to work with what we have. But the brain cells the child comes to school with must be supplied with protein and vitamins so he can use what he has.

It may be as simple as getting a better breakfast. Also, allowing free access for all children in the classroom to nuts, cheese and other bits of protein snack can calm down the wildest, most noncompliant and most disruptive children. Teachers tell me they have been successful in activating their pupils' brains by merely providing a can of mixed nuts that the children may nibble on as needed. These teachers acted on the information that a child's brain has two to three times the energy requirements of an adult's. It is impossible for many to function from breakfast to lunch without nibbling on some protein.

Try to talk the teacher into having protein snacks available in the classroom, and the principal into eliminating sugars and desserts from the lunchroom, and candy from the machine in the hall.

School Readiness*

What excitement is generated in the mind of the child when he is considered old enough to enter the public school, more often nowadays at age five than at six. Few people, parents or educators, question a child's readiness to take this step. It is often only after evidence of stress or failure that the question of readiness is fully considered.

Over the years the schools have attempted to solve their multiple problems without getting to the heart of the matter, which is in large part related to proper grade placement and the rate of growth. The schools have too long clung to *chronological* age, which is usually determined by some arbitrary cutoff date of entrance, as

---

* The entire matter of readiness has in recent years come to seem so important and so essential to successful school performance that we shall devote the rest of the chapter to this topic. For our usual information about behavior to be expected at the different ages, the reader is referred to gradients on pages 375 to 386.

a measure for deciding on time of starting school. Chronological age does give us a clue, but to a large extent it is maturity, or maturational age, that determines successful adjustment to school.

We at the Gesell Institute have long thought in terms of maturity level, though at first we did not fully appreciate its vital importance. When we conducted our own study of school readiness (1957–1967) we came to realize that the school was grappling with this problem, but mostly from a remedial point of view. The school wished through remediation to pull the immature child up to the level where it felt he should be.

But those in charge soon found that the child couldn't stay at this level unless he or she had continuing supportive help. Then the schools decided to teach the lagging child at the level where he was actually functioning. Thus, though a child might be in fifth grade, if he was functioning at a third-grade level they taught him at a third-grade level. Too often they did not realize the strain on the child of being in a class above the level where he was actually functioning.

The coming of the open classroom or of ungraded classes took off some of the pressure in some schools. Some such classes developed well, especially if they had expert teachers and not too large numbers of children. But others produced a pandemonium, did not provide an atmosphere of learning, and demanded planning and adjustment on the part of the teachers that was beyond the call of duty. Many teachers actually refused to teach in open classrooms.

As we mentioned in the Preface, it was not until we established a clinical service at the then newly formed Gesell Institute of Child Development in 1950 that we realized we were seeing child after child who was failing in school because of the unnecessary stress situation related to his lack of maturity to cope with the demands his school put upon him.

At first we thought this applied only to children in trouble enough to be brought to a clinical service. But when we started to visit schoolrooms in 1956 we realized that overplacement in school was a far bigger problem than we had surmised and that a research study was needed. We shall always remember our shock on examining the first kindergarten group to find that perhaps 40 percent of the children were not ready for this school group into which age had placed them.

Since 1956 we have been studying the problem of school placement, slowly unraveling the intricacies of each child's rate of growth. Early in our research we realized that though we were concerned with maturational age, chronological age still had a great deal to do with where a child was functioning. We saw the advantages of a child's being well into his age. Thus a child with a spring birthday who was five years eight months or five years seven months in the fall, had a great advantage over a child with a fall birth date who was not yet five at the time of school entrance. We observed that these fall-birth-date children were often in trouble in all sorts of ways. They were definitely under stress and continued so from year to year even under the best of schooling conditions. When such children were put back a grade into a situation that was geared to their maturational age, most signs of stress evaporated almost overnight.

We well remember one second-grader with an October birth date who was miserable both at school and at home. His mother came to the Institute with a long list of complaints. Examining this boy, we soon had evidence that he was a nicely endowed child who was just too young for second grade. His mother was naturally worried as to how he would react emotionally to placement back in first grade. Fortunately he needed glasses and we could use this as a scapegoat.

The very first day was a glowing success. He felt at home in his first-grade surroundings. On a follow-up visit to us two months later, the mother could hardly recall her long list of earlier complaints. They had all disappeared. And her son summed up the change rather neatly after a month's stay in first grade: "How come I was the last in everything in second grade and now I'm the first? I was the poorest runner and now I'm the fastest. I was the poorest reader and now I'm the best. How come, Mom?"

Unfortunately we have had to fight child by child this battle of seeing to it that children are correctly placed in relation to their behavior or maturity age, and more often than not it has been won only after the child's initial failure. We have come to appreciate that any marked shift in concepts takes time for growing in people's minds.

After the publication of *School Readiness* (Ilg and Ames, 1964) we were able to put our findings to the test through Title III funds in three different parts of the country—Visalia, California; Bennington, Vermont; and Cheshire, Connecticut. We trained a developmental examiner for one school in each town. Our findings were similar in all three towns and were very close to our expectations. Shockingly large numbers of the children were not ready for the grade into which their chronological age, and the law, placed them.

Though parents of children totally unready for kindergarten usually did not wish to keep their children at home, there was less resistance to placing these children in a younger, four-and-a-half-year-old group. When children were properly grouped according to their behavior age, the quality of the groups was immediately apparent to the teachers. And it became a pleasure for them to gear their activity programs according to the maturational level of their students.

All children were reexamined at the end of the year. Most were found to be progressing at the same rate they showed on entrance. Often it was hard for parents and educators to understand that a child who wasn't ready for kindergarten in the fall was still only ready for kindergarten the following year, even though he had attended a prekindergarten for a whole year. If he had stayed at home for the year, the answer would have been much the same. Growth is not speeded up by school attendance, though both parents and educators often expect that it will be. Not that school experience does not enrich a child's life and give him a good experience; but it does not accelerate growth.

The reexamination at the end of a kindergarten year produced much the same results found in the initial examinations. Few had accelerated relatively and some were still ready only for what has come to be called a readiness or five-and-a-half-year-old group, a transitional grade between kindergarten and first.

Alas! Many were the parental storms that raged in relation to these truly unready children—children who often had good potential but needed extra time for growing. Some of the parents who did appreciate the importance of readiness had had earlier sad experiences in overplacing children and welcomed the opportunity for their younger child to move more slowly, at his or her own rate.

But there were times when we couldn't convince a parent, and in some cases had to sacrifice what we considered to be the child's welfare to the parent's determination. Many parents would not permit retention until their child had clearly failed. This sometimes didn't happen until fourth grade, especially with the brighter children and especially if remedial help was brought in along the way to patch things up.

Many schools throughout the United States have become interested in what we call a developmental point of view, but it isn't easy to put a developmental placement program into operation. If the schools would at least initially think of age alone, it would help. That child does best who is fully five before she starts kindergarten (five and a half for a boy); fully six for first grade (six and a half for a boy). In fact, some countries—China, the Soviet Union, and the Scandinavian countries—prefer seven years of age as a time for first-grade entrance, and thus save themselves many problems.

If we persist in sending children to first grade at six, could we at least establish a cutoff date of July 1 or even June 1? Consider all those July and August boys who are, to us, obviously too young. They may be bright, they may be doing their work, but they are often under the tension of constant stress.

Colleges are recognizing this matter of immaturity and often encourage their students to take a year or two off to engage in some practical experience and then return to college. It would have been far better, however, to have taken this extra year way back in kindergarten or primary school. What a difference this could have made in all of those subsequent twelve years, including a readiness for college!

But a proper cutoff date is only a first step. Ideally each child needs to be examined developmentally.* Some schools emphasize merely a prekindergarten screening. Others emphasize the whole first three years, with screening before each grade. Even with a full-time examiner, this three-year load of examining can be a heavy one. We are now working on a shortened examination which can be administered by classroom teachers, under supervision. Every child would be examined developmentally each year through the sixth grade. This would help all teachers to understand better the important growth forces. It would also provide a better growth history of each child. Too often teachers isolate the child from his past, when a little forewarning could have been of help.

We ourselves have come to feel that there should be transition points at which children can be slowed down when the placement problem has not been solved correctly at the time of school entrance. Many schools have already taken on the concept of a readiness or five-and-a-half-year-old group. A next hard step could be between second and third grades. Another crucial time comes between fifth and sixth grades. Slowing down at either point could be very helpful to many children.

The open classroom has taught us much. It has emphasized the importance of special areas of interest. But the need of a child to be related to one teacher in the first three grades is more important than the advocates of the open classroom often realize. Give these young children a chance to go visiting in other classrooms when they are ready, but don't confuse them with too many teachers, too many other children.

A class size of fifteen to twenty has too often been discarded, but this is as many children as one teacher can handle comfortably. Also, it is a comfortable number for children to interact with. Many of the special teachers in art, music, remedial work, especially in the younger grades, might well be relinquished to provide needed funds for smaller classes.

---

* See *School Readiness*.

Signs of Overplacement

Even without the aid of a developmental placement examination, a child shows by his general behavior when he is not ready. Teachers should be able to pick up signs of overplacement fairly quickly. Unreadiness for kindergarten is easily indicated by crying, inability to separate from parents, or refusing to go to school at all. When there is initial difficulty, a two-week trial period should give the answer.

Some children, however, adjust well in school but show their unreadiness for the school situation by exploding at home, from the tension built up in school. Parents are rightfully disturbed by any marked shift in behavior—wild running, temper tantrums, overfatigue. The school often blames the parent or home for this behavior, since it does not occur at school. Actually, it is all too often the school situation that produces the tension. Still other children, the disruptive ones, want to come to school but behave badly once there.

In first grade, many children who even though not fully ready have coped with kindergarten now find the going too hard. They will express their tensions by vomiting in the morning before school. They may have nightmares or a return to bed-wetting. In school, their attention span is short. They are restless, frequently wander around the room. They struggle at their work, but succeed poorly. All evidence is that children with such signs and symptoms are not ready for first grade.

By second grade, children express unreadiness by dawdling at home, or by continuing to be sick to their stomach in the morning. Such children may be hard to manage at home, resistant to all suggestions. Things are just as bad or worse at school. The overplaced child is inattentive, talks out loud, whispers, bothers other children, doesn't do his work. In fact, the biggest complaint of the second-grade teacher about the over placed child is that he doesn't finish his work.

Then the school institutes all sorts of patch-up devices such as keeping him in from recess, which he so desperately needs, making him stay after school, which disorients him about going home, or sending his work home, to add to his misery there. Another complaint on the part of the second-grade teacher is that the child daydreams, his way of coping with an intolerable situation. Daydreaming should be taken seriously at this second-grade level.

The second-grader in trouble also has his complaints, the most outstanding one being that his teacher yells at him. Perhaps fortunately, there usually comes that time of explosion when the child declares his hatred of school. It is hoped that both parents and teachers will take this seriously and realize that such a child may be under unbearable stress, and may need to be placed back in first grade.

By third grade, if overplacement continues, things get increasingly worse. Many of the signs seen in second grade continue, but now the child is more obviously not doing his work. He bothers other children and may become rebellious. His teacher responds in kind. She scolds him. She may even smack him. But most of all, she isolates him, putting him out in the hall or sending him to the principal's office.

At home this stressed third-grader is often tired, irritable, and unhappy. But as soon as school is out in the summertime, his spirits miraculously recover and he becomes a different child, unless the demands of school are continued in summer school.

Other third-graders are not rebellious in these obvious ways. Rather, they do struggle to keep up, but the joy of learning is not theirs. Often they have headaches and often find it hard to make friends. They can't compete with the other children in athletics. "No friends" and "Poor in athletics" are two good clues of overplacement from third grade on.

By fourth grade it is hoped that the more obviously overplaced child will fail in his school work sufficiently for parents and school to keep him back. It is sad that many children do not fail conspicuously until the extra demand of fourth grade reveals an unreadiness that should have been picked up in kindergarten.

Actually, things have to be pretty bad for most schools to suggest that a fourth-grader repeat. Most prefer to use patch-up methods. Parents are expected to help with homework. Many a family evening is ruined with homework that is obviously too much for the child. If this isn't successful, then a tutor may be brought in.

In spite of all efforts, signs and symptoms of overplacement seldom cease. An overplaced child remains an overplaced child right through high school and even into college. One father told us that he felt he didn't catch up with himself until he was forty.

All too often the situation of overplacement is covered up by such phrases as "She could do better if she'd put her mind to it" or "He's not working up to his capacity." Rather than saying, "He could do better if he would," we prefer to say, "He would do better if he could."

Admittedly, improper grade placement is not the only cause of school failure. Proper placement is not the only cure. But it is our contention that if all children were entered in school and subsequently promoted on the basis of their behavior rather than their chronological age, perhaps 50 percent of our present cases of school failure could be prevented or corrected.

This is one of the many reasons that we consider the information about what behavior is like in the important years from five to ten, as given in the present volume, to be so vitally important for parents and teachers alike.

Home and School Relationships

A truly child-centered school will not ignore the home, but will work in partnership with it. Such a school will be concerned about the kind of home in which the child has been reared, will be interested in his biography. Every child comes to school with a long developmental career behind him. Can the school afford to remain altogether unaware of that past? Parents can be helpful both to teacher and to child by bringing significant information to the attention of the school.

When classes are too large and when teachers have been too narrowly trained, a flexible partnership between home and school is impossible. There are many questions that the two need to answer together. Should the sessions be shortened? Should the lavatory facilities be improved? Should the child be laden so heavily with formalized homework? Should the home be encouraged to supply special learning through games and an informal approach?

The total welfare of the child should determine the answers to such questions. Sometimes home and school can decide together, though there are many areas where the responsibilities of each are separate and defined. One question both should decide together is the matter of reading, since it is often made the basic factor in determining promotion. The school system tends to place excessive emphasis on the importance of the printed word. An experienced high-school principal has reminded us in forcible terms that at least a third of the entire secondary-school population (grades nine to twelve) are "incapable of mastering the stock tools of learning (reading and writing) well enough to profit from textbook instruction." Not even the attentive perusal of the comics has served to make these nonverbal millions of pupils masters of the printed page. Comics doubtless increase the reading vocabulary of the verbal multitude, but the nonverbal child suffers from limitations which are more or less constitutional.

This does not necessarily mean that he is backward or dull-witted. As a matter of fact, he is frequently talented in less verbal directions, and may be more than ordinarily wholesome in total personality make-up. He may be able to "read" music, or physiognomy, or the contours of a landscape; or even the devious ways of his fellow men. He may have excellent judgment; he may have outstanding mechanical ability, or other skills which will someday make of him a valuable citizen. In fact, there are many potential leaders among the nonverbal lower third.

If our schools were less narrowly preoccupied with typographic reading, they would discover other marked skills and potentialities early in life. We should not wait until the high-school years before we identify our nonverbal pupils. Home and school should early make this discovery together.

And home and school should continue to ask themselves this question: "Why does the child from five to ten go to school?" He goes because society should have something to offer at school which will enrich his life as an adult citizen in the culture of tomorrow, and will enrich, too, his life in the culture of today.

Growth Gradients

ADJUSTMENT TO SCHOOL

5 years—Adjusts to school with relative ease. May request to stay at home intermittently; shows fatigue occasionally.

Mother or older child may need to accompany child to school for first few days or longer.

Girls more apt to like school than boys.

May like to take a favorite toy to school.

Sometimes takes his products home.

Some children are better at home than at school, and vice versa.

Very little reporting at home about school activity.

6 years—Anticipates first grade but may have difficulty with adjustment.

May refuse to go to school because of some unpleasant experience.

Fatigue, with or without two sessions, and colds are common.

Brings and may share toys, cookies, or a book with classmates or teacher.

Loves to take his products home to show parents.

There is litle verbal reporting at home of school activities, but may report about a "bad" child in the group.

7 years—May not anticipate return to school in the fall, thinking it will be too hard. Some would prefer to remain in first grade.

Relationship to teacher is important in adjustment.

Likes to go to school with other children or alone rather than have mother accompany him.

May show fear of being late to school. If lateness probable, would prefer to stay at home.

Shows fatigue, especially with two sessions.

Brings fewer things to school, though likes to display a new possession.

Now accumulates his products in desk and takes home only occasionally.

8 years—Enjoys school and even dislikes staying at home, particularly if he will miss a special event.

Much less fatigue and fewer absences because of illness.

A few children are said to have an occasional "bad" day at school.

Some dawdle and have difficulty getting ready for school on time.

Now brings things to school that relate to school work.

Some products may be taken home.

Many children now report on their school activities.

9 years—On the whole likes school.

Takes responsibility for getting to school.

Apt to forget to take material to school unless reminded.

A few boys may take a gun or ball to school with them.

Reports some home and outside activities at school, usually in great detail. Talks at home about his standing in a school subject or about a special event.

10 years—Most say that school is "okay," and indicate that on the whole they like school. But they tend to be restless, and attention span is short. Most "hate" some subjects, but rebellion is passive and individual, doesn't come to a head in open revolt. They rebel by withdrawing.

Social relationships are important, but generally not intense. Fairly easy acceptance of one sex by the other. Much note-passing—often about the opposite sex, though notes are passed between members of the same sex. Some plan mean things to get other children into trouble. May discuss contemporaries not as whole people, but in terms of "his reading," "his arithmetic."

Beginning of a sophisticated self-consciousness in reciting or singing.

Most can get off for school on time without confusion and without losing or forgetting things.

According to Eric W. Johnson, things that annoy them most about their teachers is that they talk too much, give no time for questions, show favoritism.

Their advice to teacher: Try to be understanding; don't pick on one person; always help and encourage your students; don't get angry at kids when they do little things.

CLASSROOM DEMEANOR

5 years—Needs some assistance from teacher with dressing and undressing.

Enjoys routine and adjusts to an activity program that allows freedom yet maintains control of the sequence of separate activities.

Changes from one activity to another with relative ease.

Likes to complete a task.

Some respond well to a rest period, others resist it.

Class can enjoy a directed activity for about twenty minutes.

"Reading" and "number" work closely associated with play.

Refers to teacher for materials, to tell experiences, and to show his products.

Child works in short bursts of energy.

Kindergarten activity is not highly social.

6 years—Loves to be busy, but will avoid things he cannot do.

Is in almost constant activity. Frequently stands to work at a desk or table.

Easily distractible as he watches others, as well as within own activity.

Does not know when to ask for help.

In attempting to form a group line, will push or lean on one another.

Can be given a choice of many things to do, but may need suggestions from teacher to make decision. Then may chose opposite.

Talks about what he is doing and what neighbor is doing.

When working does not like interference until he needs help.

Tries to conform and to please teacher and self.

Some children spoil games and need individual play activity. May do better with teacher close by or may need separation from the group.

Likes a "chart" of own successes, but not ashamed of showing to others even if has only a few.

7 years—Works quietly and with absorption for periods.

Noisy and explosive during transitions.

Is impatient in demands for assistance from teacher.

May regard neighbor's work and copy from it.

May whistle and make different noises.

Accumulates all sorts of objects in desk or pockets.

Becomes concerned if does not complete a task.

Wants to know what comes next, how far to go, etc.

Is anxious for his place in the group and does not like to be singled out for reprimand or praise.

Does not like teacher to repeat instructions, but may need repetition.

When whole class gets out of order, necessary to shift to a different activity.

If teacher leaves the room, class becomes disorganized and some do forbidden things.

8 years—Eager to verbalize and to respond. Cannot wait for a slow child.

May dawdle and be slow during transitions.

Tackles work with speed. Likes to be timed in a performance.

May interfere with others by his need to verbalize.

Likes and seeks praise both from teacher and from neighbor. "My drawing isn't good, is it?"

May work better with separation from the group within the room.

Wants to have turn and wants each child to have a turn.

Some play with "gadgets."

Teacher more aware of child's process. Can explain in group how his mind is working.

9 years—Individual behavior more noticeable.

Quieter while at work, but may make sudden noise such as banging desktop.

Competitive in work and in play, and is afraid of failure.

Wants to work independently of teacher. Refers to her for assistance.

May be self-conscious when reciting before the group.

Has better critical evaluation of how he can do things best.

Knows when he is "sure" or "not too sure."

Works for longer periods and may be unwilling to stop.

Likes now to be graded and to compare his grades with others'.

Isolation to do his work is less effective than earlier.

Needs to know own process and to be given individual assistance apart from the class.

10 years—Seem most interested in concrete learning experiences, and learning of specifics. Usually love to memorize, but don't generalize or correlate facts, or care what you do with knowledge. May like to know what a thing is called but have little interest in mechanism or source of material. Often enjoy "place" geography—names of states, capitals, etc.—but vague about actual geographic characteristics.

Like to talk and listen more than work. Often better with oral and pictorial presentation than with printed words. Like to take dictation; like oral arithmetic.

Not able to plan own work, need schedules. Usually not much homework assigned. What there is they can usually manage by themselves with little help and without much complaint.

READING

4 years—Identifies several capital letters. Some associate letter with the beginning letter of a familiar name: "S for Susan."

Enjoys having adult print his name on his products.

May identify a letter without naming. "That's in my name."

5 years—May cease temporarily to identify letters formerly recognized, when attempting to print them.

Likes to identify repetitious phrases or words in familiar books, such as exclamations or sounds that animals make. Also identifies word signs such as stop and go, or hot and cold on faucets, or words on cereal boxes.

Some like to underline letters or words in a familiar book.

May read letters in sequence and ask, "What does D-O-G spell, Mommy?" Likes to spell simple words, as cat, dog, yes, no, mommy.

In identifying letter or word, often selects first or last letter on a line and reads vertically from bottom up or from top to bottom.

Recognizes own first name.

May enjoy using wooden letters to represent names of people and may use these in combination with block building.

May recognize several or all numbers on the clock, or those related to certain routines. May identify some numbers on calendar, on telephone dial, or on own house number plate.

5½ years—More familiar with letters of the alphabet.

May translate a word into more familiar meaning: coffee for cup, etc. (similar to two-year-old who names the picture of a cup "coffee").

May "read" pictures of a book.

Likes to listen to stories of children in action, such as those in a first-grade primer.

May regard print as well as pictures when read to.

6 years—Interest in small as well as capital letters.

Recognizes words and phrases, and perhaps sentences. Finds words related to picture or story. Matches words.

Likes to have material that relates to own experiences.

Beginning to develop reading vocabulary. Beginning to recognize words out of context.

Gets clues from length of word, beginning sound or letter.

Uses marker or points with finger at words.

Some like to read nursery books. May now read though earlier may have memorized.

Some like to pick out letters on a typewriter and have mother spell words for them. May supply beginning letter, but need help with rest.

Likes to listen to poems about letters, as in Sounds the Letters Make.

When can read a book, apt to read and reread it many times.

Typical errors of those who read: Words added to give balance (the king and **the** queen). May reverse meaning (come for go; I for you); substitute words of same general appearance (even for ever; saw for was; house for horse); add words (little, very, y at end). Tendency to carry down a word that was encountered on line above.

7 years—Can now read sentences. Recognizes familiar words easily and rapidly out of context.

Individual differences in reading rate are marked. In oral reading many try to maintain flow and prefer to have unfamiliar words supplied, or they guess at them. Apt to repeat word or phrase to maintain

speed. Some are excessively slow.
Likes to know how far to read. May use a marker.

In spelling may supply beginning and ending letters if cannot spell the whole word. May enjoy game of spelling words at home during routines.

Enjoys finding familiar words in a child's dictionary.

Typical reading errors: Omissions of short familiar words, (and, he, had, but, and final s or y.) Some similar additions (the, a, but, little). Substitutions are the most common error (the or some for a, come for go, was for lived, a for the). One letter substituted (pass for puss, some for same, they for then). Changed order of letters (saw for was, three for there). Letters added at beginning or end (the for he, y at end). Words of similar form (green for queen, bed for bird).

8 years—Masters new words through context, division into syllables, initial consonants, prefixes and suffixes.

Mechanics and reading for meaning now in better balance.

Begins to be able to stop and discuss what he is reading.

Reads easy material with exaggerated expression. Considers it "babyish."

Uses table of contents and index.

Book usually held easily on lap with some little shifting of head distance. Seldom needs to point to maintain place. May point or bring head closer for a difficult new word.

Reads more rapidly in silent reading, and usually prefers it. Also enjoys taking turns in reading a story orally.

Typical reading errors: Greater variety of errors but they interfere less with mechanics and meaning. More omissions than additions, chiefly the, little, and, in, then. May read words in a phrase in wrong order.

9 years—Reading now more related to various subjects.

Individual differences in abilities and interest. Now some who have been slow have a real spurt.

Utilize dictionary.

May do better in silent reading, but need to be checked by oral reading.

Many prefer silent reading, but when reading for facts and information retain reading matter better when read orally.

Typical reading errors: Repetitions are frequent, usually one or two words at a time. Substitutions of meaning (house for room, she for mother, beautiful for wonderful).

WRITING

4 years—**Letters.** Prints a few capital letters, large and irregular. Prefers circular letters, as C, G, O, Q; or angular letters, as E, H, I, L, T, A.

Selects first letters usually of familiar names, as own name or a member of family: T for Tommy, C for Charles.

Letters are often made with many parts (four parts to E).

Prints on page at random. Variable positions of letters, which may lie flat in horizontal position. Seldom reverses.

Name: May attempt to print own name (girls especially). Some print first few letters and mark for remaining ones. May split name in middle and continue on next line.

5 years—Letters. Prints some letters of varying sizes, in various positions, and usually large. May be reversed vertically.

Letters formerly made in three parts are now made in two.

Asks help in forming or identifying letters already drawn. "How do you make F?" "That isn't a [letter], is it?"

May recognize a letter that is in own name without identifying it.

May write from right to left without reversing any letters.

Some like to copy letters and frequently do so from right to left.

Name: Prints first name, or nickname, large and irregular. Printing gets larger toward end of name.

Numbers: May print certain numbers that have significance. (5 for own age; 12 for 12 o'clock.)

May copy from the clock or calendar.

Marked variation in ability to write numbers. Some can write into teens, usually reverse the position of the separate digits (31 for 13). Frequently omit a number.

Some draw on a page from right to left without reversing. Some draw in a confused manner or reverse.

6 years—Letters. Prints most of the capital letters with several reversals (usually horizontal, fewer vertical).

Prints some words. May use all capitals and may use a mixture of capitals and small letters without differentiating their size.

Letters are now more apt to be drawn with a continuous stroke.

Prints large and increasingly larger letters as proceeds across page. Certain letters may be consistently drawn larger.

Beginning to recognize reversals, but may not change.

Likes to use variety of materials: Writes on blackboard with chalk, or on large paper with crayon. Later able to handle writing at desk with a pencil.

Name: Prints first or both names and may add middle name or add Junior at end, usually in all capital letters.

Letters large and uneven. May reverse a letter (especially S). May not separate names, or may write one under the other.

Some print increasingly larger; some increase, decrease, and then increase; others maintain fairly uniform size and write with an undulating line.

Numbers: Many can write from 1 to 20. Print numbers large in horizontal rows.

May reverse order of digits in teens, either in final product or in execution (writes end digit first and places 1 in front of it).

Reverses one or two digits (3, 7, or 9 more usual).

7 years—Words. Prints or writes words and sentences, in capital and small letters.

Beginning to differentiate height of capital and small letters, but may make about the same height. Capital may be substituted for a small letter.

Writing is somewhat smaller and in a few it is greatly reduced in size.

Corrects letter reversals (usually 6½ years), but errs occasionally. May place letters in reversed order or omit a letter.

Beginning to separate words, but sentences usually run together.

Tends to reduce letters in size as writes across page.

Prefers ruled paper. Some want large space, some small.

Likes to copy sentences.

Pencil grasp is tight, with the forefinger caved in, and the shoulder is tensed. Now prefers pencil rather than crayon for writing.

Likes to write correctly and erases a good deal.

Numbers: Writes 1 to 20 or higher, usually without error. May still reverse one, sometimes two numbers. The same number may be reversed as a single digit and not

when it appears in the teens or vice versa (6 and 9 most frequent; also 4 or 7).

Figures are smaller, considerably smaller with a few children.

Usually place numbers in one horizontal row at top of page, but some write in vertical column at this age.

8 years—Words. Can write several sentences.

Considerable variation in writing. Many now do cursive writing instead of printing. Write fairly large and rather "squarely," usually with slight slant. A few still write large and very irregularly. Some write medium-size letters, somewhat evenly, though still quite straight. Letters may be wider. If writing is becoming smaller, then capitals and looped letters tend to be disproportionately tall.

Reversals are now rare.

Now beginning to space words, sentences, and paragraphs.

Tries to write neatly, though sometimes hurries and does not care.

Still may not be able to write down all the ideas he has for a story.

Name: Writes both names with good spacing and correct use of capital and small letters. Considerable discrepancy in size between capitals and small letters. Great variation from child to child in size and style of writing.

Numbers: In writing 1 to 20 does not reverse single digit. May reverse order in number 20 (02).

In written number work may still have an occasional reversal of a digit, especially when making a double number.

9 years—No longer prints, unless printing continued form of writing.

Handwriting is now a tool. Writes for extended periods.

Writing is smaller, neater, more even, and slanted. The pressure is lighter (especially in girls). Some write with upward slant and some make letters irregularly.

Letters are in good proportion.

Some now have a skillful "style."

Now use finger movements, with tension in the forearm.

Increase in speed and in volume of writing.

Occasional error when copying or in recording dictated numbers.

ARITHMETC

4 years—Counts three objects, pointing correctly.

Is reported to count to ten. May start with a number higher than one. Verbal counting without objects definitely exceeds counting of objects.

4½ years—Can give "just one," "two," or "three" cubes on request.

Counts four objects with correct pointing and answers "how many?" Some can count ten objects.

Understands the terms "most," "both," and "biggest," but not "same" and "equal."

5 years—Counting by ones: Usually stops just before a decile (19, 29). May jump from 29 to 40, or go back to a smaller number.

Counting objects: Can count and point to thirteen objects. Some difficulty maintaining regard and pointing and if loses sequence is apt to go back to beginning. May need two or three trials.

Naming coins: Names a penny. Likes to take pennies from adult to give storerkeeper for a purchase.

Writing numbers: May write some numbers from dictation. Names and verbalizes as writes. "I don't know what 7 looks like." Usually writes in confused manner (2, 5, 8) or reverses (3, 7, 9, and teens). Omits 6 and 9.

May write in horizontal line across top of paper or vertical line at left of paper. Many place anywhere on page.

Some like to copy numbers from clock. May know numbers such as 7, 3, or 12, associated with time of events in daily schedule.

May not be able to identify the number made. Asks, "What does it look like?"

Addition and subtraction: Some enjoy oral figuring and can add within five. May use objects or fingers and count by ones. Errors are usually one number more or less than correct answer. In attempts to subtract within five, counts forward from one to larger number using fingers, then counts backward to answer.

5½ years—Counting by ones: Error at decile or at 17 or 27 or omits 7.

Counting objects: Can count to twenty, pointing correctly and giving total on one or two trials.

Writing numbers: Writes from 1 to 10 or higher, with many reversals, or in teens wrong order (71 for 17) and/or reversal. Writes in confused manner: 2, 5, 6. Reverses: 3, 4, 7, 9. May omit 9. Writes horizontally across top of page. Many turn paper sideways and then write horizontally across width of paper. Verbalizes: "I can't make it"; "Down like that and over like that"; "My hand gets kinda tired."

Addition: Adds correctly within five. Counts on fingers or counts in mind, starting with the smaller of two numbers.

Subtraction: Subtracts correctly within five.

6 years—Counting by ones: Counts to thirty or more. May overestimate how high he can count: to "million," "dillion."

Counting by tens: To one hundred or to ninety and then says, "twenty."

Counting by fives: To about fifty.

Names coins and knows number of pennies in nickel and dime.

Counting pennies: Counts twenty with correct pointing and gives total.

Writing numbers: Recognizes and may write numbers to 12 or 20. Writes large, with some numbers (especially 5) larger than others. Reverses especially 3, 7, 9. Rarely omits a figure. Usually writes horizontally across top of paper.

Verbalizes: "Can't do too well because I mess them up"; "I'm tired. I'm hot, too"; "I wonder if I'm making them backward."

Addition: Many add correctly within ten. Count starting with larger number or at the one following this ($3+7$: 7, 8, 9, 10 or 8, 9, 10). Errors are usually one number more or less than correct answer. A few guess. Some know small combinations, especially balanced numbers as $3+3$ by heart.

Subtraction: Correct within five. Counts from one to larger number and then back. May add instead of subtract. A few use balanced numbers to figure from.

Likes to group objects: four of this, etc.

Interest in balanced numbers: 2 and 2, 3 and 3, etc.

Uses simple measurements: pint and quart.

7 years—Counting: Can count to one hundred by ones, fives, tens, and by twos to twenty.

Naming coins: Can name penny, nickle, dime, quarter, half-dollar, and tell how many pennies in each.

Writing numbers: From 1 to 20 or higher. Fewer errors. Some reversals, especially 4, 7, 9, or reverses positions in teens, especially 12, 17, 19, 20. May write horizontally or vertically on page. Little verbalization while writing, though small mouth movements indicate silent counting.

Addition: Correct within twenty. A few make errors of plus or minus one, suggesting that they are still counting. Others know combinations, especially even combinations, (3 + 3) by heart, and break harder ones down into known combinations and figure from there. Thus 18 + 5: 18 + 2 = 20 + 3 = 23. In the teens, may add the right-hand figures and then precede answer by 1, thus 14 + 3: 4 + 3 = 7, preceded by 1 = 17.

Subtraction: Subtracts correctly within ten. Counts backward from larger number: uses balanced number (10 − 4: 5 + 5 = 10, 5 − 1 = 4, so 5 + 1 = 6, therefore 10 − 4 = 6; changes to addition (6 − 4 = 2 because 4 + 2 = 6). Knows many combinations by heart.

When doing written work, does not shift easily from addition to subtraction on same paper.

Likes to write a number with many digits.

Learning to use fraction of one-half of a unit or a group.

8 years—Counting: Counts by threes to thirty and fours to forty.

Writing numbers: Rarely makes an error in writing numbers through 20 or higher. Spaces correctly and may put dots and dashes between. Figures are more uniform and smaller.

Addition: Knows many combinations by heart. Some count by ones from larger number; some rearrange in combinations they know by heart (8 + 5: 7 + 5 = 12 + 1 = 13). Occasional error of plus or minus one.

Subtraction: Knows some combinations by heart. In teens may subtract the right-hand figures and then precede this answer by 1. Errors mostly plus or minus one, but a few "wild" answers suggest that they are no longer counting by ones.

Learning to add and subtract one- to three-digit numbers requiring borrowing and carrying.

Multiplication: Through 4 or 6 table. Knows some low combinations by heart, especially 3 × 3, 4 × 4. May add (3 + 3 + 3 = 9), or say table.

Division: Uses simple facts of short division. Errors mostly plus or minus one of a single digit in the answer.

Can measure distances in room in terms of feet.

Fractions: Uses fractions of one-half and one-quarter.

Interest in weights of people and things.

Interest in money and relative value of coins.

Shifts process frequently. Suddenly shifts to adding when multiplying. May be aware of it and say, "I always do that!"

9 years—Writing numbers: Writes numbers accurately, though may make occasional error when dictated to or when copying from the board. Prefers to figure by writing numbers down. Does not verbalize while writing, but may not do neatly and says, "My worst numbers"; "My most careless thing." May now prefer to write a vertical column.

Addition and subtraction: Knows all simple combinations by heart. May select certain combinations when adding a column.

Can tell own process. Knows what combinations has most trouble with and may write them on a card or desk until knows by heart. Wants to analyze errors with teacher. Likes to differentiate between "good" errors and "bad" errors.

Multiplication: Through the 9 table. Errors are mostly with 7 or 9. A typical error is to substitute 6 or 8 for 7, or 8 or 10 for 9 (= one shift). Most now multiply instead of adding. May change 8×3 to 3×8. May start from even numbers ($6 \times 7: 6 \times 6 = 36 + 6 = 42$); or from one he knows by heart, and adds or subtracts from this.

Fractions: Learning to use fractions and measurement.

Division: Can, on paper, use two- to five-digit dividends and one-digit divisors, using the method of long division.

Can keep accounts and records.

CHAPTER 19

ETHICAL SENSE

This chapter deals with a prickly theme. Any discussion of morals, whether it be the morals of children or of adults, inevitably invites confusing emotions and conflicting concepts. It is almost impossible to set aside adult preconceptions of what a child *ought* to do; and so we fail to understand what the child *does*, and what he actually *is*.

Our culture is charged with moral directives and with ethical norms which must be preserved if civilization is to survive. Generation after generation, the wisest of men have argued the age-old questions of Right and Wrong. The literature of the race is laden with writings on virtue and sin, duty, discipline, punishment, justice, mercy, guilt, expiation, retribution, salvation, and transgression. Not so long ago there were sober disquisitions on inborn child depravity. Nor have all the ghosts of the past yet been laid.

This chapter describes objectively the growth of the art of good conduct in the child from five to ten. It is a complex art which depends upon the development of an ethical sense—a sense that matures by natural progressions.

What are these progressions? The growth gradients that follow indicate that the underlying growth mechanisms begin to operate in early infancy. At the age of ten years these same mechanisms are still operating. They continue throughout adolescence. When, indeed, *do* morals mature?

A child is not born with a weak ethical sense which becomes stronger as he grows older. He is born with certain dispositions and potentialities, which undergo progressive organization from day to day, and from month to month. As early as the age of six weeks the child smiles by himself. An egocentric smile! At eight weeks he smiles back at the beaming face of his mother—a responsive social smile, which relates to someone else! At twelve weeks he spontaneously initiates a similar smile—a reciprocal social smile, which has a double origin, a two-way implication! In this simple sequence we already glimpse the dynamic that governs the growth of the ethical sense.

Already the infant is sensitive to smiles of approval. Soon he will be sensitive also to frowns. Very early (about the age of thirty-six weeks) he heeds a monitory "No! No!" as a nursery game, and also as a serious command. Here we glimpse the germs of self-inhibition and of social disapproval. At one year the baby is so highly socialized that he likes to please others. At any rate, he greatly enjoys repeating performances that are laughed at by others. So far as the culture is concerned, he is already caught in a complex web of smiles and frowns—of approbation and disapprobation. His moral welfare would appear to be assured.

But behold, at the age of fifteen months he has a will of his own, so strong that he no longer heeds "No! No!" His conduct becomes self-assertive. He insists on doing things for himself. Sometimes he seems to carry this insistence to excess. He does not accept the kind of protectiveness that he welcomed at the age of one year. He casts his toys in a "self-willed" manner. But we do not make a moral issue of his obstreperous behavior. He is too young for that. Tolerantly we recognize the favorable and constructive significance of the growth changes that are taking place before our very eyes.

All too soon, however, his behavior is misconstrued through over-rigid application of standards of right and wrong. As he approaches his second birthday, more and more is expected of him. His toilet behavior may be made the object of emphatic approbation and disapprobation. At eighteen months he may hang his head in shame if he is adjudged "guilty" of the puddle for which he is "responsible." He counters by blaming the misdeed on someone else, as though groping for an alibi.

We doubt that his feeling of guilt is profound, or that it encompasses his whole personality. He is probably incapable of blushing; although in another year or two a sensitive child may indeed blush when reproved for a fault. (Darwin, by the way, regarded blushing as the most human of all emotional expressions.)

The primitive shamefacedness of the eighteen-month-old denotes a simple form of shyness and withdrawal, linked in the present instance with the function of elimination, which is closely bound up with his emotional life. Nevertheless, this disgrace gesture, with its projective reference to someone else, reveals that the personal ego is elaborating, and has even attained a measure of detachment, in its capacity to set up a flimsy alibi.

It will take years of structural growth and of patterning experience before the individual is capable of the higher forms of moral judgment. As adults we are too prone to think of the ultimate forms, rather than of the gradients that lead to them.

Fortunately the gradients have a forward reference, and even undesirable behavior sometimes signalizes a growth process which becomes constructive under skilled guidance. The two-and-a-half-year-old, for example, when confronted by two alternatives, has a way of trying out both. Opposites seem to have equal appeal. But with experience and with help, he learns to choose *within the limits* of his maturing capacity. At the age of three, he actually likes to make choices and he likes to please. Within the limits of his maturity he is becoming a moral agent, who assumes, and who should assume, suitable responsibilities.

At four years, for developmental reasons, he is apparently less anxious to please. He is less sensitive to praise and blame, and he needs new kinds of motivation when questions of obedience arise. He tends to go out of bounds. Wisely managed, he usually proves to be conforming again at the age of five. Then he invites and accepts supervision. He likes to ask permission, even of strangers. He likes to stand in well with people. His ready obedience has an attractive quality. He is very good!

But "obedience" is not an absolute trait, fixed once and for all. It is really only a general label for a diverse group of specific obedient acts of which a child happens to be capable. The patterns, the contexts, and the occasions for obedience inevitably change with age. The wise parent never makes a fetish or even a goal of obedience for its own sake. As we have already noted in our behavior profiles, the whole map of behavior undergoes deep changes in the second half of the fifth year and throughout the sixth. The psychological transformations involve the entire personality, creating new problems of conduct for the child, and new demands for guidance for his father and mother. At five his sense of goodness and his good conduct consisted largely of obedience to the commands of grownups. His ethical development between the years from five to ten is clearly traced in his expanding concepts of good and bad, particularly goodness in himself and badness in others. The two-way dynamic works like a weaver's shuttle, as he penetrates more deeply into his own ego and that of his agemates and elders. Observing others helps him to understand himself. And what he inwardly feels he also ascribes, more or less, aptly, to others. A nicely balanced two-way appraisal is no mean feat. It takes skill. It takes maturity.

No wonder the six-year-old is ethically inept when the tide of development brings him to a level where he yields to the temptation of cheating, a new form of behavior, which he partly learned by being cheated! He has an acute sense of possession; but a very poorly organized relation to his belongings. He must also have an acute sense of self-status; for he cannot gracefully bear to lose a game. He will cheat on occasion. But to even the psychological score, he denies his guilt; and he worries about the cheating of others! Perhaps he worries most at the very time when he is himself most liable to cheat.

In the seventh year there is already a decline in the amount of cheating; and a more robust insistence on the part of the seven-year-old that there should be no cheating by others. Thus he adds his own weight to the social disapprobation of dishonesty. The threads of the fabric of morals are minutely, ceaselessly woven. Children themselves help to fashion the growing designs.

Pensive SEVEN has a new type of awareness of the good *and* bad.

Home ties are loosening; he vaguely apprehends the community. He generalizes and abstracts to a degree far beyond conforming FIVE and sketchy SIX. He does not limit his thinking to specific acts. He is beginning to sense the *qualities* of goodness and badness, and to erect more universal standards of conduct to live by. He is getting a firmer grip on everyday honesty and truth. His blaming and alibiing have moral overtones, and he can even be appealed to on ethical grounds. All of which means that he is becoming more of an individual among individuals.

EIGHT with all his expansive and evaluative traits is yet more conscious both of himself and of the selves of others. His awareness of these others is more perceptive, and increasingly subtle. He shows an impressive catholicity of insight into the good characteristics as well as the shortcomings of his comrades. He grants that boy X is the best athlete, that girl Y is the most skillful artist in school, that boy Z is not always fair, but that he is the most fun in this game or that, etc., etc. The widening range and refinement of his estimates lend substance to his ethical outlook. Vigorous morals are based on acquaintance with the world.

The evaluative tendencies of EIGHT do not exclude himself. He is vulnerable to criticism. He is contrite. He will never, no, *never*, do it again! All told, he has the essentials of an advanced ethical sense. He is sensitive; he is not overcompetitive; he has a fairly tolerant insight into the psychology of his associates; he shows a strong tendency to work out his relationships with them, unaided by interference from without. He may squabble in the process; but even so, his collective behavior represents an embryonic forecast of a democratic culture.

The ten-year-old registers a further advance along these same promising developmental lines, when surrounding conditions are favorable. Cultural controls have become of increasing importance in molding the resultant patterns of social behavior. A most important period for the prevention of juvenile delinquency embraces the years between seven and ten.

The normal, well-rounded ten-year-old is already a law-abiding citizen. He is able to organize and to conduct a club, with rules, regulations, and referee. His bylaws, written or unwritten, ban lying and cheating. He follows leadership, but he also participates in discussion, and he can wait his turn in the discussion, because he has outgrown the eight-year squabble and the six-year quarrel, and the five-year compliance. Best of all, he has a sense of humor. He is able to take a joke on himself, a capacity that we would include as one of the metaphysical ingredients of the ethical sense.

But the "normal" child is not uniformly "good." He is sometimes selfish, destructive, deceitful, at least by dictionary definitions. Even the ten-year-old, whose virtues we have just proclaimed, can use his new-found ethical abilities to spite his comrades, to gang up against them, and to disrupt their club activities.

In the first ten years of life, it is unwise, and usually unjust, to impose standards of conduct *arbitrarily*. Arbitrariness leads to emotional conflicts and to intellectual confusions. Parents frequently become emotionally "burned up" by the child's poor manners—a misplaced emphasis which suggests a confused scale of values. For manners, like morals, are influenced by immaturity. They do not yield to arbitrary authority.

Harsh forms of punishment are, of course, automatically ruled out by a developmental approach to the problems of child conduct. When an adult pits himself against a child for the mere sake of preserving authority, no good follows. Care needs to be taken even in exacting apologies. Apology is a form of expiation, intended to set matters right between child and adult, or between child and child. But injudiciously demanded, it leads to insincerity or resentment, or to a sit-down strike. Forceful physical punishment is so difficult to apply beneficially in times of crisis that it is the better part of wisdom to have recourse to more enlightened methods of control.

In all disciplinary situations the adult must keep an eye on himself as well as on the child. He should feel certain that he is not demanding too much in terms of the gradients of growth. He must be sure of steps 1, 2, and 3 before he exacts steps 4, 5, and 6. He will not knowingly confuse manners with morals and will keep his eye on the one long-range goal: the mental health of the child. A sense of humor and a little skillful, face-saving banter can work miracles in discharging emotional tensions, even in the moral realm.

And perhaps we should think more in terms of emotional equilibrium, and less in the gloomier terms of expiatory punishment and of retributive justice. Because over the long pull that begins with birth, there is nothing more stabilizing than affection and mutual respect between adult and child. Morals are rooted in mutual respect, and in the reciprocity that comes with such respect. Reciprocity in turn leads to reason, and ultimately to the concepts of equity, which distinguish the mature ethical sense.

Growth Gradients

BLAMING AND ALIBIING

4 years—Blames inanimate objects. Some tattling on others.
Will sometimes admit own fault in a whisper: "An accident."

5 years—Denies own fault if questioned directly.
Blames nearest person for his own misdeeds: "Look what you made me do."

6 years—Usually denies own fault if questioned. May blame sibling, friend, or mother.
If admits fault, alibis: "He made me do it" or "His fault" or "I didn't mean to."
Can be led into admitting fault by asking, "How did you do it?" instead of "Did you do it?"
May blame inanimate objects for his mistakes in school.

Better at accepting blame for big things than for small.

7 years—Directly accuses others: "He did it" or "His fault."
Alibiing takes form of self-justification: "I was just going to do it"; "That was what I meant."
May throw book if cannot read; may throw cards if loses card game.

8 years—More responsible for his acts. Usually some justification if blames another person.
May deny guilt, but not blame others.
Blames himself. Feels need to apologize. Says he will "Never do it again."
May evaluate own action and feel guilty about it.

9 years—Wants blame apportioned fairly; much interest in who started any difficulty; tries to explain own behavior; reasons his way out.

Some can accept blame and say, "I did it and I'm sorry"; may even feel ashamed of own wrongdoing; upset if blamed for something he has not done.

Makes excuses when things go wrong (studying and practicing): "He was bothering me."

Considerable "taking it out on others," "picking at others"; if hurt, kicks the next fellow who comes along.

Self-criticism implied in "I **would** do that!"

10   years—Fairness very important; especially concerned that parents treat them fairly.

Very few take blame if they can get out of it; nearly all will try to push it off onto a sibling or someone else. Alibiing is very strong— someone else always started any difficulty. Many admit quite frankly, "I wouldn't bother taking the blame for something I did. I would say I didn't do it if they blamed my brother for something I did and he said I did it."

RESPONSE TO DIRECTION, PUNISHMENT, AND PRAISE

4 years—Less anxious to please, obey, conform than earlier.

Routines go smoothly and independently.

Out-of-bounds, resistant response to many directions. But can understand that rules and restrictions sometimes necessary. Likes to receive new privileges.

Verbal restrictions now better than physical.

Goals and competitions help motivate.

Less sensitive to praise and blame.

5 years—Needs, invites, and accepts some supervision and direction.

Asks permission. Asks, "Is this the way to do it?"

Likes to help mother at home.

Likes approval but does not demand praise. Likes to please and to do things right.

May hesitate to carry out direction, but usually does. May refuse because he can't do a task, or is too busy.

Many are described as "angels" or "perfect."

If corrected or reprimanded may become angry and cry.

6 years—Responds slowly or negatively to demand, but in time may spontaneously carry out as though it were his own idea.

If pressed, may be defiant: "No, I won't" or "How are you going to make me?"

An indirect approach is usually more effective: counting, magic word, a surprise. Needs extra chances.

Needs clear, simple directions in advance to get him started in the right direction.

Vacillates between two choices and usually ends with wrong one.

Loves praise and wants approval.

Resists punishment physically and verbally. Punishment does not improve behavior.

If criticized or blamed may become saucy, rude, argumentative, or have temper tantrum.

May respond to isolation.

7 years—Does not respond promptly; often does not hear directions. May forget easily.

May argue: "But Mommy" or "Why do I have to?" Delays: "Just a minute" (which may be several).

May start to obey and then get into a detour on the way.

Wants to be warned ahead of time. Also likes to know what punishment will be. Can plan with him to avoid disaster.

Better at helping mother than at doing household tasks alone.

Is suggestible and sensitive. Cares what people think of him.

Many respond well to praise though it is less necessary than at some ages. May be embarrassed by praise.

If criticized or if feelings are hurt, may cry.

8 years—Delays in carrying out a request; may argue and find excuses, but finally obeys with "If you insist."

Demands to be treated as an adult. Wants cues, a hint, secret codes.

Wants instructions worded just right.

Likes to work for an immediate reward, not just to help.

Responds to small deprivations for short periods. May say, "I didn't care anyway."

Loves praise and to be reminded of his improvement.

May burst into tears if blamed or criticized, or may say, "Who cares?"

Mere words or a look may suffice to help him to control his behavior.

Often cannot tolerate even a slight correction.

Feels guilty if he does wrong: "I'll never do it again."

Does not like to be teased or joked about.

Criticize and compliment each other.

9 years—Can now interrupt own activity in response to a demand from adult. Securing his attention may depend upon his interest and willingness to carry out the request; may wish to postpone until later because so busy with own interest, and then may forget.

Needs to be given detailed directions and to be reminded.

Much less "arguing back" than earlier.

If does not like directions may look sulky, cross, truculent, but if no issue is made will usually obey eventually.

May go from extreme of taking over authority for himself (unexpectedly brings a child home to lunch) to asking permission for some small thing.

May prefer reasonable appraisal of his work rather than praise, though nearly all welcome praise.

A threat, or deprivation of some desired object or activity, usually suffices to put him in line.

May be "sore" at punishment: "a gyp"; "not fair"; "just my hard luck."

Takes criticism better than formerly, but it still needs to be carefully phrased.

Says he is sorry if he does wrong and may feel ashamed of himself.

Group standards may be more important in determining behavior than parental standards.

Begins to be able to take a joke on self.

RESPONSIVENESS TO REASON

3½ years—Tends to want the opposite of whatever is offered.

4 years—For all that he is so often out of bounds, can at times be extremely reasonable.

5 years—Not much difficulty in making up mind. Decides quickly what he wants; does not present self with too many alternatives.

Likes to do things own way, but also likes to conform and to please adult. Thus adult can change his mind. May refuse because considers self unequal to demand.

6 years—Difficulty in making up own mind. Vacillates between two choices. Gets mixed up.

Will not change mind once it is made up.

If reasoned with, does not change mind, but explodes into temper.

7 years—Transition stage. Somewhat easier to make up mind, to make choices and simple decisions, especially if both alternatives appeal.

Still hard to change mind, but can occasionally listen to reason and change mind without exploding into temper.

Has standards and is trying to live up to them. Thus may be appealed to ethically.

8 years—Makes up mind rather easily, though has difficulty with little things of life.

Knows what he wants.

Frequently can listen to reason and can change mind with some ease.

However, does like to have own way.

9 years—Can make up mind easily and some can change it in response to reason, though this does not hold for all issues.

10 years—Listens to reason customarily, or at least sometimes. Tries harder to be reasonable than in the ages to follow.

Some may admit to arguing sometimes.

Most try to be polite, and most try to mind, but may sometimes ask, "Why do I have to?" Some get so mad they can't help arguing. But if he does argue, it is to win a point, not just for the fun of it.

SENSE OF GOOD AND BAD

3 years—Tries to please and conform. "Do it dis way?"

Responds positively to question "Have you been a good boy [girl]?"

May repeat prayers about "God make me a good boy [girl]."

4 years—Begins to understand about rules and ways to do things.

Some interest in good and bad, but not much understanding.

5 years—Child is "good" (from adult point of view) much of the time.

Sense of goodness and badness limited largely to things parents allow or forbid.

Child's "goodness" largely due to interest in conforming and obeying. "Is this the way to do it?"

Likes to help mother and to do other things considered by adult as good."

Likes to be in good with people and to ask permission.

Understands and respects rules—that he must get to school on time, etc.

Knows when he has been good and may plan to be good next day.

Dislikes being called "bad." May play being "bad."

5½ years—Little generalized sense of good and bad. Seems to keep in mind for each specific thing whether it is "good" or "bad"—allowed or forbidden by parents.

Likes to be made to conform; but seems often to define what he must not do by doing it.

Much interest in behavior of playmates—whether good or bad, whether they do things the right way.

May behave better away from home.

6 years—Notion of good and bad still largely connected with specific activities allowed or disapproved of by parents.

Rudiments of a sense of good and bad, and may ask, "Was I good?" (usually after he has been bad).

Very undifferentiated in ethical sense as in other fields.

Great interest in behavior of playmates—whether good or bad, whether they do things in right way. Especially report on bad behavior of playmates.

May think that other people are not fair.

Chief interest is in having own way.

Once he has started misbehaving, is not influenced by criticism of behavior.

7 years—Simple but generalized notions about goodness and badness. Knows that some kinds of behaviors (obeying, doing things willingly) are good and others bad.

Has standards of goodness for self as well as for others, and means to live up to them.

Has a sense of fair play and can be appealed to ethically.

Thinks that things are "a gyp," "not fair," and that he too must be "fair."

Judges behavior of playmates as good or bad, but not quite as verbal as at six.

Own behavior varies, sometimes quite good, sometimes not. May be better away from home.

Concerned about being good. Proud of good days. Worries about bad ones.

Realizes that being "bad" spoils things.

8 years—Aware of goodness and badness. May try to evaluate them.

Good and bad no longer just what parents permit or forbid.

Child wants and means to be "good." Wants to be appreciated.

Tries not only to live up to own standards but to what he thinks are the adult's standards.

More evaluation may lead child to believe that he or she has been "bad," or has failed to live up to standard. Then may feel guilty.

Inwardly unhappy if he does wrong. Dislikes to admit wrong-doing.

If fails to live up to standard, wishes failure to be condoned: "Do you blame me?" "Could I help it?"

Thinks of things as right and wrong, no longer simply as good and bad.

9 years—Less concern about good and bad; now thinks in terms of right and wrong.

Wants to do things the right way; may be ashamed of being wrong.

Interest in fairness of teacher, of others, and of punishment.

Evaluates behavior of other children: "He's a good sport."

Standards are those of contemporary group; disgusted with others who do not live up to these standards.

10 years—Slight majority—more girls than boys—report they can tell right from wrong. But nearly as many (far more than at other ages) admit simply that they cannot. Nearly all are definite, one way or the other; responses are only rarely qualified: "Usually, but not always. I'm not really hot at that."

Most say they distinguish by what their mothers tell them or what they learn in Sunday School, a few by conscience.

More concerned about what is wrong than what is right, and very specific in their concepts: "I'd know if an example was wrong"; "If I stepped in a brook and got my feet wet . . ."; "If you wanted to chop down a tree, the first thing you'd use a saw and not an ax if great bunches of people were around."

Most report that they try to be good most of the time, and many that they succeed. Some try and fail. "Sometimes I do a few bad things, but I try to be a good boy."

Standards for right and wrong acts of others are very high.

Most girls say their conscience does bother them; boys either allow that it does, or expect that it would if they ever did wrong. Some mention that it depends on the deed. But most are not bothered excessively. A smaller number, mostly girls, are untroubled by conscience.

A few are not sure what conscience is: "Something that tells you when you've forgotten something?"

TRUTH AND PROPERTY

4 years—Property. Much interest in possessions. Showing off and bragging about possessions: "Mine is bigger [better] than yours."

Especially proud of large possessions (big bed) of which he can boast.

Possesses parents and boasts about them.

Begins to possess his special friends.

Strong feeling for teddy bear. May treat as a real person.

An age of bartering and swapping of possessions. Most apt to share with special friends.

Shows off new clothes.

Strong personal feeling for own products made at school. Wants to take them home.

Will help feed and care for pets under parents' direction, but not dependable.

Honesty: Expansiveness leads to taking of small objects (such as labels) from store, objects of little value to either store or child.

May take home school equipment as well as own school products.

Money: May know what penny will buy and may save money to buy a more expensive object.

Can count three objects.

Objects to parting with money, even in purchase.

Truth: Tells very tall tales, often with little basis in fact.

Peak age for imaginative verbalization.

Often makes little distinction between fiction and fact.

5 years—Property. Little trouble about possessions. Child does not seem to want more than has.

May show pride in clothes, but does not take good care of them, on or off.

Likes to take school products home; also likes to take own things to school.

Other people's possessions remind him of own possessions. "I have blocks."

Much less bragging about possessions than earlier.

Money: Interest not strong.

Knows that money is used in making purchases; likes to take coin from adult to give to storekeeper.

Can name penny. Can count ten objects.

Truth: Fanciful stories and exaggerations continue, but child begins to distinguish real from make-believe and may know when he is "fooling."

5½ years—Property. Likes to have a great many possessions. Likes to have large quantities of objects.

May collect a few miscellaneous objects: toys, fancy paper, odds and ends.

Very poor at taking care of things: leaves them around, breaks them, loses them.

Takes poor care of own things, but objects to parting with them; may go to opposite extreme and be overgenerous.

Some are destructive and even like to break things.

Pride and interest in clothes, but do not take good care of them.

The phrase "Play with my doll" suggests strong feeling of possessiveness.

Likes to take things not his from school.

Honesty: May take toys or possessions of others. May also take gum or candy from stores. Now take things they really want.

Money: This is a "money for candy" age. Money is important not for itself but for what it will buy.

Many have an allowance of twenty to twenty-five cents a week. May do tasks, as clear off table, help with dishes, in return for this.

Little saving; mostly spend allowance.

Spend money slowly and carefully, taking much time to decide which object they will buy. This decision usually takes place at the counter and by means of picking up and handling many different objects.

Can name penny, nickel, dime.

Truth: Less exaggeration and untruthfulness. May tell fanciful stories, but usually distinguishes fact from fancy.

Some said to be very truthful, their word "law."

6 years—Property. Likes to take things to school to show and share; takes work home to show parents. Takes present to teacher.

Likes to have a great many possessions, but does not take care of them or keep track of them. Scatters them around house or yard. Breaks them. Loses them.

Loses toys, clothes, pocket money. Cannot keep track of anything.

Miscellaneous collecting and accumulating.

Some have pride and interest in clothes, but do not take care of them.

Bargaining, but little sense of value, so may make poor bargains.

Honesty: Needs are strong, sense of the limits of ownership weak. Thus takes what he sees and wants, regardless of who owns it.

Conversely, may give away own most valuable possessions.

In collecting and accumulating, may accumulate belongings of others.

Cannot bear to lose. Will cheat if necessary to win.

Money: Money still thought of in terms of what it will buy: Ice cream money."

Interest in the object that money buys , not in the money. Careless with money; might "steal" objects that money buys; less likely to take money.

Spends money immediately and thoughtlessly. Little saving unless motivated by parent.

Many have a formal allowance, (twenty-five cents per week). Most do some work at home in return for this: empty wastebaskets, other simple tasks.

Can name penny, nickel, dime, quarter.

Truth: Will deny fault if questioned directly. Falsehoods told often to evade blame.

Some are very "honest" verbally; but may cheat at games.

7 years—Property. Less taking things to school to show, but sometimes takes special things.

Becoming more interested in possessions and takes better care of certain things.

Some, especially girls, may take good care of clothes.

Much collecting: the goal being a large quantity.

Bartering: mostly on an "even swap" basis.

May give away own things.

Feeling of possession in relation to "school things": likes to have a schoolbag or case which contains own pencils, eraser, etc.

Honesty: Takes home school pencils and erasers.

Girls may take attractive small belongings of mothers.

Money: Increasing interest in money.

Most have an allowance and are interested in the fact of having it. Some earn this; others have a basic allowance and may supplement it with earnings.

Usual allowance is around fifty cents, with a range to $2.50.

Can name all coins and tell how many cents in each.

Many are interested in saving: piggy bank or bank account.

May also save money toward some expensive purchase, as a bicycle.

Truth: Less lying than at six.

Much concerned about wrongness of lying and cheating, especially in friends.

Quick to tattle of any breach of ethical code by others.

8 years—Property. Great interest in property and possessions.

Likes to acquire, own, and barter objects: hoards, arranges, gloats over possessions.

Wants a place of his own in which to keep things.

Some take good care of things, but most continue to be very careless.

Room and clothes usually untidy, but keeps some things neat: desk, books, certain toys.

Likes to bring to school objects related to the school subjects.

Takes shortcuts across property of others, often damaging property.

Honesty: Child needs what he wants. If not provided for, may take money, which is now meaningful in terms of what it will buy.

May take household money to "treat" friends.

Money: "Money mad"; "just loves money."

Real interest in money and in acquiring a good deal of it; likes to earn it at home.

Knows how much he has, how much is due him, what he wants to buy, what it will cost.

Plans ahead (in mind or from catalogues) as to what he will buy.

Saves up for expensive things; little squandering of money on trivialities, except comic books.

A high period for bartering. Ability improving.

Truth: Expansiveness may lead to telling tall tales and to boasting. But distinguishes fact from fancy and may size up adult to see if adult believes his stories.

Many are truthful about matters they consider really important.

9 years—Property. Beginning to be neater and does not lose things as much as he did.

Some effort (parent-instigated) at picking up room, but does not usually hang up clothes.

Usually "particular" about own things and may consider room and possessions "sacred."

Some boys interested in trading and barter.

Possessions quite numerous. Elaborate collections, carefully classified.

Honesty. Has ethical standards and may be very exacting of self and others.

May verbalize: "I'll have to be honest."

Only a few children deliberately take things not belonging to them.

If forbidden, say comic books, may read them in secret without parents' knowledge.

Many can lose in competitive games with fairly good grace.

Money: Likes idea of having large amount of money to look at, to show, to count, and to talk about.

Less interest in allowance. May forget to ask parent for it. Knows he can do chores to earn it, but may not care enough to, except on occasion. May be paid a certain amount for each chore.

Buys little needs (glue, crayons, clips, comics) and asks for money to pay for them.

Interest in how much different things cost.

Some can save up smaller sums to attain a more costly object.

Truth: Becoming more truthful. Are "essentially" truthful, but there are definite exceptions. May exaggerate, may say has washed hands, etc., when hasn't and may support friend or sibling in a lie.

10 years—Cheating. Has a strict code, and feels "cheating is awful." Most say specifically they would not cheat, though a few report one or two children at school who do.

Stealing: No children admit to stealing. Many comment that stealing is very bad. Some might be tempted, but many know they would feel "awful" if they did; others know the consequences would be too bad. Several say they know children who do steal, and remark on the badness of this.

Truthfulness: Most described as "quite" or "usually" truthful, straying only sometimes, or telling just "white lies." Many say they try to tell the truth, but a large number—boys especially— "sometimes do and sometimes don't" tell the truth. A few more girls than boys are described as "strictly" truthful, but more girls are also described as untruthful. Several admit they are untruthful, and are described by mothers as "telling whoppers."

Money: The majority depend on an allowance for money, though some do a little work in return for this and others supplement the allowance with earnings. Only a few have to earn all their money.

Weekly allowance ranges in amount from fifty cents to two dollars, the middle figure being one dollar. Most are reasonably satisfied with the amount, though a few think it too small. Not required to do much with this allowance; most spend it as they choose.

Many are very casual about money —forget to ask for their allowance, leave it in a pocket, lose it. Parents say, "Irresponsible"; "Not interested"; "Money means nothing to him."

Some save a little; others save nothing. Some worry that family money will not last.

Work: Most are not good about helping at home: "I hate it"; "I'm tired and I don't want to help"; "Not too good at it." Parents say, "Never does a thing but what she groans." Slow about responding to requests for help: delay, object, dawdle. Most do not openly rebel.

Most work best away from home. Boys do better outdoors than indoors.

Some are paid for work, others are expected to work in return for allowance. Among regular tasks: set table, do dishes, make bed, clean room, take out trash or garbage, mow lawn, garden, shovel snow, sweep, dust, feed dog. Some care for younger siblings, but most do not yet babysit outside of home.

CHAPTER 20

PHILOSOPHIC OUTLOOK

Man has lived on this swirling globe for a million years. It has taken him a long time to get acquainted with himself and to become aware of the universe in which he has his being. The day before yesterday he discovered that the earth is but a speck in a vast cosmos. Only yesterday he discovered the cosmic energy contained in the atoms that constitute this planetary speck. Even with the help of Einstein he has not yet solved the riddles of time and space. Only a few hundred years ago America was unknown; and medieval Europe lived in a "dream of eternity," which, Lewis Mumford suggests, did not dissolve until the thirteenth century, when campaniles and belfries were erected to announce the passing hours. This imparted a new sense of time and tempo.

There remained, however, many childlike beliefs about human fate and evil, life and death, nature and deity. Modern science and technology reconstructed these beliefs and is still reconstructing them. Copernicus revolutionized the naïve ideas concerning the canopy of heaven. Darwin gave us a new outlook on the origins of plants, animals, and mankind. The *Encyclopaedia Britannica* in 160 miles of linotype gives a large-scale account of transformations of human thought and action which have taken place throughout the ages. And now a new atomic age is with us. Never was philosophy more needed!

Man is continually engaged in the task of reconciling the known and the unknown. He is forever seeking orientation to the realities and the unrealities that surround him. If he is a professional philosopher he may formulate his outlook into weighty tomes and bring a conscious logic and science to bear upon thoughts.

Needless to say, the child from five to ten is not a philosopher in this articulate sense. Nevertheless, the modern child spontaneously develops notions about natural phenomena which bear striking analogy to the concepts of the early philosophers of ancient Greece. He also has spontaneous ideas of physical causality which do him no little credit. And he, like his forebears, is continually engaged in reconciling the known and the unknown. Long before the age of five, he thinks thoughts that once constituted major achievements in the mental evolution of the race.

The term "philosophy" can be variously defined. As systemized knowledge, it is the general science which integrates all sciences. At its highest levels it is a codification of man's reflections on his relations to the universe. Now, children do not deliberately codify their concepts; and yet they have characteristic modes of thinking and acting, which express their relations to the knowable universe. They have intellectual orientations and tendencies which constitute the essence of a philosophy in the making. It is difficult to draw a line between a complete and an incomplete philosophy, because even at adult levels no final philosophy has been achieved. We surely would not wish to say that the five-year-old has no philosophy at all. His intellectual orientation to the world is already so advanced that we must trace the threads of development back to infancy to find the antecedents of his philosophical outlook.

The newborn baby is immersed in the cosmos whence he came! But when he wakens from his natal sleep to search for the breast, and when he opens his eyes to look upon the world, he is already at the threshhold of the riddles of time and space. He promptly begins to solve these riddles at a pragmatic level. The ego that philosophers ascribe to him begins to expand; so that he steadily disengages himself from the cosmos which held him so intimately in its grasp at birth. Under the surge of growth he pushes frontiers toward the unknown. Whenever he is startled by a novelty or a surprise, he reacts with a movement, a feeling, a shift of attention, an exclamation, a word, a sentence. And thereby he becomes an embryonic philosopher! We cannot begin to catalogue the cumulative conquests of his fast-widening horizons; so we shall content ourselves with a condensed sketch of his intellectual progress in four classic areas of the philosophic domain: (1) *Time and Space*; (2) *Ego and World Society*; (3) *Life and Death*; (4) *Cosmos and Deity*.

Time and Space

The eyes take the lead in making a pathway into cosmic space. On the very first day of life, an infant may briefly fixate one of his open eyes upon an approaching object. During the first week he can sustain fixation on a *near* object. By the end of the first month he can fixate *far* as well as near objects. In another month he can coordinate both eyes to explore his surroundings with *roving inspection*. The conquest of space is well under way.

Having cleared a trail with his nimble eyes, he must now use his hands to penetrate the spatial wilderness. Thereby he refines his estimates of near distances (and stops reaching for the moon, if he ever did!). When he gains better command of his legs, he will creep and walk, thereby refining his knowledge of far distances.

But practical (and philosophic) space is a manifold of many sectors, indicated by numerous prepositions and adjectives: on, under, in, above, in front of, behind, high, low, thin, thick, vertical, horizontal, oblique etc. The infant invades and conquers these varied sectors of space through a joint use of eyes and hands fine and gross muscles, postures and locomotion. He probes the third dimension with index finger. He learns the properties of container and contained in his poking, filling, and pouring play at sand pile or seashore. He rediscovers the elementary architecture of space by building vertical towers, horizontal walls, lintels, and arches with his blocks. These rediscoveries have a lawful developmental sequence, because they are inherent in the architecture of the nervous system itself.

"Nature geometrizes," said the philosopher Plato. The infant confirms the philosopher by demonstrating a geometry of growth in the ontogenesis of geometry itself. Held in his mother's arms at the age of one year, he wriggles to get *down*; he gestures to be taken *up*. At two years he has an expanding vocabulary of prepositions and place words. At three years he has a definite sense of destination. At five years he likes to make a simple map picturing a road that goes somewhere.

This is prophetic of an almost revolutionary reorientation which gets under way at six years. At that age he is still the center of the universe, but he is less space-bound, and takes a new and rangy interest in the sun, his own planet, and other heavenly bodies. At seven years he is interestedly aware that there are other places than those just "right here." At eight years he has a new awareness of foreign lands. By ten years he has a fairly comprehensive feeling of the earth as his home, the points of the compass, the significance of parallels of latitude and longitude. He has made immense strides since he first cast his eyes on a moving shadow on the ceiling above his crib. He is spatially oriented to the *basic* geography of his world. To that extent he has a philosophic outlook.

He becomes oriented in time in much the same manner. For time has much of the essence of space, and most of our time words are space words. Time is long and short, near and far, two-part and three-part, before long (soon), endless; it fills an interval. Here and now, and then and there, are closely united in the psychology of growth. The calendar is a kind of space map of time.

Time, however, is in a sense more abstract and inflexible than space. It has only two sectors or dimensions (backward and forward). In an unsophisticated way the infant is aware of the flow of time; but not of the units of time. By association he learns to *place* events in his accustomed surroundings and his accustomed daily schedule. (Note that the word "place" has a spatial connotation). By experiences of *place* expectancy, he identifies *times*. By deferments he learns to wait and to appreciate units of time. His capacity to expect punctual happenings, and to wait for deferred happenings, determines his elementary sense of time. As he matures he is able to manipulate and to foresee potential time in the same way that he learns to manipulate plastic space. Some individuals are more adept than others in this manipulation of time; and this, by the way, fundamentally colors their philosophic outlook as children and as adults. Some of the most durable individual differences of childhood pertain to this very trait.

A glance at the growth gradients shows that the child progresses from appreciation of personal time to interpersonal and to more abstract nonpersonal time. At two years he comprehends the words "soon," "wait," and "pretty soon," particularly if the inflection is emotionally reassuring. It must be a tangible and prompt transaction. At three years there can be more interval in the bargain, and the child knows what he will do on the morrow. At four years he uses past, present, and future time words with similar facility. At five years he is so symmetrically oriented in both time and space that he seems to live in a relatively stable world of *here* and *now*.

At six years he takes a new type of interest in the ages of young and old, and in the babyhood of his mother. This is more than a perception of *duration*. It is a beginning apprehension of a *time cycle*, a higher order of insight, a more philosophic outlook. At seven years he not only tells time by the clock, but is interested in time schedules—a cultural kind of time. At eight years he likes to consult the schedules as they are posted on the bulletin board. He is getting time bearings in a restricted province. But he is still color blind for historic time. For all he knows, George Washington is mentioned in the Bible.

At ten years, however, the child is better oriented with respect to historic time, and he is yet more precisely oriented to local community time, life-cycle time, and personal time. He is at home with units of time. He knows the date; the day of the week; the exact minute of the next television program. His timing and tempo are more highly geared than the bells of the medieval campanile. As he grows older he will move nearer to Emerson, who enjoins us to have faith in the years and the centuries, so that we may restore the minutes to their proper perspective. Philosophy again!

Ego and World Society

By the ego we mean the personal self, and the nonpersonal—the individual who by progressive detachment becomes a partial entity in the vast human family. The process of detachment is slow and also paradoxical; for the ego takes form only as the infant becomes more and more aware of other individuals. The process begins with the mother. A drama of reciprocal identification, projection, and separation ordinarily takes place in a household. The presence of other persons helps the baby realize his own status. This psychological mechanism is a little like stereoscopic vision. The baby senses himself to be in others; but he also senses himself in his own physique; the two experiences offset each other; they are sufficiently different to build up a sharpening image of his own integral self.

As early as the age of thirty-two weeks he senses strangers as something different from familiars, although he does not recognize himself in the image which stares at him from a mirror. At two years he has a heightened sense of self-identity. He calls himself by his own name; he calls all men and women "mommies" and "daddies"; he calls every child "baby." And he has taken one short step beyond the confining boundary of the household: he feeds and toilets a doll. Even if he prefers a teddy bear, we may consider that he has begun to relate himself actively to other selves. He enjoys simple pictures of persons as well as of things. At three years he likes to hear stories about them—a definite step beyond egocentrism.

The noteworthy bargaining ability of the three-year-old must again be cited as a symptom of a changing (philosophic) outlook upon the world. At five years he likes to feel grown up, and significantly he asks, "Could a baby do this?" meaning, of course, that a baby couldn't.

At six years the child is emotionally in a paradoxical, a two-way state, so far as ego and the world are concerned. He is certainly the center of his universe, even though he is emotionally embroiled with his mother. And he is inordinately interested in himself; he is intrigued with his own babyhood, and inquisitive about his anatomical make-up. Notwithstanding, he is eager to participate in the world's work, and is earnestly concerned about his school work. From the latter standpoint he is not so egocentric after all.

The world is widening. At seven years he may be provincial enough to want his own set place at the table or in the automobile; but he is also seeking a place orientation in his school and community. He shows a dawning interest in government and in civilizations. In another year this interest comes to expansive expression. The eight-year-old, though his temperamental traits of individuality are now more marked than ever before, identifies himself with foreign peoples, and foreign cultures. He can hardly wait to grow up.

The ten-year-old has begun to read adult magazines, and is reflecting seriously on the vocation he will follow when he is grown up. Accordingly he reads biography and history with deepened perspective. He listens to the radio and watches television for communications from the outer world. In time he follows the news commentaries with a factual, almost adult, interest. He takes interest in problems of war, but fundamentally his psychology is preparing a foundation for a potentially peaceful philosophic view of a world society.

Philosophic outlook is in the making!

Life and Death

It took no little insight on the part of our racial forebears to make a biological distinction between life and death; and there is a period in the development of the child when he unites the two phenomena so closely that he believes in reversible death. This interesting notion rises in the mind of the five-year-old child, at the very time when the distinction between the quick and the dead dawns upon him. He recognizes the immobility of the dead. His attitude is factual, unemotional. He may even do a little experimental killing of lower forms of life. But his concepts are vague. He does not think of himself or of the aged as dying. He has an inkling of finality, but does not sorrow. The idea of the reversibility of death is, of course, implicit in primitive and modern religions. Religious beliefs are akin to philosophies.

The three-year-old has little or no understanding of death; but he is making a definite approach to the problem of the origins of life. He does so through his interest in babies. He likes them; he wants the family to have one right away. He may ask groping questions: Where does the baby come from? Where was it before it was born? What can the baby do when it comes? The questions are not as profound as they seem to be on the surface; but they do denote an interest in origins. Mythologies, which express the philosophic outlook of primitive peoples, are replete with theories of origin and genesis. The four-year-old living in a commercial culture may cling to the idea that babies are purchasable; or in his more private thinking he often maintains that the baby is born through the navel. The five-year-old is somewhat matter-of-fact about the birth of babies, as he also is about the finality of death. In a vague way he associates movement with life; and probably does not make a consistent distinction between animate and inanimate objects when the latter seem to have the power of movement.

But with the forward pulse of growth that comes at six years, the child has a new awareness both of life and death. An appreciation of the negation of death serves to sharpen his perception of manifestations of life. He shows a more concerned interest in babies and asks many questions about them. He makes general inquiries about the process of gestation and of birth. He may show a beginning interest in the reproduction of animals.

At seven his interest is less outspoken and more reflective. He does not need the concrete stimulus of an actual baby to start a short train of theoretical reflections. The mechanical aspects of birth may chiefly engage his attention.

The eight-year-old characteristically shows a definite expansion in the scope of his comprehension. He sees the necessity of a long uterine period of growth prior to birth; and he is beginning to understand that the father plays a part in procreation. His thinking, however, is relatively concrete and he may retain naïve notions about the floating clouds, the current of rivers, the action of the wind, and the movements of sun, moon, and stars.

The ten-year-old is less naïve. He still thinks vaguely of forces behind all movements; but he has grasped the significance of spontaneous movement, so he arrives at the rationalistic conclusion that animals—and plants—are endowed with life. For all practical purposes he has made a distinction between animate and inanimate. The distinction cannot be final, for even now scientists and philosophers are debating whether the protein molecule of a virus is animate or inanimate.

Death poses the distinction in new forms. As already suggested, the six-year-old is becoming more aware of the meaning of death, emotionally as well as intellectually. Self- and mother-centered as he is, he begins to worry about his mother's dying and about the separation that will result. In an aggressive mood he may invoke death upon parent or playmate. His vehemence may astound; but often it is purely verbal. However, he feels the passing shadow of the curse of Cain; for he is acquiring the idea of death by violence— death as a condition that results from killing! (War has not delayed this insight.)

For the seven-year-old the death idea becomes somewhat more personal. He suspects that he himself will someday die; but since this suspicion is in tender and timid beginnings, he also denies that he will die. While Six might verbally visit death upon another, Seven, true to his inwardizing psychology, may verbally complain, "I wish I were dead." But even more than Six, he has a realistic curiosity about the objective appurtenances of death: coffin, burial, and cemetery.

The eight-year-old progresses from an interest in graves and funerals to an interest in what happens after death. His comprehension is more general, and he acknowledges that "All men must die."

The ten-year-old accepts this philosophic dictum more completely. He confronts the fact of death as a natural phenomenon; he does not limit his interest to its appurtenances and consequences. He thinks of life as having a physiological basis in nutrition, growth, blood, and breathing. Death comes when these essentials fail. Death is a negation of life, a biological process. True to his maturity traits, the ten-year-old again approximates and foreshadows the outlook of the adult.

Cosmos and Deity

The newborn infant, as already suggested, is immersed in the cosmos. Perhaps that is the reason he has about him an "air of infinite wisdom" which tends to vanish when mere mortal intelligence develops.

Thoreau hints as much: "In a sense the babe takes its departure from Nature as the grown man his departure out of her, and so during its nonage is at one with her, and as a part of herself."

Our growth gradients attempt to tell something about how this generic babe disengages himself and makes the developmental departures toward a state of maturity where he can contemplate the cosmos that gave him birth! It is a long journey, which begins with his first steps in the early conquests of time and space; which continues in his endless questions: What's that? Why? How?; and which ultimately brings him to the sacred and the secular literatures that deal with nature and with God. The culture answers his childhood and adult questions through sciences and religions.

The cosmology of the infant is delimited by the nursery. His world system consists of furniture, feeding utensils, crib, clothes, and domestic trappings. In his perambulator he may note the waving trees against the horizon; he glimpses the come and go of other vehicles; he senses vast masses of houses against the sky; but as yet he is scarcely conscious of either earth or sky, for he makes no distinction between the two. He is space-bound by what immediately impinges on his needs, his economy.

With his increasing powers of locomotion, his hitherto constricted world system enlarges and takes on structure. He walks on curbs and walls with a thrilling sense of distance and destination. He begins to know that pathways and streets lead somewhere. He may name his own street, his village or city, neighboring cities. In time the drugstore, the marketplace, the nursery school and kindergarten become part of his "cosmology."

If he could draw a map of his universe we can be pretty sure of what he would include, because his cosmology, up to the age of five, is highly personal.

At six and seven his interests become somewhat more impersonal. He displays at least a picture-book interest in foreign places; he makes inquiries about both the astronomical and theological heavens. In his efforts at orientation he tries to ascertain the precise spatial location of an overruling deity. He is curious about the elements, the earth's crust, fire, the wind, the weather, clouds, the melting of snow and ice, the origins of rivers, lakes, and sea, mountains and deserts, flora and fauna. A tree is no longer a mere moving blotch against a background. It is a plant. But how did it get there? Where does the wind come from? Or does the tree make the wind by nodding? What are stones made of? And, Mommy, where did you find me? Where was I when you were at school? And *who* took care of the very first baby? And does Superman make supermen?

With such a welter of questions, one might wonder how the child is ever able to escape confusion. And yet he fashions for himself an orderly universe. To begin with, he doesn't ask the questions all at once. He asks in relation to a specific spot on the frontier of *his* unknown. If you try to tell him too much and too early, you are more likely to bewilder him. He is not lost; he simply wants to take one step; that is the *next* one, and always one at a time. He would not ask the questions at all if there were no immanent order in the universe of which he is a very important fragment. He feels himself in a world of lawful forces, some of which he controls. For this reason his questionings and his thinking take him toward and into the realms of the natural sciences and of cosmogony. In his naïveté he may even ask, "Well, who made God?" or "Was God born?" And a seven-year-old skeptic argues, "I have never seen God in school."

When skepticism makes its appearance in a child's thinking, we may be sure that the mind is becoming conscious of itself. This leads the child to an increasingly objective view of nature. At the same time the sense of self is becoming more defined; and the concepts of deity undergo corresponding changes. During the earlier preschool ages, the child's relation with the cosmos is so close, and in the child psychologist Piaget's sense, so egocentric, that he attributes purpose and feeling to the events of nature. Many of the child's spontaneous notions are then probably colored by animism; and occasionally by magic. Frequently his notions bear a striking resemblance to some phase of primitive mythology.

Within the limits of his intelligence and experience, however, the child of six and younger is capable of drawing rational deductions; and he can think in the nonmystical terms of physical causality. At first he thinks of specific causes. By the age of ten he may think of general, mechanical causes. He is less naïve; his errors of interpretation are fewer. His modes of thinking and his attitudes toward cause and effect become truly scientific in their essence. But the most remarkable feature of his intellectual development is not an increase of knowledge and accuracy. More remarkable is his interest in causes, which expresses itself in "Why?" even before the age of three.

Whence this why? which becomes particularly insistent at the ages of four, five, and six. It is an untaught tendency of the child's growing mind. It is as instinctive as his play and fantasy. It resembles a startle response evoked by new or strange situations, and is based on the inborn capacity to wonder.

The corollary of "Why?" and "How?" is "I don't know" and "I can't." The child's questionings reflect and direct the growth of his critical ability. His sense of self becomes more discriminating. He no longer considers himself all-powerful; and gradually, or perhaps suddenly, he perceives that his parents are not all-powerful. This necessitates a revolutionary revision of his philosophic outlook. He looks upon the world and upon the household in a changing light.

All children, even the less gifted, pass through an anteadolescent phase during the crisis of the sixth year or thereabouts. The dethronement of Father as omnipotent is, after all, not too drastic. Life with father goes on. The qualities of omnipotence and omniscience are perpetuated in the child's developing concepts of a heavenly father—and also in a popular figure who comes down a chimney once a year. With good reason Santa Claus is sometimes called Father Christmas. He is a true folk phenomenon. At his best he remains a jolly and kindly embodiment of a beneficent parenthood.

Perhaps our culture should do more to preserve him, by preventing overcommercialization, and also over multiplication; for the susceptible believer is subject to numerical and other confusions. But usually a child can assimilate, adore, and in time deny him without suffering any scars of disillusionment. Indeed, this substantial saint, in contributing to the spirit of Christmas, assists the child to attain a more abstract concept of a spiritual deity.

The prevailing culture and the religion of the household have a marked effect upon the child's ideas of God; but the general character of the ideas is basically determined by developmental factors.

These factors are neatly reflected in the growth gradients for the Santa Claus myth. Up to the age of two and a half years the physical Santa is usually feared. He is a strange and formidable threat to the child's security. A year later he begins to be somewhat meaningful and interesting. Most three-year-olds are aware of Santa long before they are aware of God. The four-year-old is a true believer and accepts every detail of the myth. The five-year-old embraces the realism of Santa's clothes, his laugh, his reindeer. The six-year-old hears doubtings, but he fiercely repels all suspicion. His belief is more emotional; his enjoyment more intense. If he has a lively mind he images not only old Santa himself, but Santa's wife, home, workshop, and the ledger in which the names and deeds of good children are enrolled.

Reflective Seven has moments of skepticism—or moments of constructive criticism. His natural science (which includes the measurement and displacement of physical bodies) does not permit him to believe that Santa comes down the chimney. He may repudiate still other details, but he adheres to the core of his faith and of his enjoyment. At age eight, the notion of Santa Claus is more etherealized, but it is by no means entirely surrendered. The spirit of Christmas is taking shape as an observed and felt reality.

By the age of nine or ten, the Santa myth has been generally abandoned; but who can doubt that it may play an enriching role in the development of personality? The child's reactions to the myth reflect at least the mechanisms and the stages by which he reaches the higher levels of religious thought. In the early preschool period he regards his parents as omniscient, but he admits Santa into his pantheon, and ascribes to him parental attitudes when a philosophical need arises. Coincidentally he admits angels and heaven into the gallery of his imagination. (His imagination and interest are particularly rich at the age of six.) Parents, once made everything in the world. Now there are other agencies; and even Santa may prove to be a bridge to the concept of God as a creator and governor. The ten-year-old is less naïve, more rationalistic. He ascribes natural origins and natural processes to nature and to man, and over the cosmos he is erecting a supreme deity. He has attained a preliminary stage of maturity where he can combine science and religion in his philosophic outlook.

One of the great tasks of today's education is to impart the life sciences and the physical sciences in a manner that will preserve both rational and spiritual values.

Stages of Thought

Though in our *own* thinking, and our own writing, we have not separated thinking from the child's total activity—even an infant thinks when he views a desired object, gets to his hands and knees and creeps toward it—in view of the vast current interest in the work of Jean Piaget on the subject of thought, we present here, in very brief summary, Piaget's own summary of the development of thought in the child.

According to him, the first stage may be labeled *Sensorimotor.* It involves perception, recognition, means-end coordination, and lasts from birth till somewhere around two years of age.

This is followed by the *Preoperational* stage, from two to seven years, in which thinking involves comprehension of functional relations and symbolic play.

Next, from eight to eleven years of age, comes the stage Piaget calls *Concrete Operational,* emphasizing the invariant structure of classes, relations, numbers. And lastly the *Formal Operational* stage comes in from eleven through thirteen years, when propositional and hypothetical thinking is achieved.

Growth Gradients

TIME

3 years—Most common basic time words now in child's vocabulary.

More time words added to vocabulary between two and a half and three years than in any other equal period.

Many different words now used for past, present and future. Most for future.

Adult can bargain with the child, can persuade him to wait for things.

Expressions of duration—"all the time," "for two weeks"—come in.

Pretense of telling time and spontaneous use of clock-time phrases, usually inaccurate.

Much use of the word "time" alone or in combination: "It's time," "lunchtime."

Child can tell how old he is, when he goes to bed, and what he will do next day.

3½ years—Great variety of expressions indicating past, present, and future now used spontaneously, to about an equal extent.

Many complicated expressions of duration: "for a long time"; "for years"; "a whole week"; "in the meantime."

Increase in refinement of expression: "It's almost time"; a nice long time."

Expresses habitual action: "On Fridays."

May refer to future happenings as if in the past: "I'm not going to take a nap yesterday."

Ability to answer questions about time not much increased since 3 years.

4 years—Spontaneously speedy, but slows down under pressure. If urged to hurry, usually goes more slowly.

Has reasonably clear understanding of when events of the day take place in relation to each other.

Past, present, and future words continue to be used freely and about equally.

Many new time words or expressions are added.

The word "month" comes in; also such broad concepts as "next summer," "last summer," but "yesterday" and "tomorrow" have more immediate meaning even if they are confused.

5 years—Child lives in the here and now.

Knows when events of day take place in relation to each other.

Dramatic house play involves sequences in time, routines of the day.

Most of the time words commonly used by adults now in the child's vocabulary.

Free verbal handling of the more common aspects of time.

Can name days of the week, at least in rote fashion.

Can answer questions such a "How old will you be on your next birthday?" "What day is it"

Cannot conceive of not being alive, of dying, or of anyone living before him.

Interest in clocks. Likes to play with toy clocks.

Interest in calendars; likes to find birthday and holiday dates.

6 years—Child tends to dawdle in most routines.

Increasing knowledge of duration. Can roughly discriminate time intervals; but "You may play for twenty minutes" is not useful unless implemented.

An understanding of the seasons, in terms of activities suitable for each.

If asked, "What is time?" may say, "Time to get out of bed."

Interest in own and/or mother's babyhood.

Can answer questions such as "What time do you go to school?" "How long do you stay in school?" "What do you do in the spring?"

Begins to understand that oldest people usually die first.

Some interest in time being different in different parts of the world.

May be mixed up about past and

present. Clings to the old yet scoffs at it, and wants the new.

7 years—Adult needs to be aware of child's natural tempo and give time for performance.

Child may dawdle almost until deadline, then speed up and finish with a spurt.

Interest in school schedule as to what subject follows what.

May be afraid of being late for school.

Can tell what time it is; also how many minutes past, or of, the hour.

Can tell what season it is; what month it is; how many minutes in an hour.

If asked "What is time?" may answer, "Time is to be ready for school."

Spontaneously uses concepts such as how many years till some event, in thinking and in conversation.

8 years—Child is very "speedy" and likes anything that is speeded up.

"Can't wait" for future events or to be grown up.

Likes to consult bulletin board about school schedule.

Can tell time, but still depends on parent to be told that it is bedtime, etc.

Can tell what day of the month it is.

Can name months; can tell what year it is.

Asked "What is Time?" may tell what part of the day it is, what time it is.

Beginning of interest in primitive peoples and in times past.

Not very clear about times past; thus not know whether or not George Washington is mentioned in the Bible.

9 years—Child can tell time, but does not as a rule take responsibility of depending on his watch to know when to do things.

Practical time sense not too good. Cannot report in any detail what daily school schedule is. Can tell time for recess, and time to go home.

Can telephone home if going to be late.

May plan schedule of day, or may plan way ahead to an adult future.

Child may feel pressed for time, he is so busy.

May be challenged competitively by timing of a performance.

Interested in biography: the life sequence of the individual.

Marked interest not only in history but in prehistoric times.

Will do a task if told how much there is to do, and how long it will take.

10 years—Concept of time is typically static, specific, and concrete. "Time is something the watch tells"; "A clock tells time." A few think of time more dynamically:

"Time is something that passes" or "Time is days past or future; time is seasons; time is centuries."

SPACE

3 years—Says; "in the train," "back," "over," "over here," "fits," "gone away," "around," "in New Haven."

Can tell what street he lives on but usually not the number.

Can carry out commands in regard to: over, under, big, high, long, tall.

Puts ball on, and under, chair.

Out for a walk, definitely has destination in mind. Always likes to follow the same route.

3½ years—Says, "go there," ("go" meaning belong), "found," in school," "over there."

Puts ball on, under, behind chair.

Can tell his street and city.

If asked how to get to a certain place, will answer, "On the bus", "In the car." Cannot tell route.

4 years—Uses space words more exactly, and in combinations.

Carries out commands in regard to: on top, behind, bumpy, deep, pointed, shallow.

Puts ball on, under, in front of, behind chair.

Plays hide-and-seek.

Makes road in sand for toy car. Dramatic rather than spatial use of "store," "home," etc.

Goes on errands outside home, without crossing street. Visits neighbors.

Out for a walk, runs ahead of adult and can wait at crossing.

Likes to go "different" ways when on walks.

If asked how he gets to a certain place, may try to describe the route. More likely to say "the goat way" or "by the ball place."

5 years—Child is here and now. Very literal and factual. Also focal.

Remains close to home base; close to mother.

Needs things in close juxtaposition spatially.

Needs parent to be right where he himself is; at his level.

Is interested in own home and in immediate neighborhood.

Likes to do errands around the house; will go to the store usually accompanied by an adult. Can cross streets with traffic lights. Can learn to go to kindergarten by self.

Can point out simple routes he takes between near and familiar points.

Can carry out commands in regard to: few, forward, backward, tiny, smooth, high.

Likes to trace journeys on maps and make simple maps indicating the route he takes to school, etc. Indicates specific landmarks.

Interested in the space that is here but not so much in spatial relations.

Is interested in distant cities and

states if someone he knows lives there. ·

Likes to go on excursions with mother.

6 years—Environment is expanding. Now includes relationships between home, neighborhood, and an expanding community.

Home and school both very important, but child has trouble orienting to the combination of these two different worlds.

Home interests now include: people, keeping house, pets, animals, outdoors, amusements, sources of food, preparation of food, clothing, books, holidays.

School interests now include, materials, equipment, library, various rooms, playgrounds.

Child is the center of own universe, but is also interested in the sun, moon, planets, the whole world.

A rangy orientation to schoolroom: oriented to the whole room.

A minimal, picture-book type of interest in children of other lands.

Marked interest in heaven—how you get there, etc. A similiar interest in the devil and hell.

Very undifferentiated in regard to space, as in all fields.

Can distinguish left and right on own body, but not on others.

May be able to tell points of compass from a familiar starting point; can name nearby streets.

May begin to realize that same programs on other people's television as on his own.

Some interest in what rest of school building is like. Enjoys exploring it with his group.

If he goes on shopping excursions, must buy something.

7 years—Somewhat similar to 6, with deepening of meanings and more understanding of relationships throughout the whole community.

School and home both important.

Community interests include details about: grocer, policeman, fireman, etc.

An interest in the elements: earth's crust, stones, heat, fire, sun, geology.

Not ready for study of far times and places.

Interest in God in heaven now more clear and more spatial.

In school is oriented toward the teacher.

Interested in having "own place."

Interested in the fact that "there are other places than just right here."

Marked improvement in understanding of orientation in regard to cardinal points of the compass.

Can play hide-the-thimble.

Can go from home room to another familiar room, but wants specific directions.

8 years—Definite expansion into deeper understanding of wider community relationships.

Foreign countries and world relationships are better understood.

Beginning of interest in primitive

people and times past: Indians, Pilgrims.

Child is expansive and evaluative; adventurous; willing to try new things and new places.

Interest in barriers: likes to set own barriers.

Out-of-bounds encroaching on neighbors' property. Likes shortcuts.

Speedy: covers much ground—in every way.

Interest and apparent understanding (to own satisfaction) of going to heaven when he dies.

Can distinguish right and left on bodies of others.

Can go to city on bus if put on and met by someone.

9 years—Can go to familiar places on bus, getting on alone; or go downtown alone.

Interest in expanding community life: community problems of health, life, property; mercantile businesses; manufacturing industries; agricultural industries; transportation; weather, animal and plant life in community; holiday and seasonal activities.

Environment widens to include the whole earth. Studies culture outside his own. Understandings, attitudes, and concepts become worldwide: China, South America, Russia.

Communication with somewhat distant places through correspondence.

Likes geography (maps) and history; other countries and other times.

Beginning to like biography (whole development of one person).

Strong interest in details of life in foreign countries and in primitive times.

10 years—Relates space to air: "Space is an empty piece of something."

LANGUAGE AND THOUGHT

2½ years—Vocabulary increases rapidly. Language now a useful tool for child.

Spontaneous language often rhythmical and repetitive.

Long monologues with fluent use of language.

Verbally asserts domination over members of family.

Uses such forms as "I," "me," "you."

More time words appear in next six months than during any other equal period.

Adult now handles child by words instead of physically.

Key words effective in handling child: "need," "has to have," "when you are finished," "it's time to."

"Preoperational" stage of thinking.

Ritualistic. Likes to hear same story over and over.

In examination, child refuses situation by shaking head "No," saying "No," asking verbally for other materials.

3 years—More command of language. Uses language fluently and with confidence.

Can use words to control and can be controlled by words.

Interest in new words. Adult can use key words effectively in handling the child: "surprise," "secret," "could help," "might," "new," "different," "maybe."

Listens when reasoned with.

Listens with interest to adult conversations. Increasing span of interest in listening to stories.

Stuttering (3½ years).

In examination, child refuses situations by saying, "I don't know." Suggests other materials. Verbal reference to mother.

4 years—Out of bounds verbally: talks a great deal; exaggerates; boasts; tells tall tales.

Talks with and about imaginary companions.

Much questioning: "Why?" "How?" as much to keep conversartion going as seeking information.

Profanity, mild obscenities; verbal play about elimination.

Calls names; threatens; uses slang.

Likes nonsense words; silly language and rhyming; new and different words.

Many grammatical mistakes, and misuse of words.

Can listen to stories and be read to with sustained interest.

Less need for key words. Adult can talk to child in more mature way. Whispering may be effective and child may be willing to whisper an answer he will not give aloud.

In examination, child refuses situations by saying, "I can't"; "I don't know." Boasts about irrelevant subjects, questions examiner; says, "You tell me"; "Hey"; "Ow."

May say he thinks with his mouth or his tongue.

5 years—Likes to talk and will talk to anyone. Some talk "constantly."

Interest in using new and large words; interest in the meaning of words.

Asks, "What does . . . spell?"

Innumerable questions; now really seeks information.

Grammar now reasonably accurate; usually one or two inaccurate forms. Criticizes wrong use of grammar in others.

"Loves" to be read to.

Uses language conformingly: "Is this the way to do it?"

In examination, begins to use language thoughtfully: "I think"; "I forget." Evaluates tasks: "That's hard"; "That's easy."

Can define simple words.

Difficulty in distinguishing between fantasy and reality.

"Magic" is an accepted answer to the child's "how" questions.

May believe that everything active is alive; that man made everything.

May say he thinks with his eyes.

Figures things out for self. Makes own generalizations after even one occurrence of an event. If both his grandfathers died first he may ask, "Do daddies die first?" If by chance he has been told that two brown dogs were females and two black ones were males, he will conclude that all brown dogs are female and all black ones are male.

6 years—Uses language aggressively: calls names, threatens, contradicts, argues.

Slang and mild profanity.

Asks many questions. Very talkative.

Uses telephone. Some can dial.

Likes to use big words.

Loves television.

Usually good pronunciation and fairly accurate grammatical form. Can detect own mistakes and may accept correction.

Considerable stuttering, especially in boys.

In examination, is conscious of multiplicity of tasks: "So many words." Interest in beginnings of tasks: "I can't do it far"; "I'll go as far as I can."

Can tell differences between two simple objects.

Increased ability to differentiate fantasy and reality.

Interest in magic strong: child plays that he is magic, has magic ears, etc. Counting is magic. Puts baby teeth under pillow and believes that fairies substitute coins.

Everything that moves may be thought alive in contrast to that which is inert; child believes that God made everything.

7 years—Uses language complainingly: nobody likes him, people are mean and unfair, he has nothing to play with.

If angry, may retreat into silence instead of, as earlier, into angry verbalization.

Interested in meaning and spelling of words. Some use of pictorial dictionary.

Considerable social telephoning to friends.

Use of slang and clichés.

Variable pitch of voice: voice generally loud, but may speak softly or mutter complaints.

Reading, listening to radio, watching TV, silent verbal planning.

In examination, estimates own ability: "I've never done that"; "I guessed it."

Criticizes own performance: "What's the matter with me?" Delays: "Got to think it over." Interest in endings: "I've got all up to here."

Can give similarities between two simple objects.

Now relates thinking to head or mind: "You have to think it up in your head"; "It went out of my mind."

Great interest in magic, wishing stones, tricks, riddles.

May play at magic, that he has a magic wand, or that he "is" magic.

May believe everything that moves is alive and that God made everything.

End of Piaget's "Preoperational" stage of thinking.

8 years—Out of bounds verbally (as at 4 years): talks a great deal, exaggerates, boasts, tells tall tales.

Uses language fluently, almost as adult does.

Much social use of telephone.

Some slang and profanity; raises voice when angry or tired.

Reading and television interests strong.

Good pronunciation and good grammar, as a rule.

Beginning of code language; use of Pig Latin or Double Dutch; secret passwords.

Can give similarities and differences between simple objects.

Differentiation between fantasy and reality established.

Less belief in magic, but interested in magician's tricks and may like to perform simple card tricks.

Can verbalize ideas and problems.

Begins to understand cause-and-effect relationships.

Distinguishes between original and acquired movement: to be alive is to move by one's self.

Beginning of Piaget's "Concrete Operational" stage of thinking.

9 years—Language now used more as a tool, less for its own sake.

No longer out-of-bounds verbalization, as at 8 years.

May return to many incorrect grammatical uses.

Writes out lists and plans.

Uses language to express subtle and refined emotions: disgust, self-criticism.

Reading and television interests increase.

Considerable verbal criticism of parents' actions.

Extended use of code language.

Emergence of independent critical thinking.

Increasingly realistic conception of the world; does not like fairy stories.

Less belief in magic, but strong belief in luck, and some superstition.

DEATH

4 years—Very limited concept of death. Uses the word with some vague notion of its meaning.

No particular emotion related, though may verbalize a rudimentary notion that death is connected with sorrow or sadness.

5 years—Concept becoming more detailed, accurate, and factual. Some recognition of the finality of death, "the end." Though may think it is reversible (5½ years).

Recognize the immobility of the dead.

Attitude quite matter-of-fact and unemotional.

Bodily actions may come in, associated with death: avoids dead things, or may enjoy killing.

Seems to know as a fact, though apparently does not understand or feel emotionally, that death is related to age and that oldest often die first.

6 years—New awareness of death. Beginning of an emotional response to the idea of death.

Worries that mother will die and leave him.

Connects killing, possibly illness and hospitals, as well as old age, with death.

Idea of death as result of aggression or killing.

Some preoccupation with graves, funerals, burial.

Disturbed by pictures and stories of children or animals dead or dying.

Does not believe that he himself or she herself will die.

7 years—Similar to 6 years, but more detailed and realistic; better understanding.

Still looks at appurtenances: coffin, burial rites, etc.

Rather marked interest in causes of death: old age, violence, disease.

Interest in visiting cemeteries.

Still thinks of death in terms of specific human experience.

Futher connection of old age with death, oldest dying first.

May complain, "I wish I were dead."

Suspects that he himself will die. Denies that he will die.

8 years—Progresses from an interest in graves and funerals to interest in what happens after death.

Usually refers death only to humanity, though earlier included other species.

Feels that he understands the concept better.

May accept fact that all people, including self, die.

9 years—Reference now made to logical or biological essentials: "not living"; "when you have no pulse and no temperature and can't breathe."

Now looks straight at death, not just at the periphery: i.e., coffins, graves.

Accepts quite realistically fact that when he is older he will one day die.

Not a marked interest with most at this age.

10 years—Concrete and matter-of-fact. If asked what happens after people die, says, "You get buried" or "You go to heaven."

Most seem relatively unconcerned.

DEITY

4 years—Marked interest in and many detailed factual questions about God. The concept is usually introduced by parents in answer to questions of "why" and "how." Comments and questions likely to be extremely "inappropriate."

Has religion of parents: child believes parents to be omniscient, all-powerful, eternal.

Enjoys prayers and elaborates them from the original.

Enjoys Sunday school and may sit through part of church services—as music.

Firmly believes in Santa Claus, in every detail.

5 years—Many continue 4-year-old interest in and questions about

God. Some are already losing this marked interest.

Some believe that God is responsible for everything. If child falls, God pushed him.

Enjoys prayers and makes up own.

Likes Sunday school but may be very restless in church. May enjoy the pageantry.

Realistic approach to God and Santa Claus. Thinks of them as persons living in houses, etc.

6 years—Grasps idea of God as creator of the world, of animals, of beautiful things.

Asks to go to Sunday School. Loves story of little Lord Jesus. Emotional interest in this. Interest in angels.

Enjoys a short ritualistic service. May enjoy Sunday school very much.

Prayers are important and child expects them to be answered.

Feeling of two forces: heaven and hell, God and the Devil, good and bad.

Profanity involves name of God.

Very firm about belief in Santa Claus; insistent and emotional. Fiercely denies any hint that he is not real.

7 years—More thoughtful interest in God and heaven. Questions becoming more "appropriate."

Beginning of slight skepticism and distinguishing what he knows from what he has merely been told.

Less praying as child takes more responsibility for own night routines.

Sunday school interest; and interest in Bible stories continues.

Beginning skepticism about Santa Claus. Denies some aspects, as that he comes down the chimney. Multiplicity of Santa Claus seen on street may confuse child.

8 years—Interested in information that soul only, not body, goes to heaven.

May conceive of death as an immediate act of God, result of disease, or as resulting from disease which in turn is a punishment from God.

Not too much preoccupation about God.

Some still believe in Santa Claus. May deny that he is real, but "protest too much." May be able to substitute a "spirit of Christmas" or of "giving" for the more physical Santa Claus.

Likes Bible stories and passages from Bible. Likes to say prayers with mother.

9 years—In general, interest in God and religious matters is not strong.

May pray spontaneously on occasion if in great need or danger.

Most do not believe in Santa Claus.

Sunday school may be of continued interest if well taught or if associated with "clubs."

Bible story interest shifts to portions

of Old Testament, especially historical books. Enjoys memorizing Psalms and passages from Bible, enjoys singing in the choir.

10 years—A belief in God is expressed positively by a majority. A large minority, however, say they do not believe, question God's existence, or are "less interested" than formerly.

God is conceived of as "a spirit" by most, as "a man" by some. Few believe that "God makes things happen to you" (though more do now than at later ages), but more feel they are influenced by thoughts of God. Prayers are said by a small number—including some who say they do not believe in God.

A majority attend Sunday School regularly, while a few say that they have never attended. Of those who go, most say they enjoy going ("The family likes to have me go, but it's fun anyway"). A smaller number attend but do not enjoy it, saying that their families make them go. And quite a few admit that they and other children—especially the other children—act badly in Sunday school.

POSTSCRIPT

It will be clear by now that in our opinion human behavior develops in a patterned, predictable manner, ages of equilibrium rhythmically alternating with ages of disequilibrium. Thus the typical child may be in good, cooperative equilibrium at five; in disequilibrium at six; withdrawn and anxious at seven; exuberant and outgoing at eight; once again in difficulty, especially with those around him, at nine; and in calm, golden equilibrium at ten.

These things we can predict as the average or typical path of development. But each individual has his own timetable and manner of development. Some operate always on the difficult side of life, some on the smooth. Some go to great extremes, others vary less from one age to another.

That is, every child interprets the more or less typical or expected age changes in his own way. And every child, whatever the age or function in question, expresses himself differently from every other child, depending on his own physical structure. We agree with Dr. William Sheldon that behavior is a function of structure and that to a large extent we behave as we do because of the way our bodies are built.

Thus at the present time we can to quite an extent measure and predict. What we understand less about—but at least the importance of this area is being recognized—is the chemical and physical functioning of each individual body, genetically determined. Why are some children allergic to certain stimuli in the environment? Why is the behavior chemistry of some boys and girls so inadequate that their behavior is affected adversely?

If we are to live with and work with children effectively we must not only know age and individuality differences, but we must at least try to understand the interaction between any organism and its environment. Our senior author first commented on the importance of this interaction in 1940: "The organism always participates in the creation of its environment, and the growth characteristics of the child are really the end-product expressions of an interaction between intrinsic and extrinsic determiners. Because the interaction is the crux, the distinction between these two sets of determiners should not be drawn too heavily."

Parents can perhaps make their greatest contribution to the happy and effective functioning of their children if they will implement their normal parenting skills with a simple understanding of age changes and by paying vast attention to individual differences. And since such a substantial portion of any child's time is spent in schools as we have emphasized, one of the most important things a parent can do for a child is to see that the child starts school, and is subsequently promoted, on the basis of his or her behavior age rather than, routinely, on the basis of birthday age alone.

If we wish to do justice to the child's personality, we must think in terms of growth, in terms of developmental maturity. This means a philosophy that recognizes the relativities of the life cycle.

Developmentalism is the name for such a philosophy. Developmentalism is the very opposite of totalitarianism, for it acknowledges the individuality of the child and wisely concedes that all his behavior is subject to the natural laws of human growth. These natural laws can be comprehended only through science and yet more science.

We live in a technological age; we know something of the precision and the beauty of engines and machines. The rising generation of parents can readily absorb a science of child development that acquaints them with the mechanisms of growth—with the machinery of behavior. That will be sound self-knowledge. It would make for tolerance and understanding, and a more penetrating appreciation of the meaning of infancy and childhood. Developmentalism is in harmony with the spirit of democracy.

The nature of man is almost as terrifying as the unleashed atom: terrifying until we comprehend, and thereby govern, his inner forces. Only through profound self-knowledge can the human mind bring itself nearer to individual and collective control. For such self-knowledge we need vast and even dramatic extensions of science, both basic and applied. We need a new *science of man* and we need it urgently.

A true and effective science of man would involve many different kinds of knowledge. It would include a full understanding of the patterned age changes in behavior, a perfection and elaboration of the kind of information included in the present volume. Assuming that to a large extent behavior *is* a function of structure, it should include a thorough understanding of the kinds of behavior that might be expected of individuals of different body types and kinds of physical and chemical functioning. And it inevitably would include a better evaluation than has yet been arrived at of the relative contributions of organism and environment as they interact in the living human being.

But before we are in a position to make this evaluation, it seems certain that we must arrive at a much better understanding than is now available of the substantial differences in body chemistry that make some individuals so highly vulnerable to stress, whether from sight, sound, pain, bacteria, or pollution.

We cannot conserve the mental health of children, we cannot make democracy a genuine folkway, unless we bring into the homes of the people a developmental philosophy of child care rooted in scientific research.

A science of man, accordingly, becomes a most creative force in the atomic age. It will heighten and multiply human values. In a more sincerely sustained effort to understand children, men and women of maturity will better comprehend themselves and their fellows.

REFERENCES AND READINGS

Ames, Louise Bates. "Children's Stories." *Genet. Psychol. Monog.* 73, (1966): 337–96.

———. *Is Your Child in the Wrong Grade?* New York: Harper & Row, 1966.

———. *Child Care and Development.* Philadelphia: Lippincott, 1970.

———. "Learning Disabilities: The Developmental Point of View." In *Progress in Learning Disabilities,* ed. Helmer Myklebust. New York: Grune & Stratton, 1969.

Ames, Louise Bates, and Chase, Joan Ames, *Don't Push Your Preschooler.* New York: Harper & Row, 1974.

Ames, Louise Bates, Gillespie, Clyde, and Streff, John. *Stop School Failure.* New York: Harper & Row, 1972.

Ames, Louise Bates, and Ilg, Frances L. *Parents Ask.* Syndicated daily newspaper column. New Haven, Conn.: Gesell Institute, 1951–.

———. The developmental point of view with special reference to the principle of reciprocal neuromotor interweaving. *J. Genet. Psychol.,* 1964, 105, 195–209.

———. *A Trilogy: Your Two Year Old; Your Three Year Old; Your Four Year Old.* New York: Delacorte, 1976.

Austin, John J., and Lafferty, J. Clayton. *Ready or Not? The School Readiness Checklist.* Muskegon, Mich.: Research Concepts, 1963.

Beck, Helen. *Don't Push Me. I'm No Computer.* New York: Mc-Graw-Hill, 1973.

Bernard, Jessie. *The Future of Motherhood.* New York: Dial, 1974.

Braga, Laurie, and Braga, Joseph. *Learning and Growing: A Guide to Child Development.* New York: Prentice-Hall, 1976.

Brazleton, T. Berry. *Infants and Mothers.* New York: Delacorte, 1969.

———. *Toddlers and Their Parents.* New York: Delacorte, 1974.

Briggs, Dorothy Corkill. *Your Child's Self Esteem.* Garden City, N.Y.: Doubleday, 1970.

Brutten, Milton, Richardson, Sylvia O., and Mangel, Charles. *Something's Wrong with My Child. A Parents' Book about Children with Learning Disabilities.* New York: Harcourt Brace Jovanovich, 1973.

Callahan, Sidney Cornelia. *Parenting: Principles and Politics of Parenthood.* Garden City, N.Y.: Doubleday, 1973.

Carl, Barbara, and Richards, Nancy. *School Readiness: One Piece of the Puzzle.* New Hampshire State Title III Office, 64 N. Main St., Concord, N. H., 1965.

Chase, Joan A. "A Study of the Impact of Grade Retention on Primary School Children." *J. Psychol.* 70 (1968), 169–77.

———. "Differential Behavioral Characteristics of Non-Promoted Children." *Genet. Psychol. Monog.,* 86 (1972), 219–77.

Chess, Stella. *How to Help Your Child Get the Most out of School.* Garden City, N.Y.: Doubleday, 1975.

Collier, Herbert. *The Psychology of Twins.* Twins, Phoenix, Ariz.: 1974.

Comer, James P., and Poussaint, Alvin F. *Black Child Care.* New York: Simon & Schuster, 1975.

Darwin, Charles. *The Expression of the Emotions in Man and Animals.* New York: D. Appleton & Co., 1897.

Davis, Clara. "Self-selection of Food by Children." *American J. Nursing* 35 (1935), 401–10.

Decter, Midge. *Liberal Parents, Radical Children.* New York: Coward, McCann & Geoghegan, 1975.

Delacato, Carl H. *The Ultimate Stranger.* Garden City, N.Y.: Doubleday, 1974.

De Rosis, Helen. *Parent Power/Child Power*. New York: McGraw-Hill, 1975.

Dodson, Fitzhugh. *How to Parent*. Los Angeles: Nash, 1970.

———. *How to Father*. Los Angeles: Nash, 1974.

Feingold, Ben F. *Why Your Child Is Hyperactive*. New York: Random House, 1975.

Forer, Lucille K. *Birth Order and Life Roles*. Springfield, Ill.: C. C. Thomas, 1969.

Furth, Hans. *Piaget for Teachers*. Englewood Cliffs, N.J.: Prentice-Hall, 1970.

Gardner, Richard A. *The Boys and Girls Book About Divorce*. New York: Science House, 1970.

———. *Understanding Children*. New York: Aronson, 1973.

———. *MBD—The Family Book of Minimal Brain Dysfunction*. New York: Aronson, 1973.

Gesell, Arnold, Ilg, Frances L., and Ames, Louise B. *Infant and Child in the Culture of Today*. Rev. ed. New York: Harper & Row, 1974.

———. *Feeding Behavior of Infants: A Pediatric Approach to the Mental Hygiene of Early Life*. Philadelphia: Lippincott, 1937.

Ginott, Haim. *Between Parent and Child*. New York: Macmillan, 1965.

Grollman, Earl A., ed. *Explaining Death to Children*. Boston: Beacon Press, 1967.

———. *Explaining Divorce to Children*. Boston: Beacon Press, 1969.

Harrison-Ross, Phyllis, and Wyden, Barbara. *The Black Child: A Parents' Guide*. New York: Peter Wyden, Inc., 1973.

Hartley, Ruth E., and Goldenson, Robert M. *The Complete Book of Children's Play*. New York: Crowell, 1970.

Hughes, Richard. *A High Wind in Jamaica*. New York: Modern Library, 1932. (Fiction)

Ilg, Frances L., and Ames, Louise B. *Child Behavior*. New York: Harper & Row, 1955.

———. *Parents Ask*. New York: Harper & Row, 1962.

———. *School Readiness*. New York: Harper & Row, 1965.

Jensen, Arthur R. *Understanding Readiness. An Occasional Paper.* Urbana, Ill.: University of Illinois Press, 1969.

Johnson, Eric W. *How to Live Through Junior High School.* Rev. ed. Philadelphia: Lippincott, 1975.

Kappelman, Murray. *Raising an Only Child.* New York: Dutton, 1975.

Kirk, Samuel A., and Elkins, John. "Learning Disabilities: Characteristics of Children enrolled in the Child Service Demonstration Centers." *J. Learning Disabilities,* 8, no. 10 (1975), pp. 630–37.

Kraskin, Robert A. *You Can Improve Your Vision.* Garden City, N.Y.: Doubleday, 1968.

Kruger-Smith, Bert. *Your Non-Learning Child: His World of Upside Down.* Boston: Beacon Press, 1968.

Liepmann, Lise. *Your Child's Sensory World.* New York: Dial, 1973.

Maddox, Brenda. *The Half-Parent.* New York: Evans, 1975.

Mayle, Peter. *Where Did I Come From?* New York: Lyle Stuart, 1973.

McIntire, Roger W. *For Love of Children.* Del Mar, Calif. CRM Books, 1970.

Maynard, Fredelle. *Guiding Your Child to a More Creative Life.* Garden City, N.Y.: Doubleday, 1973.

Moak, Helen. *The Troubled Child.* New York: Henry Holt, 1958.

Postman, Neil, and Weingartner, Charles. *The School Book.* New York: Delacorte, 1973.

Pulaski, Mary Ann Spencer. *Understanding Piaget.* New York: Harper & Row, 1971.

Rimland, Bernard. *Infantile Autism.* New York: Appleton-Century-Crofts, 1964.

Skousen, Willard C. *So You Want to Raise a Boy?* Garden City, N.Y.: Doubleday, 1962.

Smith, Lendon H. *The Children's Doctor.* Englewood Cliffs, N.J.: Prentice-Hall, 1969.

———. *Improving Your Child's Behavior Chemistry.* Englewood Cliffs, N.J.: Prentice-Hall, 1976.

Thomson, Helen. *The Successful Stepparent.* New York: Harper & Row, 1966.

Von Hilsheimer, George. *How to Live with Your Special Child.* Washington, D.C.: Acropolis Press, 1970.

Wenar, Charles. *Personality Development from Infancy to Adulthood.* Boston: Houghton Mifflin, 1971.

Wender, Paul H. *The Hyperactive Child: A Guide for Parents.* New York: Crown, 1973.

Wunderlich, Ray. *Allergy, Brains and Children Coping.* St. Petersburg, Fla.: Johnny Reads Press, 1973.

Zuk, Gerald H. *Family Therapy.* New York: Behavior Publications, 1972.

INDEX